ORDOLIBERALISM, LAW AND THE RULE OF ECONOMICS

Ordoliberalism is a theoretical and cultural tradition of significant societal and political impact in post-war Germany. For a long time the theory was only known outside Germany by a handful of experts, but ordoliberalism has now moved centre stageafter the advent of the financial crisis, and has become widely perceived as the ideational source of Germany's crisis politics.

In this collection, the contributors engage in a multi-faceted exploration of the conceptual history of ordoliberalism, the premises of its founding fathers in law and economics, its religious underpinnings, the debates over its theoretical assumptions and political commitments, and its formative vision of societal ordering based upon a synthesis of economic theories and legal concepts. The renewal of that vision through the ordoliberal conceptualisation of the European integration project, the challenges of the current European crisis, and the divergent perceptions of ordoliberalism within Germany and by its northern and southern EU neighbours, are a common concern of all these endeavours. They unfold interdisciplinary affinities and misunderstandings, cultural predispositions and prejudices, and political preferences and cleavages. By examining European traditions through the lens of ordoliberalism, the book illustrates the diversity of European economic cultures, and the difficulty of transnational political exchanges, in a time of European crisis.

Ordoliberalism, Law and the Rule of Economics

Edited by
Josef Hien
Christian Joerges

·HART·

OXFORD · LONDON · NEW YORK · NEW DELHI · SYDNEY

HART PUBLISHING
Bloomsbury Publishing Plc
Kemp House, Chawley Park, Cumnor Hill, Oxford, OX2 9PH, UK

HART PUBLISHING, the Hart/Stag logo, BLOOMSBURY and the Diana logo are
trademarks of Bloomsbury Publishing Plc

First published in Great Britain 2017
First published in hardback, 2017
Paperback edition, 2020

A catalogue record for this book is available from the British Library.

Library of Congress Cataloging-in-Publication Data

Names: Ordoliberalism as an Irritating German Idea (conference) (2016: Berlin, Germany) |
Hien, Josef, 1981 - editor. | Joerges, Christian, editor. | Hertie School of Governance. organizer.

Title: Ordoliberalism, law and the rule of economics / edited by Josef hien, christian Joerges.

Description: Oxford; Portland, Oregon: Hart Publishing, an imprint of Bloomsbury Publishing Plc, 2017. |
Based on the conference "Ordoliberalism as an Irritating German Idea" held at the Hertie School of Governance
in Berlin from the 13 to the 14 of May 2016, co-funded by the Thyssen Foundation and the RESCEU project
at the University of Milan.—ECIP preface. | Iincludes bibliographical references and index.

Identifiers: LCCN 2017039021 (print) | LCCN 2017041276 (ebook) | ISBN 9781509919055 (epub) |
ISBN 9781509919048 (hardback)

Subjects: LCSH: Economic policy—Congresses. | Law and economics—Congresses. | Liberalism—Congresses.

Classification: LCC HD82 (ebook) | LCC HD82.O627 2018 (print) | DDC 330.1—dc23

LC record available at https://lccn.loc.gov/2017039021

ISBN: HB: 978-1-50991-904-8
PB: 978-1-50993-750-9
ePDF: 978-1-50991-906-2
ePub: 978-1-50991-905-5

Typeset by Compuscript Ltd, Shannon

To find out more about our authors and books visit www.hartpublishing.co.uk. Here you will
find extracts, author information, details of forthcoming events and the option to sign up for
our newsletters.

Preface and Acknowledgements

The editors of this volume have worked extensively on ordoliberal theorems and traditions for quite some time upon the assumption that, outside of Germany, the theory was known only to experts of German economics and law.[1] We were more than surprised when, with the European sovereign debt crisis, the theory all of a sudden was on everyone's lips and had moved centre stage in the debates about the future of European integration. We come from very different disciplinary backgrounds, and our concerns and perspectives mirror this disciplinary diversity. While Josef Hien, a historical sociologist with a keen interest in conceptual history, explored the ideational roots of ordoliberalism, Christian Joerges is particularly interest in the synthesis of legal concepts, economic theory and constitutional projects in the ideational legacy of ordoliberalism. What both of us nonetheless share is an uneasiness with the front lines in the current debates. The treatment of ordoliberal ideas by most of the commentators seemed too superficial to both of us, and we further felt that its influence was all too often conjectured rather than thoroughly traced. We concluded that political ideas such as ordoliberalism should be studied in their own right before we can use them as independent variables for our explanations of political preferences and orientations, economic policies and governance practices. This motivated us to prepare a two-day conference at the Hertie School of Governance in Berlin from the 13 to the 14 of May 2016, co-funded by the Thyssen Foundation and the REScEU project[2] at the University of Milan. The title of the conference was: 'Ordoliberalism as an Irritating German Idea'. The conference title reflects the critical perception of ordoliberalism beyond German borders. The objective of our initiative was to explore more thoroughly the complex facets of this tradition and the reasons for the irritation that it provokes in so many non-German quarters, whereas it is perceived as commonsensical within Germany.

We brought together 24 pertinent experts on ordoliberalism from both outside and inside Germany, and we had them discuss, debate, eat, drink and argue with one another for two days. The results of the conference went far beyond our expectations. Now we know much more about ordoliberalism and its functioning in the European crisis than we would have ever imagined. We would like to thank the

---

[1] See, in particular, Josef Hien, 'Competing Ideas: The Religious Foundations of the German and Italian Welfare States', PhD Thesis EUI Florence, 2012, available at: http://cadmus.eui.eu/handle/1814/24614?show=full; Josef Hien, 'The Ordo that never was', (2013) 12 *Contemporary Political Theory*, pp 349–358. Christian Joerges, 'What is Left of the European Economic Constitution? A Melancholic Eulogy', (2005) 30 *European Law Review*, pp 461–89, available at: http://papers.ssrn.com/sol3/papers.cfm?abstract_id=635402.

[2] Reconciling Economic and Social Europe: the role of ideas, values and politics (REScEU) is a European Research Council funded project at the University of Milan exploring the possibilities for a balanced social and economic integration of Europe. Principal Investigator is Maurizio Ferrera. ERC Advanced Grant No. 340534.

Thyssen Foundation for their generous support, Maurizio Ferrera and REScEU, a European Research Council-funded project at the University of Milan, for intellectual and monetary contributions, Chris Engert for his editing of our continental English and tireless copy-editing, Ines Andre-Schulze for her fantastic organisation, our student assistant from Canada, Michael Davies Venn, and, last, but not least, Fleur Diggines at Hertie for her advice on the submission of our application and further administrative help.

Josef Hien and Christian Joerges
Milan and Berlin, May 2017

Table of Contents

List of Contributors

Bruno Amable is Professor of Economics at the University of Geneva and at the University Paris I Panthéon—Sorbonne, from which he is currently on leave. His research is on comparative capitalism and the political economy of institutions and institutional change. He is the author of *The Diversity of Modern Capitalism*, (2003), and *Structural Crisis and Institutional Change in Modern Capitalism: French Capitalism in Transition* (2017), both published with Oxford University Press.

Thomas Biebricher is currently Professor of Political Theory and Philosophy at the Goethe-Universität in Frankfurt. He received his doctorate at the Albert-Ludwigs-Universität Freiburg with a dissertation on the works of Habermas and Foucault. From 2003 to 2009, he was DAAD Visiting Assistant Professor at the Department of Political Science at the University of Florida in Gainesville; from 2009 to 2012, he was a Junior Research Group Director at the Cluster of Excellence 'The Formation of Normative Orders' in Frankfurt. He is interested in the political thought of neoliberalism.

Werner Bonefeld is Professor of Politics at the University of York (UK) and is currently Leverhulme Research Fellow. Before coming to York, he taught at the Universities of Frankfurt and Edinburgh. His research focuses on critical theory, the critique of political economy, ordoliberalism and European integration. His most recent book publications include *Critical Theory and the Critique of Political Economy*, (Bloomsbury, 2014, 2016) and *The Strong State and the Free Economy*, (Rowman and Littlefield, 2017).

William Callison is a PhD candidate in Political Science with a designated emphasis in Critical Theory at the University of California, Berkeley. He has held DAAD fellowships at the Humboldt-Universität zu Berlin, where he received an M.A. in Philosophie, and at the Goethe-Universität, Frankfurt am Main, where he was a visiting scholar at the Institut für Sozialforschung and the Exzellenzcluster Normative Orders. His research interests include the history of modern political thought, contemporary democratic and legal theory, and critical social theory. He is special issue editor of 'Rethinking Sovereignty and Capitalism' in the journal *Qui Parle*, co-edotor of the issue 'europe at a Crossroads' in *Near Futures Online*, and co-editor of a forthcoming collected volume on neoliberalism and biopolitics.

Malte F Dold is a PhD student at the University of Freiburg, a research affiliate of the economics department at New York University, and a member of the Freiburg Advanced Centre of Education. His research interests lie in behavioural economics, economics and ethics, and philosophy of economics. In his PhD thesis, he discusses the role of expert decision-making in libertarian paternalism ('nudging'), welfare concepts in behavioural economic theories, and the impact of procedural preferences on individual behaviour. He holds an MA in philosophy and economics and a BA in philosophy and economics from the University of Bayreuth.

Kenneth Dyson is Visiting Research Professor in the School of Law and Politics at Cardiff University and Honorary Visiting Professor in the School of Politics and International Studies at Leeds University. His most famous books are *The State Tradition in Western Europe*, with K. Featherstone (Choice academic book of the year and chosen by the European Parliament as one of the 100 'best reads' on European Integration); *States, Debt and Power: 'Saints' and 'Sinners' in European History and Integration*, (UACES Book of the Year); and *Elusive Union*. He is a Fellow of the British Academy and holds an honorary doctorate from Aston University.

Michelle Everson is Professor of Law at Birkbeck College, University of London. She has written widely on European Constitutional and Economic Law. Her interest in German ordoliberalism dates from her PhD studies, which also revealed the practical difficulties of the implementation of ordoliberal approaches within the regulation of the German private insurance market (See M. Everson, 'Regulating the Insurance Sector', Niamh Moloney, Ellis Ferran and Jennifer Payne (eds), *The Oxford Handbook of Financial Regulation*, (Oxford University Press, 2014).

Maurizio Ferrera is Professor of Political Science at the University of Milano, Italy. His research focuses mainly on comparative politics and public policy, the welfare state and European integration. He has taken part over the years in many commissions and Working Groups set up by the Italian government, the European Union, the OECD and the ILO and currently sits on the *Exzellenzkommission* of the *Deutsche Forschungsgemeinschaft* (DFG). He is President of the Network for the Advancement of Social and Political Studies (NASP) among the universities of Lombardy and Piedmont and a member of the Board of Directors of the *Centro di Ricerca e Documenzazione Luigi Einaudi* of Turin. Since 2004, he has been an editorialist on the *Corriera della Sera*. His latest book in English is *The Boundaries of Welfare*, (Oxford University Press, 2005). In 2013, he received an Advanced Grant from the ERC, to carry out a five-year project on 'Reconciling Economic and Social Europe' (REScEU).

Josef Hien is a post-doctoral fellow at the REScEU project. Funded through a European Research Council advanced grant and hosted at the University of Milan, REScEU aims at reconciling social and economic Europe. Hien is interested in the ideational and cultural foundations of European political economies. He received his PhD from the European University Institute and has worked as a post doc at the Max Planck Institute for the Study of Societies (Cologne), at the Collegio Carlo Alberto (Moncalieri/Turin) and the Berlin Social Science Centre (WZB, Berlin).

Christian Joerges is Professor of Law and Society at the Hertie School of Governance in Berlin and Co-Director of the Centre of European Law and Politics at the University of Bremen. Until 2007, he held the chair for European Economic Law at the European University Institute, Florence. In 2009, he was awarded an honorary doctorate from the University of Fribourg i.Ue. His research focuses on European and international economic law and the legitimacy problems of pertinent government arrangements and practices. His most discussed book is the *Darker Legacies* *of Law in Europe: The Shadow of National Socialism and Fascism over Europe and its Legal Traditions* (with Navraj Singh Ghaleigh).

Tim Krieger has been the Wilfried Guth Professor of Constitutional Political Economy and Competition Policy at the Albert-Ludwigs-University Freiburg. He holds a master's degree in empirical economics from the University of Kiel, Germany, and received his PhD in economics from the University of Munich, Germany. He worked as an assistant or interim professor at the Universities of Mainz, Marburg and Paderborn, Germany. He works in the tradition of the Freiburg School of Economics mainly on economic, social and education policies in aging and globalising societies. In addition, he specialises in the economics of conflict, terrorism and crime. He has published in several scholarly journals in both economics and political science (including the *Journal of Public Economics*, the *European Journal of Political Economy*, *Public Choice*, the *Journal of Conflict Resolution* and the *Journal of Peace Research*.

Arnaud Lechevalier is *Maître de Conférences* at the University Paris 1 Panthéon-Sorbonne and researcher at the *Laboratoire Interdisciplinaire pour la Sociologie Economique* (CNRS-CNAM, Paris) and at the Centre Marc Bloch (French-German research centre in the social sciences centre of the Humboldt Universität, Berlin). He was Visiting Professor at the European University Viadrina from 2007 to 2013, and has developed research on the dynamics of the welfare state in a French-German comparative perspective, on the Europeanisation of social policy and on social Europe. With Jan Wielgohs, he has recently published the volume entitled: *Social Europe: A Dead End. What the Eurozone Crisis is doing to Europe's Social Dimension*, (DJØF Publishing, 2015).

Philip Manow is Professor of Comparative Political Economy at the University of Bremen in the Department of Political Science. He held Professorships at the universities of Konstanz and Heidelberg and was director of a research group at the Max-Planck Institute of Studies, Cologne. He was visiting scholar at the Center for European Studies, Harvard, Sciences Po, Paris, and the Institute for Advanced Studies, Berlin. His research interests include comparative political economy, in particular comparative welfare state research, the German political system, European integration and political theory. He has published, amongst others, in the *British Journal of Political Science*, the *European Journal for Political Research*, *Politics and Society*, *Legislative Studies Quarterly*, *Comparative Political Studies*, and *Socio-Economic Review*. He is editor (with Kees van Kersbergen) of *Religion, Class-coalitions and Welfare States*, (Cambridge University Press, 2009), and author of the forthcoming book: *Social Protection, Capitalist Production: The Bismarckian Welfare State and the German Political Economy, 1880–2010*.

Stephan Pühriger is a post-doctoral research associate at the Institute for Comprehensive Analysis of Economy (ICAE) at the University of Linz in Austria. In recent research projects, he has been working on the politico-economic history of German economics after WW2 and the current paradigmatic status and ideational foundations of economics after the global financial and economic crisis. His main interests include the history of economic thought, the political and societal consequences of economics and the role of economists in neoliberal think tanks. See http://www.jku.at/isae/content/e246965.

Stefano Solari is associate professor of Political Economy at the Department of Economics and Management of the University of Padua in Italy. His research interests include the study of comparative capitalism, with a particular focus on territoriality and social law, from a broadly defined institutionalist perspective; the study of state-economy relationships; and the history and philosophy of political economy.

Albert Weale is Emeritus Professor of Political Theory and Public Policy at University College London. He has written on European Union policy theory including *Environmental Governance in Europe: An Ever Closer Ecological Union?*, (with G. Pridham, M. Cini, D. Konstadakopulos, M. Porter and B. Flynn) (Oxford University Press, 2000), *Democratic Citizenship and the European Union*, (Manchester University Press, 2005), as well as articles in such journals as *Public Administration*, *Journal of European Public Policy*, *Government and Opposition* and *European Political Science Review*.

Jonathan White is Professor of Politics at the European Institute of the London School of Economics and Political Science. He gained his doctorate at the European University Institute (EUI) in Florence, and has been a visiting scholar at the Institute of Advanced Studies (*Wissenschaftskolleg*) in Berlin, Harvard University, Sciences Po in Paris, the Australian National University and the Humboldt University of Berlin. His work has appeared in *American Political Science Review*, *Journal of Politics*, *Political Studies*, *Modern law Review*, *Political Theory*, *Journal of Common Market Studies*, the *British Journal of Political Science*, *British Journal of Sociology*, and the *Boston Review*. He is the author of *Political Allegiance after European Integration*, (Palgrave MacMillan, 2011), and, with Lea Ypi, *The Meaning of Partisanship*, (Oxford University Press, 2016).

Angela Wigger is Associate Professor of Global Political Economy at the Radboud University, The Netherlands. She is specialised in capitalist competition and competition regulation. In addition to book chapters, she has co-authored the book *The Politics of European Competition Regulation: A Critical Political Economy Perspective*, (Routledge, 2011), and published in journals such as *New Political Economy*, *Review of International Political Economy*, *Journal of Common Market Studies*, *Comparative European Politics*, *Capital and Class*, and *Economy and Society*.

David Woodruff is Associate Professor of Comparative Politics at the London School of Economics and Political Science. He is the author of *Money Unmade: Barter and the Fate of Russian Capitalism*, (Cornell University Press, 1999) and a number of articles on Russian and Soviet political economy. His prior work also includes 'Governing by Panic: The Politics of the Eurozone Crisis', *Politics & Society*, Vol 44 No 1, which includes a discussion of the role of ordoliberalism.

Brigitte Young is Professor (em) of International Political Economy at the University of Münster in Germany, and has been an expert advisor to the EU Commission, DG Research and Innovation since 2008. She was awarded the Kaethe-Leichter State

Prize of Austria for 2016. Her research focuses on global financial market govern-ance and monetary policy, European economic and monetary integration, and femi-nist economics. Her most recent (co-edited) book is on *Financial Cultures and Crisis Dynamics*, (Routledge, 2015); a Special Issue on German Ordoliberlism, *European Review of International Studies*, volume 2/2015; and 'Imaginaries of German Economic Success: Is the Current Model Sustainable?', *Near Futures Online 1*, 'Europe at a Crossroads', (March 2016), available at: http://nearfuturesonline.org.

List of Abbreviations

AG	Advocate General
AGS	Annual Growth Survey
BC	Before Christ
BDI	*Bundesverband der Deutschen Industrie*
CDU	*Christlich Demokratische Union Deutschlands* (Christian Democratic Union of Germany)
CEO	Chief Executive Officer
CJEU	Court of Justice of the European Union
DG	Directorate General
DNA	Deoxyribonucleic Acid
EBA	European Banking Authority
EC	Economic Community
ECB	European Central Bank
ECJ	European Court of Justice
ECSC	European Coal and Steel Community
EEC	European Economic Community
EMU	European Monetary Union
ERM	Exchange Rate Mechanism
ESCB	European System of Central Banks
ESM	European Stability Mechanism
ESU	European Social Union
EU	European Union
FDP	*Freie Demokratische Partei* (Free Democratic Party)
FED/Fed	Federal Reserve System (US)
FMS	Free Market Study (financed by the Volker Fund)
FRG	Federal Republic of Germany
G7	Group of Seven: Canada, France, Germany, Italy, Japan, the United Kingdom, and the United States
GATT	General Agreement of Trade and Tariffs
GB	Great Britain
GCC	German Constitutional Court
GCEE	German Council of Economic Experts
GDP	Gross Domestic Product
IAGS	Independent Annual Growth Survey
IMF	International Monetary Fund
INSM	Initiative for New Social Market Economy/*Initiative Neue Soziale Marktwirtschaft*
IR	Industrial Relations
LSE	London School of Economics
MP	Member of Parliament

MPS	*Mont Pèlerin Society*
NBER	National Bureau of Economic Research
NIE	New Institutional Economics
NSDAP	*Nationalsozialistische Deutsche Arbeiterpartei* (National Socialist German Workers' Party)
OCA	Optimal Currency Areas
OFCÉ	*Observatoire Français des Conjunctures Économiques*
OMT	Outright Monetary Transactions
REScEU	Reconciling Economic and Social Europe
SGP	Stability and Growth Pact
SPD	*Sozialdemokratische Partei Deutschlands* (Social Democratic Party)
TEU	Treaty on European Union
TFEU	Treaty on the Functioning of the European Union
TTIP	Transatlantic Trade and Investment Partnership
UK	United Kingdom
US/U.S./USA	United States of America
WVF	William Volker Foundation
WWII	The Second World War

Introduction

Objectives and Contents of the Volume

JOSEF HIEN AND CHRISTIAN JOERGES

T HE SPECTRE OF ordoliberalism is haunting Europe. The socio-economic theory, known before the Euro crisis only to a handful of insiders outside of the German-speaking world, has made a formidable career during the past five years. Commentators in the media[1] and from universities[2] have identified it as a variable that could explain the position of Germany during the European sovereign debt crisis. The discussion on the contemporary influence of ordoliberalism follows the same geographical fault lines as the Euro-crisis. Commentators from Southern European countries see ordoliberalism as an 'ideational superpower' that is at work amongst the German élites. Germans are reluctant to admit to being 'remote controlled' by ordoliberal ideas. They think that Germany's reply to the crisis was commonsensical. In the following introduction, we will probe some aspects of the

---

[1] Suffice it here to mention *The Economist* of 9 May 2015 ('German Ordoliberalism has had a big influence on policymaking during the Euro crisis'), *The Guardian* of 2 March 2012 ('Let us introduce you to "Ordoliberalism"'), and *The New York Times* of 16 November 2014 ('The wacky economics of Germany's parallel universe'). We could add a good number of similar statements from France and Italy. An analysis from Helsinki has documented 'the struggle between Germany's ordoliberal orthodoxy and alternative, more Keynesian solutions' meticulously, (Timo Harjunienu and Markus Ojala, 'Mediating "the German Ideology"? Ordoliberalism and its Alternatives in the Press Coverage of the Eurozone Crisis', Paper for the European Studies Day, University of Helsinki, 25 August 2014).

[2] See, in particular, Mark Blyth, *Austerity: The History of a Dangerous Idea*, (Oxford: Oxford University Press, 2013), p 141: 'Germany's response to the crisis, and the crisis itself both spring from the same Ordoliberal instruction sheet'; but also Volker Berghahn and Brigitte Young, 'Reflections on Werner Bonefeld's 'Freedom and the Strong State: On German Ordoliberalism' and the Continuing Importance of the Ideas of Ordoliberalism to Understand Germany's (Contested) Role in Resolving the Eurozone Crisis', (2013) 18 *New Political Economy*, pp 768–78; Simon Bulmer, 'Germany and the Eurozone Crisis: Between Hegemony and Domestic Politics', (2014) 37 *West European Politics*, 1244–63; Simon Bulmer and William E. Paterson, 'Germany as the EU's Reluctant Hegemon? Of Economic Strength and Political Constraints', (2013) 20 *Journal of European Public Policy*, pp 1387–1405; Sergio Cesarotti and Antonella Stirati, 'Germany and the European and Global Crises', (2010) 39 *Journal of Political Economy*, pp 56–86; Pierre Dardot and Christian Laval, *The New Way of the World: On Neoliberal Society*, (London: Verso Books, 2014), first published as *La nouvelle raison du monde: Essai sur la la société néolibérale*, 2009; Sebastian Dullien and Ulrike Guérot, 'The Long Shadow of Ordoliberalism: Germany's Approach to the Euro Crisis', European Council on Foreign Relations Policy Brief 22 (2012); Rainer Hillebrand, 'Germany and its Eurozone Crisis Policy: The Impact of the Country's Ordoliberal Heritage', (2015) 33 *German Politics & Society*, pp 6–24; Peter Nedergaard and Holly Snaith, '"As I Drifted on a River I could not Control": The Unintended Ordoliberal Consequences of the Eurozone Crisis', *Journal of Common Market Studies*, 53 (2015), 1094–1109.

'ordoliberalisation of Europe' thesis by giving a brief introduction to the theory's development trajectory in post-war Germany and Europe. Our strategy is twofold: first, we re-construct the original content of the theory and how it has evolved since the 1930s. Thereafter, we take a closer look at its political impact in Germany and Europe. Our assessment bears mixed results. On the one hand, we find that ordoliberalism's political impact was—even in its heydays in the 1950s and 1960s—never as straightforward or as strong as today's debate seems to suggest. Moreover, we find that ordoliberal theory has, from the 1980s onwards, moved considerably in the direction of the Anglo-Saxon neo-classical mainstream economics. Nonetheless, we see that ordoliberals have been key epistemic and political actors both in post-war Germany and during the formative years of the European single market. Moreover, we conclude that ordoliberal theory might have become diluted through the influence of neo-classic mainstream economics but, paradoxically, its historical legacy has, at the same time, been strengthened. Today, ordoliberalism has become an item of the common national container, a rallying-point for German collective cultural memory, one which is frequently used by politicians and economic élites to communicate with the public.

I. RE-CONSTRUCTIONS: WHAT KIND OF THEORY IS IT?

Law and ethics distinguished ordoliberals from other branches of neoliberalism and classic *laissez-faire* liberalism in the 1930s, 1940s and 1950s. An interest in this specificity of ordoliberalism surfaced only recently with the re-discovery and re-publication of Michel Foucault's lectures at the *Collège de France*, which had already rigidly categorised ordoliberalism in the 1970s.[3] Is the ordoliberal triangle of institutional economics, law and ethics that framed the original ordoliberal embedding of markets still central for contemporary ordoliberal thinkers, or has it evaporated in recent decades under the influence of ever-greater global market integration and the dominance of Anglo-Saxon neoliberal economics? Could it be that the type of synthesis between economic and legal concepts that characterised the ordoliberal ordering of the economy through law in its foundational period can no longer be realised after the deepening of economic integration in Europeanisation and globalisation processes, as Christian Joerges suggests? Did these processes foster the formation of a *de facto* assimilation alliance between German and non-German neo-liberalism?

To get a better idea of what kind of theory ordoliberalism is, our re-constructions focused on the three components of ordoliberal thought which are key to its comprehensive understanding: (1) the ordering functions of law; (2) the normativity of 'the economic'; and (3) the ethical foundations of ordoliberalism. All of these components surface in today's European debate on ordoliberalism and Germany. However, they do so as anecdotes, rather than in conceptual analyses.

---

[3] Michel Foucault, *The Birth of Biopolitics: Lectures at the Collège de France 1978–79*, (Basingstoke: Palgrave-Macmillan, 2008).

A. The Ordering Functions of Law in Changing Contexts

The foundational literature of the ordoliberal tradition synthesised legal and eco-nomic scholarship. This is particularly true for the legendary Ordo Manifesto of 1936.[4] This remains a truth for the leading scholars of the Freiburg School after World War II. Franz Böhm defined the constitutive importance of law with out-standing clarity: the *ordo* of the economy is a *legal* order ('*Wirtschaftsordnung ist Rechtsverfassung*'); this legal order is an order of freedom ('*Freiheitsordnung*'), albeit one that requires a strong state which ensures its respect and functioning. It is an order of constitutional validity, ensuring both material freedom and the equality of social chances.[5] Ordoliberalism dominated German economic law scholarship for some decades through such renowned exponents as Kurt Biedenkopf and Wolf-gang Fikentscher and many others. However, the ordoliberal project of an 'economic constitution' which the legislature had to respect experienced serious setbacks in seminal constitutional controversies (for example, *Investitionshilfe* judgment of 20 July 1954, BVerfGE 4, 7; *Mitbestimmungs-Urteil* of 1 March 1979, BVerfGE 50, 290). A re-conceptualisation of the ordoliberal legacy of paradigmatic dimen-sions occurred under the intellectual leadership of Friedrich A. von Hayek and Ernst-Joachim Mestmäcker. This renewal affected the core of the theory, namely, the conceptualisation of the system of undistorted competition.[6] It therefore seems to us that Pierre Dardot and Christian Laval,[7] in their analyses of the politi-cal meaning of the integration project, have valid reasons to characterise this re-orientation as 'neo-ordoliberalism', and rightly underline its affinities with the Austro-American forms of neoliberalism. Does the more recent turn to constitutional economics repeat this move?[8] We see continuity in the search for both workable and normatively justifiable frameworks of rules and institutions which are expected to orient policy-making. But constitutional economics seems to operate at a level of abstraction at which the formerly close ties between the two disciplines are sig-nificantly loosened. The 'conflicts-theoretical perspective' promoted by Tim Krieger[9]

[4] Franz Böhm, Walter Eucken and Hans Großmann-Dörth, 'The Ordo Manifesto of 1936', in: Alan Peacock and Hans Willgerodt (eds), *Germany's Social Market Economy: Origins and Evolution*, (London: Palgrave MacMillan, 1989), pp 15–26.

[5] Franz Böhm, *Wirtschaftsordnung und Staatsverfassung*, (Tübingen: Mohr Siebeck, 1950).

[6] Friedrich A. von Hayek, 'Wettbewerb als Entdeckungsverfahren (Kiel 1968)', Nachdruck in Friedrich A. von Hayek, *Freiburger Studien. Gesammelte Aufsätze*, (Tübingen: Mohr Siebeck, 1969), pp 249–265; [Competition as a Discovery Procedure, (2002) 5 The Quarterly Journal of Austrian Economics, pp 9–23]. See, eg, Ernst-Joachim Mestmäcker, 'Wettbewerbsfreiheit und Wohlfahrt Ein ideengeschichtlicher Beitrag zum Verhältnis von Ökonomie und Recht', (2012) 63 *ORDO*, pp 429–448.

[7] Dardot and Laval, n 2 above, p 208 et seq.

[8] Initiated by Viktor Vanberg, '"Ordnungstheorie" as Constitutional Economics—The German Conception of a "Social Market Economy"', (1988) 39 ORDO, pp 17–31, and renewed, eg, by Lars P. Feld, 'Eine Europäische Verfassung aus polit-ökonomischer Sicht', (2003) 54 *ORDO*, pp 289–317; and Lars P. Feld and Ekkehard A. Köhler, 'Ist die Ordnungsökonomik zukunftsfähig', (2011) 12 *Zeitschrift für Wirtschafts- und Unternehmensethik*, pp 173–195.

[9] Tim Krieger, 'Any Solution in Sight to Europe's Crisis? Some General Thoughts from a Conflict Theoretical Perspective', in: Tim Krieger, Bernhard Neumärker and Diana Panke (eds), *Europe's Crisis: The Conflict-Theoretical Perspective*, (Baden-Baden: Nomos, 2015).

and Bernhard Neumärker[10] remains committed to the *ordnungs*-theoretical tradition, albeit without the backing of congenial allies in legal scholarship who would translate their re-orientation into legal concepts. It may be a confirmation of such retractions from law that many critical comments on ordoliberalism in the current debate, such as those mentioned above (Section I), and not even those of sophisticated jurists,[11] fail to explore the importance of law and legal scholarship in the ordoliberal tradition.[12]

B. Ordoliberalism and the Normativity of 'the Economic'

Both the older and the more recently widespread critique of ordoliberalism tend to equate the ordoliberal advocacy for markets[13] with the mainstream of neoliberalism, and, hence, to downplay the differences between these liberalisms which were discerned by Foucault in his legendary lectures of 1978–1979 at the *Collège de France*.[14] *Michelle Everson* emphasises that this equation does not do justice to the leading proponents of the tradition, in particular the lawyers. Franz Böhm's *Wettbewerbsordnung* was a normative construct and the exercise of economic freedoms was socially adequate (to wit, 'just') only in view of their embeddedness in the ordo of 'the economic' which law was to constitute. *David Woodruff* has re-constructed the normative communalities between law and economics in the ordoliberal tradition: competitive markets deserve moral recognition both if, and, if so, because '*Leistungswettbewerb*' ('achievement' or 'performance competition') will ensure that economic success is a moral desert. It seems but logical to conclude that the moral standing of the market should be protected by an economic constitution which derives its legitimacy from precisely this, as normative quality must hence be insulated against democratic will formation. In sharp contrast to classical *laissez-faire* liberalism, ordoliberals never believed in the self-constitution and auto-regulation of markets. Ordoliberals argued that free competition had to be guaranteed not only through an enshrining in law of 'the visible hand of law', but also in ethics. '[S]ociological liberalism' should replace 'sociologically blind' paleo-liberalism and help to 'embed' the market economy into a 'higher total order'.[15] It was based not only upon anthropological assumptions on the nature of human behaviour, but also included prescriptions for a 'moralisation of economic life' (*Versittlichung des Wirtschaftslebens*).[16] Hence, ordoliberal sociology emphasises a twin strategy of

---

[10] Bernhard Neumärker (ed), Konflikt, Macht und Gewalt aus politökonomischer Perspektive, (Marburg: Metropolis, 2011).

[11] Michael A. Wilkinson, 'The Specter of Authoritarian Liberalism: Reflections on the Constitutional Crisis of the European Union', (2013) 14 *German Law Journal*, pp 527–560.

[12] But see recently Thomas Biebricher, 'Neoliberalism and Law: The Case of the Constitutional Balanced-Budget Amendment', (2016) 17 *German Law Journal*, pp 747–762.

[13] Programmatically: 'Mehr Mut zum Markt', *Kronberger Kreis* 1983.

[14] Foucault, n 3 above, p 77 et seq.

[15] Wilhelm Röpke cited in Dieter Haselbach, *Autoritärer Liberalismus und Soziale Marktwirtschaft: Gesellschaft und Politik im Ordoliberalismus*, (Baden-Baden: Nomos, 1991), p 172.

[16] Alfred Müller-Armack, 'Die Wirtschaftsordnungen sozial gesehen', (1947) 1 *ORDO*, pp 125–155, at 147.

the 'legal curbing' of such behaviour at the aggregate level (cartels and monopolies) and the moral formation of society that went all the way down to moral prescriptions and institutional incentives for behaviour at individual level. The moral and religious underpinnings of the economic *ordo* are, as Josef Hien underlines, inaccessible to the mainstream of contemporary economic thought. Legal scholarship, however, is less indifferent. Even the leading exponent of the 'second generation', Ernst-Joachim Mestmäcker,[17] has quite emphatically distanced himself (and, by the same token, the Hayekian 'competition as a discovery procedure' from the commitment to economic efficiency as defended by the American economic analysis of law scholars, most famously by Richard Posner.[18] It is, of course, not by accident that law and its normative *proprium* are mentioned increasingly less in the current debates of ordoliberalism. The differences between Anglo-Saxon and ordoliberal traditions have become practically ever less visible, *Christian Joerges* has argued in his contribution, and it is likewise obvious that the formerly close ties between lawyers and economist have become very loose.

C. Social Justice: The Ethical Foundations of Ordoliberalism

The 'social market economy' and ordoliberalism have become equated in the debates about ordoliberalism and Europe. This has plausible political reasons and rhetorical advantages. The conceptual basis of the connection between ordoliberalism and the 'social market economy', however, is fragile.[19] The German conceptual background of this notion is richer, and the debate about its post-war success in the early years of the Federal Republic remains controversial. The understanding of the social market economy by Alfred Müller-Armack, who first coined this notion,[20] is adequately characterised as a categorically-distinct vision which does not represent ordoliberalism, although he himself asserted the compatibility of his suggestions with the concepts of the Freiburg School.[21] Positive accounts of the *soziale Marktwirtschaft* by non-German authors are rare.[22]

---

[17] Ernst-Joachim Mestmäcker, *A Legal Theory without Law. Posner v Hayek on Economic Analysis of Law*, (Tübingen: Mohr Siebeck, 2007).

[18] Richard A. Posner, *Economic Analysis of Law*, 9th ed., (New York: Wolters Kluwer Law & Business, 2014).

[19] Christian Joerges and Floran Rödl, '"Social Market Economy" as Europe's Social Model?', EUI Working Paper Law No. 2004/8, available at: https://ssrn.com/abstract=635362.

[20] Alfred Müller-Armack, eg, *Wirtschaftslenkung und Marktwirtschaft*, (Hamburg: Verlag für Wirtschaft und Sozialpolitik, 1947); 'Die Soziale Marktwirtschaft nach einem Jahrzehnt ihrer Erprobung', in: Alfred Müller-Armack (ed), *Wirtschaftsordnung und Wirtschaftspolitik: Studien und Konzepte zur sozialen Marktwirtschaft und zur Europäischen Integration*, (Freiburg: Rombach, 1966), pp 251–265; and 'Die Wirtschaftsordnung sozial gesehen', in: *Wirtschaftsordnung und Wirtschaftspolitik*, this note, pp 171–199.

[21] Christian L. Glossner, *The Making of the German Post-War Economy: Political Communication and Public Reception of the Social Market Economy after World War II*, (London-New York: Tauris Academic Studies, 2010), pp 31–46; Joerges and Rödl, n 19 above.

[22] But see Maurice Glasman, *Unnecessary Suffering: Managing Markets Utopia*, (London-New York: Verso Books, 1996), p 55 et seq. His analysis is inspired by Polanyi's economic sociology. He underlines institutional innovations and social accomplishments which contrast markedly with strictly neoliberal positions.

The divergences between the political *praxis* and institutional instalment of the 'social market economy' and ordoliberal positions becomes most obvious in how both approach the welfare state. While it is a central element of the German model of capitalism and the social market economy, it is a thorn in the side of ordoliberal thinkers. Ordoliberals saw the troubles of the Weimar Republic as a result of a capturing and overburdening of the welfare state by the 'interest mob'[23] who were enabled by parliamentarism and corporatism. This led to what has been described as the 'total catastrophe of state and society'.[24] Ordoliberals had a distaste for the Bismarckian welfare state as they identified, in its self-administration, the gateway for the capturing of Weimar through interest from capital and labour. The Beveridge type of welfare state, in the early ordoliberal perception, is also a gigantic moral hazard machine that would erase both any and all incentive for individual action.

Instead, as Glasman has shown, ordoliberals espoused a romantic middle-European idea of a small property-holding society. According to Glasman, the ordoliberal embedding of the market was pro-active, instead of re-active, based upon the establishing of equal starting conditions, residual universal social provisions, a strong emphasis on education and training, the promotion of home ownership, the vision of an equally distributed small shareholder society all seen as a means of creating equal starting conditions and of overcoming both concentration of wealth and concentration of economic power.[25]

II. ORDOLIBERALISM IN EUROPE

So far, we have discussed ordoliberalism both in its conceptual development and in its empirically observable *praxis* and have to conclude that its lasting legacy of legislative influence and institutional embeddedness in Germany is much less clear-cut as the current debate that we cite at the beginning makes us believe. Upon the basis of the preceding re-constructions of the ordoliberal legacy, we turn to the debate about our main concern, namely, the impact of ordoliberalism on the European integration process in general, and its functions in the present financial crisis in particular. The line drawn with this distinction can, in our view, be justified by the importance of the Treaty of Maastricht with the establishment of the Monetary and Economic Union (EMU), and the concomitant and present turmoil. Maastricht, we submit, should be understood as a turning-point in the history of the integration project.

---

[23] Wilhelm Röpke, *Gesellschaftskrisis Der Gegenwart*, (Erlenbach-Zürich: Eugen-Rentsch Verlag, 1948), p 310.

[24] ibid, p 364.

[25] Wilhelm Röpke, *Civitas humana : Grundfragen der Gesellschafts- und Wirtschaftsreform*, (Bern: Paul Haupt, 1949), pp 257–258; Walter Eucken, *Grundsätze der Wirtschaftspolitik*, (Bern: Francke, 1952), p 334 and 336.

A. From Rome to Maastricht

There was, initially, hesitation on the part of ordoliberals in identifying with a merely 'regional' Economic Community.[26] However, this hesitation was soon replaced by a strong commitment to the integration project. This commitment is unsurprising, in view of the affinities between the institutional structure of the EEC and the ordo-liberal agenda. This affinity became apparent after the constitutionalisation of the EEC Treaty through the foundational jurisprudence of the European Court of Justice (ECJ). The principles which the ECJ established were fully compatible with the ordo-liberal reading of the four freedoms and the Treaty provisions on competition policy as the core of a European 'economic constitution'.[27] Is this compatibility indicative of an ordoliberal impact on the integration project? A test case of exemplary impor-tance can be found in European competition policy, a core concern of ordoliberalism and a field in which the ordoliberal impact has, indeed, been held to have been very considerable, at least in the earlier phases of the integration project.[28] Another insti-tutional test case is the ordoliberal defence of non-majoritarian institutions which were, however, not established in the field of competition policy.[29] What remains puzzling, in view of the present intense debates on ordoliberalism, is the disregard of this school of thought in European law scholarship. What reached a broader public were the controversies between France and Germany about *planification and Ordnungspolitik*.[30] These controversies foreshadowed the current debates about the responses to the crisis. The same holds true for the disputes about industrial policy during the negotiations about the Maastricht Treaty.[31] And yet, the course of the integration project was much more significantly determined by two further objectives: (1) the efforts of the Delors Commission to complete the internal market; and (2) the striving for an 'ever closer Union', an expansion of European compe-tences and policy-fields which were to include moves towards a 'more social Europe' and, later, to the commitment to a 'highly competitive social market economy' in Article 3 TEU. While the internal market initiative was strongly supported by the

[26] Milène Wegmann, *Früher Neoliberalismus und europäische Integration: Interdependenz der nation-alen, supranationalen und internationalen Ordnung von Wirtschaft und Gesellschaft (1932–1965)*, (Baden-Baden: Nomos, 2002).

[27] Joerges, n 1 above.

[28] *Kiran Klaus Patel and Heike Schweitzer*, 'EU competition law in historical context: Continuity and change in', in: Heike Schweitzer and *Kiran Klaus Patel (eds)*, *The Historical Foundations of EU Competi-tion Law* (Oxford: Oxford University Press, 2013), pp 207–230; much more sceptical is Wigger's chapter in this volume (Ch 10) which departs from her earlier work; see Angela Wigger, 'Competition for Com-petitiveness: The Politics of Transformation of the EU Competition Regime', Dissertation, Department of Political Science, Vrije Universiteit Amsterdam, 2008.

[29] See Yannis Karagiannis, 'The Causes and Consequences of the Collegial Implementation of European Competition', (2013) 19 *European Law Journal*, 682–704.

[30] Alexander Nützenadel, *Stunde der Ökonomen. Wissenschaft, Expertenkultur und Politik in der Bundesrepublik 1949–74*, Kritische Studien zur Geschichtswissenschaft, Bd. 166, (Göttingen: Vandenhoeck & Ruprecht, 2005), p 40; Ernst-Joachim Mestmäcker, 'Towards a Concept of a Workable European Competition Law: Revisiting the Formative Period', in: Kiran Klaus Patel and Heike Schweitzer (eds), n 28 above, pp 191–206, at 196–198.

[31] Mestmäcker, previous note, pp 198–200.

Scientific Advisory Council of the Federal Ministry of Economics,[32] the successive adoption of the notion of a 'highly competitive social market economy' by the European Convention and the Treaty of Lisbon was more ambiguous. The formula mirrored the tension between Böhm and Müller-Armack to which we have pointed above (Section II C).[33] How likely is it that, under such circumstances, the proponents of ordoliberalism would be finally able to realise their project of a European economic constitution through the establishment of the EMU? To be sure, Ernst-Joachim Mestmäcker, in particular, had, back in 1973, predicted that, under the constraints of a common currency, economic and fiscal policies would converge.[34] But this expectation concerned a smaller and more homogeneous Community. The perceptions and evaluations of the EMU differ very considerably among both the opponents and the adherents of ordoliberalism. Tellingly enough, the Maastricht Treaty and the EMU met with considerable reserve amongst ordoliberals.[35] Manfred E. Streit elaborated his critique on Hayekian premises,[36] while Lars P. Feld endorsed the understanding of the EMU as a Stability Union, which the German Constitutional Court has defended in its judgment on the Treaty of Maastricht.[37] He also stressed that this remained a theoretical vision which was not sufficiently backed by effective policy instruments, was unprepared for responses to economic crises, and, hence, was overwhelmed by factual constraint and political pressure (but he also criticised this Treaty for its failure to provide for the effective means to respond to the failures of its functioning).[38]

B. Responses to the Crisis

'With the benefit of hindsight' we see more. But, for a good number of years, the common currency seemed to be functioning quite smoothly. Only after the outbreak of the financial crisis in 2008 did public and scholarly attention shift to the

[32] BMWi, 1986, 'Wissenschaftlicher Beirat beim Bundesministerium für Wirtschaft, Stellungnahme zum Weißbuch der EG-Kommission über den Binnenmarkt', Schriften-Reihe 51, Bonn.

[33] Christian Joerges and Florian Rödl, 'The 'Social Market Economy' as Europe's Social Model?', in: Lars Magnusson and Bo Stråth (eds), *A European Social Citizenship?: Preconditions for Future Policies from an Historical Perspective*, (Brussels: P. Lang, 2005), pp 125–158.

[34] Ernst-Joachim Mestmäcker, 'Power, Law and Economic Constitution', (1973) 11 *The German Economic Review*, pp 177–192.

[35] Manfred E. Streit and Werner Mussler, 'The Economic Constitution of the European Community. From "Rome" to "Maastricht"', (1995) 1 *European Law Journal*, pp 5–30; Peter Behrens, 'Die Wirtschaftsverfassung der Europäischen Gemeinschaft', in: Gert Brüggemeier (ed), *Verfassungen für ein ziviles Europa*, (Baden-Baden: Nomos Verlag, 1994), pp 73–90; summarising Markus C. Kerber, 'Den Bock zum Gärtner machen? Eine ordnungspolitische Hinterfragung der Bankenunion', (2014) 65 ORDO, pp 75–98.

[36] Manfred E. Streit, 'Zur Krise des Euro. Ein Währungspolitisches Problem und seine Ordnungsfolgen', (2011) 62 ORDO, pp 517–522, at 520.

[37] Judgment of 12 October 1993, BVerfGE 89, 155; *Brunner v European Union Treaty*, (1994) 57 *CMLR*, p 1.

[38] Lars P. Feld, 'Ein Scheitern ist nicht eingeplant. Oder: Ordnungspolitische Prinzipien der Europäischen Währungsunion, Impulsreden zur Sozialen Marktwirtschaft', (Berlin: Wirtschaftspolitischer Club Deutschland e.V., 2011).

institutional configuration of the EMU and its defects—and started with hectic rescue operations. The commitment to the balancing of national budgets, the avoidance of excessive deficits and the averting of macroeconomic imbalances became enshrined in the so-called Fiscal Compact signed by all but two Member States, and a comprehensive regulatory machinery was established to ensure the implementation of the new agenda.[39] Is this new mode of European economic governance characterised by an ordoliberal imprint? This is what so many of the commentators cited in Section I assume. Leading proponents who are clearly committed to the ordoliberal legacy disagree. Lars P. Feld has, on several occasions, underlined the discrepancy between the concept of a stability union and the actual framing of the EMU.[40] Ernst-Joachim Mestmäcker has rigorously objected to the transformation of states into semi-autonomous polities and even of the ECB into a stakeholder with interests of its own in distributional conflicts.[41] Another *proprium* of the ordoliberal legacy, which the present crisis politics disregards, is a synthesising of law and economics, which implies that economic policy must be guided by law and justiciable criteria.[42] What we observe, instead, is a de-legalisation *of policy-making and its replacement by highly discretionary powers,*[43] and, in this sense, a de-legalisation of the European project.[44]

III. AN ALTERNATIVE RESEARCH AGENDA

Despite all the above-mentioned doubts regarding the straightforwardness of the ordoliberalisation of Europe thesis, we still think it is worth exploring the connection between ordoliberalism, Germany and European integration. Since the 1980s, Germany has experienced a remarkable renaissance of the legacy of Ludwig Erhard. In parallel to the Christian Democratic and liberal coalition under Chancellor Helmut Kohl taking office and proclaiming 'a spiritual and moral renewal', a network of think tanks had emerged in the early 1980s

[39] For details, see Mark Dawson, Henrik Enderlein and Christian Joerges, *Beyond the Crisis: The Governance of Europe's Economic, Political, and Legal Transformation*, edited by the Hertie School, (Oxford: Oxford University Press, 2015).

[40] Feld, n 38 above; idem, 'Europa in der Welt von heute: Wilhelm Röpke und die Zukunft der Europäischen Währungsunion', HWWI Policy Paper 70, Hamburg: Hamburgisches Welt Wirtschafts Institut, 2012.

[41] Ernst-Joachim Mestmäcker, 'Der Schamfleck ist die Geldverachtung', [The Shaming Flaw is the Disdainfulness of Money], *Frankfurter Allgemeine Zeitung*, 18 November 2011; idem, 'Ordnungspolitische Grundlagen einer politischen Union', [Foundational Principles for the Ordering of a Political Union], *Frankfurter Allgemeine Zeitung*, 12 November 2012.

[42] Mestmäcker, n 34 above.

[43] Dariusz Adamski, 'Europe's (Misguided) Constitution of Economic Prosperity', (2013) 50 *Common Market Law Review*, pp 47–86; Fritz W. Scharpf, 'Monetary Union, Fiscal Crisis and the Disabling of Democratic Accountability', in: Wolfgang Streeck and Armin Schäfer (eds), *Politics in the Age of Austerity*, (Cambridge: Polity Press, 2013), pp 108–142.

[44] Christian Joerges, 'The Overburdening of European Law through Economic and Monetary Union', in: Tim Krieger, Bernhard Neumärker and Diana Panke (eds), *Europe's Crisis: The Conflict-Theoretical Perspective*, (Baden-Baden: Nomos, 2015), pp 155–173.

(for example, *Kronberger Kreis* and *Stiftung Marktwirtschaft*).[45] When the world financial crisis de-legitimised Anglo-Saxon mainstream neoclassical economics in Germany, politicians searched for salvation in the Freiburg tradition. In 2013, Angela Merkel made a trip to Freiburg to hold a lecture for the anniversary of the 125th anniversary of the birthday of Walter Eucken.[46] In 2016, a public controversy erupted over a new economic research institute that the finance ministry wanted to establish in Brussels to promote German ordoliberal economic ideas.[47] Key German politicians frequently used ordoliberal concepts and ordoliberal economists as reference-points to communicate with their voters during the sovereign debt crisis.[48] While the original ordoliberal theory has become considerably diluted through public choice and new institutional economics, and has seemingly abandoned its formerly close connection to law, ordoliberalism paradoxically experienced a remarkable renaissance as a cultural reference-point for German élites and voters. Since the 1980s, it has come to a re-interpretation of the ordoliberal legacy. Many quintessentially anti-ordoliberal institutions such as co-determination, collective wage bargaining and the '*Ordnungspolitik der sichtbaren Hand*' (ordering politics by the visible hand) of the federal ministry of the economy, all trademarks of the German model of capitalism, have—in public and political discourse—become associated with the theory of the Freiburg School but not of ordoliberalism.[49] A good number of contributors to this volume resort to notions such as 'tradition' (*Dyson*) or 'cultural predispositions' (*Hien*) when framing ordoliberalism.[50] Indeed, the following volume might open the doors to a new research agenda dealing with the persistent impact of ordoliberalism on policy preferences and in societally widespread 'thinking about the economy'.[51]

---

[45] Walter Ötsch, Stephan Pühringer and Katrin Hirte, *Netwerke des 'Marktes': Ordoliberalismus als Politische Ökonomie*, (Springer, forthcoming 2017).

[46] Angela Merkel, Freiburg, 13 January 2016, available at: www.bundeskanzlerin.de/Content/DE/Rede/2016/01/2016-01-14-rede-walter-eucken.html.

[47] *Frankfurter Allgemeine Zeitung*, 28 February 2017, available at: www.faz.net/aktuell/wirtschaft/wirtschaftspolitik/forschungsauftraege-gezerre-um-schaeubles-bruessel-initiative-14901219.html.

[48] Josef Hien, 'The Religious Roots of the European Crisis', (2017) *Journal of Common Market Studies*, (forthcoming).

[49] Werner Abelhauser and Christoph Klopper, 'Ordnungspolitik der sichtbaren Hand. Das Bundeswirtschaftsministerium und die Kunst der Wirtschaftspolitik', in: Werner Abelhauser (ed), *Das Bundeswirtschaftsministerium in der Ära der Sozialen Marktwirtschaft. Der deutsche Weg der Wirtschaftspolitik*, (Berlin-Boston MA: Springer Verlag, 2016).

[50] Lars P. Feld, Ekkehard A. Köhler and Daniel Nientiedt, 'Ordoliberalism, Pragmatism and the Eurozone Crisis: How the German Tradition Shaped Economic Policy in Europe', CESifo Working Paper Series No 5368, 2015, available at: https://ssrn.com/abstract=2613901.

[51] Sabine Frerichs, 'Integration durch Recht', in: Maurizio Bach and Barbara Hönig (eds), *Europasoziologie: Handbuch für Wissenschaft und Studium*, (Baden-Baden: Nomos, 2017, forthcoming).

Section I

Irritations/Perceptions of Ordoliberalism and of German Politics

1

Dirigisme *and Modernism* vs *Ordoliberalism*

BRUNO AMABLE

ABSTRACT

This contribution compares French neoliberalism with ordoliberalism. The origins and specificities of French neoliberalism are exposed in the first section. The importance of other attempts to find a 'third way' between laissez-faire and Soviet-style economic planning in the 1920s and 1930s for the French brand of neoliberalism is stressed. In this respect, modernism has exerted a significant influence and the synthesis of neoliberalism and modernism was achieved in the dirigiste period after the Second World War, as is shown in the second section. The third section emphasises more specifically the differences between French neoliberalism and ordoliberalism, and explains them by the differentiated levels of industrial development of France and Germany as well as the particular sociology of each school of thought.

I. INTRODUCTION

I N A PUBLICATION that compared French neoliberalism with German ordoliberalism,[1] French economist François Bilger recalled that, while writing his doctoral thesis on the German liberal thought,[2] he was struck by the similarities between *Ordoliberalismus* and eighteenth-century *physiocratie*. Following Bilger, both schools of thought had one key founder (respectively, Walter Eucken and François Quesnay), they had taken inspiration from another science (respectively, medicine and legal studies), they had proposed a doctrine for an economic order in which philosophy and theory were tightly knit, they had manifested a certain scientific dogmatism, and they had tried to exert an influence on political élites. When it came to the comparison with the French neoliberal school, however, Bilger noted

---

[1] François Bilger, 'La pensée néolibérale française et l'ordolibéralisme allemand. Contributions du Colloque du 8 et 9 décembre 2000'. Edited by Patricia Commun. CIRAC/CICC. Travaux et Documents du CIRAC (2003).

[2] idem, *La Pensée économique libérale dans l'Allemagne contemporaine*, (Paris: Librairie générale de droit et de jurisprudence, 1964).

the absence of a unified framework as a specificity. There was no French equivalent of the *Freiburger Schule*.

French neoliberalism and German *Ordoliberalismus* have a partly common history, which takes place in the various inter-war attempts to overcome the limits of *laissez-faire* and renew the liberal thought. The *Colloque* Walter Lippmann, held in Paris in 1938 to celebrate the publication of Walter Lippmann's book, *The Good Society*, in French, gathered contributors to what was going to be broadly labelled neoliberalism,[3] in particular, for Germany, Wilhelm Röpke and Alexander Rüstow, as well as Jacques Rueff, Louis Marlio and Robert Marjolin for France. Various strands of (neo-) liberal thought, united at the time around an 'Agenda for Liberalism', emerged from the *Colloque*.

Ordoliberalismus had already emerged when the *Colloque* of 1938 took place. The German approach to neoliberalism was known and appreciated in the French liberal circles in the 1950s and 1960s:[4] Jacques Rueff considered the post-war German economic miracle as the logical outcome of the application of neoliberal (ordoliberal) principles, and even Pierre Mendès-France, the figurehead of the 'non-Communist left' in France, lauded the pattern of intervention of the German authorities, and considered this to be genuine 'modernism'.

As Bilger points out,[5] another specificity of French neoliberalism, was that the doctrine, compared to its German counterpart, was less systematic, more pragmatic and conceived as an empirical practice implemented by the administration that was theorised *ex post*. As is exposed in what follows, this characteristic derives from the particular historical and economic context in which French neoliberalism emerged.

II. FRENCH MODERNISM AND NEOLIBERALISM

Like *Ordoliberalismus*, French neoliberalism emerged between the two World Wars, in a context in which several 'neo' movements were gaining momentum (neo-capitalism, neo-socialism, neo-corporatism ...),[6] and when the search for a third way between *laissez-faire* and the Soviet-style planned economy, between economic anarchy and economic dictatorship,[7] led to a re-consideration of what the role of the state could be in an economy with 'free' markets.

François Denord distinguishes three different positions regarding state intervention at the time of the *Colloque* Walter Lippmann of 1938, which is considered to

---

[3] Bilger, n 2 above. François Denord, *Néo-libéralisme version française. Histoire d'une idéologie politique*, (Paris, Demopolis, 2007); Pierre Dardot and Christian Laval, *La nouvelle raison du monde. Essai sur la société néolibérale*, (Paris: La Découverte, 2009).

[4] idem, 'Néo-libéralisme et "économie sociale de marché": les origines intellectuelles de la politique européenne de la concurrence' (1930–1950), (2008) 27 *Histoire, économie & société*, pp 23–33.

[5] Bilger, n 1 above.

[6] Denord, n 3 above.

[7] Bilger, n 1 above, p 297.

be the launching event of neoliberalism.[8] The first one was that state intervention was directly or indirectly responsible for the violations to the competitive order. This was the position of the Austrians (von Mises, von Hayek) and partly that of the ordoliberals, who, however, were more clearly associated with the second position, according to which the state was the main actor that could and should fend off and resist the attacks against competition, such as cartels and monopolies. Finally, some of the French participants[9] tended to consider so-called market imperfections to be potentially functional to economic development, and viewed concentration as an inevitable consequence of the evolution of markets and technologies. The role of the state would then be to use market 'imperfections' in the search for the greater good and, if need be, to foster concentration for the sake of economic efficiency.

Two elements can explain the particular attitude of (some of) the French participants on the joint issue of competition and state intervention. The first element concerns the comparative sociology of the participants to the *Colloque* Lippmann. Some of the French participants, who were also contributors to the various 'neo' debates were businessmen and/or engineers (Auguste Detoeuf, Louis Marlio, Ernest Mercier), ie people who were immersed in the practical problems of competition and efficiency, rather than academics for whom issues of competition could be conceived from a more abstract point of view and had no particular *a priori* reasons to sympathise with business interests. Auguste Detoeuf, for instance, published a book of aphorisms,[10] in which he expressed the idea that competition was stimulating when taken in small doses, but poisonous in large doses. A certain French pragmatism vis-à-vis the liberal doctrine also bore the influence of the scientific education of the French participants to the *Colloque*. Louis Marlio considered that the liberal economy (private property, competition, division of labour ...) was the most efficient mode of production, but, in parallel with the laws of physics, which are valid under specific conditions (pressure, temperature ...), the laws of economic liberalism only applied when a series of social, economic, technological and even psychological conditions were satisfied.[11]

The second element to take into account is the relative backwardness of the French economy in the first half of the twentieth century. In 1912, French GDP *per capita* was 58% of that of the US, to be compared with a figure of 79% for Germany and 95% for the UK. In 1938, the situation had changed only a little, the French relative GDP *per capita* had increased to 69%, but the figures for Germany and the UK were respectively 84 and 95%.[12] The theme of the necessary 'modernisation' of the economic structures became a *leitmotiv* for a growing fraction of the industrial and administrative élites as well as workers' unions.[13] The positions adopted by the

---

[8]   Denord, n 4 above.

[9]   Jacques Rueff's opinion on the matter was close to that of the Austrians.

[10]   Auguste Detoeuf, *Propos de O.L. Barenton, confiseur*, (Paris: Eyrolles, Edition d'Organisation, 1986). Originally published in 1937.

[11]   Serge Audier, *Le colloque Lippmann. Aux origines du 'néo-libéralisme'*, (Lormont: Editions Le Bord de l'Eau, 2012), p 227.

[12]   Data source: Stephen Broadberry' EuroGDP2 dataset.

[13]   Richard Kuisel, *Le Capitalisme et l'État en France. Modernisation et dirigisme au XXe siècle*, (Paris: Gallimard, 1984).

French participants to the *Colloque* Lippmann were therefore influenced by the concern, widely shared in the various 'neo' movements, about the low efficiency of the French productive and social system. Broadly agreeing with the superiority of 'free' markets over central planning, the French 'modernists' were nevertheless not ready to put the respect of abstract rules of competition before the search for productivity improvements.

The deficiencies of the French productive system had made themselves felt during the First World War, and the inability of the private sector to sustain the war effort had led the state to step in and administer more or less directly foreign procurements and domestic production. Besides, the war effort involved a certain degree of social peace, which implied relinquishing the *laissez-faire* approach to industrial relations and associate workers' unions to the productivity-improving efforts. The dogmatic liberalism that was dominant before the war condemned any type of public intervention in the economy, except when it came to the protection of specific interests against foreign competition, in particular, in agriculture.[14] This liberalism was then blamed for failing to provide a sufficiently competitive environment for incumbent firms while, at the same time, neglecting the social question.

Some economists, managers and public servants looked for another type of state intervention, which would be subordinated to the objective of economic modernisation. 'Modernism' was a broad movement oriented towards the promotion of technical and organisational change, enabling productivity improvements and a rise of the standard of living, in opposition to the so-called 'Malthusianism' of *laissez-faire* liberalism. Some industrialists, mostly engineers trained in the élite *grandes écoles* (Polytechnique, Centrale, etc) who had acquired a certain rationalist ethos during their studies,[15] were willing to extend the type of governance that they had promoted in their firms to the administration of the whole economy, aiming to diffuse widely the Taylorist principles of scientific work organisation. During the 1920s and 1930s, they formed several movements in order to spread their ideas on how to promote the development of the French economy: *le redressement français* (Ernest Mercier), *les Nouveaux Cahiers* (Auguste Detoeuf), *X-Crise* (Jean Coutrot) …

Valuing competence, the modernists considered that an administration populated by technocrats could work together in a partnership with private firms. Such a partnership would bypass the traditional political channels because politicians were held to be too receptive to demands emanating from traditional sectors or specific firms, which were taken to be responsible for economic backwardness in the first place. Modernisation would be led by a competent élite that would not be hindered by the various political opposition that their plans for the transformation of the French economic structures were bound to raise.

Nevertheless, modernism incorporated social aspects and criticised *laissez-faire* for its lack of consideration of labour, taken to be a mere commodity. In accordance with a certain spirit of the times, 1930s modernism considered corporatism

[14] ibid.
[15] ibid.

favourably for its contribution to social peace, which was instrumental in the diffusion of productivity-improving management methods.

In fact, the economic progress expected from the modernisation of the economic structures was also considered to be a solution to social problems and class conflict. Modernisation would lead to an increase in productivity that would, in turn, raise the standards of living. The less affluent part of the population would more than proportionately benefit from these changes, and the improvement in their economic security would keep the working classes away from the temptation of a socialist revolution. Economic development would, with the help of 'social dialogue', lead to the end of 'ideologies' and the conversion of both the masses and the élite to a common ideal of prosperity and social consensus.

Modernism, in practice, was rather limited before the Second World War, but nevertheless inspired several attempts to devise an 'economic policy' during the 1930s. The modernist influence is also present during the War both in the collaborationist Vichy administration and in the provisory government of the French Republic in London. After the Second World War, the figurehead of the post-WWII modernist movement was Pierre Mendès-France, a left deputy before the Second World War, who had joined de Gaulle in London during the war and became the minister of the national economy in the first post-liberation government in 1944. He was briefly Prime Minister (*président du conseil*) for eight months in the 1950s. But the modernist influence was particularly strong under the de Gaulle presidency.[16]

French modernism influenced French neoliberalism, and, although one should not mistake one for the other, they do share significant common characteristics. They both developed from a critique of *laissez-faire* 'paleo-liberalism' and looked for an alternative to the nightwatchman conception of the state. The state would be instrumental in the stimulation of the modernisation of the productive system and the rationalisation of management methods and economic structures (modernism), or the promotion and defence of an economy based upon the efficiency of competitive mechanisms (neoliberalism). Both movements shared a common rejection of central planning, socialism, Marxism and Communism. They incorporated a rather high dose of élitism and defiance towards political/democratic mechanisms, suspect of being under the influence of pressure groups. And, more simply, the same individuals were associated with both modernism and neoliberalism, such as Auguste Detoeuf and Robert Marjolin, modernists who took part in the *Colloque Lippman*.

III. *DIRIGISME*: A SYNTHESIS BETWEEN MODERNISM AND NEOLIBERALISM

As previously mentioned, the heydays of modernism were the de Gaulle presidency (1958–1969), a period commonly characterised as that of '*dirigisme*'. This term is

---

[16] André Gauron, *Histoire économique et sociale de la Vème République. Tome 1. Le temps des modernistes*, (Paris: La Découverte/Maspero, 1983).

commonly associated with a rather strong influence of the state in the economy. That *dirigisme* is the opposite of laisser-faire is relatively obvious, but how does it relate to the role of the state that the different approaches to neoliberalism envisage? The question revolves around the way the various doctrines consider the way the economy should be steered or directed, and this was already a matter of debate around the time of the *Colloque* Lippmann.

The efforts to renew the liberal doctrine implied to relinquish the notion that the state should limit itself to the role of a night watchman while still respecting the fundamental principles of a 'free' economy. In that perspective, the terms used in the various discussions were all open to more or less divergent interpretations. *Dirigisme* was already a term used at the time of the colloque Lippmann, either to characterise the 'command economy', which the various strands of neoliberalism strongly opposed, or more modestly an economy which would preserve competition and 'free' markets, but given a direction compatible with the respect of certain social and economic objectives as well as the promotion of moral values.

The various interpretations of the same terms could even be found among the French neoliberals. Jacques Rueff thought that an *'économie dirigée'* was an economy with a dictator, whereas other French neoliberals would interpret the notion as an economy that had a direction, in the spirit of a 'liberal interventionism', to which Rüstow and Röpke were favourable, for instance,[17] or even a *'"dirigisme libéral'*. According to another French participant to the *Colloque* Lippmann, the economist Roger Auboin, there was a difference of nature between the Anglo-Saxon *dirigisme*, which respected and used economic mechanisms, and the fascist or Communist *dirigisme*, which tried to obstruct those mechanisms.[18] To confuse matters even more, Louis Rougier, the organiser of the *Colloque* Lippmann, made a distinction between *dirigisme* and interventionism, the latter being considered as being compatible with neoliberalism because of its respect of the 'price mechanism', while the former was taken to be incompatible. Another French participant to the *Colloque*, the economist Louis Baudin, spoke of a 'guided liberalism'. Rougier stated in a later contribution that neoliberalism justified an 'institutional and judicial' interventionism as well as a social interventionism, provided that all this was compatible with the respect of the price mechanism as well as public finance equilibrium.[19] Echoing the position of Louis Marlio mentioned earlier, he considered that the hostility of dyed-in-the-wool liberals towards state intervention stemmed from a neglect of the particular conditions in which such an intervention would take place, and, in particular, to neglect the social environment.

The ambiguity persisted when *dirigisme* was the orientation of the French economic policy under de Gaulle's presidency. De Gaulle's conception was that the state had to give an impulse to economic activity and harmonise the rules.[20] An episode here illustrates the ambiguity of *dirigisme*. A discussion took place in 1961

---

[17] Denord, n 4 above.
[18] Audier, n 11 above, p 248.
[19] Serge Audier, *Néo-libéralisme(s). Une archéologie intellectuelle*, (Paris: Grasset, 2012), p 85.
[20] Charles De Gaulle, *Mémoires d'espoir*, (Paris: Plon, 1970).

between de Gaulle and Pierre Massé, then in charge of planning. De Gaulle asked Massé's advice on a speech that he was meant to deliver a few days later, wherein he would state that the state should run (*diriger*) the economy. Massé thought that this was too strong a word, and proposed 'orientate' (*orienter*), instead of *diriger*. De Gaulle deemed the word too weak, and chose 'lead' (*conduire*), instead.[21]

But the evolution of French planning after the war showed that Massé's view was the one that prevailed. French planning increasingly turned towards an 'indicative', rather than 'prescriptive', direction as the economy progressively got out of the period of shortages which immediately followed the Second World War. Progressively, the 'price mechanism' and competition became the dominant regulating mechanisms in order to achieve economic efficiency, and the efforts of planners became directed towards improving, rather than replacing, the price mechanism. The compatibility of planning and neoliberalism is best summed up by the efforts of Maurice Allais to theorise a 'competitive planning' which combined the advantages of a market economy with those of state intervention. The ambition of what he later called 'institutional planning' was to obtain a de-centralised economy, that is, an economy guided by the price mechanism, which would operate within the institutional structures that only the state could define.[22]

Studying that period, Richard Kuisel simply considered post-war *dirigisme* as a 'neoliberal order'.[23] *Dirigisme* was, in a true neoliberal spirit, an alternative to both *laissez-faire* and central planning, an ordered economy that was not led at every moment but let to be free within certain limits set by the state. The economy was given an objective: to achieve the modernisation of the productive structure.

IV. FRENCH NEOLIBERALISM AND *ORDOLIBERALISMUS* COMPARED

As mentioned above, French neoliberalism and German ordoliberalism have common origins, and followed broadly similar ambitions. The context in which both approaches emerged was that of the decade-long crisis of liberalism, the discredit of *laissez-faire* in the context of the Great Depression, and the competition of other ideologies, in particular, socialism. The moral aspect present in certain strands of neoliberalism is central in *Ordoliberalismus*, and was also present in the original contributors to French neoliberalism. Auguste Detoeuf thought that getting out of the (1930s) crisis would imply a moral transformation that would spread over several generations.[24] Jean Coutrot (*X-Crise*) thought that the core of the 'co-ordinated economy' he wanted to see emerge would be composed of managers characterised by their competence and their high morals.

---

[21] Henri Weber, *Le parti des patrons. Le CNPF (1945–1986)*. (Paris: Seuil,1986), p 125.

[22] Arnaud Diemer, 'La planification concurrentielle: théories et application', in: Arnaud Diemer, Jérôme Lallement and Bertrand Munier (eds), *Maurice Allais et la Science économique*, (Paris: Clément Juglar, 2010).

[23] Kuisel, n 13 above.

[24] Denord, n 3 above.

The two approaches have also some specific characteristics. Table 1 presents a brief synthesis of the most notable differences. Going back to that pointed out by François Bilger,[25] between a theory-based *Ordoliberalismus* and a more pragmatic French neoliberalism, one may actually argue that the real difference is between a more philosophical approach on the German side, opposed to an economic theory-based approach for the French side.[26] In fact, if one follows Kuisel[27] and considers the *dirigisme* and indicative planning period as representative of the application of neoliberal ideas in France, one cannot fail to observe the importance of the '*calcul économique*' (economic computation), ie the application of mathematical economics to concrete economic problems, such as public investment, for instance.

Table 1: Comparison between French neoliberalism and *Ordoliberalismus*

	Dirigisme/Modernisme/French neo-liberalism	*Ordoliberalismus*
'Sociology'	Industrialists (engineers), high-level civil servants, policy-makers, 'engineer-economists'	Academics, law professors, economists
objectives	Fight against the vested interests responsible for economic backwardness; modernisation of the productive structure	Fight against cartels and monopolies, which are a danger for liberties
means	Administration-controlled emulation of competitive mechanisms	Competition-preserving legal framework and monetary stability
evolution	Away from directive planning under the 5th Republic and increased importance of market competition and the 'price mechanism'	Diminished importance of anti-cartel actions
specificities	Keynesian ideas influential	Virtual absence of Keynesian elements

The development of these methods follows a French tradition going back at least to the nineteenth century with Jules Dupuit and the 'engineer-economists', a tradition that lived on in the twentieth century with contributors such as Pierre Massé, Marcel Boiteux and Edmond Malinvaud. The basic idea underlying the application of mathematical economics to real-life economic problems is that one could try to come as close as possible to the optimal equilibrium that would be obtained in a first-best world by letting the price mechanism work, but not with the prices that would prevail if the actual markets were characterised by many imperfections. The actual prices would not be the 'right' prices in a context of market imperfections.

---

[25] Bilger, n 1 above.
[26] The economic-theoretical reference would be the modern version of Walras' general equilibrium that mathematical economists developed during the 1950s and 1960s.
[27] Kuisel, n 13 above.

In this perspective, it is up to the state to build an institutional and regulatory environment within which market mechanisms would orient society in a socially desirable direction.

This perspective is rather different from the German view, which expects the achievement of socially-desirable goals from a competitive environment as perfect as possible. In contrast, the French view, at least during the period when indicative planning had a significant influence on the path of economic development, was to consider the issue of actual competition as secondary as long as it was impossible to reconcile competition with economic efficiency, as in the case of 'natural monopolies', for instance. This opposition was already present at the time of the *Colloque* Lippmann, when the French participants, or at least the engineers/managers among them, were worried about the lack of efficiency of the national productive structures, and thought that the German participants neglected the potential benefits that industrial concentration could bring in terms of productivity improvements. If both the French and German neoliberals agreed with the necessity of public intervention in the economy, the character of this intervention differed across the two countries: mostly legislative and, indirectly for the ordoliberals, mostly administrative and direct for the French. The Germans, in contrast, wanted to create the conditions of perfect competition, the French merely wanted to emulate perfect competition.

2

Why and How has German Ordoliberalism Become a French Issue? Some Aspects about Ordoliberal Thoughts we can Learn from the French Reception

ARNAUD LECHEVALIER

In the second half of the twentieth century
(…) liberalism is a word that comes to us
[to France] from Germany.

Michel Foucault, *The Birth of Biopolitics*, p 22

ABSTRACT

In recent years, as evidenced by several books, essays and political controversies, the German ordoliberal doctrine has become part of the public debate in France. In the main, this has to be understood against the backdrop of the Eurozone crisis. But, in actual fact, it is since the beginning of the 1960s that one can speak of a French corpus concerning the reception and discussion of the German ordoliberal doctrine. This chapter looks at three major waves of how the ordoliberal school of thought was received in France in order to analyse what we can learn from its reception: to wit, from the beginning of the 1960s onwards, at the turn of the century, and since the outset of the Eurozone crisis. Through these developments, four main issues are addressed. First, we present the theoretical re-reading of the content and scope of ordoliberalism with a view to the (neo-) liberal tradition in the light of another national cultural tradition. Second, we synthesise the discussion on ordoliberalism's contribution to the German miracle after WWII, and, upon this basis, show that the French reception of ordoliberalism has enriched the content of the theoretical, as well as the empirical, debates on the 'German model'. Third, ordoliberalism is considered as a key controversy—especially between both sides of the Rhine—not only about the relevant economic policy, but also as a means of justifying neoliberal policies in France. Fourth, in the context of the responses brought to the Eurozone crisis, ordoliberalism has, on the French side of the Rhine, been a major topic for debates on the European integration project, in terms of both its process and its methods.

I. INTRODUCTION

NOWADAYS, IN FRANCE, the German ordoliberal doctrine has become an integral part of the public debate. Indeed, over the last years, the ordo-liberal legacy has been much more discussed in France than in Germany. Let us take some recent examples of this pervasiveness in the public debate. Upon the basis of Donald Tusk's statements, François Denord, Rachel Knaebel and Pierre Rimbert published a long contribution in *Le Monde diplomatique* entitled 'Ordo-liberalism, an iron cage for the old continent'.[1] Some time before, a famous publica-tion for secondary school teachers in social sciences, with an educational purpose, devoted an issue to the Ordoliberalism.[2] Jean-Luc Mélanchon, a leftist candidate for the 2017 presidential election, published a pamphlet against Germany in 2015, which targeted, among other things, the German 'ordoliberal credo'. Conversely, a former senior civil servant who had become the CEO of one of the biggest French banks published an essay on the alleged 'neurotic' relationship of the French people with economic matters handled by Germany, thanks to its ordoliberal tradition, a model which was supposed to have established the foundations of the 'Rhine-land model' (sic).[3] Recently, some leaders of the French liberal-conservative party (*Les Républicains*) have claimed to be 'ordoliberal',[4] and, according to commentators, 'more than the neoliberalism of Margaret Thatcher, it is ordoliberalism that makes it possible to understand the coherence of François Fillon's political programme'— the main candidate of the conservative camp for the 2017 presidential election.[5] Over the period from 2013 to 2016, the items 'ordoliberal' and 'ordoliberalism' led to some 20 articles in the newspaper '*Le Monde*', but almost nothing before 2012. A biography published in 2016 by a journalist has been 'rewarded' with a preface by Wolfgang Schäuble because of its accurate portrayal of Jacques Rueff, an economist and former political advisor of Charles de Gaulle, as an ordoliberal.[6]

Hence, in recent years, in the wake of the Eurozone crises, of the European Union's crisis and that of Greece, the ordoliberal tradition has thus experienced a

---

[1] François Denord, Rachel Knaebel and Pierre Rimbert, 'L'ordolibéralisme allemand, cage de fer pour le Vieux Continent', *Le Monde diplomatique*, August 2015.
[2] Frédéric Farah, 'L'Ordolibéralisme', *Ecoflash*, no 281, October 2013.
[3] Jean Peyrelevade, *Histoire d'une névrose, la France et son économie*, (Paris: Albin Michel, 2015).
[4] ie, Hervé Mariton on the programme 'Questions Politiques', on Sunday 19 February 2017.
[5] Jean-Louis Thiériot, 'François Fillon et Margaret Thatcher: même combat, vraiment?', *Le Figaro*, 24 November 2016.
[6] Gérard Minart, *Jacques Rueff: Un libéral français*, with preface by Wolfgang Schäuble, (Paris: Editions Odile Jacob, 2016).

peak of interest in France. However, beyond these recent events, one can speak of a French *corpus* concerning the reception and discussion of the German ordoliberal doctrine. In this chapter, we will look at three major waves of the ordoliberal school of thought's reception in France. The first one took place from the early 1960s onwards: its main concern was to situate ordoliberalism in the history of ideas in Germany. At the same time, it aimed at assessing its contribution to the 'German miracle' after WWII as well as its contribution to what has often been portrayed, not only in France, as a 'German model'. After the turn of the century, the second wave began with the post mortem publication of Michel Foucault's lectures on the ordoliberalism at the *Collège de France*. This major work has nurtured several publications, which have tried to re-assess ordoliberalism's own contribution as an original version of the neoliberalism. Third, against this background, several pieces of research have attempted to re-appraise the influence of the ordoliberalism on the European integration process from its very inception onwards, but especially in the wake of the Eurozone crisis.

If the reception of the German ordoliberalism in France is of particular interest, it is because, through these developments, four main issues will be addressed: first, the theoretical re-reading of the content and scope of ordoliberalism in the light of another national cultural tradition; second, the discussion of ordoliberalism as an element—or not—of the 'German model'; third, ordoliberalism as a key controversy—especially between both sides of the Rhine—about the right economic policy; and last, but not least, ordoliberalism as a major topic for debates on the project of the European integration process and its methods.

II. ORDOLIBERALISM, THE LIBERAL TRADITION, AND GERMANY

At the very beginning of the 1960s, the first reception of German ordoliberalism in France was mainly focused on the history of ideas as well as on economic policy. The first issue was to explain the revival of a liberal doctrine in a country which was famously recalcitrant about it, and to analyse the content of ordoliberal thought as well as past continuities and breaks with its views on the liberal tradition. The other main issue was to discuss the contribution of ordoliberalism to the economic 'German miracle', and then to the distinctive features of the German model. Nearly four decades later, at the turn of the century, several works published in France contributed to a re-discovery of the topic.

A. The First Reception of Ordoliberalism in France in the 1960s

The first work published on ordoliberalism in France after WWII was François Bilger's thesis, which he defended at the University of Strasbourg in June 1960. The thesis director was Daniel Villey (1911–1968), a neoliberal economist, who tried to reconcile French Catholics to economic liberalism. A member of the Mont Pèlerin Society from the 1950s, then vice-president from 1965 onwards, and even briefly president before his death, he worked for the creation of a new liberal school in France. He was not a direct proponent of German ordoliberalism, whose 'productivism' he saw as a 'concession to the materialism of our time and an unfortunate subordination of freedom to social purposes', François Bilger wrote in a tribute dedicated to him in 1971.[7] In his foreword to the edited thesis, Villey explains ironically the meaning of the enterprise:

> It seems obvious to us [in France] that the market economy is no more than a museum piece, a past system, an outdated historical category. Our students use the past tense to speak about the "liberal era". Mr Bilger reminds us that in Germany the simple present tense is used to speak about it. And it is mainly the future tense, which is used to speak about it.[8]

The fact is even more surprising that the 'German spirit' had remained profoundly impermeable to ('Anglo-French') liberalism.

> It was against it [Anglo-French liberalism] that Germany unified, and step-by-step constituted itself into a nation.[9]

This is why it is important not only to understand how it was possible for (ordo-) liberalism to win in Germany, but also to analyse its main distinguishing features compared to 'paleoliberalism'.

The purpose and content of Bilger's thesis was precisely to understand how the ordoliberalism had conquered post-war German society and what this might mean. The first part of his thesis was devoted to the life and works of Walter Eucken—who is presented here as the subject of a glowing portrait—and of Franz Böhm, and to the connexions which made the Freiburg School possible. The second part was dedicated to the German liberal doctrine (the ordoliberal philosophy, the economic regime, and the economic policy which it produced), and the third was explored the resurgence of liberal economical ideas (the liberalism of the German economic policy, the doctrinal resonance of ordoliberalism, liberalism and public opinion).

Ordoliberalism is viewed as a profound reaction to the general ideas that had been prevalent in Germany from the beginning of the nineteenth century, first and foremost, the ideology of materialism.[10] Materialism nurtured the idea that there were absolute natural laws, which, in general, present constraining factors for a society. Therefore, materialism was also at the origin of the harmful *laissez-faire* doctrine and also led to the neglect of the spiritual dimension of humanity. German liberals elaborated their doctrine, which was conceived as a common defence of values in opposition to this 'resignation' in the West. It was also viewed as a scientific response

---

[7] François Bilger, 'Daniel Villey, Professeur de liberté', (1971) *Revue d'Economie Politique*, pp 581–583.

[8] Bilger, Foreword of thesis.

[9] ibid.

[10] Somewhat curiously, Bilger missed one key piece of the intellectual puzzle: Eucken's wish for emancipation concerning the programme of the German historical school after the 'Methodenstreit'. A few years ago, this issue was discussed in details in the Franco-German PhD thesis of Sylvain Broyer, *La pensée théorique et politique de Walter Eucken à la lumière des écoles historiques allemandes. Die Hinterlassenschaft der historischen Schule in Walter Euckens Ordnungstherorie und dem deutschen Ordoliberalismus*, University Lyon 2, (2006).

in the face of the ecological, political and social crisis. By analysing the economic philosophy of ordoliberalism in three successive parts (ontology, gnoseology, and axiology), Bilger identified what he considered to be at the heart ('the vital centre') of the perspective's reversal realised by ordoliberalism with regard to 'classical' liberalism. According to him, if both philosophies believe in reason, the classical form of liberalism uses it only as an instrument of knowledge and human liberation. Unlike the ordoliberalism, it does not believe 'in the creative, constructive power of reason in relation to nature'.[11]

Against this background, what are the aims of political economy? Walter Eucken and Wilhelm Röpke answer: A social order worthy of human beings. Due to Bilger, it is therefore the view of what humankind means that has to define the aims of economic policy. On this matter, the Freiburg School is part of the Kantian heritage; a human being requires two related rights: natural freedom and equality before moral law.[12] The freedom claimed by individuals is no longer that of *laissez-faire*, it becomes the freedom to act in accordance with moral law, thereby ensuring the equality of all. Franz Böhm as well as Leonhard Miksch, define market mechanisms as a 'plebiscite', according to which everyone is free because he or she is subject to the same general law. 'Fair action' is indeed an action which is in conformity with the 'general will' in the sense of Rousseau. For instance, to receive a wage determined by supply and demand is 'fair', because supply and demand are the expression of the general will. In this way, the 'new liberalism' surely represents a form of idealism. Yet, this idealism is based upon laws derived from the nature of things and from the nature of reason through science, for example, Kant's moral idealism is tempered by the realism of knowledge. 'We can speak of "scientific idealism". Idealism is guided by social science, but at the same time science must avoid scientism, and idealism has to draw the natural and moral limits of science. What a difference with the hedonistic philosophy of the old liberalism!' sums up Bilger.[13]

While the 'old liberalism' claimed the compliance of the economic regime with the 'state of nature', the first requirement of the 'new liberalism' is the establishment of an economic regime freely defined both by the people and for the people. According to the ordoliberal doctrine, the general principle of the ideal economic regime should have the character of the *Rechtsstaat* (the state under the rule of law). This is why the first economic act of a free people must be to give itself an economic constitution at the same time that its political constitution is conceived. The fundamental principle of this economic constitution would be that of achieving a price system resulting from perfect competition. The other main principles are based upon a stable currency, free access to markets, freedom of contract, and consistency of economic policy. In addition, regulatory principles, which should govern not the framework but the economic process, concern the regulation of competition, the distribution of income (the existence of a social safety-net) and corrective measures

[11] François Bilger, *La pensée économique libérale dans l'Allemagne contemporaine*, (Paris: Librairie Générale de Droit et de Jurisprudence, 1964), p 131.
[12] Surprisingly, the influence of Husserl on Eucken's work was almost totally ignored by Bilger.
[13] Bilger, n 11 above, p 140.

to mitigate negative external effects. Concerning social policy, Bilger remarks that 'the Freiburg School demands, in the name of its own effectiveness, that the social policy of purchasing power re-distribution should be as limited as possible, since it almost necessarily dampens economic development'.[14] The ordoliberals want to limit social policy to marginal cases, that is to say, a social policy has to be linked to certain thresholds of income. The steady improvement in the level of national income is supposed to enable and to allow everyone to secure by their own means an increasing share of their needs. Short-term, anti-cyclical economic policy should be a classic monetary policy led by an independent central bank.

The third part of the thesis is devoted to the explanation of the resurgence of the (neo-) liberalism in Germany after WWII and its influence on the economic policy pursued in West Germany, as it was seen in France in the early 1960s. At the beginning of the first chapter, Bilger quotes two books—one from André Piettre published in France in 1952 and another from Henry C. Wallich published in England in 1955—which point out the renaissance of the ordoliberalism as key factor of the 'German miracle'.[15] In Bilger's opinion, there is a major actor in this context, 'the Turgot of the ordoliberals': namely, Ludwig Erhard.[16] After the war, he was first in charge of the economic administration of the Anglo-American Bizone and he was responsible for nominating the scientific council, which had been formed alongside the administration of the Bizone as an independent body. This council included several ordoliberals (Walter Eucken, Franz Böhm, Alfred Müller-Armack, Leonhard Miksch) picked by Erhard; the other half of the members was made up of representatives of the Christian Democratic Union (CDU) (Oswald von Nell-Breuning) or of the 'socialists' (Karl Schiller, Gerhard Weisser). Among other things, this council advocated the rapid liberalisation of prices, which was implemented as soon as 20 June 1948 (see, also, above). Bilger explains the resistance that Erhard had to face in the administration as well as in his own party (the CDU) after his nomination as a Minister for Economics in Konrad Adenauer's government in 1948, even though the CDU adopted the social market economy approach in 1949. The first success attributed to its policy provided Erhard fairly soon with the support of public opinion.

> The presence close to the Minister, then to the chancellor, of the Secretary of State, Müller-Armack, the influence of Röpke's opinions on him, the permanent existence of a scientific council in which the members of the Freiburg School occupied a prominent place from the beginning onwards, all these things show the influence of liberal thinking on German politics.[17]

Indeed, according to Bilger, if the basic law of 1949 included the recommendations of the Freiburg School only partly (in particular, the enumeration of quite a

---

[14] ibid, p 178.

[15] André Piettre, *L'Économie allemande contemporaine*, (Paris: Medicis, 1952); Henry C. Wallich, *The Mainsprings of the German Revival*, (New Haven CT: Yale University Press, 1955).

[16] 'It is a rare opportunity for a scientific school to have a maker as faithful to his ideas and a statesman, who is so adroit to persuade crowds and so close to the scientists', writes Bilger, p 215.

[17] Bilger, n 11 above, p 215.

few of the fundamental economic freedoms), one can assume that the economic policy led by Erhard matched the ordoliberal view through the liberalisation of prices and wage-setting as well as that of external trade. The ordo-policy was also implemented through the privatisation of public companies. Clearly, the success of the German economy cannot be attributed exclusively to the influence of the ordoliberal doctrine.

> In fact, since the end of the 19th century, Germany had a production potential quite comparable to that of England at the beginning of the 20th century (...). Yet the primary cause of the liberal success in Germany has been the very rapid realization of the liberalization of external trade by the German government under the influence of L. Erhard and the liberals.[18]

Bilger acknowledges that under the pressure of the trade unions the policy led 'has deviated from the model', with the implementation of the *Mitbestimmung* as well as by softening the anti-monopolistic policy under the pressure of the employers' association. Yet, in the third part of his work he insists on the influence of the ordoliberalism on the change of German social democracy (Bad Godesberg) and even beyond on the public opinion thanks to its relays in the media.

B. From the Early 1960s to the Turn of the Century: The Controversies Concerning the Contributions of Ordoliberalism to the Genuine German Model

François Bilger refused to 'rally the opinion' of those who 'try to deny the doctrinal inspiration of this policy [for example, the economic policy led]'.[19] Indeed, this debate took place in France in the 1950s and 1960s and actually continued even later on. Several French authors denied or put in doubt the influence of the ordoliberalism; ie more precisely, the fact that the policy implemented in Germany was really liberal. One of the most significant examples is Pierre Mendès France (Prime Minister from June 1954 to February 1955 and a prominent figure of the political centre-left after WWII), who, in 1954, published an article in the *Le Monde* with the title 'Liberal policy or realistic policy?'. He mainly argued that the 'Erhard method', which had determined the success of Germany's economic recovery, was not, in fact, as liberal as it claimed. This success was, first and foremost, due to the monetary reform of 1948 and to the Marshall Plan. This aid applied to a war-production system which remained powerful enough to get the production system back afloat in spite of the dismantling of the productive system imposed by the allies. In the same vein, the economist André Piettre began an article published in the *Revue économique* in 1962 with the following question: 'Has the fatherland of List, Bismarck or Dr. Schacht, become nowadays the country of liberalism?'[20] Piettre defended a thesis

---

[18] ibid.
[19] ibid, p 232.
[20] André Piettre, 'L'économie allemande est-elle vraiment libérale?', (1962) 13 *Revue Economique*, pp 339–354.

according to which Germany had indeed, in a dialectical way, implemented a liberal policy for its economic *mechanisms*, but, at the same time, had implemented it in favour of *structures* which remained much less liberal.

He emphasised not only the anti-Keynesian monetary and fiscal policy, but also the external free-trade policy pursued by Erhard ('alone against all'). On other occasions, he observed that German industry as well as the German bank system had become more concentrated than ever before, with a cartel office which had been 'easy going' on this issue. Abundant tax revenues had boosted public investment, the high level of which was one of the secrets of Germany's economic recovery. Piettre considered the contrast between German neoliberalism and French planning as a simplification.

In his handbook on *West Germany*, published in 1970 in the series *Politiques économiques*, and used by generations of students, Jean François-Poncet, diplomat and later on Minister of Foreign Affairs Minister (1978–1981) in Prime Minister Raymond Barre's government, took part in this debate.[21] On the one hand, he outlined that the Freiburg School realised the synthesis of classical liberalism, to which the German intelligentsia had remained allergic, with the traditional aspirations of the 'Germanic soul'.[22] On the other hand, after having emphasised the 'fortuitous circumstances' of Erhard's decisive role, he suggested that the success of the German economy was also due to external factors (the Marshall Plan, the London Agreement on German External Debts implemented in 1953). He added also that, in spite 'of a somewhat solemn and readily verbose infatuation for the ordoliberalism', the economic policy being pursued was, in fact, 'often pragmatic, and sometimes perfectly anti-liberal'. Yet 'by providing the government with a doctrine, the ordoliberal school of thought gave governmental action an authority and a consistency it would doubtless have benefited from otherwise'.[23]

This issue re-surfaced at the beginning of the 1990s with the publication by a senior civil servant who had become the chief executive of a big insurance company, Michel Albert, of an essay on modern capitalism.[24] Following some scientific works on the variety of capitalism, Albert opposed both Anglo-Saxon and 'Rhineland capitalism'—an expression that afterwards flourished in France. Moreover, he presented ordoliberalism, first, as a pillar of the Rhineland model, and, second, drew equivalence between the former and the social market economy. Compared to Anglo-Saxon capitalism, the Rhineland model was characterised in Albert's book by the role of the banks, which offered 'patient capital' for financing business, a form of corporate governance conceived in the interests of all stakeholders, the role of unions and the social consensus, as well as the importance of the ordoliberal doctrine. The latest was seen through the lens of a state limited to the role of a rule-setter. Some commentators noted that the book is, in this respect, interesting because it

---

[21] Jean François-Poncet, *L'Allemagne occidentale*, (Paris: Sirey, coll. Politiques économiques, 1970).
[22] 'Independently of their own value, the Freiburg School presents liberalism from a point of view best suited to seduce the German mind. Its emphasis placed on moral values, the notion of order, the important mission assigned to the state, the scientific, systematic or even closed character of the doctrine, are made to please' (François-Poncet, n 21 above, p 65).
[23] ibid, p 66.
[24] Michel Albert, *Capitalisme contre capitalisme*, (Paris: Édition du Seuil, 1991).

contains two major biases of the French view on the relationship between the state and the economy in Germany.[25] The first one opposed a 'colbertist' French state, pervasive and interventionist, to a German state, the holder of the precepts of the social market economy, which acts only as a rule-setter of the framework within which the economic game takes place. Upon this basis, the comparative analysis of public intervention concretely forgets the key role of the *Länder* and Gemeinden most of the time. The second one is the role devoted to ordoliberalism, which is regarded as the matrix of the social market economy, which was supposed to have organised post-war German capitalism according to liberal principles. In fact, several features of the 'German model' clearly contradict the ordoliberal doctrine;[26] these include, among other things, the high degree of concentration of industrial big companies, the Bismarckian social insurance system, as well as the collective bargaining system (*Tarifverträge*) or the *Mitbestimmung*. Indeed, several works since then have stressed the ambiguity and the polysemy of the expression 'social market economy' due to the successive versions of the concept[27]—beginning with the different approaches to this topic among the ordoliberals themselves (see above). More globally, by constructing a model opposed to that which was prevalent in the Anglophone countries, Albert 'blends inputs of liberal provenance and social-democratic correctives to them'.[28] The book by Michel Albert was not the first one on the 'German (economic) model'.[29] Yet, it has contributed to re-launch a debate in France on the main components of the German model, mainly conceived in terms of 'institutional complementarities',[30] and the role played in this regard by the ordoliberal doctrine; a debate which has remained uninterrupted since then.

Moreover, at the turn of the century, the role of institutions in the ordoliberal doctrine drew the attention of some French economists of the 'regulation school',

---

[25] Jean-Daniel Weisz, 'L'intérêt pour une approche régulationniste du detour par l'ordolibéralisme', in: Patricia Commun (ed), *L'Ordolibéralisme allemand. Aux sources de l'économie sociale de marché*, (Paris: CIRAC/CICC, 2003), pp 49–66.

[26] Christophe Strassel, 'La France, l'Europe et le modèle allemand', (2013) 151 *Hérodote*, pp 60–82.

[27] See Pierre Dardot and Christian Laval, *La nouvelle raison du monde. Essai sur la société néolibérale*, (Paris: La découverte, coll. Poche, 2009), Ch 11; *The New Way of the World: On Neoliberal Society*, trans. Gregory Elliot, (London-New York: Verso, 2014), Ch 7; Arnaud Lechevalier, 'Eucken under the Pillow: The Ordoliberal Imprint on Social Europe', in: Arnaud Lechevalier and Jan Wielgohs (eds), *Social Europe: A Dead End: What the Eurozone crisis is Doing to Europe's Social Dimension*, (Copenhagen: DJØF Publishing, 2015), pp 49–102, at 64–68.

[28] Dardot and Laval, n 27 above, p 226.

[29] The first masterpiece of the comparative analysis between France and Germany was due to the book by Marc Maurice, Sellier François Sellier and Jean-Jacques Silvestre, *Politique d'éducation et organisation industrielle en France et en Allemagne*, (Paris: Puf, 1982), which has also been the trigger factor of a methodological reflexion on the comparative analysis upon the basis of the French-German comparison (see Anne Labit and Jens Thoemmes, '20 ans de comparaison France-Allemagne: de l'effet sociétal à l'analyse de l'articulation des régulations globales et locales', in: Michel Lallement and Jan Spurk (eds), *Stratégies de la comparaison internationale*, (Paris: Editions du CNRS, 2003), pp 23–38.

[30] For some recent contributions, see Fabrice Pesin and Christophe Strassel, *Le modèle allemand en question*, (Paris: Economica, 2005); Christopher Lantenois, 'L'Allemagne à l'épreuve de la réunification et de la financiarisation', doctorate thesis in economic science, Université de Paris XIII. (2008); Rémi Lallement, 'Le régime allemand de croissance tirée par l'exportation: entre succès et remise en cause, Document de travail du Centre d'Analyse Stratégique', (2010); Fabre, n 2 above; Arnaud Lechevalier, 'La grande transformation de l'Allemagne réunifiée dans le contexte européen', (2013) 60 *L'économie politique*, pp 17–34.

who compared both methodological and theoretical approaches.[31] Concomitantly, in the context in Germany of the Kohl era and subsequently of the creation of the '*Initiative Neue Soziale Marktwirtschaft* (INSM)' in the year 2000, which is a period of 'a return to the sources' accompanied by a challenge to the 'social drift of the social market economy', a new interest in ordoliberalism—its main characteristic features, its sources, its influence—re-appeared among French specialists of German studies.[32]

III. FOUCAULT'S *BIRTH OF BIOPOLITICS*: ORDOLIBERALISM AS A NEW MODE OF GOVERNMENTALITY

After this first analysis in the 1960s, Michel Foucault played a key role in the re-discovery of German ordoliberalism in his lectures of 1978 and 1979 at the *Collège de France*, which were published in 2004, long after his death in 1984. It should be noted that François Bilger's thesis seems to have been one on the main sources for Foucault on ordoliberalism. Both lectures focus on the 'genealogy of the modern state' (Lecture 5 April 1978). Foucault coins the concept of 'governmentality' as a 'guideline' for the analysis: the semantic linking of governing ('*gouverner*') and modes of thought ('*mentalités*') indicates that it is not possible to study the technologies of power without an analysis of the political rationality underpinning them.[33] From this point of view, the lectures on *Securité, territoire, population* and on the *Naissance de la biopolitique*[34] held at the *Collège de France* in 1978 and 1979 expressed a shift of Foucault's focus from 'subjection' to the 'exercise of freedom'. This shift expresses Foucault's new awareness of the limits and inadequacies of a reflection on the social order which mainly focuses on discipline and constraints, because this approach does not account for the more recent forms of governmentability. Thus, Foucault questions the genealogy of the notion of government.[35]

---

[31] Agnès Labrousse and Jean-Daniel Weisz (eds), Institutional Economics in France and Germany. German Ordoliberalism versus the French Regulation School, (Berlin-Heidelberg-New-York: Springer Verlag, 2001).

[32] Patricia Commun (ed), *L'Ordolibéralisme allemand. Aux sources de l'économie sociale de marché*, (Paris: CIRAC/CICC, 2003). It could come as a surprise for German readers, that the sole French review on the German economy, ie *Regards sur l'économie allemande*, has been for years in the hand of German studies' specialists, who have remained close to the neo- and ordoliberal tradition. See, for a significant example, the publication of the paper of Berthold Busch and Jürgen Matthes, 'Gouvernance de la zone Euro: comment prévenir la défaillance du politique? Le point de vue allemand', (2012) 105 *Regards sur l'économie allemande*, pp 5–25.

[33] Thomas Lemke, 'Foucault, Governmentality, and Critique', (2002) 14 *Rethinking Marxism*, pp 49–64.

[34] As noted by Foucault himself at the beginning of his lesson of 1 February 1978 (Foucault 2004/2007), a more accurate title for the course would have been 'a history of governmentality'.

[35] In fact, the interest of Foucault at that time in neoliberalism and especially in ordoliberalism has triggered a controversial debate on the scope and sense of this research with regard to its global work. See, among others, for French references: Jacques Donzelot, 'Foucault et l'intelligence du libéralisme', (2005) *Esprit*, November 2005, pp 60–82; Jacques Bidet, 'Foucault et le libéralisme', (2006) 40 *Actuel Marx*, pp 169–185; Serge Audier, *Le colloque Lippmann. Aux origines du 'néo-libéralisme'*, (Paris: éditions du bord de l'eau, coll. Poch, 2012); Frédéric Gros, Daniele Lorenzini, Ariane Revel and Arianna Sforzini (eds), 'Les néolibéralismes de Michel Foucault', (2013) 52 *Raisons politiques*.

This led Foucault to investigate the issue of liberalism understood 'not as a theory or an ideology, and even less, obviously, as a way in which "society" "represents itself," but as a practice, that is to say, a "way of doing things" directed towards objectives and regulating itself by continuous reflection'.[36] This interpretation of liberalism cannot claim to be comprehensive: it is 'a possible level of analysis, that of "governmental reason," of those types of rationality that are implemented in the methods by which human conduct is directed through a state administration'.[37] According to Foucault, liberal thought does not start from the existence of the state, but from society, which exists in a complex relation of exteriority and interiority vis-à-vis the state. Against this backdrop, the question is no longer 'How can one govern as much as possible at the least possible cost?'. Instead, the question becomes: 'Why must one govern? That is to say: What makes government necessary, and what ends must it pursue with regard to society in order to justify its own existence?'[38]

From this point of view, the most interesting moment is the second half of the eighteenth century, when an 'internal limitation of governmental reason' emerged after the reign of the '*raison d'État*'. This change was made possible through the emergence of the political economy in a broad sense (as 'a sort of general reflection on the organization, distribution, and limitation of powers in a society'). According to Foucault, it was political economy that made it possible to ensure the self-limitation of governmental reason:

> The political economy does not discover natural rights that exist prior to the exercise of governmentality; it discovers a certain naturalness specific to the practice of government itself. The objects of governmental action have a specific nature. There is a nature specific to this governmental action itself and this is what political economy will study.[39]

With the emergence of political economy 'an important substitution, or doubling rather, is carried out, since the subjects of right on which political sovereignty is exercised appear as a *population* that a government must manage'.[40] Indeed, why does the political economy change the governmental practice? It is this invention of the notion of population, through which the principle of self-limitation of government action was implemented. As a social object, the population is characterised by regularities that can be described as natural. There are two kinds of them.[41] First, as progressively discovered by statisticians, the population is characterised by constant, stable or probable proportions (number of deaths, patients, etc). Second, governmental reason no longer speaks in the name of authentic divine or natural political rights, but instead places the 'nature' of humans, especially of the population, at the

---

[36] Michel Foucault, *Naissance de la biopolitique: Cours au Collège de France 1978–1979*, ed by M. Senellart under the dir. of F. Ewald and A. Fontana, (Paris: Gallimard/Seuil, 2004); *The Birth of Biopolitics*, translated by Graham Burchell, New York: Palgrave-MacMillan, 2008, p 318.

[37] ibid, p 322.

[38] ibid.

[39] ibid, p 16.

[40] ibid, p 22.

[41] Jean-Yves Grenier and André Orléan, 'Michel Foucault, l'économie politique et le libéralisme', (2007) 62 *Annales. Histoire, Sciences Sociales*, pp 1155–1182, at 1160.

centre of regulations. Yet, there is a behavioural invariant, one which confers to the population a unique driving force: the pursuit of individual interest.

> In the (historic) moment when people speak in the name of the market, when there is veridiction, it is no longer the right of a subject that needs to be promoted or changed, but the interest, which is administered in the name of freedom.[42]

The nature of mankind, of its freedom and interests, is correlated with the interest of the whole population through market economy, whereas political economy is the science of the management of the population; that is to say, the intellectual model from which we have to think of the government.[43]

After having explained the role of the political economy in the emergence of liberalism, Foucault ends his first lesson with a rather surprising statement:

> So, if you like, after having situated the historical point of origin of all this by bringing out what, according to me, is the new governmental reason from the eighteenth century, I will jump ahead and talk about contemporary German liberalism since, however paradoxical it may seem, liberty *in the second half of the twentieth century*, well let's say more accurately, *liberalism, is a word that comes to us from Germany*.[44]

Indeed, Foucault devoted five out of his twelve lessons to ordoliberalism during the years 1948–1962, and two lessons to the American liberalism of the Chicago School.

> In both cases, liberalism arose in a very precise context as a critique of the irrationality peculiar to excessive government, and as a return to a technology of frugal government, as Franklin would have said.[45]

However, it is not possible at this point to tackle all the issues raised by Foucault's reading on ordoliberalism. Consequently, we intend to target three main questions here: First, why and how does Foucault highlight the unique role played by economic freedom as a vector to legitimise the (re-) foundation of the state? Within this framework, what is the role of the state, in particular with regard to the logic of competition in society, and, conversely, how has the rationality of state intervention been regulated by the requirements of competition? All the issues are also decisive with a view to the third part of this contribution, which is devoted to the French perception of the influence of ordoliberalism on the European integration.

In the first two lectures on the ordoliberalism (Lessons III and IV of the book), Foucault explains the main differences between classical liberalism and the ordoliberal approach. These differences are not only due to the historical context, but also due to theoretical reasons.[46] The originality of German ordoliberalism, which Foucault pointed out, lies in its responses to the imperatives of the aftermath

[42] Nils Goldschmidt and Hermann Rauchenschwandtner, 'The Philosophy of Social Market Economy: Michel Foucault's Analysis of Ordoliberalism', (2007), Freiburg discussion papers on constitutional economics, No. 07/04, p 8.
[43] Grenier and Orléan, n 41 above.
[44] Foucault, n 36 above, p 22, emphasis added.
[45] ibid, p 322.
[46] Michel Senellart, 'Michel Foucault: la critique de la *Gesellschaftspolitik* ordolibérale', in: Patricia Commun (ed), *L'Ordolibéralisme allemand. Aux sources de l'économie sociale de marché*, (Paris: CIRAC/CICC, 2003), pp 37–49.

of WWII (re-building, planning, social objectives). Concretely, the scientific Council, which had been formed alongside the German economic administration in the Anglo-American Bizone wrote:

> The Council is of the view that the function of the direction of the economic process should be assured—as widely as possible by the prices mechanism.[47]

Ludwig Erhard, himself in charge of the economic administration of this zone at that time, as we have already seen, demanded the liberalisation of the price system in his discourse in front of the Assembly of Frankfurt.[48] This specific principle is inscribed within a much more general principle according to which interventions by the state should generally be limited. But, according to Foucault, there is a broader and, at the same time, more sophisticated meaning to Ludwig Erhard's statement: only a state that recognises economic freedom and thus makes way for freedom and the responsibility of the individual can speak in the name of the people.[49] The state is supposed to set an 'institutional framework X', which establishes a space of (economic) freedom. The establishment of this framework implies consent on the part of the citizens:

> to any decision which may be taken to guarantee this economic freedom or to secure that which makes this economic freedom possible (…) In other words, the institution of economic freedom will have to function, or at any rate will be able to function as a siphon, as it were, as a point of attraction for the formation of a political sovereignty.[50]

In summary, here, on the one hand, we have a historical problem: the re-construction of a state after the Nazi period and, on the other hand, a theoretical solution: the idea of a legitimising (re-) foundation of the state upon the basis of market freedom. It was precisely in post-war Germany that Foucault saw an example of a state in which economic development and economic growth was producing sovereignty: 'it produces political sovereignty through the institution and institutional game that, precisely, makes this economy work'.[51] Yet for ordoliberals—and this is why they were so interesting for Foucault—market freedom would not only help to legitimise the state, but would also limit its scope and guide its actions. For ordoliberals, this means that, instead of calling for a state which monitors the market—according to the opinion of the original liberal project—they want the market to have a regulatory effect on state actions.[52] In the fifth lesson, Foucault explains the rupture of the ordoliberal approach in comparison to the liberalism of the eighteenth and

---

[47] Quoted in Michel Foucault, *Sécurité, territoire population: Cours au Collège de France, 1978–1979*, ed by M. Senellart under the dir. of F. Ewald and A. Fontana, (Paris: Gallimard/Seuil; 2004), *Security, Territory, Population*, translated by Graham Burchell, (New-York: Palgrave-MacMillan, 2007), p 80.

[48] Discourse in front of the 14th Vollversammlung des Wirtschaftsrates des Vereinigten Wirtschaftsgebietes 21 April 1948, reprinted in W. Stützel et al (eds), *Grundtexte zur Sozialen Marktwirtschaft. Zeugnisse aus zweijahrhundert Jahre ordnungspolitischer Diskussion*, Bonn-Stuttgart-New-York, Ludwig Erhard Stiftung 1981, 39–42.

[49] Foucault, n 36 above, p 82.

[50] ibid, p 83.

[51] ibid, p 84.

[52] Dardot and Laval, n 27 above; Grenier and Orléan, n 41 above.

nineteenth centuries: for neoliberals, the most important thing about the market is not the exchange, 'that kind of original and fictional situation imagined by eighteenth century liberal economists', but market competition. The shift in focus from exchange to competition in liberal theory had already become discernible from the end of the nineteenth century. In contrast to the former liberal approach, under the influence of Husserl, ordoliberals such as Walter Eucken formed the opinion that market competition was not a natural phenomenon which the state has to protect by *laissez-faire* policies:

> Competition is an eidos (...), which will only appear and produce its effects under certain conditions which have to be carefully and artificially constructed (...) Competition is therefore an historical objective of governmental art and not a natural given that must be respected.[53]

In the sixth lesson on the nature of government interventions, this leads Foucault to develop the question of 'conformable actions' based upon the *Grundsätze* of Eucken. His main issue concerning neo-liberalism is now focusing on how the overall exercise of political power can be modelled on the principles of a market economy: 'A state under the supervision of the market rather than a market supervised by the state.'[54] By quoting texts from Röpke or Böhm at the Walter Lippmann Colloquium in 1939 as well as Eucken, Foucault explains that the main issue is not the scope of the state's intervention, but its content or the 'governmental style'. It is precisely the content of the intervention which represents a starting point for understanding what it is specific to the neo-liberal policy. He looks at three main examples: the question of monopoly, the issue of what the 'neo-liberals call a conformable economic action' and the question of social policy.

In the book about the '*New Way of the World: On Neoliberal Society*', which explicitly borrows from Foucault's work, Pierre Dardot and Christian Laval start from the crisis of traditional liberalism as the 'crisis of liberal governmentality'.[55] They conceive traditional liberalism as the search for the right limits to governmental interventionism in contrast to the intellectual re-foundation made by neoliberalism in the twentieth century. In their book which received resonance beyond the circle of specialists, they define neo-liberalism not, first and foremost, as an ideology or as a political economy, but as 'a normative system' and, fundamentally, as a 'rationality'. And what is as the heart of this rationality? 'The principal characteristic of neoliberal rationality is the generalization of competition as a behavioural norm and of the enterprise as a model of subjectivation'.[56] From this point of view, Dardot and Laval emphasise the key role of German ordoliberalism in having conceptualised the state as the main engine to introduce and universalise the logic of competition in society.[57] Like Foucault himself, Dardot and Laval place the distinction made

---

[53] Foucault, n 47 above, pp 120–121.
[54] ibid, p 116.
[55] Dardot and Laval, n 27 above.
[56] Preface of the English version, p 8.
[57] For Dardot and Laval the link with the current crisis in Europe is direct. See n 27 above.

by Eucken in *Grundsätze* between 'organising actions' and 'regulatory actions' to define the 'conformable economic action' of the state at the centre of their analysis. They show how the ordoliberals use free competition as an object of a fundamental political choice. To establish a stable framework for the optimal functioning of an economic process based upon free competition and the price mechanism, a 'fundamental decision' (Eucken) is required: the institutionalisation of the free market economy in the form of an economic constitution as part of the constitutional law.[58] The main principles of the economic constitution are well known; they all aim at the implementation of a price system of perfect competition. Yet the order has to be extended to the cultural and social spheres as well.

As pointed out by Foucault, neoliberal intervention is no 'less dense, frequent, active, and continuous than in any other system', but the point of intervention is not the same: neoliberal government does not have to correct the 'destructive effects of the market on society', but to intervene in society, 'in its fabric and depth' so that competitive mechanisms can play a regulative role within society 'at every moment and at any time'.[59] This is exactly what *Gesellschaftspolitik* means. From this point of view, the *homo oeconomicus* whom ordoliberals want to value is not the man of trade, not the man of consumption, but the man of entrepreneurship and production.[60]

The role of social policy has to be understood against this backdrop. In fact, there are several approaches for this issue among ordoliberals. For Eucken himself and some of his followers such as Erhard, social policy must not compensate for or eliminate the anti-social effects of competition. Social policy should make sure that the market broadens and deepens, because it is the best way to allow individuals access to private property and capitalisation mechanisms while facing social risks. As stated by Foucault, the only one and true social policy is economic growth, because it allows for an increase in productivity, and, 'supposedly', from there, the trickle-down effect(s). As Ludwig Erhard summarised, 'the concepts "free" and "social" are congruent; the freer an economy is the more social it is and the greater will be the macroeconomic utility created'.[61] This statement clearly showcases the approach adopted in the social programme of the Treaty of Rome (see above). Allocation and re-distribution are always linked,[62] and the competitive order ensures that the formation of income is subject to the right rules of the game. This is the key issue: 'The ordoliberal state "intervenes" not for discernible social ends, but for undistorted

---

[58] This point is of tremendous importance regarding the debates on the European 'constitutional treaty' during the referendum campaign in France in 2005 and the outcome of the consultation: Opponents of the treaty protested that the inclusion of economic principles in a text of 'constitutional value' was undemocratic, because a constitution cannot pre-empt the outcome of democratic processes regarding a desirable economic policy. On this issue, see Arnaud Lechevalier and Gilbert Wassermann, *La Constitution européenne. Dix clés pour comprendre*, (Paris: La Découverte, coll. Sur le vif, 2005).

[59] Foucault, n 47 above, p 145.

[60] Dardot and Laval, n 27 above, Ch 4.

[61] Cited by Hans Tietmeyer, *The Social Market Economy and Monetary Stability*, (Paris: Economica, 1999), p 6.

[62] Eucken Walter, *Die Grundlagen der Nationalökonomie*, Siebente Auflage, (Berlin-Göttingen-Heidelberg: Springer Verlag, 1959).

competitive relations.'[63] Yet, because competition policy is not sufficient to solve all of problems, one must consider 'special social policy areas' that reach beyond the order issue and commutative justice as defended by Hayek. Moreover as it is well known, Müller-Armack defended a much more interventionist and redistributive approach.[64]

In his last lesson on the ordoliberalism, Foucault explains how the 'German model' ie 'the model of a possible neoliberal governmentality' has spread to France up to the 1970s. He put forward three main elements of context. The diffusion of the German neo-liberal model has taken place in France 'on the basis of a strongly state-centred, interventionist, and administrative governmentality', in a context of an 'acute (economic) crisis', and the agents of the spread and implementation of this model 'are precisely those who administer and direct the state in this context of crisis'.[65] Foucault discusses at length the role of the President Valéry Giscard d'Estaing (1974–1981) and of his Prime Minister, Raymond Barre (1976–1981),[66] and of the high-level administration, their discourses and their economic and social policy. He explains that during the seventies the main problem in France arises of 'the overall transition to a neo-liberal economy, that is to say, roughly, catching up and inserting the German model'.[67] Thus, according to Foucault, under the leadership Giscard d'Estaing and Barre, the neoliberal turn in France can be directly linked to the requirements of the French economy's 'unrestricted integration' in the European and world market.

IV. HOW ORDOLIBERALISM HAS SHAPED THE EU-INTEGRATION'S PROCESS: A NEW PHASE OF DISCUSSION IN FRANCE

In France, after the turn of the century and following the publication of Foucault's lessons at the *Collège de France*, a new wave of research on ordoliberalism appeared. Most of these publications[68] focused this time on the way in which ordoliberalism

---

[63] Werner Bonefeld, 'Freedom and the Strong State: on German Ordoliberalism', (2012) 17 *New Political Economy*, pp 633–656, at 639.

[64] Alfred Müller-Armack, 'Die zweite Phase der sozialen Marktwirtschaft. Ihre Ergänzung durch das Leitbild einer neuen Gesellschaftspolitik', in: Egon Tuchfeldt (ed), *Wirtschaftsordnung und Wirtschaftspolitik*, 2nd ed., (Bern-Stuttgart: Verlag Paul Haupt, [1960] 1976), pp 267–292.

[65] Foucault, n 36 above, p 192.

[66] Professor of economics at the University Paris 1, former European Commissioner responsible for economic affairs and finance and Vice-President of the European Commission (1967–1973), Raymond Barre, translator of Hayek in French, knew very well the German Ordoliberal tradition and was the first to introduce neoliberal economic policy in France (Frédéric Lebaron, 'La croyance économique dans le champ politique français', (2016) 18 *Regards croisés sur l'économie*, pp 32–44).

[67] Foucault, n 36 above, p 192.

[68] See François Denord, 'Néo-libéralisme et économie sociale de marché: les origines intellectuelles de la politique de la concurrence', (2008) 1 *Histoire, économies et sociétés*, March, pp 23–34; Dardot and Laval, note 27 above; Christophe Strassel, 'Le modèle allemand de l'Europe: l'ordolibéralisme', (2009) 39 *En Temps Réel—Cahier*, June; Serge Audier, 'Une voie allemande du libéralisme? Ordo-libéralisme, libéralisme sociologique, économie sociale de marché', (2013) 60 *L'économie politique*, pp 48–76; Frédéric Lordon, *La Malfaçon: monnaie européenne et souveraineté démocratique*, (Paris: Les liens qui libèrent, 2014); Lechevalier, n 27 above; Patricia Commun, *Les ordolibéraux. Histoire d'un libéralisme à l'allemande*, (Paris: Les belles lettres, coll. Penseurs de la liberté, 2016), Ch 4.

shaped the European integration's process from the project's very beginning until the management of the Eurozone crisis. First, the influence of the ordoliberal school of thought on the Treaty on the European Economic Community and subsequently on the architecture of the Economic and Monetary Union (EMU) will be presented upon the basis of these works. Against this background, the content of the debates between the French and the German governments on some key issues of the economic policy will be highlighted. Second, the responses addressed to the crisis at European level will be analysed with regard to the imprint of German ordoliberalism.

A. Rome and Maastricht: The Ordoliberal Footprint on European Integration

The history of the relationship between ordoliberalism and European construction is a complex business, extending over four decades from resistance by the ordoliberals to their ideological victory.[69]

Ordoliberalism provided the basics of the doctrinal foundation of current European construction before it became subject to the new global rationality.[70]

Indeed, as several authors remind us,[71] initially the relationship between German ordoliberalism and the Treaty of Rome was tricky because most ordoliberals were divided on this topic and were opposed to the content of the treaty, which was seen as being too 'interventionist'. What ordoliberals had in common was their support for global free-trade.[72] Preferential regionalism was accepted in so far as it did not lead to a common commercial policy, except as a step towards global liberalisation.[73] However, one pole, represented at the foreign office by Hans von der Gröben, politically close to Walter Hallstein, was in favour of a European 'relaunch' even at the price of the abandonment of sovereignty.[74] Another pole, unified around Ludwig Erhard and the Ministry of the Economy, feared a project which threatened the liberalisation of markets, German exports and a greater union between free nations,[75] while Alfred Müller-Armarck tried to mediate between both poles.[76]

---

[69] Dardot and Laval, n 27 above, p 227.

[70] ibid, p 217.

[71] Bilger, n 11 above; Audier, n 66 above.

[72] Bilger, n 11 above, p 182.

[73] Finally, art 110 of the Treaty of Rome on the 'commercial policy' stated: 'By establishing a customs union between themselves, Member States aim to contribute, in the common interest, to the harmonious development of world trade, the progressive abolition of restrictions on international trade and the lowering of customs barriers.'

[74] Bilger sums up in 1964 how the treaty of Rome could be viewed by a contemporary pro-European neoliberal: 'The European liberal is rather persuaded that the next stage of economic unification can only be achieved by relying on the common denominator of national economic policies: namely, the monetary policy. Concerning fiscal policies, a day will necessarily arrive at which it will be requested from the Federated States what today they demand from their regional and local authorities: a balanced budget.'

[75] Especially Röpke—who had for the same reasons already advised Adanauer in 1950 to exclude the European Coal and Steel Community project—was resolutely against the common market, viewed as a vector of an European bureaucracy and as a wish for an European planification (Bilger, n 11 above, p. 183; Audier, n 68 above, p 70).

[76] Audier, n 66 above.

Second, the Treaty of Rome was, in fact, a twofold compromise within the German government (hammered out at Eicherscheid), on the one hand, and, on the other, between the German and the French governments against the background of the Spaak Report.[77] In his capacity as head of the department for fundamental issues at the Federal Ministry of Economics, Alfred Müller-Armack had a pivotal influence not only in the two political fields, but also as a representative of Germany at the preparatory intergovernmental conference on the treaty. In so doing, he played a key role in eliminating most of *dirigist* measures in the wake of the negotiations.[78] Ludwig Erhard shouldered the political responsibility. As a Directorate General for Competition (DGIV) Commissioner of the European Commission, Hans von der Gröben played an important role in implementing the ordoliberal potential of the treaty, particularly with Regulation (EEC) 17/62, which enshrined a very binding system concerning supranational trust agreements.

Indeed, the ordoliberal approach played a key, yet not exclusive, role in the architecture of the Treaty of Rome. The French administration was against the content of the Spaak Report of April 1956, which paved the way towards the common market. As attested by the memorandum of October 1955, at the beginning of the negotiations, the French administration requested a four-year probationary period for the trade liberalisation, which could not be implemented without the prior harmonisation of certain social standards, demanded by the French government in the name of employers' associations, and without the introduction of an investment fund at European level.[79] After the modification of the French position with the new (Guy Mollet) government in January 1956 and the change on the part of the French employers' union, the German Minister of Economics succeeded in imposing key points in the negotiation: market liberalisation without prior fiscal and social harmonisation,[80] as well as precise constraining rules regarding competition, designed to bolster a liberal policy.[81] The Treaty of Rome contained already the 'essentials of the doctrine of European construction. From 1957 onwards, the basis economic liberties assumed a constitutional value, recognized by the European Court of Justice as fundamental rights of European Citizens'.[82] Upon this basis, the social programme

---

[77] Dardot and Laval, n 27 above.

[78] Commun, n 68 above, Ch 4.

[79] Laurent Warlouzet, *Le choix de la CEE par la France. L'Europe économique en débat de Mendès France à de Gaulle (1955–1969)*, (Paris: Comité pour l'histoire économique et financière de la France, IGPDE, 2011), pp 30–35.

[80] 'In exchange for accepting an industrial customs union, the French government forwarded the demands of the *Patronat*—prior harmonization of social regulations concerning the length of paid vacation, gender equality of wages and the workweek, the right to withdraw of veto continuation to the "second stage", after the first 25 percent tariff cut, the right to invoke clauses and impose border taxes in the case of a balance of payment crisis–plus an agriculture policy. ... By late October 1956 ... France renounced the right to withdraw unilaterally and conceded that social policy might be harmonized at the beginning of the second stage, but reasserted its positions on safeguards and the veto. Erhard, apparently seeking to block the EC and mobilize German business behind the Free Trade Agreement, rejected the compromise.' (Andrew Moravcsik, *The Choice for Europe: Social Purpose and State Power from Messina to Maastricht*, (Ithaca NY: Cornell University Press, 1998), p 144).

[81] See Art 3.f: 'the institution of a system ensuring that competition in the common market is not distorted.'

[82] Dardot and Laval, n 27 above, p 222.

of the Treaty of Rome was conceived as a by-product of market integration.[83] According to the programme of Erhard ('Prosperity for all') and Müller-Armack, the EEC was supposed to be social because its 'orientation to consumption is in fact equivalent to a social service of the market economy (...). The enhancement of productivity guaranteed and constantly imposed by the competitive system, also acts as a source of social progress'.[84] Moreover seeing the ordoliberal imprint it seems tempting to talk about the EEC in similar terms Foucault used about the German state:

> In the new German economic-political regime one started by giving oneself a certain economic functioning (...) one gave oneself this economic framework, and it is then that the legitimacy of the state emerged as it were.[85]

With the Treaty of Rome, it was not simply an economic theory on the effectiveness and utility of market freedom which was implemented; it was a type of governmentality by which the common market was supposed to legitimise the European integration. The inversion between politics and economics will be confirmed by the treaty of Maastricht with the supposedly same foundational role for the monetary regime—like in the FRG in 1949.[86]

The influence of the ordoliberal doctrine on the Treaty of Maastricht is even easier to trace, because the tenants of the ordoliberal legacy were initially *against* the monetary union. As soon as 1988, with the Genscher's Plan, the West German government envisioned sharing German monetary sovereignty while imposing binding rules based upon institutional ordoliberal principles. Helmut Kohl wanted to secure the national central bank's acceptance for a proposal, made by Delors because of his pro-European beliefs,[87] which later on were strengthened in the context of the fall of the Berlin wall.[88] Hence, the European Council of Hannover decided in June 1988 to invite central bank governors to envision the path to a single currency. In this group, which worked out the so-called 'Delors Report', the approach of the *Bundesbank* advocated by its president Karl-Otto Pöhl played a major role and paved the way for later developments. Relying on its dominant position in the negotiation process and presenting itself as the negotiation partner with the greater assets and therefore as the state which might suffer the greatest potential loss, Germany prevailed on the majority of the key issues.[89]

Finally, the part of the Maastricht Treaty devoted to the Economic and Monetary Union includes four main elements. First, it is based upon the principle of an open market, which secures the four fundamental freedoms of the single market.

---

[83] Lechevalier, 'Eucken under the Pillow', n 27 above.

[84] Quoted in Hans Tietmeyer, 1999, p 6.

[85] Foucault, n 36 above, p 90.

[86] Grenier and Orléan, n 41 above, p 1177.

[87] Jacques Delors, with Jean-Louis Arnaud (2004), *Mémoires*, (Paris: Plon, 2004), p 333; Jörg Bibow, 'At the Crossroad: the Euro and its Central Bank Guardian (and Savior?)', (2012), Levy Economics Institute Working Paper 738.

[88] Femke van Esch, 'Why Germany wanted EMU: The Role of Helmut Kohl's Belief System and the Fall of the Berlin Wall', (2012) 21 *German Politics*. p 34–52.

[89] Moravcsik, n 80 above.

Second, based upon 'binding rules', the institutional framework of the monetary union aims to ensure the primacy of monetary policy by subordinating the functioning of the Eurozone to an inflation target defined by the European Central Bank, the constitution of which was inspired by the *Bundesbank* experience.[90] The objective of economic growth is thus subordinated to price stability, and the ECB has no mandate to monitor financial markets. Third, fiscal decisions 'would have to be placed within an agreed macroeconomic framework and be subject to binding procedures and rules'.[91] In addition to the Maastricht criteria, which were later anchored in the Stability and Growth Pact (SGP), the role of national budget policies is limited to smoothing out business-cycle fluctuations in accordance with the subsidiarity principle. Where required, the sanction mechanisms have to ensure that discretionary spending policy in the Member States does not damage ECB objectives. Fourth, the prohibition on the ECB monetarising sovereign debt and the 'no bailout' clause between Members States in the case of crises of solvency affecting one Member State contributes to the same end: they aim to prohibit moral hazard behaviour and to ensure the liability principle of each Member State. 'In this respect the entire Maastricht framework reflects core principles of ordoliberalism.'[92] The resulting institutional balance has led the EMU to move closer towards the ordoliberal model than Germany itself has never done.[93]

As a result, this architecture has been criticised in France for several reasons. However, in the context of the extensive literature, we want to limit our observations here to three main criticisms which deal with principles which lie at the core of the Economic and Monetary Union's ordoliberal legacy. On the other hand, it should be borne in mind that German negotiators had, of course, to compromise concerning different national, social and political logics on other key issues.

As is well-known, during the process of negotiation, German representatives focused on price stability and binding rules to avoid excessive deficits, whereas French representatives put forward the necessity of co-ordination of national policies through a—rather vague—'economic government'. This opposition between rules and discretionary policies has been at the heart of a first fundamental political critique: by fostering a mode of integration which consists mainly in containing the prerogatives of the Member States within binding norms, it has gradually emptied the seat of national sovereignty without investing in that of European sovereignty. 'In fact, the government of the European Union resembles a government by rules more than a government by choices', summarised Jean-Paul Fitoussi,[94] the former director of the OFCE, the centre for economic research at Science Po, Paris.[95]

[90] Strassel, n 26 above, p 76.

[91] Jacques Delors, *Report on Economic and Monetary Union in the European Community*, Committee for Study of Economic and Monetary Union, 1989.

[92] Jens Weidmann, 'Krisenmanagement und Ordnungspolitik', Walter-Eucken Vorlesung, Rede. Freiburg, 11 February 2013.

[93] Strassel, n 26 above.

[94] Jean-Paul Fitoussi, *La règle et le choix. De la souveraineté économique en Europe*, (Paris: Seuil, coll. La République des idées, 2002), p 7.

[95] Since 2012, among others, in collaboration with the *Institut für Makroökonomie*, the OFCE has produced the Independent Annual Growth Survey (IAGS), which has been conceived as an alternative to the Annual Growth Survey (AGS) published by the European Commission.

The problem did not so much present itself in the loss of national sovereignty as in the inability to offer the populations concerned anything other than 'negative integration'—in the sense of Fritz Scharpf—and a default policy.[96] By shifting power towards 'enlightened despots' (ie bodies such as the ECB or the European Commission's DG competition) with their own political priorities (price stability, budget balance, and competition), bodies which are not accountable to any political authority, the ordoliberal rule-based approach has led to a deprivation of democratic sovereignty in the Eurozone.[97] In fact, very soon the governance-by-rules approach did not pass the test of reality, because in hard times political choices are needed.[98] Yet, French governments were unable to propose an alternative in order to promote further co-ordination of national policies according to the Article 121 (ex-99), because of contradictory preferences: on the one hand, the supranational consequences of an interventionist approach to macroeconomic policy, and, on the other, the will to retain sovereignty as much as possible and to insist upon intergovernmentalism in EU-level macroeconomic policy-making.[99]

Second, the Eurozone architecture inherited from the ordoliberal tradition has also been criticised for several economic reasons;[100] its anti-growth bias has, in particular, been denounced. Compared to that of the US Federal Reserve, the policy pursued by the ECB, which was mainly preoccupied with its search for 'credibility' in the context of a 'chicken game' with national fiscal authorities,[101] has dampened economic growth by doing 'too little, too late'.[102] Apart from these technical aspects, at the end of the 1990s, the sociologist Pierre Bourdieu became a virulent critic of what he called 'Tietmeyer's thought' in one of his contributions,[103] that the latter only aimed at 'reinsuring financial markets' by holding a 'neoliberal discourse'. In political essays, Bourdieu fought a theory, 'which gives authority to the words of M. Trichet or M. Tietmeyer'—who themselves 'transform economic trends into destiny'—and which, at the same time, 'reduces the supranational state to a bank'.[104] Yet, the anti-growth bias of the Maastricht Treaty can also

---

[96] Fitoussi, n 94 above.

[97] Lordon, n 67 above, Ch 3.

[98] Jean Pisani-Ferry, 'Only One Bed for Two Dreams: A Critical Retrospective on the Debate over the Economic Governance of the Euro Area', (2006) 44 *Journal of Common Market* Studies, pp 823–844.

[99] David J. Howarth, 'Making and Breaking the Rules French Policy on EU "gouvernement économique"', (2007) 14 *Journal of European Public Policy*, pp 1061–1078.

[100] The institutional design of the monetary union was also due to the New classical macroeconomics; see Jérôme Creel, 'Par-delà le pacte de stabilité et de croissance, la coordination des politiques budgétaires', in: Olivier Beaud, Arnaud Lechevalier, Ingolf Pernice and Sylvie Strudel (eds), *L'Europe en voie de constitution: pour un bilan critique des travaux de la Convention*, (Brussels: Bruylant, 2004), pp 537–556.

[101] Jérôme Creel, Thieey Latrielle and Jacques Le Cacheux, 'Le Pacte de stabilité et les politiques budgétaires dans l'Union européenne', (2002) *Revue de l'OFCE*, special issue 'La mondialisation et l'Europe', pp 246–297.

[102] Jérôme Creel and Jean-Paul Fitoussi, 'How to Reform the European Central Bank?', (2002) Centre for European Reform, available at: www.cer.org.uk/sites/default/files/publications/attachments/pdf/2011/p343_ecb-1682.pdf.

[103] Pierre Bourdieu, 'La pensée Tietmeyer', in: *Contre-feux: Propos pour servir à la résistance contre l'invasion néo-libérale*, (Paris: Raisons d'agir, 1998), pp 50–56.

[104] Pierre Bourdieu, 'Pour un nouvel internationalisme', in; *Contre-feux: Propos pour servir à la résistance contre l'invasion néo-libérale*, (Paris: Raisons d'agir, 1998), pp 65–74, at 60 and 67.

be explained with regard to the fiscal pillar (the excessive deficit procedure based upon Article 126 (ex-104)). The reasons given for limiting the ceiling of public deficit at 3% of GDP were regarded as awkward,[105] and the 'rationale for a medium-term balanced budget' had 'no clear economic justification either', but reflected an anti-discretionary fiscal policy ideology.[106]

Within this framework, economic growth is supposed to come from structural reforms aimed at the smooth working of markets—first and foremost, the labour market—as well as at reducing the size of the government in the economy and its 'distortionary effects'. On the one hand, cost reduction through fiscal competition and progressive dismantlement of the welfare state (social competition) are the only form of policy available to national governments that have to react to idiosyncratic shocks. On the other hand, they respond to the more general objective of reducing the weight of the state in the economy, a pillar of the 'Brussels-Frankfurt-Washington' Consensus.[107] Moreover, this institutional framework has created an incentive for notional non-cooperative strategies of 'competitive disinflation', resulting from wage stagnation and cuts in the welfare state aimed at gaining market shares at the expense of other Member States. This incentive is particularly strong for small national economies because of the high share of exports in their GDP. Yet, wage moderation up to the mid-1990s as well as the 'Agenda 2010' have been viewed in France as a deliberate strategy chosen by the (big) German economy in this new framework. It is as if Germany, for the sake of its own interests, had preferred to play the role of a 'little economy' at global level, instead of assuming its responsibility as the strongest economy within the monetary union.[108]

Last, but not least, the status of the Euro has been questioned. Indeed, the ECB issues a common currency for all citizens of the monetary union. Yet, in the absence of a lender of last resort, the Euro has become a foreign currency with a fixed exchange rate for all Member States. The Member States of the Eurozone have been deprived of the direct relationship that exists everywhere between the central bank and the sovereign state when the state is the ultimate guarantor of the capital of the central bank and the central bank is the lender of last resort of a financial system in which public debt plays a pivotal role.[109]

In the opinion of some French researchers, the influence of German ordoliberalism on the EMU has been over-estimated: In fact, the main culprit of the Eurozone crisis should have been the US 'Chicago style' neoliberalism and its dissemination

---

[105] Indeed the ceiling of 3% of GDP for public deficit was in fact proposed by France, even if this criterion is the product of a historical contingency without any economic fundaments. See Guy Abeille, 'A l'origine du déficit à 3% du PIB, une invention 100% ... française', *La Tribune*, 1 October 2010.

[106] Catherine Mathieu and Henri Sterdyniak, 'How to Deal with Economic Divergences in the EMU?', in: Jesús Ferreiro, Giuseppe Fontana and Felipe Serrano (eds), *Fiscal Policy in the European Union*, (Basingstoke: Palgrave Macmillan, 2008), pp 157–183; Creel, n 100 above.

[107] Jean-Paul Fitoussi and Francesco Saraceno, 'The Brussels-Frankfurt-Washington Consensus Old and New Tradeoffs in Economics', OFCE Working-Paper No. 2004-02.

[108] Jérôme Creel and Jacques Le Cacheux, 'La nouvelle désinflation compétitive européenne', (2006) 98 *Revue de l'OFCE*, pp 7–36.

[109] Michel Aglietta and André Orléan, *La monnaie entre violence et confiance*, (Paris: Odile Jacob, coll. Economie, 2002; Michel Aglietta, *Zone euro: éclatement ou federation*, (Paris: Michalon, 2012).

on a global scale.[110] However, many authors, and not only in France,[111] are of the opinion that, from the onset of the crisis, the Eurozone governance reforms have not only re-inforced the influence of the ordoliberal tradition—but have also shown its weaknesses.

B. The Predominant Ordoliberal Responses to the Eurozone Crisis

The Eurozone crisis has been viewed—especially in France—as a product of the Eurozone's functioning being shaped by the ordoliberal tradition. Indeed, this institutional architecture has fostered divergences between national economies, and these divergences or discrepancies are fundamentally at the core of the current crisis. Moreover, it has placed national economic policies under the surveillance of financial markets,[112] and this has allowed the contagion of the Greek crisis to spread to other Member States. The responses addressed to the crisis have often been presented as a compromise between a German neoliberal strategy and a more interventionist and cohesive French ambition. In fact, the Eurocrisis has actually fostered a convergence in views towards a more modest ordoliberal view, rather than a greater divide between Germany and France.[113]

The first element is that the current European crisis has demonstrated the extent to which the foundations of European construction (the 'order of free, undistorted competition') have led to growing asymmetries between the Member States. It is precisely the imperative of 'competitiveness', 'universally vaunted as the sole "remedy"', which accounts for the specificity of the current European crisis. 'The race for competitiveness, on which Germany embarked at the start of the 2000s with growing success, is simply the effect of implementing a principle written into the "European Constitution": competition between the economies of Europe, combined with the existence of a single currency administered by a central bank ensuring price stability, in fact constitutes the very basis of the European Union's edifice and the dominant axis of national policies,' wrote Pierre Dardot and Christian Laval in the introduction to the English edition of their book.[114] In France, some analyses have

---

[110] According to this thesis, neither the competition policy led by the EU nor the form of the Central Bank's independency can be ascribed to the ordoliberal tradition. See Bruno Théret, 'Dette et crise de confiance dans l'euro: analyse et voies possible de sortie par le haut', (2013) 12 *Revue Française de Socio-Economie*, pp 91–124.

[111] See among others Sebastian Dullien and Ulrike Guérot, 'The Long Shadow of Ordoliberalism: Germany's Approach to the Euro Crisis, European Council on Foreign Relations', Brief Policy 49, February 2012; Mark Blyth, *Austerity: The History of a Dangerous Idea*, (Oxford: Oxford University Press, 2013); Thomas Biebricher, 'The Return of Ordoliberalism in Europe – Notes on a Research Agenda', (2014) 21 *i-lex*, opp. 1–24, available at: http://www.i-lex.it/articles/volume9/issue21/biebricher.pdf; Peter Nedergaard and Holly Snaith, '"As I Drifted on a River I could not Control": The Unintended Ordoliberal Consequences of the Eurozone Crisis', (2015) 53 *Journal of Common Market Studies*, pp 1094–1109.

[112] Lordon, n 67 above.

[113] In fact, this global diagnosis should be nuanced according to the issue (European Rescue Funds, Regulation to strengthen national budgetary surveillance, Banking Union) at stake. For more details, see Sinah Schnells (2016), 'Deutschland und Frankreich im Krisenmanagement der Eurozone. Kompromisse trotz unterschiedlicher Präferenzen?', (2016), Dissertation zur Erlangung des akademischen Grades Dr. rel. Pol., Freie Universität Berlin.

[114] Dardot and Laval, n 27 above, p 18.

explored more precisely the causes of these persistent and increasing disparities. According to this view, the benefits of the Eurozone for the Member States catching-up, but, above all, the weaknesses of the euro area economic policy framework and the implementation of non-cooperative domestic policies, which have induced excessive competition and insufficient co-ordination between national economic policies, explain these growing disparities.[115] In a consistent manner with regard to the power structures in economics and economic policies in post-war Germany,[116] the narrative of the crisis put forward by the German government can be explained by the 'profligacy' of several Member States, which has led to unsustainable levels of debt. This narrative has played a crucial role in recasting the crisis as an issue of public finance and competitiveness. Essentially, 'the central aim of Merkel's patterns of arguments brought forward by a variety of discursive strategies [has been] the re-establishment of market forces, which is based upon the strong belief in the superiority of rational market mechanisms over (active) economic policy measures'.[117] If the mainstream economist thinking has also been predominant in the French academic field over the last years, the 'Manifesto of appalled economists' launched in France in 2010 and signed by more than 300 economists explicitly insists on market deficiencies as a source of the Eurozone crisis.[118]

Against this background, what have been the main responses to the crisis from this point of view? To understand their content, it is important to keep in mind that the management of the crisis has been marked by the rise of the intergovernmental approach. Moreover, the crisis bargaining was constrained by the path dependency of the design of the monetary union.[119] Therefore, the main new features of Eurozone governance can be traced back to the preferences and discourses of national governments and to the compromises between Member States, mainly between France and Germany, as stressed by several researches, which portray a 'Battle of Ideas'[120] between 'Titans' differing in terms of paradigms, norms and values.[121] In fact, for several reasons,[122] the duo 'Merkozy' was asymmetric and

[115] Mathieu and Sterdyniak, n 106 above.

[116] Stephan Pühringer, 'Think Tank Networks of German Neoliberalism. Power Structures in Economics and Economic Policies in Post-war Germany', ICAE Working Paper Series, no 53, September 2016; Peter Bofinger, 'German macroeconomics: The long shadow of Walter Eucken', in: George Bratsiotis and David Cobham (eds), *German Macro: How it's Different and Why that Matters*, European Policy Centre, 2016, available at: www.epc.eu/documents/uploads/pub_6497_german_macro_how_it_s_different_and_why_that_matters.pdf.

[117] Stephan Pühringer, 'Markets as "Ultimate Judges" of Economic Policies: Angela Merkel's Discourse Profile during the Economic Crisis and the European Crisis Policies', (2015) 23 *On the Horizon*, pp 246–259, at 251.

[118] Crisis and debt in Europe: 10 pseudo 'obvious facts', 22 measures to drive the debate out of the dead end. See in German: *Manifeste d'économistes atterrés. Empörte Ökonomen. Eine Streitschrift. Ökonomisches Alphabetisierungsprogramm*, (PAD Pädagogische Arbeitsstelle Dortmund: Bergkamen 2011).

[119] Lechevalier, 'Eucken under the Pillow', n 27 above.

[120] Markus K. Brunnermeier, Harold James and Jean-Pierre Landau, *The Euro and the Battle of Ideas*, (Princeton NJ: Princeton University Press, 2016).

[121] Amendine Crespy and Vivien Schmidt, 'The Clash of Titans: France, Germany and the Discursive Double Game of EMU Reform', (2014) 21 *Journal of European Public Policy*, pp 1085–1101.

[122] Arnaud Lechevalier and Jan Wielgohs (eds), *Social Europe: A Dead End*, n 27 above.

the leeway of successive French governments was limited.[123] As a result, the policy response to the Eurozone crisis under German leadership has actually fostered a convergence towards a more modest ordoliberal view.[124] It could be deemed essentially ordoliberal because the new economic governance of 'packs and pacts'[125] has primarily aimed to create more restrictive rules for public finance so as to ensure monetary stability and 'sound' public finance, and to encourage greater competition between national spaces of labour allocation. A pre-requisite for this competition has been the implementation of structural reforms (especially of the labour market and social protection systems) as well as the 'internal devaluation' of labour costs (which touches both wages and social benefits) in order to restore competitiveness and correct trade imbalances.[126] In fact, given the limited success of this approach in resolving the main macroeconomic issues, additional measures were taken by the European Central Bank with its 'non-conventional policy' that has broken with the ordoliberal approach.

V. CONCLUSION

One could say that the reception of German ordoliberalism in France has shown how Germany has misleadingly been portrayed in certain representations which reveal far more about France's self-image in relation to its neighbour, than about Germany itself.[127] For sure, this statement contains some truth. Yet, as we have tried to show, the story is far more comprehensive. Four main issues have been addressed. First, several key French contributions have undoubtedly proposed far-reaching theses about the scope and the meaning of ordoliberalism from a theoretical, as well as from a political, point of view. Indeed, the German ordoliberal doctrine was the subject of an early reading in France which was attentive to the reasons for the success of the ordoliberal doctrine in Germany as well as to the fact that the post-war German economic system was also the product of other influences and other traditions. Further analyses, starting with that of Michel Foucault, contributed to a critical perspective on the meaning and scope of ordoliberalism in terms of new governmentality, and on its originality with regard to other variants of neoliberalism.

Second, the French reception of the ordoliberalism has enriched the content of the theoretical as well as the empirical debates on the constitutive core elements (institutional complementarities) of the 'German model'. From this expert (typology

---

[123] Ben Clift and Magnus Ryner, 'Joined at the Hip, but Pulling Apart? Franco-German Relations, the Eurozone Crisis and the Politics of Austerity', (2014) 12 *French Politics*, pp 136–163.

[124] Femke van Esch, 'Exploring the Keynesian—Ordoliberal Divide. Flexibility and Convergence in French and German Leaders' Economic Ideas During the Euro-Crisis', (2014) 22 *Journal of Contemporary European Studies*, pp 288–302.

[125] Hacker Björn, 'Under Pressure of Budgetary Commitments: The New Economic Governance Framework Hamstrings Europe's Social Dimension', in: Lechevalier and Wielgohs (eds), *Social Europe: A Dead End*, n 27 above, pp 133–158.

[126] Lechevalier and Wielgohs (eds), *Social Europe: A Dead End*, n 27 above.

[127] Strassel, n 26 above.

of capitalisms), fascinating, as well as conflicting, relationship with the 'German model' and its neo-liberal dimension, it emerges that (West) Germany's social market economy was, in fact, not so liberal before the re-unification. There are thus strong limitations to ascribing the performance of the German economy to the ordoliberal legacy. Conversely, since the launch of the euro, European integration has had a leverage effect for re-introducing neoliberalism in Germany.

Third, over the past years, the German ordoliberal tradition has been an asymmetrical object of intellectual, as well as political, debates in France—many commentators were ostensibly critical but some were more discreetly approving[128]—especially with regard to the relevant economic policy to follow. As shown by the initial reception of ordoliberalism in France, as well as by the compromises on the Eurozone management accepted by French governments in the wake of the Eurozone crisis, ordoliberalism has become a means for neoliberal policies in France, and also the symptom of its acceptance among the governing élites.

Last, but not least, in the wake of the Eurozone crisis, ordoliberalism in France has been more than ever at the centre of controversies about the European project and content of European integration. The reception of ordoliberalism in France has acted as a revealing factor for the conflicting and ambiguous relationship of many French people towards the European integration. It has revealed a conflict between national cultures—beyond the point of view of the relevant economic policy. If Germany is not merely ordoliberal, as the works on the German model have shown, the French reception of ordoliberalism has emphasised that European integration has led to an attempt to export a German 'culture of stability' into France, one which lacks several institutional complementarities particular to German society. The cautiousness of the alternative proposals to reform the EMU has demonstrated the ambivalent reactions of the French governing élites to this evolution. Yet, criticism formulated in France against the ordoliberal influence on the European integration process, against its political predominance, itself anchored in the European treaties, and against the responses to the Eurozone crisis promoted by the Merkel-Schäuble's government have given rise to credible alternative proposals for the Eurozone,[129] whose existence is currently still threatened.

---

[128] Ariane Bogain, 'Demons, Ants, Giants and Dwarves: The Construction of Germany's Handling of the Euro Crisis in French Political Discourses', (2014) 22 *Journal of Contemporary European Studies*, pp 7–23.

[129] Thomas Piketty et al, 'Manifeste pour une union politique de l'euro', *Le Monde* on 18 February 2014; Michel Aglietta and Nicolas Leron, *La double démocratie. Une Europe politique pour la croissance*, (Paris: Seuil, 2017).

3

Ordoliberalism's Trans-Atlantic (Un)Intelligibility: From Friedman and Eucken to Geithner and Schäuble

WILLIAM CALLISON

ABSTRACT

This chapter examines German ordoliberalism and its relation to American neo-liberalism, highlighting trans-Atlantic (mis)perceptions of the German framework from the post-war period to the present. It begins with a comparative analysis of the early Freiburg and Chicago Schools and then traces the American evolution towards a more monopoly-friendly and monetarist-oriented framework entailing market and financial de-regulation. The second part of the chapter explores the shadow of this trans-Atlantic divide in Wolfgang Schäuble and Timothy Geithner's conflicting approaches to the European sovereign debt crisis. Geithner's own narrative of the EU's 'crisis management' not only (unwittingly) demonstrates their distinct political rationalities with respect to financial markets, balanced budgets, and central banks, it also reveals the relative unitelligibility of the ordoliberal framework, which appeared to Geithner as a stubborn commitment to 'Old Testament justice' and a refusal to govern according to the (speculative) logic of the market. The chapter concludes with the importance of ordoliberalism for understanding the German approach to monetary and fiscal policy as well as the EU's 'economic constitution', rooted in principles of market stability, growth, competitiveness, and austerity. Given the recent fault lines produced by German-led Europe, the theoretical and institutional logics of ordoliberalism may become increasingly intelligible targets of democratic contestation and transformation.

I. INTRODUCTION

Even the best ideas only bear fruit when they are put into practice. One could perhaps say that it was a stroke of luck in German history that, after the Second World War, the right principles of Walter Eucken met the right politician in Ludwig Erhard. The economic model sketched by Eucken also proved itself to be a firm pillar in practice while the Federal Republic of Germany was still in its infancy. Indeed, Erhard also had some very exciting exchanges with the Allies when, in times of rationing, as it were, he came upon the genius idea of setting prices free, thereby also sending signals of scarcity, in order to kick economic initiatives into gear. This principled decision to turn from an economy of distribution and rationing to one of free activities proved to be a groundbreaking paradigm shift. The miracle occurred: the success of the social market economy did not take long. The shelves filled themselves with commodities, the economy's circulatory system was set in motion, and the German economic miracle, as we call it today, took its course … Time and again [Eucken's] ordoliberal political principles help to ensure that we do not lose sight of the whole. They are comprehensible and they provide orientation. The uninterrupted interest in the work of Walter Eucken and the Freiburg School is therefore not surprising in the least.[1]

WHILE 'NEOLIBERALISM' AND 'social market economy' are familiar, if contested, terms of political and academic debate, 'ordoliberalism' has never enjoyed a spotlight on the international stage—that is, until the recent Euro crisis. Many scholars began speaking of the 'return of ordoliberalism', implying that the market principles and technocratic approach of this uniquely German model of political economy had been transposed into the European Union's economic, monetary and governmental institutions. Suddenly, it seemed imperative to ask: Whence ordoliberalism, what role does it play today, and what is its future?

To venture answers to these questions, recent receptions of post-war ordoliberalism are an instructive starting place. Chancellor Angela Merkel's speech on the legacy of Walter Eucken and Ludwig Erhard, for example, represents a distinctly ordoliberal obsession with—and repression of—economic crisis.[2] Shrouded in myth like all good origin stories, with Eucken and Erhard as founding fathers of the so-called 'economic miracle', the speech confirms the significance, while covering over the contested beginnings, of the post-war political economy—a decisive development, as Friedrich von Hayek prophesised, for the fate of Western liberalism.[3] Leaping from the past to the present, Merkel then goes on to frame the European Union's crises as a set of timeless, yet resolvable, political-economic problems: German *Ordnungspolitik*, she declares, provides the right economic approach for

---

[1] Excerpt from Chancellor Angela Merkel's speech commemorating the work, legacy, and 125th birthday of Walter Eucken. The speech was delivered at the Walter Eucken Institute in Freiburg, Germany on 13 January 2016 (my translation).

[2] Having already formally announced her campaign for another six-year term as Chancellor, Angela Merkel's latest speech was delivered in December at the CDU's conference after this chapter was written. Yet this speech is just as exemplary as the one discussed below. In the name of the social market economy, Merkel again reaffirms the government's commitment to a balanced budget (*Schwarze Null*), is the 'trademark' of the party. Such a 'grandiose accomplishment' is not to be taken for granted and 'should always be connected to the name Wolfgang Schäuble'. The focus on stable finances is part of a programme for 'hard working people'. Merkel additionally argues that financial markets must be better regulated so as to prevent the speculative financial crises; that tax avoidance must be prevented; and that competitiveness must be strengthened across Europe. 'CDU-Parteitag: Rede von Angela Merkel am 06.12.2016', available at: www.youtube.com/watch?v=rUqZHSK7Rt4.

[3] Friedrich von Hayek said the following in a speech delivered on 28 February 1944: 'Whether we shall be able to rebuild something like a common European civilization after this war will be decided mainly by what will happen in the years immediately following it … [T]he future of Europe will largely be decided by what will happen in Germany.' (F. von Hayek quoted in R.M. Hartwell, *A History of the Mont Pèlerin Society*, (Indianapolis IN: Liberty Fund, 1995), pp 27–8).

Germany, for the Eurozone, and even for the recent refugee crisis.[4] As German finance minister Wolfgang Schäuble explained with similar clarity during the Greek sovereign debt negotiations, the means and ends of crisis management are straight-forward: implement the ordoliberal recipe for a competitive market order. Whether as myth or reality (or both), the spectre of ordoliberalism is haunting Europe.

To approach its spectral presence from a different and comparative angle, this chapter examines ordoliberalism vis-à-vis past and present American perspectives. Comprised of two parts, it first explores the shared theoretical premises of the Freiburg School ordoliberals and the Chicago school neoliberals, marking their break as the latter evolved from the 1950s onwards. Thereafter, a newly de-regulation-and monetarist-oriented perspective helped to shape a theoretical and policy framework that was more open to speculative free market finance, and less concerned with monopoly and balanced budgets than is the case in the German tradition. Placing such divergences in their historical and theoretical contexts, I suggest, elucidates an epistemic incongruity and relative unintelligibility between them that persists to this day.

Viewed against this mid-century backdrop, the second part of the chapter turns to the European sovereign debt crisis as an exemplary instance of ordoliberal governance, the underpinnings of which are importantly missed even by many of its critics. According to the narrative of Timothy Geithner, the Obama administration's Treasury Secretary, German finance minister Wolfgang Schäuble and other officials of German-led Europe showed dangerous disrespect for the speculative 'truth' of the market and an 'Old Testament faith' in balanced budgets, which resulted in a punitive approach to debt-ridden countries such as Greece, Ireland, Portugal, Spain and Italy. What Geithner misses throughout his account, however, is the distinctly *ordoliberal* framework underpinning the EU's economic governance. Budgets balanced by debt breaks, an inflation-focused central bank, a disregard for structural inequalities, a Union built upon principles of 'stability', 'growth' and 'competitiveness', and yet dominated by a single export-oriented economy—there is an order and rationality to this 'economic constitution' that is greater than the sum of its parts. Criticism of the EU should not simply focus, then, on the democratic deficits, moral failures, or conflicting national interests that thwart its real and aspirational legitimacy. It is also necessary to grasp and challenge the ordoliberal principles that underpin German-led Europe's technocratic governance, anti-Keynesian framework, and inequitable outcomes.

---

[4] 'What does this challenge presented by the refugees mean for us now in Europe? We don't just have a German internal market but also a single European market and a shared currency. The definition of the market indeed plays an exciting role in the question "How do I apply the ordopolitical conceptions of Walter Eucken?" ["Wie wende ich die ordnungspolitischen Vorstellungen von Walter Eucken an?"] ... A part of the search for a European solution to the refugee question involves, when we also include economic aspects, the question of the single market, the question of the shared currency and the necessary conditions such that both can in reality to come into operation' (Merkel 2016, my translation). For another example of how this (non-) debate reappears in German media, see Josef Joffe, 'Der böse Kapitalismus. Warum der Unmut? Das Gegenmodell DDR ist total gescheitert', in: *Die Zeit*, Nr 47/2014, p 13: 'Jeder Zweite findet den Kapitalismus 'nicht mehr zeitgemäß', aber nur jeder Vierte sagt das über die 'Marktwirtschaft'. Auf den ideologisch aufgeladenen Begriff kommt es also an. Ludwig Erhard, der 1948 gegen die Planwirtschaftler der CDU siegte, darf in Frieden ruhen.'

II. TRANS-ATLANTIC BRIDGES AND BREAKS: FREIBURG
ORDOLIBERALISM AND CHICAGO NEOLIBERALISM

Before the 'Freiburg School' came to be associated with the journal *Ordo*,[5] founded by Walter Eucken and Franz Böhm in 1948, a series of personal exchanges and collaborative projects established an intellectual firmament. In 1926, for example, Eucken joined forces with Wilhelm Röpke, Alexander Rüstow and others to form 'the German Ricardians'. Led by Rüstow, a lapsed Marxist, this group aimed at overcoming the dominance of the German Historical School by lending 'greater validity and influence to the doctrine of free trade within economic theory'.[6] From the very beginning, these scholars shared a more or less culturally conservative diagnosis of the political and economic crisis of Weimar Germany, an economically liberal desire to combat the rise of the modern welfare state, and a commitment to a strong, autonomous state that could establish and secure a competitive market order. Thereafter, a blossoming network of ideas, scholars, politicians, and business interests crystallised in the interstices of Röpke and Rüstow's 'sociological neoliberalism' and Eucken and Böhm's politico-legal programme for 're-ordering' the economy.[7] When the Nazis took power, Röpke and Rüstow fled the country while Eucken and Böhm remained and focused on the scientific elaboration and possible implementation of their 'ordo' programme. But, when the war ended, they were already mobilised, with allies at their side such as Alfred Müller-Armack, Leonhard Miksch and, most importantly, Ludwig Erhard.[8]

[5] Full title: *ORDO: Jahrbuch für die Ordnung von Wirtschaft und Gesellschaft*.

[6] Once a student of Franz Oppenheimer, who famously preached the 'third way' between socialism and capitalism, Rüstow was a 'radical socialist and Marxist' and a member of Paul Tillich's circle of 'Religious Socialists' before he made an official break with the group in 1925; see Hauke Janssen, 'Zwischen Historismus und Neoklassik: Alexander Rüstow und die Krise in der deutschen Volkswirtschaftslehre', (HWWI Research Paper), 2009, p 104. See, also, Rüstow's speech at a meeting of the *Verein für Socialpolitik*, entitled 'Freie Wirtschaft—Starker Staat'; see. Alexander Rüstow, 'Freie Wirtschaft—Starker Staat (Die staatspolitischen Voraussetzungen des wirtschaftspolitischen Liberalismus)', in: Franz Boese (ed), *Deutschland und die Weltkrise, Schriften des Vereins für Socialpolitik*, Bd. 187, (Dresden: Duncker & Humbolt, 1932), pp 62–69. For their personal letters, see Hans Otto Lenel 'Walter Euckens Briefe an Alexander Rüstow', (1991) 42 *ORDO Jahrbuch*, pp 11–14; regarding the name 'German Ricardians', consider the following: 'The reference to Ricardo evokes a model theoretic, deductive approach to economic theory that would have made him an obvious adversary of the German Historical School', (Introduction to Friedrich August von Hayek), in: Hansjoerg Klausinger (ed), *Business Cycles: The Collected Works of F.A Hayek, Part I*, (Chicago IL: University of Chicago Press, 2012), p 3.

[7] See, eg, the 1936 mission statement penned by Böhm, Eucken and Grossmann-Doerth: 'The task before us may be defined as one involving critical analysis. We need only to turn our criticism into a positive force in order to identify clearly the lines along which we must work if we are to return law and economics to their proper place ... [W]e wish to bring scientific reasoning, as displayed in jurisprudence and political economy, into effect for the purpose of constructing and reorganizing the economic system.' Franz Böhm, Walter Eucken and Hans Grossmann-Doerth, 'The Ordo Manifesto of 1936', in: Alan T. Peacock and Hans Willgerodt (eds), *Germany's Social Market Economy: Origins and Evolution*, (Basingstoke: Palgrave, 1989), pp 22–23. Originally published as 'Unsere Aufgabe', in: *Ordnung der Wirtschaft*, No 2, (Stuttgart and Berlin: W. Kohlhammer, 1936).

[8] Having already elaborated their theory at length in publications and personal letters over the past decade, the public dissemination commenced: they met with German business groups, organised seminars, co-founded the Mont Pèlerin Society, served on local and federal policy committees, and struck close ties with political figures in the CDU and the FDP. Their strategy was not centred on political parties but on networks of influence. Some of the ordoliberals, like Miksch, even joined the SPD. Böhm became a

In 1948, before the *Grundgesetz* (Basic Law) was written, before the West German state even existed, the ordoliberals assisted Erhard in constructing the now famous, but then controversial,[9] economic and currency reforms that introduced the *Deutsche Mark* and lifted nearly all price controls. Amidst the dire economic conditions of post-war Germany, their decrees to abolish the rationing of even the most basic goods needed for survival, to liberalise commodity prices, and to 'unleash' the market forces of competition were without precedent. They were the first to buck the dominant trend across the Euro-Atlantic towards social welfare-oriented 'state planning'. Erhard implemented the reforms against the Keynesian objections of the Allied authorities, the Social Democrats, and the labour unions.[10] By the Bad Godesberg conference of 1959, however, corporate and governmental campaigns on behalf of 'the social market economy' (a concept coined and crafted by the ordoliberals) had proven so successful that the Social Democratic Party (SPD) opposition came to accept several of its key tenets. The socialist goal was no longer to overthrow and replace liberal capitalism, but to reform it according to principles of social justice.

Notwithstanding the importance of these and subsequent developments to how ordoliberalism was (or was not) 'applied' in practice—for example, both the dominance and the concessions of conservative coalitions between 1949–69—there is reason to reflect on the ordoliberal tilling of the post-war soil. The mythical origin story of the 'economic miracle' credited to German *Ordnungspolitik* tends to erase the contested and technocratic features of its political founding, and it is worth recalling that the market economy and its corresponding monetary and banking framework were rapidly installed under conditions of crisis; that these decrees were made with minimal democratic checks and without any popular legitimation; and that

CDU representative in the *Bundestag* from 1953–65; he also worked as the minister of cultural affairs in Hessen and served on the *Institutsrat* at the Frankfurt School's *Institut für Sozialforschung*. I am grateful to Hermann Korcyba for sharing his research on Böhm's activities in Frankfurt.

[9] 'In den ersten Monaten nach der Währungsreform schien es, als würden die Skeptiker recht behalten, die Erhards Kurs für falsch hielten. Solche gab es auch in den Reihen von CDU und CSU … In den ersten Tagen waren die Läden leer gekauft worden, dann reagierten die ratlosen Konsumenten erbost gegen die Hektik, mit der die Preise in die Höhe kletterten. Ein großer Teil der Presse verlangte den Abbruch des marktwirtschaftlichen Experiments und die Entfernung des allem Anschein nach unfähigen Politikers Erhard. Im Frankfurter Wirtschaftsrat stellte die Opposition im Sommer und Herbst 1948 zweimal Misstrauensanträge gegen ihn. Die Gewerkschaften der britischen und amerikanischen Zone—die viereinhalb Millionen organisierte Arbeiter repräsentierten—riefen schließlich im November 1948 zum Generalstreik "gegen die Anarchie auf den Warenmärkte und gegen das weitere Auseinanderklaffen von Löhnen und Preisen" auf. Etwa neun Millionen Arbeiter folgten der Aufforderung am 12. November 1948 und demonstrierten mit einer 24-stündigen Arbeitsniederlegung gegen die Marktwirtschaft.' Bundeszentrale für politische Bildung, 'Wirtschaftsentwicklung von 1945 bis 1949', (13 July 2005), www.bpb.de/izpb/10077/wirtschaftsentwicklung-von-1945-bis-1949?p=all.

[10] An exchange between Ludwig Erhard and General Clay was recorded in 1948 during the month of Erhard's decrees, which had the approval of neither the Allies nor many CDU officials: 'General Clay: "Herr Erhard, my advisers tell me what you have done is a terrible mistake. What do you say to that?" Ludwig Erhard: "Herr General, pay no attention to them! My advisers tell me the same thing."' See A.J. Nichols, *Freedom with Responsibility: The Social Market Economy in Germany, 1918–1963*, (Oxford: Oxford University Press, 1994), and Alfred C. Mierzejewski, *Ludwig Erhard: A Biography*, (Chapel Hill NC: The University of North Carolina Press, 2004), p 67.

the criteria of *economic* 'success' (for example, growth, stabilisation, and market integration with the transatlantic West) preceded and perhaps even authorised the institution of West German *political* sovereignty. In a stateless territory disbarred of sovereignty due to its total surrender and its wartime atrocities, economic legitimation prefigured political self-determination. Seen in an ordoliberal light, an 'economic constitution' both appropriately framed and produced political institutions. This was a transformative moment in the turbulent history of liberalism.

Ordoliberals would not have had it any other way. With only minor individual deviations, they advocated a competitive order (*Wettbewerbsordnung*) that would, inter alia, privilege the price mechanism, construct a legal framework for the economic 'rules of the game', promote entrepreneurial subjectivity and self-reliance through de-centralised control and 'de-proletarianisation', cultivate conditions of market competition, and establish an insulated central bank with technocratic control over currency and inflation. The order itself, in the first and last instance, requires a strong, active and autonomous state, which serves as a 'market police' and rule-enforcer for minimising monopoly and maximising competition. A related end of the strong state is to 'free economic activities' and 'suppress the class struggle' through a set of 'decisive rules' that maintain economic order[11] and potentially allow for what Rüstow called 'dictatorship within the bounds of democracy'.[12] The 'Third Way' between *laissez-faire* capitalism and collectivism is the *only* programme, they claimed, capable of resolving the perpetual crisis of liberalism. For, when economic policy is subjected to 'de-stabilising' corporate cartels and 'irrational' democratic input, they argued, liberal capitalism will collapse into totalitarianism or (what, for them, was the same) socialism.

Chicago School neoliberalism, much like Freiburg School ordoliberalism, emerged from the political economic crises of the interwar period. Both schools believed themselves to hold the solution for overcoming crisis; both propagated programmes with explicit anti-socialist and anti-Keynesian impetus; and both saw themselves as possessing greater scientific objectivity than any of their predecessors or contemporaries. Indeed, the vast majority of these positions had already crystallised before they convened at the 1938 '*Colloque* Walter Lipmann' in Paris and then re-convened to form the Mont Pèlerin Society in 1947, thanks to the co-ordinated efforts of Friedrich von Hayek and Wilhelm Röpke. Although disagreements were abundant in Mont Pèlerin, a sense of shared mission only deepened the convictions of this trans-Atlantic vanguard.

'Neoliberalism' emerged as a potential self-descriptor which, though tabled at the time, was later applied to this ascendant intellectual and political movement. Despite the concept's polysemic evolution, then, neoliberalism has consistently aimed at the critical revision and programmatic transformation of liberal capitalism

---

[11] Alfred Müller-Armack, *Staatsidee und Wirtschaftsordnung im neuen Reich*, (Berlin: Junker & Dünnhaupt, 1933), p 41.
[12] Alexander Rüstow, n 6 above. See, also, Werner Bonefeld, 'Freedom and the Strong State: On German Ordoliberalism', (2012) 17 *New Political Economy*, pp 633–656, as well as Werner Bonefeld's contribution to this book (Ch 17).

itself.[13] Before 'ordoliberalism' became associated with the Freiburg journal *Ordo*, Rüstow coined 'neoliberalism' as an alternative to 'neo-capitalism', 'social liberalism', and other possible signifiers at the 1938 colloquium in Paris. Being, by nature, conceptual entrepreneurs, Rüstow and Röpke made occasional use of the term in the 1950s to distinguish their own scientific programme from the mistaken creeds of the past, the *'Neuliberalen'* from the *'Altliberalen'*, 'neoliberalism' from 'paleoliberalism'.[14] Other members of the group would try the category out for size, but ultimately decide against it, for reasons that were both strategic and highly ambiguous.[15]

Even if Milton Friedman, like von Hayek, eventually chose to popularise his immutable truths under the banner of 'liberalism', unmoored by prefix, this was not always his conceptual or political strategy. Before his arrival in Chicago, Friedman worked at the US National Resources Committee in 1935–37 under Wesley C. Mitchell, the director of the NBER whose approach to economics incorporated statistics and intuitionalism. Both Mitchell and Friedman believed that 'economics could be established as a predictive science with a broad scope capable of yielding objective claims', and both saw economists 'as heavily involved in policy making, where they would not serve as partisan advisers but as neutral scientists who clarified available means and predicted the outcomes of various actions'.[16] Mitchell's critique of neoclassical price theory didn't go over so well in Chicago, however. Friedman gradually, yet successfully, assimilated into Frank Knight and Henry Simons' programme, which included Econ 301 with Jacob Viner as right of passage, a course always taught by the programme's star economist and 'stern disciplinarian' of price theory.[17] A turning-point came when Viner and Oskar Lange left the programme

[13] In this vein, see the accounts in Hartwell, n 3 above; Dieter Plehwe and Bernhard Walpen, 'Wissenschaftliche und wissenschaftspolitische Produktionsweisen im Neoliberalismus Beiträge der Mont Pèlerin Society und marktradikaler Think Tanks zur Hegemoniegewinnung und -erhaltung', (1999) 115/29 Nr. 2. *PROKLA: Zeitschrift für kritische Sozialwissenschaft*, pp 203–235; and Thomas Biebricher *Neoliberalismus zur Einführung*, (Hamburg: Junius Verlag, 2015).

[14] See, eg, Alexander Rüstow, 'Sozialpolitik diesseits und jenseits des Klassenkampfes', in: idem: *Aktionsgemeinschaft Soziale Marktwirtschaft: Sinnvolle und sinnwidrige Sozialpolitik*, (Ludwigsburg: Hoch, 1959), p 20.

[15] See, eg, Walter Eucken, *Grundsätze der Wirtschaftspolitik*, (Stuttgart: Mohr Siebeck UTB, [1952] 2004); on this conceptual ambiguity, see, also, Philip Mirowski, 'The Political Movement that Dared not Speak its own Name: The Neoliberal Thought Collective under Erasure', (INET Working Paper No. 23, 2014).

[16] In this vision, Thomas Stapleford rightly adds, 'the expansion of scientific economics was simultaneously the rationalization of politics. Given this emphasis on prediction and empiricism, it should be unsurprising that both Friedan and Mitchell saw strong parallels between the physical sciences and economics. Just as the physical sciences provided objective, predictive theories for the behavior of nonhuman objects, so too would economics provide objective, predictive theories in the social realm'; idem, 'Positive Economics for Democratic Policy: Milton Friedman, Institutionalism, and the Science of History', in: Robert Van Horn, Philip Mirowski and Thomas A. Stapleford (eds), *Building Chicago Economics: New Perspectives on the History of America's most Powerful Economics Program*, (Cambridge: Cambridge University Press, 2011), pp 4–5.

[17] See Jamie Peck, 'Orientation: In Search of the Chicago School', in: Van Horn, Mirowski and Stapleford (eds), n 16 above, p xxv, at xxviii, and Reder, cited in Johan Van Overtveldt, *The Chicago School: How the University of Chicago Assembled the Thinkers who Revolutionized Economics and Business*, (Chicago IL: Agate, 2007), p 77: 'The teaching of 301 has always been the prerogative of

between 1945–6, spurring the rise of Friedman's views in Chicago over the next two decades.[18] Pulled together by von Hayek's internationalist vision, Friedman, Knight, Aaron Director and George J. Stigler became the Chicago contingent and co-founders at the Mont Pèlerin Society in 1947. For Friedman, these meetings helped root the disciplinary stakes of economics within a political battle against 'collectivism', ie the shared neoliberal enemy encompassing socialist 'state planning', the Beveridge Plan, Keynesianism, and a range of other perceived threats. In a tellingly titled essay from 1951, 'Neo-Liberalism and its Prospects', Friedman writes:

> A new faith must avoid both errors [of *laissez-faire* capitalism]. It must ... explicitly recognize that there are important positive functions that must be performed by the state. The doctrine sometimes called neo-liberalism which has been developing more or less simultaneously in many parts of the world and which in America is associated particularly with the name of Henry Simons is such a faith. No one can say that this doctrine will triumph. One can only say that it is many ways ideally suited to fill the vacuum that seems to me to be developing in the beliefs of intellectual classes the world over. Neo-liberalism would accept the nineteenth century liberal emphasis on the fundamental importance of the individual, but it would substitute for the nineteenth century goal of *laissez-faire* as a means to this end, *the goal of the competitive order*. It would seek to use competition among producers to protect consumers from exploitation, competition among employers to protect workers and owners of property, and competition among consumers to protect the enterprises themselves. *The state would police the system, establish conditions favorable to competition and prevent monopoly, provide a stable monetary framework, and relieve acute misery and distress.* The citizens would be protected against the state by the existence of a free private market; and against one another by the preservation of competition.[19]

Multiple influences shine through this short declaration, which also marks a turning point in Friedman's own development. The call for a shift from '*laissez-faire*' to 'competitive order' is quintessentially ordoliberal; the critique of nineteenth-century liberalism's purely passive view of the state, however, forms a bridge between Chicago and Freiburg traditions of thought. Simons and Knight, mentors of Friedman and avid readers of Austrian and German economic theory, held 'ordoliberal' positions on anti-trust measures, the formal 'rules of the game' governing economic and monetary policy, and the principle of economic competition, understood as a condition for a functional market order and for human freedom more generally. Like the ordoliberals, Henry Simons also considered it the task of the government to set up the 'framework' which would ensure the proper functioning of market

the department's big guns and over the years has been identified successively with Viner, Friedman and Becker ... Course 301 has always been tough and its teachers have been stern taskmasters.'

[18] Roger E. Backhouse, 'The Rise of Free-market Economics since 1945', in: Peter J. Boettke and Steven G. Medema (eds), *The Role of Government in the History of Economic Thought*, (Durham NC: Duke University Press, 2005), p 372.

[19] Milton Friedman, 'Neo-Liberalism and its Prospects,' *Farmand*, 17 February 1951, p 3, my emphasis.

competition.[20] Without the 'important positive functions performed by the state', as Friedman put it, the 'price system could not discharge effectively the tasks for which it is admirably fitted'.[21]

From the 1930s through the early 1950s, Simons, Knight, Friedman, Stigler, Thorstein Veblen and other Chicagoans were all concerned with the negative effects of monopoly. But the transatlantic harmony on this question would only briefly out-last the suicide of Henry Simons in 1946. Led by Aaron Director, the budding law and economics movement of the post-war era played a key role in revolutionising the Chicagoan perspective. As Van Overtveldt observes, 'Director's major innova-tion was to look at monopoly and antitrust legislation through the lens of price theory'.[22] This generated a critique of US anti-trust legislation based on the view that 'important efficiencies were frequently realized through these practices, that the exercise of monopolistic power should not be exaggerated, and that often-assumed practices of monopoly, such as predatory price cutting, simply did not occur in real life'. Relatedly, the foundations of the post-Simon period were built upon the con-crete support of politically motivated corporate foundations and think tanks such as the Volker Fund,[23] which helped both guide and materialise Chicago's more radi-cally free market approach to political economy. For instance, von Hayek persuaded Aaron Director to conduct the WVF-funded Chicago Free Market Study (FMS) on monopoly with Friedman and Edward Levi, the dean of the law school, which reached a monopolistic conclusion in 1952.

> Though avowed to study and describe "a suitable legal and institutional framework of an effective competitive system",[24] the FMS predominantly researched the issues of monopoly and corporations, transforming the fundamental economic approach to these issues and giving birth to a significant tenet of neoliberalism.[25]

---

[20] Despite the contradictory signifier of Simons' *A Positive Program for Laissez Faire* (1934), his vision entailed the following framework: 'Eliminate all forms of monopolistic market power, to include the breakup of large oligopolistic corporations and application of anti-trust laws to labor unions. A Federal incorporation law could be used to limit corporation size and where technology required giant firms for reasons of low cost production the Federal government should own and operate them ... Promote economic stability by reform of the monetary system and establishment of stable rules for monetary policy ... Reform the tax system and promote equity through income tax ... Abolish all tariffs ... Limit waste by restricting advertising and other wasteful merchandising practices'; Henry C. Simons, *A Positive Program for Laissez Faire: Some Proposals for a Liberal Economic Policy*, (Chicago IL: The University of Chicago Press [1934] 1949). See, also, Friedman's statements on Simons in Rob Van Horn and Matthias Klaes, 'Intervening in *Laissez-faire* Liberalism: Chicago's Shift on Patents', in: Van Horn, Mirowski and Stapleford (eds), n 16 above, 231, and Daniel Stedman Jones, *Masters of the Universe: Hayek, Friedman, and the Birth of Neoliberal Politics*, (Princeton NJ: Princeton University Press, 2012), p 98.

[21] Friedman, n 19 above, p 3.

[22] See George Stigler, *Memoirs of an Unregulated Economist*, (Chicago IL: University of Chicago Press, 1988), cited in Van Overtveldt, n 17 above, p 73: '[Director's] work stimulated related research by others, including Ward Bowman, Robert Bork, John McGee, and Lester Telser.'

[23] Rob Van Horn and Matthias Klaes, 'Intervening in Laissez-Faire Liberalism: Chicago's Shift on Patents', in: Robert Van Horn, Philip Mirowski and Thomas Stapleford (eds), *Building Chicago Economics*, (Cambridge: Cambridge University Press, 2011).

[24] Ronald Coase, 'Aaron Director', Paul Newman (ed), *The New Palgrave Dictionary of Economics and the Law*, (New York: Macmillan, 1998), p 603.

[25] Van Horn and Klaes, n 20 above, p 205.

As the Chicago School developed, monopolies came to be seen as benign (because always temporary) so long as competition can do its magic and the state does not get involved. When Friedman published his own popularisation of Chicago School doctrine in 1962, in *Capitalism and Freedom*, he explicitly contrasted this interpretation of monopoly with the alternative, but respectable, views of Henry Simons and Walter Eucken.[26] Simons generally argued against state intervention, but accepted state ownership of particular industries in cases where market competition could not possibly be obtained. For Eucken and the ordoliberals, pure competition is only realised when the size and power of corporations is checked by anti-trust regulations, lest big business become parasitic on the state and obstructive to competitive market forces. But now, according to Friedman, even if 'technical monopoly' may result from market forces, private behemoths are best left untouched by state intervention or regulation because they will eventually be undone by the very forces of competition themselves:

> both public regulation and public monopoly are likely to be less responsive to [the conditions of a rapidly changing society], to be less readily capable of elimination, than private monopoly.[27]

Beyond these evolving views on monopoly, differences in the American and German positions can also be seen as extensions of their respective historical, cultural and geographic roots.[28] Such trans-Atlantic differences are additionally reflected in configurations of monetary policy, finance, and budget deficits. On one side, ordoliberalism has always held the stability of currency as the highest priority,[29] treasured the *Haftungsprinzip* (liability principle) against the threat of 'moral hazard', considered de-centralised competition a means for dissolving economic power blocks, and permitted only 'market conforming' state interventions that respect the price mechanism. The traditional ordoliberal model of finance is one in which a relatively large number of privately-owned firms compete against each other and—as was the case in West Germany—remain locally grounded by virtue of drawing their finances from loans provided by local and regional banks. This model also relies on an independent central bank—as was also the case with the West German *Bundesbank*—to secure the stabilising effect of 'sound money' and to prevent excessive inflation. In addition, governments are to focus on saving and cost-cutting. These austerity-oriented positions are based upon a conception of stability and crisis most recently articulated by Wolfgang Schäuble in response to his critics. 'While US policymakers like to focus on short-term corrective measures,' Schäuble writes, 'we take the longer view and are therefore more preoccupied with the implications of excessive deficits and the dangers of high inflation.' Here, even Schäuble admits that such 'aversion

---

[26] Milton Friedman, *Capitalism and Freedom*, (Chicago IL: Chicago University Press, [1962] 2002), p 28.

[27] ibid, p 28.

[28] Stedman Jones, n 20 above, p 125. Josef Hein, 'The Ordoliberalism that Never was', (2013) 12 *Contemporary Political Theory*, pp 349–358.

[29] Eucken, n 15 above, p 256, called this the primacy of monetary policy in the ordoliberal framework: 'alle Bemühungen, eine Wettbewerbsordnung zu verwirklichen, [sind] umsonst, solange eine gewisse Stabilität des Geldwertes nicht gesichert ist.'

to deficits and inflationary fears ... have their roots in German history in the past century'.[30]

On the other side, while the Chicagoan evolution towards monopoly and monetarism engendered a trans-Atlantic rift, there remained a more foundational disagreement with Freiburg over the importance of balanced budgets. Accordingly, Friedman and his colleagues moved with the free market tide during the 1950s and 1960s,[31] unconcerned by the ordoliberal obsession with budget deficits. In the historical context of an American economy dominated by corporations in which ownership and management were dissociated—an important difference from the German model—the Chicagoan trajectory dovetailed with the rise of rational choice theory[32] and with a 'revolutionary' managerial theory which dictated that managers work for the good of the shareholders, rather than for their own interests.[33] Competition, then, accorded to the logic of managers competing among each other in order to attract investors and to satisfy shareholders.[34] And to organise this kind of competition, a de-regulated capital market was required. Financialisation would soon pair well with this form of shareholder governance, and with the neoliberal imperative to de-regulate, all to the benefit of large corporations.[35]

Following the end of the Bretton Woods system and the stagflation crisis of the 1970s that called Keynesian assumptions into question, the Chicago School's ready-made doctrine found interested audiences at the highest levels of government and industry. Having learned its post-war lesson from the ordoliberals, Friedman and others knew well that the 'tide' of policy and opinion could be turned through exploiting moments of crisis. Thus, by the 1980s, Friedman had achieved what, in 1951, was a mere utopian pining, an article of faith:

> neo-liberalism offers a real hope of a better future, a hope that is already a strong cross-current of opinion and that is capable of capturing the enthusiasm of men of good-will everywhere.

After winning a Nobel prize, as well as the ears of Augusto Pinochet and Ronald Reagan, Friedman recapitulated his 1951 theory of crisis in a 1982 preface to his 1962 book:

> There is enormous inertia—a tyranny of the status quo—in private and especially governmental arrangements. Only a crisis—actual or perceived—produces real change. When

---

[30] 'To the question of what caused the recent turmoil in the eurozone, there is one simple answer: excessive budget deficits in many European countries.' Schäuble, cited in 'German Treasurer: US Should Learn From Us,' *Newsmax Finance* 29 June 2010. For his response to George Soros' criticism (available at: www.ft.com/content/504fa87a-7eec-11df-8398-00144feabdc0), see Wolfgang Schäuble, 'Why Europe's monetary union faces its biggest crisis', available at: www.ft.com/content/2a205b88-2d41-11df-9c5b-00144feabdc0.

[31] Van Horn and Klaes, n 20 above, p 215.

[32] Sonja Amadae, *Rationalizing Capitalist Democracy: The Cold War Origins of Rational Choice Liberalism*, (Chicago IL: University of Chicago Press, 2003).

[33] Gerald Davis, *Managed by the Markets: How Finance Re-Shaped America*, (Oxford: Oxford University Press, 2009).

[34] Michel Feher, *Rated Agencys*, (Brooklyn NY: Zone Books, 2018).

[35] 'The intellectual roots of the derivatives market can be found at the University of Chicago. As the story goes, Friedman played the role of catalyst.' (Van Overtveldt, n 17 above, p 268).

that crisis occurs, the actions that are taken depend on the ideas that are lying around. That, I believe, is our basic function: to develop alternatives to existing policies, to keep them alive and available until the politically impossible becomes politically inevitable.[36]

With a crisis-focused, quasi-Marxist approach to the question of theory and *praxis*, this patient discursive practice proved indispensable for the historical materialisation of ordoliberal and neoliberal rationality within forms of law, knowledge and governmental practice.[37]

III. TRANS-ATLANTIC DIVIDES DURING THE EUROCRISIS: TIMOTHY GEITHNER AND WOLFGANG SCHÄUBLE

In the context of globalisation, the lived practices of ordoliberalism and neoliberalism have evolved into what many post-Keynesian economists call export-based and debt-based growth models. The former model is about competing for foreign customers; the latter is about competing for foreign investors. At present, the two models have key features in common—such as keeping labour costs and public spending down—and they are partly complementary in that export industries need credit-subsidised consumers to sell their products. Yet, their priorities are not the same and their divergence on budget deficits reflects the rifts examined above. Indeed, these models continue to irritate one another—for example, when Timothy Geithner worries that Wolfgang Schäuble and his allies punish indebted people, instead of helping them become solvent, if still indebted, consumers again. Conversely, German ordo-liberals are worried when banks—especially their own, as with the recent case of *Deutsche Bank*—get lured into the dangerous business of derivatives and investment banking, putting at risk the very export industries that they are supposed to finance. In at least these ways, the original Freiburg-Chicago divide maps onto more recent trans-Atlantic rifts concerning modes of crisis management.

Whether or not the practitioners perceived it themselves, the sovereign debt crisis drove home this divide between neoliberal and ordoliberal styles of reasoning. Timothy Geithner's *Stress Test: Reflections on Financial Crises*[38] unwittingly reproduces the divide through his American take on the European troubles that he witnessed first-hand.[39] In 2010, 'Europe was burning again,' writes Geithner, but at the G-7 meeting called in response, the Europeans 'did not seem to have the tools or the desire to contain the fire'.[40] Unsurprisingly, German and French leaders were unre-

---

[36] idem, n 26. p xiv.
[37] In forthcoming work, I discuss this Marxian element of neoliberalism with a focus on ordoliberalism.
[38] Timothy Geithner, *Stress Test: Reflections on Financial Crises*, (New York: Broadway Books, 2014.
[39] 'Based on published data, between January 2010 and June 2012, Geithner had 168 meetings and telephone discussions with Eurozone officials and 114 with the IMF.' (www.tovima.gr/en/article/?aid=595745). Thereafter, when Schäuble received the Jewish Museum's Prize for Understanding and Tolerance on November 2014 in Berlin, Geithner gave a speech underscoring the relationship between the Germans and the Americans during the crisis: 'Roughly 40 years ago, Henry Kissinger asked his famous question about Europe: 'Whom do you call?' ... For the US, Wolfgang Schäuble became a large part of the answer to Kissinger's question. We called Minister Schäuble.'
[40] Geithner, n 38 above, p 443.

ceptive to Geithner's proposed means and regarded him as 'the walking embodiment of moral hazard'. 'They still blamed our Wild West financial system for the meltdown of 2008,' he recounts, and they 'weren't going to be swayed by suggestions from the reckless Americans that they should take it easy on the reckless Greeks. In reality, Europe had enjoyed a wild credit boom of its own, with much of the risky borrowing in the periphery funded by risky lending by banks in the German and French "core".'[41] From Geithner's perspective, the Europeans were demanding devastating austerity cuts while making low-ball loan offers to Greece, 'at most 25 billion euros, which wouldn't even cover its borrowing needs through the spring, combined with harsh demands for tax increases, spending cuts, wage freezes, and other austerity measures'. While Athens protested the proceedings, several German politicians declared that Greece should auction off the Acropolis. For his part, Wolfgang Schäuble said that, 'Germany would slash its own budget in solidarity with the rest of the continent, to show that it wouldn't ask for sacrifices it wouldn't make itself'. This would only make the problem worse, Geithner thought, since 'in the near term, the German government and German citizens need to do more spending and less saving'. Thinking aloud, he replied to Schäuble: 'You know you sound a bit like Herbert Hoover in the 1930s. You need to be thinking about growth.'[42] For Geithner, the only pacifying reports were to be found in subtle signals that catastrophic risk was off the table. Chancellor Merkel told Geithner and Obama, 'we won't do a Lehman', suggesting by way of insult that Greece would not default on her watch. Geithner respected Merkel, but the feeling wasn't exactly mutual: 'she turned to me in that meeting with the President and said Paul Volcker had told her I was "very close to the markets," which I don't think she meant as a compliment.'[43]

Ironically, for Geithner, Merkel's non-compliment was well taken. For his most consistent criticism of German-led Europe is not that they were pointlessly cruel with their structural adjustment imperatives but that these leaders didn't understand, much less respect, the market. Wolfgang Schäuble and Christine Lagarde were not just harsh, but non-strategic: 'still insisting on draconian budget cuts, their harsh Old Testament rhetoric was roiling the markets, undermining the power of their aid.'[44] Though Greece needed to rein in its deficit, Geithner argued, 'imposing

[41] Geithner, n 38 above, p 443. In leaked interviews that Geithener conducted in preparation for his book, this was put in somewhat starker terms: 'the Europeans came into that meeting basically saying: "We're going to teach the Greeks a lesson. They are really terrible. They lied to us. They suck and they were profligate and took advantage of the whole basic thing and we're going to crush them," was their basic attitude, all of them …' Select excerpts of the interviews are available at: www.ft.com/content/5704c0bf-43de-3787-a981-dd1e952f8120.

[42] ibid, n 38 above, p 447. To gauge the character of Schäuble' self-defence against American criticism, see the discussion in Adam Tooze, 'After the Wars', (2015) 37 *London Review of Books*: 'In November 2010 Schäuble replied [to the Americans], dismissing Ben Bernanke's Quantitative Easing 2 as "clueless". Meanwhile, Germany's corporate giants such as Deutsche Bank can barely disguise their relief at the more expansive course being followed by the European Central Bank under Mario Draghi in the face of protests from Schäuble and his allies at the Bundesbank.'

[43] ibid, n 38 above, p 448.

[44] ibid, p 445.

too much austerity too quickly would be counterproductive, further depressing its economy, shrinking its tax revenues, and actually increasing its deficit ... The desire to impose losses on reckless borrowers and lenders is completely understandable, but it's terribly counterproductive in a financial crisis'.[45]

The Wild West of American neoliberalism seemed to be showing a Keynesian streak.[46] But the opposition at home (congressional Republicans) and the allies abroad (German-led Europe) still had austerity on the mind. Frighteningly, remarks Geithner, the Republicans' rhetoric about forcing 'the federal leviathan to live within its means ... sounded more committed to austerity than the Germans'.[47] Austerity is fine in principle, Geithner explains, except when the already wounded markets want you to spend. Though his own analysis does not take him so far, Geithner's logic runs something like this: Europe is far too ordoliberal. If it cannot swing a bit of Keynesianism for the time being, it should at least follow neoliberal common sense: the truth of the market must determine state action; or, in other words, to achieve economic growth, you should always govern *with* the market, not *against* it. Beneath this neoliberal critique of ordoliberal rationality, however, lies an unseen split between two different conceptions of 'the market' itself. For ordoliberals, austerity measures and balanced budgets are good because deficit spending distorts 'the market', primarily understood in terms of the 'price mechanism', and the negotiations that produce the 'equilibrium' or 'market-clearing price'. For Geithner, the market is clearly less about the negotiation than about the speculation of agents concerning what they think others think a security is worth.[48] Thus the market whose truth Schäuble disrespects is a financial and speculative one. In good times, such speculative truths lead to the neoliberal promised land; in bad times, they must be heeded, lest market crises and other punishments ensue.

---

[45] ibid, pp 444–445.

[46] While Geithner uses such language on occasion in his memoir, a deeper reading of this and previous texts reveal an (unsurprising) commitment to a rather non-Keynesian American economic and financial system. In his 2009 reports to Elizabeth Warren, 'April oversight report: assessing Treasury's strategy, six months of TARP', for instance, Geithner showed concern that the Europeans were less willing to play the game of boom and bust capitalism (ie to bail out banks whenever necessary) than the Obama administration. Here, he goes so far as to defend the (pre-crisis) American financial industry, warning against 'unreasonable' responses like nationalisation: 'The Europeans must contend not only with the issues arising out of linked currencies, but also with the issues arising out of their linked economies. Germany has been the most vocal regarding concerns that they will be asked not only to provide rescue packages for their own financial services industry, but for those of their poorer neighbors as well ... [Regarding the U.S.] we believe that a viable plan should be given the opportunity to work. Speculation on alternatives runs the risk of distracting our energy from implementation of a viable plan and needlessly eroding market confidence. Market prices are being partially subjected to a downward self-reinforcing cycle that could be exacerbated by unwarranted consideration of more radical solutions such as nationalization. This positive assessment of Treasury's view on the underlying causes of the financial crisis is not meant to suggest that the housing bubble should be re-inflated. But we do admit to being confident that the long-term values of mortgage-related assets secured by American homes remain a good investment.' Timothy Geithner in *United States Congressional Oversight Panel.* (Letters between Timothy Geithner and Elizabeth Warren), (Washington DC: U.S. G.P.O., 2009), p 75. On the post-election shadow of Geithner's bank rescue and the Obama administration's monopolistic sympathies, see www.washingtonpost.com/posteverything/wp/2017/01/12/democrats-cant-win-until-they-recognize-how-bad-obamas-financial-policies-were/?postshare=4791484249068024&tid=ss_fb-bottom&utm_term=.61d4f35d24e8.

[47] Geithner, n 38 above, p 450.

[48] See, also, Davis, n 32 above, and Feher, n 33 above.

At this juncture, things were bad on both sides of the Atlantic. 'The early fires of the European crisis,' Geithner laments, 'contributed to the disappointment of our Recovery Summer.' While a bad economy drove up deficits, austerity fever continued to spread:

> Ireland's support for its failing banks was on the verge of bankrupting its government ... Spain and Portugal slashed spending in fruitless attempts to avoid ratings downgrades ... Meanwhile, Germany was pushing for a European fiscal union with the power to restrain the borrowing and spending of its members.[49]

By June 2012, Geithner writes, the crisis was burning hotter than ever:

> Austerity measures were prompting riots and strikes on the periphery while depressing growth across the continent. Spain, with its jobless rate approaching 25 percent, needed a 100 billion euro credit line for its bank rescues. The debt-to-GDP ratios of Italy, Portugal, and Ireland all topped 110 percent, while Greece's neared 150 percent even after it haircut its bonds. Bank deposits were fleeing those countries as well, and their governments were too deep in debt to do anything about it. Europe had failed to persuade the world that it would not allow a catastrophe. Its firewall still looked flimsy. Its politics were still a mess. Every time its leaders announced new measure to try to control the crisis, they undercut their message with bad execution, strict conditions, and moral hazard rhetoric emphasizing their limited ability and desire to rescue their neighbors. Its loan packages were often more stigmatizing than stabilizing. And the markets still thought there was a meaningful possibility of a cascade of defaults by countries or banks, or a devastating breakup of the eurozone.[50]

Both sides were stressed as German-led Europe was failing its test.[51] Whereas Geithner and Obama let politics serve the market, the Europeans were butting heads with it in the service of other ends, including 'competitiveness', 'stability', inflation, and the supposed sovereignty of rules. All the while, from the American perspective, they were dangerously ignoring both what the market *thought* and what it might *do* to them. As if stubborn, old school Europe had never heard about the theory of (market) performativity. Yet, from the inverse angle, a German might say, Geithner's narrative displays no awareness of cultural and political difference—say, that a different rationality might be guiding a different governmental framework. The design of an 'economic constitution', the *raison d'être* of ordoliberal Europe, remained more or less unintelligible to American eyes.

---

[49] Geithner adds: 'The United Kingdom pivoted to austerity after David Cameron and the Tories ousted Gordon Brown, and would soon lapse back into recession. ... French President Nicolas Sarkozy was understandably cool to the idea of giving Germany power over the budgetary decisions of other countries. Unfortunately, he defused this threat to French sovereignty by persuading Merkel to back off the fiscal union in exchange for his support for the German mandatory haircut policy. In other words, a European government would have to restructure its debt to be eligible for assistance from the European rescue fund. Not only was Europe failing to make a credible commitment that it wouldn't allow a Lehman, it looked like it was committing to regular Wamus', n 38 above, pp 448–9.

[50] Geithner, n 38 above, p 481.

[51] For an account of the policy errors between 2011–12, see, also, Martin Sandbu, *Europe's Orphan: The Future of the Euro and the Politics of Debt*, (Princeton NJ: Princeton University Press, 2015). I am grateful to Stefan Eich for this and other suggestions.

Meanwhile, and behind the scenes, Geithner spoke with his close colleague Mario Draghi, whom he encouraged to use the ECB to curtail the recklessly anti-market, crisis-inducing conduct of these European leaders. 'Draghi knew he had to do more,' Geithner observes, 'but he needed the support of the Germans to do it, and the Bundesbank representatives on the ECB kept fighting him.'[52] For Geithner, this situation directly paralleled the US collapse in 2008; his deliberations with Draghi were reminiscent of talks with Ben Bernanke, who ultimately decided 'he would rather be hung for his own judgments than the judgments of the Feds' inflation hawks'. Geithner explains that, in the ECB's case, 'there was no way any plan that could actually work would get Bundesbank support. He had to decide whether he was willing to let Europe collapse'. Thus, the imperative he gave Draghi: 'You're going to have to leave them behind.'[53]

It was in this context that Geithner flew to meet Wolfgang Schäuble on the German island of Sylt, his regular vacation spot. Geithner recounts the following about their conversation:

> He told me there were many in Europe who still thought kicking the Greeks out of the eurozone was a plausible—even desirable—strategy. The idea was that with Greece out, Germany would be more likely to provide the financial support the eurozone needed because the German people would no longer perceive aid to Europe as a bailout for the Greeks. At the same time, a Grexit would be traumatic enough that it would help scare the rest of Europe into giving up more sovereignty to a stronger banking and fiscal union. The argument was that letting Greece burn would make it easier to build a stronger Europe with a more credible firewall.[54]

Geithner found Schäuble's proposition 'terrifying' and described his calls for austerity as coloured by a vision of 'Old Testament justice'.[55] Geithner left Sylt more concerned than ever; a Grexit would create 'a spectacular crisis of confidence'. After stopping by Frankfurt to see Draghi once more, he returned to Washington and consulted President Obama, who was also deeply worried:

> The U.S. economy was still growing steadily but modestly; a European implosion could have knocked us back into recession, or even another financial crisis.[56]

---

[52] These Germans, Geithner continues, 'didn't have a plan to save Europe, but they knew what they were against. They took a strict interpretation of the limits of the ECB's legal authority, and they opposed anything that could create moral hazard, which included just about any strategy that had a chance of calming the crisis', n 38 above, p 482.

[53] Geithner, n 38 above, p 482.

[54] ibid, p 483.

[55] As Adam Tooze, n 42 above, observes, Geithner may not have been so far off in his religious interpretation of Schäuble's motivations: 'Schäuble's ultimate source of optimism is the spiritual history of Europe. "The Reformation, already, was an answer to the search for orientation in uncertain times at the end of the Middle Ages," he said last year. "Luther found an anchor in the freedom of Christian humanity. The West again and again draws on this strength, to face the unchained forces that threaten our freedom, our understanding of self-determination and human rights."'

[56] Geithner continues: 'As countless pundits noted, we didn't want that to happen in an election year, but we wouldn't have wanted that to happen in any year. Two days after I saw Draghi, the ECB laid the groundwork for a program it announced in early September called "Outright Monetary Transactions," where it committed to buy the sovereign bonds of eurozone countries in secondary markets. The program was essentially a "Draghi Put," a promise to put a floor under bond prices in European countries, lowering their borrowing costs and making it clear that they would not be allowed to default. Draghi did not

Beyond 'their belated and often ineffectual attempts to imitate us', he says, the Europeans had made a host of mistakes. However, he self-satisfyingly concludes, at least their failure 'provides a pretty good advertisement for our crisis response'. Even this irritatingly Americentric angle leads to the same conclusion that many scholars of the EU have reached themselves.[57]

> A currency union without unified fiscal policies, banking policies, or political representation was not ideally situated to handle a monumental emergency. It was more proof that the American system, for all its faults, had a lot of strengths we took for granted.[58]

Just like his own actions between Wall Street and Washington—ie as a New York central banker turned governmental crisis manager turned private equity investor[59]—Geithner's narrative of the Euro crisis corresponds to the outline of what Claus Offe has called, with less self-congratulation, a 'crisis of crisis management'. Having recently remapped his previous account in *Europe Entrapped*,[60] Offe offers a damning take on an economically uneven, poorly designed, and democratically deficient European Union. But even Offe overlooks the significance of its 'ordoliberal' bearings, a concept that makes no appearance in the book despite the significant attention paid to Germany. The dilemma is, in Offe's eyes, a structural one: Germany is a powerful, self-interested country that privileges its own export-oriented economic model. 'As there is no longer a 'national' currency,' he writes, 'the export surplus becomes sustainable endlessly, if only at the expense of others.' To this, he adds that 'Germany, the global extreme case of an export surplus economy,

---

consult Merkel and Schäuble in advance, but they supported him publicly, even though the Bundesbank's ECB representatives voted no. The announcement of the new bond-buying program—and Merkel's vital support—persuaded the markets that the Europeans were serious about keeping the Eurozone intact ... When central banks and governments take catastrophic risk off the table, markets become investable again.' Geithner, n 38 above, p 484.

[57] Claus Offe, *Europe Entrapped*, (Cambridge: Polity, 2016).

[58] Geithner, n 38 above, pp 484–85.

[59] 'After an appropriate stint at a think tank to write his memoir and a quiet transition to Wall Street, President Obama's first Treasury secretary, who left office in 2013, is now ready to make millions thanks to help from a big bank he used to regulate ... Geithner has gotten a line of credit from JPMorgan Chase, the nation's biggest bank, to invest in a new $12 billion fund at the private equity firm where he works, Warburg Pincus ... [E]xecutives are signing up for a total $800 million and Geithner, as a top officer, is probably getting a sizable chunk of that. The returns on the private equity investment are bound to be much higher than whatever interest Geithner will be paying on the loan, so he is virtually guaranteed to make many millions in profit on the deal ... There is nothing illegal in Geithner's actions—provided his tax software or advisor can correctly calculate what he will owe the IRS—but his willingness to cash in on his time in government completes the picture of him as a poster child for much of what ails our current financial system', available at: www.usatoday.com/story/money/2016/02/09/ex-treasury-secretary-geithner-cashing-wall-street/80057762. See, also, Geithner's most recent political commentary: 'Of all the challenges facing economic growth, former Treasury Secretary Timothy Geithner believes the U.S. political situation is the worst. "I think the scarier things are really about politics, the scary erosion of the pragmatic center in politics, the diminished capacity to make sensible economic choices, something governments really have to do," Geithner said at the CNBC/Institutional Investor 2016 Delivering Alpha conference in New York', available at: www.cnbc.com/2016/09/13/bridgewaters-dalio-says-the-us-has-a-limited-ability-to-produce-economic-stimulus.html.

[60] See, also, Claus Offe, (interviewed by William Callison, Jonathan Klein, and Johann Szews), 'The Fate of an Impasse: Europe, Year 2015', (2016) *Near Futures Online* 1, 'Europe at a Crossroads' (March), for a comparative discussion of the European and American federalism.

has a strong interest in internal *re*valuation of its labor and public sectors, meaning an increase in infrastructure investment and public services, the strengthening of consumer demand through wage increases, and the raising of both minimum wages and maximum income'.[61] Offe thus sees reason to believe that the centre may not hold: Germany will be forced to recognise that Member-State economies are fundamentally and necessarily uneven, and to reconcile its interests with theirs for the common good of all. At the end of Chapter 3, in one of only a few sanguine conclusions to the book, Offe opens up to an optimism that comes, of all places, from an American perspective:

> As American observers such as the prominent trade expert Fred Bengsten have argued, Germany must and eventually will cease to pursue its vital interest in the preservation of the common currency through financing the deficit of the losers alone; instead, it will turn to a (domestically as well as within the Euro zone) much more popular strategy of *internal* adjustment, its self-transformation into a less export-addicted economy. Rather than forcing cuts of wages and pensions in Greece and elsewhere at great costs in terms of political integration, why not increase wages and public spending in Germany and other core countries to the economic and political benefit of the EU as a whole?[62]

This (American) optimism about German-led Europe is belied, as Offe would surely admit, by the CDU and the grand coalition's annual re-commitment to Schäuble's passionate attachment, the *Schwarze Null* (balanced budget).[63] In Schäuble's understanding, as we saw above, Germany's own balanced budget is an act of 'solidarity' with the rest of Europe, one that implements mandatory austerity measures. Other forms of 'solidarity' were scant, of course, when the so-called 'periphery' needed them most. Although this German sleight of hand deserves to be criticised on its own terms—say, for covering over inequalities of power and downplaying the very human suffering that it reproduces—its (less apparent) *normalising* function is equally deserving of attention. That is to say, within the extant framework of 'ever greater integration'—ie not a Social Europe modelled on a transfer union but a fiscal pact mandating debt breaks for bank loans—German *Ordnungspolitik* guarantees, through its very framing of domestic and transnational possibilities, that there is and will be no alternative.

---

[61] Offe, n 57 above, p 46, italics in original.
[62] Offe, n 55 above, p 47.
[63] Proposals from neo-Keynesians, both sanguine and realist, likewise aim at internal reform beginning with Germany; see, for example, Heiner Flassbeck and Costas Lapavitsas, *Only Germany can Save the Euro*, (*Nur Deutschland kann den Euro retten: Der letze Akt beginnt* (Frankfurt aM: Westend Verlag, 2015). Recently, and with good reason, some post-Keynesians saw the arrival of refugees in Germany as a potential boon that could lead to increases in state spending, employment and wages. Schäuble's *Schwarze Null* stood in the way, however, as did a SPD that was generally unwilling to risk linking the task of refugee assimilation to a project of state infrastructure and social spending. For an example of this brief moment of opening and closure, see the conclusion that follows from Brigitte Young's discussion of the German model, written between December 2015 and January 2016: 'Minister Wolfgang Schäuble has recently declared that the integration of refugees takes priority over the zero fiscal target. This may open the lock to a new imaginary of a domestic-led growth model in Germany. In the process, it may also return the Eurozone to a much-needed balanced current account regime.' idem, 'Imaginaries of German Economic Success: Is the Current Model Sustainable?', (2016) *Near Futures Online* 1, 'Europe at a Crossroads' (March).

It is as if the obvious *fact* of German power distracts observers from perceiving how these ostensible policy 'choices' are part and parcel of a larger normative model rooted, since its very inception, in principles of technocratic control, 'competitiveness', and export-oriented growth. German ordoliberalism is thus 'frustrating' because economic 'interests' are constructued by principles of political reasoning and techniques of governance. Many observers were recently fooled, for example, by Schäuble's intentions during his last-minute 'intervention' to cancel the fines on Spain and Portugal's deficit-to-GDP ratio. The stated aim of maintaining political (not economic) 'stability' in southwestern Europe was then revealed as an attempt to defer the fines until after the Spanish elections, ensuring that the leftist opposition, *Podemos*, could not politicise the EU's punitive actions and that Rajoy's conservative party would remain in power. It was exactly this, of course, that came to pass. That a single finance minister could direct and execute such an exceptional manoeuvre is, at this point, less than shocking; what remains remarkable, however, is that such a highly political act was met with only minimal resistance and had no consequences at all—indeed, it went exactly as planned. A parallel 'intervention' famously came a year prior during the *Troika's* 2015 negotiations with Syriza officials on Greece's debt. After Syriza won a democratic referendum against the German-designed austerity package, Schäuble infamously remarked, 'Elections change nothing. There are rules'.[64] With equal clarity this time around, Jean-Claude Juncker explained Germany's religious authority on how rules and exceptions work in the EU:

> We must not be more Catholic than the Pope, but please make it known that the Pope wanted a fine of zero.[65]

Such fluctuation between punitive inflexibility and pragmatic manoeuvring should not be mistaken for a rule-bound process of democratic deliberation or for proof of 'ideological impurity'. Rather, this form of technocratic governance—with a decade of Merkel 'leading from behind' and Schäuble ensuring outcomes are decided beforehand and preferably behind the scenes—is a domestically celebrated and quintessentially ordoliberal legacy of the postwar period. Critics such as Christian Joerges and Werner Bonefeld[66] have described the recent conduct of the *Troika* in terms of an *informal* and *extra-legal* approach to governance, an 'authoritarian liberalism' whose principle aim is to secure its own vision of economic order. Through these and other means, German officials and their European allies can continuously refer to a pre-established framework in order to defer and negate even the first steps toward internal or systemic reforms of a more 'social' nature.

---

[64] Jean-Claude Juncker clarified: 'There can be no democratic choice against the European treaties.'

[65] 'Wolfgang Schäuble bails out Spain, Portugal: Germany's finance chief intervenes to stop Commission sanctions against Iberian free spenders, partly to help political ally Mariano Rajoy in Madrid', available at: www.politico.eu/article/wolfgang-schauble-bails-out-spain-portugal-sanctions-juncker-german-finance-minister. Recent results redeem Schäuble's deceptive strategy of long-term deferral: 'To comply with Brussels-mandated budget deficit reduction targets, the government aims to introduce a €118 billion spending cap for 2017 (€5 billion less than this year)', available at: www.politico.eu/article/spains-pm-announces-economic-deal.

[66] See Chs 12 and 17 of this volume, respectively.

As we saw in Geithner's case, and as Jan-Werner Müller reiterates, whether or not ordoliberalism is intelligible to actors and analysts may make a world of difference:

> Ordoliberalism is what Angela Merkel wants for the Eurozone as a whole: rigid rules and legal frameworks beyond the reach of democratic decision-making ... She is interested in power, not in ideology. And power means domestic power—she would never risk anything for broader European objectives in the way Kohl did (but Schröder didn't). Germany, it seems, is becoming more German ... What is much less likely, however, is that they will ever abandon ordoliberalism.[67]

Foregrounding ordoliberalism's roots in a German tradition of political economic thought displaces the hope of many onlookers that—in the unlikely event that they win enough seats to form a coalition without the Christian Democrats—the Social Democratic Party would initiate a change of course.[68] As if Sigmar Gabriel's consistent support of the Chancellor during the Greek debt negotiations was not enough, the SPD's lack of vision for 'a different Europe' and its non-opposition to Schäuble's *Schwarze Null* shows the depth of ordoliberal commitments across party lines.

What I am suggesting is that the debate on German-led Europe requires greater attention to ordoliberalism as an economic tradition, institutional framework, and political rationality.[69] Within Europe, this would entail a different approach to politicisation and resistance as well as a different assessment of what must be overcome in the movement for a 'different Europe'—a largely empty phrase that has disguised a lack of real reflection and commitment concerning alternative principles of distribution, transfer, participation and justice.[70] Within Germany, this would

---

[67] Jan-Werner Müller, 'What do Germans think about when they think about Europe?', (2012) 34 *London Review of Books*.

[68] See Dyson (Ch 5 in this volume) on ordoliberalism as a 'tradition' as opposed to an 'ideology'. Regarding the legacy and cross-party reach of ordoliberalism's economic vision, see Ulrike Guérot and Sebastian Dullien, 'The Long Shadow of Ordoliberalism', (2012) *Social Europe*, 30 July 2012, available at: www.socialeurope.eu/2012/07/the-long-shadow-of-ordoliberalism: 'some elements of the German approach to the euro crisis are unlikely to change, even if majorities shift. The mainstream neoclassical belief in the need for stricter fiscal rules is shared by the Social Democrats and also has strong support inside the Green party. The same goes for the question of current account imbalances. There is a broad consensus that the burden of adjustment should be borne by deficit countries. Although some Social Democrats would like to implement elements of an expansionary wage and fiscal policy that might lower Germany's current account surplus, this is not official party position. A significant portion of the SPD still thinks that "Germany cannot be punished for its export successes." A change in government would therefore not overly affect the German position in this regard. The most decisive difference between the government and the SPD in the euro crisis is the different focus on growth. While the Social Democrats have been arguing that growth enhancing policies including fiscal stimuli are important in the crisis solution, the government has long held the position that structural reforms are good, but no additional money should be spent on growth programs.'

[69] Among the recent books that take a similar position, see Markus K. Brunnermeier, Harold James and Jean-Pierre Landau, *The Euro and the Battle of Ideas*, (Princeton NJ: Princeton University Press, 2016).

[70] For an analysis of the neoliberalisation of social democratic parties and the demise of 'Social Europe'—from Blair's 'Third Way' to Schröder's 'Agenda 2010'—see David J. Bailey, Jean-Michel De Waele, Fabien Escalona and Mathieu Vieira (eds), *European Social Democracy during the Global Economic Crisis: Renovation or Resignation?*, (Manchester: Manchester University Press, 2014), as well as Bailey, De Waele and Escanola's individual contributions to 'Europe at a Crossroads', available at: http://nearfuturesonline.org.

involve a critical engagement with the stakes and trajectory of a popular, yet highly ambiguous, heritage. Beyond the techniques of Merkel and Schäuble, discussed above, consider two recent attempts to claim the past and craft the future of German ordoliberalism, coming from opposing ends of the political spectrum. On one side, the German economist Hans-Werner Sinn has argued that left critics of 'neoliberalism' are dishonest because they do not distinguish between the 'radical concepts of Milton Friedman and the Chicago School' and the 'true' concept of neoliberalism.[71] 'In reality', the 'true' form of neoliberalism (ie ordoliberalism, though the term is not used here) is the 'exact opposite' of the Americans' reckless de-regulation that caused the financial crisis. Just as a fair soccer game requires clear rules and a referee, neoliberalism relies on 'the self-steering of the economy within an ordered framework [*Ordnungsrahmen*], though it doesn't believe that this ordered framework can be created by the economy itself'. According to Sinn, a strong state and framework itself is what produces trust, prevents chaos, and allows market competition to develop its beneficent forces. From the other side, *Die Linke* politician and economist Sahra Wagenknecht lays claim to the ordoliberal legacy of the 'social market economy'. In *Freiheit statt Kapitalismus: Über vergessene Ideale, die Eurokrise und unsere Zukunft*,[72] Wagenknecht argues that, in order to oppose (American) neoliberalism and to develop an alternative political economic programme, the left can find important tools and forgotten ideals in the work of Eucken and Erhard. Based upon legislation that crushes corporate monopolies and tames speculative banking and financial markets, this movement would construct a 'mixed economy' using markets and re-distribution oriented to social justice. 'Only a *creative socialism*,' Wagenknecht concludes,[73] can redeem Ludwig Erhard's promise of '*Wohlstand für Alle*', welfare and prosperity for all. Whether or not they prove effective, Sinn and Wagenknecht's shared critique of American neoliberalism and appeal to the ordoliberal legacy (even, perversely, from the latter's leftist perspective) represents an intriguing and distinctly German strategy for political economic hegemony.

The historical and analytic distinction between Freiburg School ordoliberalism and Chicago School neoliberalism thus possess an actuality that few foresaw and many still cannot perceive today. Whether or not they are intelligible, as such, these legacies remain alive for critics of both sides. German intellectuals and political practitioners have actively or passively drawn on ordoliberal principles both to construct legal and political institutions and to criticise the outcomes of American neoliberalism. From the other side, far from a Keynesian perspective, Geithner unknowingly criticised the EU's ordoliberal priorities of strict rules, austerity measures, and balanced budgets during the Euro crisis—ie what, in his eyes, looked like a moralised concept of fiscal discipline and a religiously inspired condemnation of debtor's justice. Not only did this approach ultimately prevail with minimal transnational

---

[71] Hans-Werner Sinn, 'Der wahre Neoliberalismus braucht klare Regeln', *Die Welt*, 15 May 2010.
[72] Sahra Wagenknecht, *Über vergessene Ideale, die Eurokrise und unsere Zukunft*, (Frankfurt aM: Campus Verlag, 2012).
[73] ibid, p 61.

resistance (social democratic parties included), it was also embraced by the German media and citizenry: after the final all-night negotiation on Greece's Memorandum of Understanding in July 2015, polls showed continued domestic support for Merkel and Schäuble's course of action.[74] An (un-)intelligible spectre that often manifests without a corresponding concept, ordoliberalism remains a normative model of technocratic rationality and an object of popular investment, the political implications of which are manifold.[75] Analysts and opponents of the EU's 'crisis of crisis management' would thus do well to engage with—rather than ignore or dismiss— the deep investments and living legacies of ordoliberalism when forging a path for future alternatives.

[74] An ARD survey conducted on 13 July 2015 showed that 87% of Germans thought the conditions for Greece were adequate or too soft while 13% thought they were too tough. Two-thirds approved of Schäuble and Merkel's leadership during the negotiations. For the long-term stability of Schäuble's domestic approval rating (around 75%), see www.tagesschau.de/multimedia/bilder/crchart-1705~_v-videowebl.jpg.

[75] Though it lies beyond the scope of this article, another important question in this regard concerns the relationship between the framework guiding German-led Europe and the rise of extreme right-wing movements and political parties across the continent. Schäuble made has made his position quite clear on these matters—ie increasing levels of xenophobia and Euroscepticism—and famously so when he blamed the rise of the AFD on the policies of the European Central Bank. When asked '[i]f the economic medicine in the euro zone is the right one and is working, then how do you explain why there's such a big voter backlash against the political establishment now?,' Schäuble (2014) replied: 'Perhaps the cause is that, when people have the feeling they're actually doing quite OK, democratic public opinion keeps a critical distance from the decision makers. Maybe that's one of the reasons why democratically elected governments quickly lose support after they take office. Maybe it's not such a bad thing. A critical public is something you have to deal with.'

4

The Tepid Reception of Ordoliberalism in Italy and Present-Day Dissent

STEFANO SOLARI

ABSTRACT

The Italian economic depression of 2011–2015 has been attributed to austerity policies politically enforced with the support of the German government and inspired by the principles of ordoliberalism. In the first part of this chapter, the roots of Italian liberalism are analysed and discussed in comparison to German liberalism. It will be highlighted how and who has been affected by ordoliberalism or had a theoretical position close to it. Then, the political reception of liberal principles in Italy is briefly discussed. In the latter part of the chapter, the present-day discomfort with European policies and the German influence on them will be discussed, by looking at the scholars that have pointed to ordoliberalism (or to 'the Germans ...') as the cultural-political cause of austerity policies.

I. THE TENETS OF ORDOLIBERALISM AND THE EUROPEAN PERIPHERY CRISIS

ORDOLIBERALISM IS INTENDED here as a policy framework which aims at obtaining a liberal regime by limiting private economic power and assuring the dignity of man (*menschen Würdig*).[1] Based upon the experience of the German economy, this approach worries about the self-destructive effects of unregulated competition that led to monopolies and concentrated economic power in the past. Consequently, ordoliberalism studies how to shape institutions appropriately in order to preserve the competitive economic process. This means that it supports state intervention based upon general and coherent rules, and is against both day-to-day intervention and Keynesian demand management policies that cause the

---

[1] Nils Goldschmidt and Hermann Rauchenschwandtner argue that ordoliberalism has a marked Kantian ethical perspective on the relationship between market processes and the law; see Nils Goldschmidt and Hermann Rauchenschwandtner, 'The Philosophy of Social Market Economy: Michel Foucault's Analysis of Ordoliberalism', 2007, Freiburg Discussion Papers on Constitutional Economics, 07/4.

distortion of prices.[2] Sound monetary policy to achieve a solid currency is a further fundamental objective of *ordo* thought. Walter Eucken originally based this framework upon the phenomenological philosophy and this led him to think of *forms* and *ideal-types*. Contemporary ordoliberals switched their method to the rationalistic epistemology of mainstream economics. In both cases, this approach particularly emphasises the role of individual responsibility.

These principles inspire two kinds of policies: the *Ordnungpolitik* and the *Prozesspolitik*. *Ordnungpolitik* consists of setting a competitive order in accordance to the economic constitution. The *Prozesspolitik* consists of correcting the existing order with the help of the regulating principles illustrated above. According to Walter Eucken,[3] we have six constitutive principles of *conforming intervention policies*[4] and four fundamental *regulating principles*.[5]

In the difficult times that followed the financial crisis which began in 2008, ordoliberalism began to be identified as the ideological reference of *austerity* as well as of *internal devaluation* policies in EU periphery. This theory has been identified as an opponent to 'American-style' liberalism, which was favourable to the expansion of monetary supply (albeit with the primary intent of preserving the global financial order). The consequence is that, especially after the second slump of 2012, ordoliberalism and its supposed *austerity policies* have progressively been questioned by many scholars and public commentators.

Actually, the financial crisis of 2008 represented a huge asymmetric shock for the Eurozone. In Italy, it took the form of a sharp fall in export demand and in a sudden stop in credit supply of banks. However, up until the year 2011, the Italian government succeeded in controlling public spending and the economy was slowly recovering. The second crisis in 2011 was primarily caused by a speculative attack, and was followed by the austerity policies of the Mario Monti's technical government, which aimed to restore confidence in the viability of the Italian public debt vis-à-vis the financial markets. This policy led the economy into a long period of stagnation and to severe difficulties for banks.[6] As a result, there is a commonly held belief that austerity was the cause of this crisis.

---

[2] Some economists, such as Wilhelm Röpke, were open to state intervention in cases of *secondary depressions*.

[3] Walter Eucken, *Grundsätze der Wirtschaftspolitik*, (Tübingen: J.C.B. Mohr, [1952] 1990).

[4] Constitutive principles: give priority to monetary policy to assure the efficiency of markets; avoid the rise of monopolies through the opening of markets and the elimination of any barrier; provide the definition and enforcement of property rights; assure freedom of contract; institute the principle of responsibility for economic actions (also for reasons related to the governance of companies); offer non-distortion of individual action plans with changes in policies, as the government should not surprise citizens with its operations.

[5] Regulating principles: an independent anti-trust authority should constantly monitor economic processes, sanctioning abuses of dominant positions (not eliminating concentration); there should be progressive taxation to re-distribute resources without affecting savings decisions; the correction of negative externalities; the monitoring of the labour market to avoid both disequilibria as well assure minimum standards.

[6] In fact, there was nothing particularly wrong with the Italian economy at that time that could have justified such a speculative attack. Italy had difficulties in controlling inflation and registered about approximately 1% yearly gap in comparison with Germany from 1997 to 2010, which, combined with

Consequently, the general rise of Italian dissent towards German-backed austerity policies began after the onset of the disastrous recession of 2012–15 caused by *internal devaluation* policies,[7] and by *prudential* banking regulation. In fact, credit policies enacted by the European Banking Authority (EBA) first, and then by the European Central Bank (ECB), have been based upon high capitalisation requirements for banks, with a particular penalisation for simple credit-oriented banks. Italian banks, found themselves unable to assure liquidity to their clients, and, in a few years, accumulated a large amount of bad credit. In an under-capitalised, bank-dependent production system, non-performing bank loans were therefore created by the increase of capitalisation standards.[8] At the time, austerity began to appear an absurd self-defeating policy to most Italians, and even to the same liberals who supported these policies. Both the conservative and the progressive media began to point to German politics as the source of austerity. Ordoliberalism was identified with deflationary policies and with de-contextualised non-expansionary monetary policies. Many commentators began to describe the German government's economic consultants as being rigidly anchored to unreasonable principles of budget equilibrium and a strong currency. A general suspicion that the Germans were imposing policies on Europe that were functional to the German domination on the Continent was cited in the right-wing media.[9] The right-wing press, once favourable to the euro—as it was expected to act as a guarantee for the savings of the middle class—became immediately contrary to austerity policies and developed a certain aversion to the whole European architecture. Only a few commentators were able to refer this policy framework competently to the theoretical tenets of ordoliberalism.

the sharp 30% re-evaluation of the *lira* prior to the fixing of parities, caused difficulties for the Italian balance of payments for a whole decade. Actually, the economy was not growing, but profitability was improving. The budget prepared by Giulio Tremonti was even stricter than the one that was to be prepared by Mario Monti at the end of 2011. Tremonti's budget met with criticism from Silvio Berlusconi, and the disagreement between the two was a relevant factor in the ensuing political instability. Actually, the *Lega Nord* (Northern League), part of the government, was against a severe reform of pensions, which was seen as a loose budgetary position, but the original budget included higher taxes and expenditure cuts. Today, many commentators argue that the Italian government was planning an exit from the euro and that the financial crisis of late 2011 was triggered by some German and French interests (the sudden selling of 7 billion euro of Italian Government bonds by *Deutsche Bank*, which is presently being investigated by the Italian authorities) in order to bring about the downfall of Berlusconi's government (based upon Timothy Geithner's memoires).

[7] Such policies are generally judged as wrong today, as they are too much based upon boosting exports. The Italian economy did not react as expected (the fiscal multipliers were estimated at 0.3, and were then revealed to be more than 1.7 ...), and the debt grew further.

[8] Banks had to cut lending (credit) to meet capitalisation standards and this caused non-performing credit by firms unable to reduce their exposure also because of fiscal restrictions.

[9] In fact, moderate and liberal left-wing scholars, as well as the newspaper *Repubblica*, who were favourable to the euro and to the recent treaties, did not criticise the entire set of austerity policies. The latter simply insistently criticised ECB German-inspired monetary policy and demanded the adoption of monetary expansion following the example of FED. Thus, they diffused this belief in the expansionary power of monetary policy (which is not Keynesian) and in the extension of ECB's powers as *lender of last resort*, which is mainly functional to the interests of large financial conglomerates and not specifically to the Italian economy. As a marginal note on the ECB policy of low interest rates, in 2015, Italy had saved 6 billion euro of interest paid on public debt. Unfortunately, it paid 7 billion euro in derivatives underwritten to protect itself from the risk of an increase in interest rates. This has a disorienting effect with regard to which policy is more convenient.

In this context, it is interesting to study the reception of German liberalism in Italy, and, more broadly, the position of Italian liberal scholars on these issues, particularly the position of liberal-conservative economists. In order to understand the different theoretical positions, both the scholars of both the past and the present will be briefly studied to highlight some diverging foundational elements. In the second section, the historical position of Italian liberal economists with an ethical or social tendency will be discussed. Then, the third section will analyse the political reception of these ideas. Section four will review the contemporary economists working on ordoliberalism, while the fifth will analyse how present-day scholars have cited ordoliberalism in their papers and blogs.

II. THE TRADITION OF ETHICAL LIBERALISM AND THE ACADEMIC RECEPTION OF ORDOLIBERALISM

While the label of *Social Market Economy* had, and still has, a certain success in both Italian politics and in academia, ordoliberal thought obtained some marginal appreciation, but no relevant followers nor a thorough discussion. The former met with the appreciation of right-wing Catholics due to its ethical and practical orientation (including contemporaries such as Francesco Forte and Flavio Felice). With regard to the latter, despite the good relationship between Luigi Einaudi and the philosopher Carlo Antoni with the German members of the *Mont Pèlerin Society*, we find only very superficial consideration of ordoliberal ideas. Even the most prominent Italian liberal, Luigi Einaudi, who openly appreciated the work of Wilhelm Röpke and invited him to Italy several times, had a less intense relationship with Walter Eucken.[10]

The first element that we can consider in order to understand the feeble reception of ordoliberalism is the specific development of Italian liberalism. From the middle of the nineteenth century, we can find two main streams of liberalism in Italy, which clearly emerge from a quarrel in 1874. The most orthodox stream, which is found in Francesco Ferrara, who was an important figure, and ethical liberalism, which was led by Marco Minghetti and Luigi Luzzatti. In 1874, they had a famous quarrel about the direction of policies and on the accusation of *Germanism* addressed by Ferrara to Luzzatti (who was also the main expert on trade policies at the Ministry of the Economy). Ferrara accused Luzzatti of obtaining his inspiration from German schools of thought (*Katheder*-socialism and Historicism). Actually, the ethical and practical approach was effectively leading Luzzatti to a very pragmatic and contextual formulation of policies, far from the *a priori* rationalistic formulas supported by Ferrara.[11] This caused an enduring division between liberals with the more orthodox,

---

[10] See the study of A. Giordano, 'A (neo)Liberal Friendship in a Time of Crisis: Wilhelm Röpke, Luigi Einaudi and the Future of European Civilization', paper presented at the Röpke memorial conference, Geneva, 14–15 April 2016.

[11] F. Ferrara, 'Il germanismo economico in Italia', (1874) 26 *La Nuova Antologia*, pp 928–1008, and idem, 'Gli equivoci del vincolismo', (1874) 15 *L'Economista*, pp 24–26; L. Luzzatti, 'L'economia politica e le scuole germaniche', (1874) 27 *La Nuova Antologia*, pp 174–192.

Turin centred liberalism, which viewed the German theories with suspicion, and which related more favourably with British and US scholars. Moreover, the progressive stream of liberalism which developed after the Second World War also tended to assume British Cambridge as a reference-point. The orientation to read and discuss German contributions remained a feature peculiar to Social Catholicism and of the follow-up of the 'historical right' wing of politics. This stream, however, had a very pragmatic orientation that degenerated into nationalistic positions that were partially at odds with liberalism. Nonetheless, the generation of ethical liberalism, to some degree, oriented to the dynamical theorisation of the economy and to understand the role of the context emerged and constantly obtained inspiration from both German economic history and theories—at least from those who could read German.[12]

A second major reason for the non-permeation of Italian liberalism by German influences is due to the specific conception of 'competition'. Many Italian economists[13] developed their microeconomic theory following Pareto. The Paretian way of modelling microeconomics constituted a rigorous, although closed, rationalistic and static system (price taking) that did not induce scholars to focus on the juridical framework of competition. The latter was mainly defined according to the number of firms and not by the specific institutional context. Subsequently, a general change in the conception of competition was produced by the diffusion of the Chicago focus on contestability, but little attention was paid to the *realistic* and *contextual* idea of competition of ordoliberalism. The idea that the law is needed in order to assure both freedom and competition is diametrically the opposite of Chicago economics. Consequently, the notion of market power has been understudied in Italy (or studied according to the Cambridge framework) and the idea that the economy needs a normative reference-point to reveal and restrict private market power remained mostly extraneous to Italian liberalism.

Nonetheless, some Italian liberal scholars were interested in the German context. Costantino Bresciani-Turroni (1882–1963) was a liberal economist who had a particular interest in the German economy. He studied in Padova and Berlin (with both Wagner and Schmoller).[14] His first two books *Mitteleuropa*[15] and the *Happenings of the German Mark*,[16] testify to his interest in and knowledge of the developments of the German economy. He self-exiled himself (similarly to Röpke) in Egypt in the late stages of fascism and published some fundamental works on political economy and economic policy. In these works, he advances some remarkable arguments that come close to German ordoliberalism.[17]

---

[12] V. Gioia and H.D. Kurz, *Science, Institutions and Economic Development. The Contribution of 'German' Economists and the Reception in Italy (1860–1930)*, (Milan: Giuffre, 2000).

[13] Those following a mathematical method.

[14] In Padua, ethical liberalism was still constituting an intellectual reference thanks to Giulio Alessio.

[15] Costantino Bresciani Turroni, *Mitteleuropa: L'Impero Economico dell'Europa Centrale*, (Rome: L'Universelle, 1918).

[16] idem, *Le Vicende del Marco Tedesco*, (Milan: Università Bocconi, 1931).

[17] idem, *Liberalismo e Politica Economica*, (Bologna: Il Mulino, [1945] 2006), and, idem, *Corso di Economia Politica, vol.2, Problemi di Politica Economica*, (Milan: Giuffré, 1962).

First of all, Bresciani-Turroni theorises the interdependence of social and economic equilibrium. Even if he has a different view of competition (taken by Maffeo Pantaleoni's competition as selection), his approach is nonetheless compatible with Eucken's phenomenology. He also shares with the Freiburg School the idea that liberty needs a legal order managed by the state (even though he cites Proudhon, instead of Eucken ...). In the same way, free competition is not spontaneous but the result of a juridical system shaped by the state.[18] At the same time, he was afraid of state interference in competition. For this reason, he made a distinction between public intervention that modifies 'data', from intervention that interferes with the price mechanism, which he was against. The ends of state intervention are political, aiming at economic prosperity and at social equilibrium. He also made a list of the state's functions: 1) to set-up a legal framework to establish competition; 2) to pay attention to inequalities (by taxes that do not affect savings; he was favourable to inheritance tax); 3) to fight monopolies; 4) to set-up social legislation and regulate workers' salaries; 5) to pursue full employment; 6) to favour workers' participation to companies' profits; 7) to favour the middle class(es) and small- and medium-sized companies; and 8) to promote education and cultural enhancement. All these points are remarkably similar to the ordoliberal framework. Moreover, Bresciani-Turroni favoured a solid monetary order.[19] He was moderately in favour of a counter-cyclical economic policy, but he expressed criticism of Keynesianism. Remarkably, Bresciani-Turroni warned that liberalisation should be cautious because he feared de-industrialisation, which is a still a crucial theme in the present crisis, which has not been sufficiently debated by contemporary politics.

Although we find no citations of German liberals in his writings, Bresciani-Turroni's ideas were developed out of similar sources and interests, and have been exposed to similar political problems (fascism). Apparently, however, there is no direct influence of ordoliberalism on his work (or vice-versa). Moreover, Bresciani-Turroni did not, unfortunately, leave a relevant follow-up in terms of a school of thought. In conclusion, the view of Bresciani-Turroni is certainly close to the ordoliberal tradition, but it appears more open to compromise solutions, and is not shaped by Kantian ethics with regard to the role of rules.

Luigi Einaudi, in contrast, was a friend and an admirer of the work of Wilhelm Röpke. In the last years of fascism, he flew to Geneva where he met him. He also knew Walter Eucken and the ordoliberal theory. We may affirm that his approach, which we can label as *social liberalism*, was not so different from the economic humanism of Röpke, although it was not structured in a well-ordered systematic framework, as ordoliberalism is.[20] Apparently, Einaudi's *Lezioni di Politica Sociale*[21]

---

[18] Bresciani Turroni, *Liberalismo e Politica Economica*, n 17 above, pp 83–84.

[19] Piero Bini, 'Costantino Bresciani Turroni: The Eulogy of Monetary Stability', in: Warren J. Samuels (ed), *European Economists of the Early 20th Century*, vol 2, (Cheltenham-Northampton MA: Edward Elgar Publishing, 2003), pp 1–36.

[20] Resico and Solari have attempted to systematise Röpke's economic theorising: Marcelo Resico and Stefano Solari, 'The moral foundations of society and technological progress of the economy in the work of Wilhelm Röpke', in: Patricia Commun and Stefan Kolev (eds), *Wilhelm Röpke (1899–1966). A Liberal Political Economist and Conservative Social Philosopher*, (Berlin, Springer Verlag, 2016).

[21] Luigi Einaudi, *Lezioni di Politica Sociale*, (Turin: Einaudi, 1949).

tends to display a more practical and open-ended approach compared to that of ordoliberalism. In particular, Einaudi, although contrary to demand management and to other forms of government intervention, never denied their utility in specific circumstances.[22] He was older than most of the Freiburg scholars, and, in the period following the Second World War, he held the posts of Governor of the Bank of Italy and President of the Italian Republic. As a consequence, he developed most of his work before the full development of the Freiburg School.

In the history of thought, we find other scholars with a similar attitude. Bruno Leoni adhered to *Mont Pèlerin Society*, but held a position similar to von Hayek's on the spontaneity of law, and not to the view of Eucken.[23] However, he was not an economist and he was not very influential (in contrast to Einaudi). The fact is that, on the one hand, scholars belonging to ethical (or social) liberalism, such as Giovanni De Maria,[24] while sharing the same concerns and experiences of the German liberals, had their own trajectory. They studied the German literature and displayed interest in the methodology, but kept to their own path. On the other hand, after the war, the cultural reference turned to the US and concepts and debates progressively evolved in that direction, instead of developing strong connections in Europe. Moreover, left-wing-oriented liberals took the British Cambridge School as their reference, neglecting the German literature.

When the last generation of Italian ethical liberalism exited from academia (retiring in the 1970s–1980s), they were replaced by a new generation of scholars educated in the US (particularly at the Bocconi University), methodologically far from German liberalism. This Americanisation of liberalism also occurred in Germany where the same ordoliberals underwent a process of methodological hybridisation, and the insertion of a different culture, namely, monetarism. This tore the two *milieux* increasingly apart.

III. THE POLITICAL RECEPTION OF ORDOLIBERAL PRINCIPLES

In the period immediately following the war, Italian politics was in contact with German liberalism. The Italian *Partito Liberale* (Liberal Party) invited Wilhelm Röpke to give speeches at its meetings. The books and works of the leading scholars were translated into Italian thanks to the interest of Luigi Einaudi (through his son's publishing company, *Giulio Einaudi*). The humanistic interpretation of liberalism and the so-called *third way* appeared a viable capitalistic philosophy to oppose Communism. It avoided the past mistakes of liberalism and its programme of de-centralisation and re-inforced both the middle class(es) and its political interests.[25]

---

[22] ibid.
[23] See Andrea Favaro, *Bruno Leoni. Dell'Irrazionalità della Legge per la Spontaneità dell'Ordinamento*, (Naples: ESI, 2010).
[24] Giovanni de Maria shared with ordoliberalism the interest for the institutional framework of the economy as well as the belief in the need of a solid currency.
[25] See Marcelo Resico and Stefano Solari, 'The Social Market Economy as a Feasible Policy Option for Latin Countries', (2016) *History of Economic Thought and Policy*, Issue 2, pp 27–52.

However, one of the main points of ordoliberalism, *competition policies* and *anti-trust*, had little following in Italian liberalism. It is very difficult to find documents which testify to any interest in breaking up the concentration of economic powers or the *interlocking directorates* that characterised Italian finance. When the Liberal Party broke-up (in the late 1960s), its progressive constituent part, the *Partito Radicale* (the *Radical Party*) was more interested in civil rights, while the conservative part simply tended to represent the interests of the rich. Even the liberal revolution of Berlusconi (mid-1990s) displayed little interest in controlling the concentration of private power.[26] Anti-trust was a reform that the European institutions pushed for but one which found no internal initiative.

After the Second World War and up to 1992, Italian governments were dominated by the *Democrazia Cristiana* or Christian Democrats. The political culture of the Christian Democrats was shaped by Social Catholicism, and thus was in harmony with *Soziale Marktwirtschaft* (SMW), or social market economy, and the politics of Konrad Adenauer and Ludwig Erhard. The right-wing part, or *corrente*, of the Christian Democratic Party was particularly close to the principles of the SMW, but not so favourable to rigorous compliance with rules, as they preferred political discretionary behaviour. Nonetheless, liberalism was influential thanks to the role of Luigi Einaudi, who gave the Italian economy a set-up that was clearly aligned to the international system of prices, which was in line with the principles of German liberalism.[27] The choice, therefore, was of an export-oriented, open economy based upon low labour costs and for a thrifty style of government action.

Changes in the political orientation towards *social democracy* happened in the 1960s, as a result of the changing weight or balance of internal *correnti* within the Christian Democratic Party which brought about substantial modification of the *policy style*.[28] This change led to more direct state intervention, to the public supply of *universalistic* services, such as health-care and to the distribution of pensions, which was used to curb the costs of structural adjustment. In this change, Italy did not find inspiration in liberalism, but in progressive-interventionist theories. All this led Italy onto a different path to that of Germany, particularly with regard to deficit spending and wage dynamics. The fact is that the Italian governments, in contrast to their German counterparts, were not able to maintain social peace without continuous excess expenditure.

In 1982, the *divorce* between the Bank of Italy and the Treasury was performed by Beniamino Andreatta, a progressive scholar affiliated to the Christian Democractic Party and inspired by British Cambridge theories.[29] Leaving the Treasury with the financial markets as its only source of financing public deficits, led to an uncontrolled increase in the public debt. Real interest rates passed from minus 2 or

---

[26] Berlusconi's political parties were mostly inspired by the US *neo-con* movement.

[27] This fact has been underlined by Augusto Graziani, *L'Economia Italiana dal 1945 ad Oggi*, (Bologna: Il Mulino, 1989), and I thank Marco Ranone for reminding me of this.

[28] Christian Democrats had the same political culture, but different economic visions. Moreover, Italy had to tackle the problem of territorial dualism—a problem that Germany faced only after re-unification, a problem that is still open.

[29] Luca Sandonà, 'Nino Andreatta and Italian Economic Policy (1963–1999)', paper presented at AISPE conference, in Lecce, in 2016.

3%, to plus 3 or 4%. In this way, Andreatta hoped to impose some discipline on the public budget, but this did not happen for a variety of political and institutional reasons that reveal the lack of coherence of the national institutions. The result was an explosion of public debt which doubled in just a few years thanks to the payment of abundant interest (to the delight of the bond-holders). This represented a major undervaluation of the notion of economic order, which, in contrast, is so relevant in the German tradition.

Even in the most recent set of reforms, those induced by the Treaty of Maastricht and by the EMU, the theoretical reference for the regulation of the Italian economy was a liberal-progressive conception of the economy.[30] In this more progressive action, little inspiration was taken from the German model or from the social market economy (with the notable exception of Carlo Azeglio Ciampi's attempt at a social pact in order to reduce inflation in 1993).

Again, the neglect of the idea of a *coherent order* led to progressive incremental reforms that mainly had counter-intuitive effects.[31] In particular, reforms that followed the 1992 political crisis attempted to turn the system in the direction of Anglo-Saxon capitalism—reforms driven by the interests of the financial markets and by a vision of the economy favourable to high flexibility and to a relative centralisation of capital allocation (concentrated in a few private hands). This is a view in total contrast to the original ordoliberal spirit of de-centralisation and of the equalisation of economic power through competition. This led to a whole series of inconsistencies in an economic system dominated by small- and medium-sized enterprises, with low growth and a decline in productivity.[32] In this *disorder*, only a continuous fiscal stimulus is able to produce the minimum of growth able to keep the viability of both public and private debt. It is no surprise that a deflationary policy in this context produces unbearable social strains and a particularly dangerous increase in debtor defaults ultimately resulting in non-performing loans for banks.

IV. CONTEMPORARY INTEREST IN THE FREIBURG SCHOOL

In the present-day landscape of economic research, there is not much interest in ordoliberalism, apart from studies on the history of economic thought concerning law and economics. However, in the last ten years, we may highlight the study by Lapo Berti of markets and of anti-trust, which also discussed and welcomed the ordoliberal approach as a viable and necessary intervention in the economy.[33]

---

[30] Berlusconi's governments were not very incisive and had more the role of slowing down changes than reverting to a conservative policy style.

[31] Marcelo Rangone and Stefano Solari, 'From the Southern-European Model to Nowhere: Italian Capitalism Evolving, 1976–2011', (2012) 19 *Journal of European Public Policy*, pp 1188–1206.

[32] ibid.

[33] Lapo Berti, *Il Mercato Oltre le Ideologie*, (Milan: Università Bocconi, 2006), and Lapo Berti and Andrea Pezzoli, *Le stagioni dell'antitrust. Dalla tutela della concorrenza alla tutela del consumatore*, (Milan: Università Bocconi, 2010).

On the other hand, most of citations concerning ordoliberalism refer to the studies by Massimiliano Vatiero of models of competition and of the specific view of ordoliberalism.[34] In these studies, the specific epistemology of the competition envisioned by ordoliberalism is contrasted with other conceptions prevailing in various traditions and in other schools of thought. However, in these studies only a part, albeit the fundamental part, of ordoliberalism is discussed, privileging the microeconomic aspect.

Another source of citation of ordoliberalism is that in writings which deal with *Soziale Marktwirtschaft*. In Italy, the social market economy is still a brand which attracts supporters (including the author of this chapter). We may cite Flavio Felice—who collaborated with Massimilano Vatiero,[35] Francesco Forte,[36] and Dario Velo,[37] who used this framework to study European integration, among its supporters. Also, some legal researcher as Alessandro Somma display a robust interest in this approach.[38] The position of these scholars relative to the policies enacted in Europe and concerning the euro have not been clearly expressed. Although Francesco Forte is in favour of austerity, in a blog he defended the quantitative easing of BCE, and, at the same time, supported the rejection of a single guarantee fund for the European banking union.[39] Therefore, we might say that he is close to, but not perfectly aligned with, the German liberal positions.

In any case, sure of not offending these scholars, we may argue that, in the last twenty years, they have not been very influential on Italian policy-making—even if some political parties still refer to this approach.

V. SOME REMARKABLE POSITIONS AMONG ITALIAN SCHOLARS RELATIVELY TO AUSTERITY

Some Italian scholars have either explicitly or implicitly addressed the ordoliberal principles of the ruling German administration as unsuitable to solve the present crisis. The most critical has been Giulio Sapelli.[40]

---

[34] Massimiliano Vatiero, 'The Ordoliberal Notion of Market Power: An Institutionalist Reassessment', (2010) 6 *European Competition Journal*, pp 689–707; idem, 'Ordoliberal competition', *Concorrenza e Mercato*, 29 July 2010, pp 371–381; and, idem, 'The Ordoliberal Notion of Market Power: An Institutionalist Reassessment', (2010) 6 *European Competition Journal*, pp 689–707.

[35] Flavio Felice and Massimiliano Vatiero, 'Ordo and European Competition Law', in: Luca Fiorito (ed), *A Research Annual*, (2015) 32 *Research in the History of Economic Thought and Methodology*, Emerald Group Publishing Limited, pp 147–157.

[36] Francesco Forte and Flavio Felice (eds), *Il Liberalismo delle Regole. Genesi ed Eredità dell'Economia di Mercato Sociale*, (Soveria Manelli: Rubettino, 2010).

[37] Dario Velo and Francesco Velo, *A Social Market Economy and European Economic Monetary Union*, (Bern: Peter Lang, 2014).

[38] Alessandro Somma, 'L'economia sociale di mercato: 1. Il fascino della terza via: torna di moda un passato mai passato', *Biblioteca della Libertà* XLIV no 195, pp 1–16, and, idem, 'L'economia sociale di mercato: 2. dal Nazionalsocialismo all'Ordoliberalismo', *Biblioteca della Libertà* XLV no 198, pp 1–20.

[39] Interview with Francesco Forte, on Il Sussidiario.net: 'Così la Germania può far esplodere l'euro', 21 April 2016. His position in favour of austerity can be found in Silvia Fedeli and Francesco Forte, 'Deficits, Tax Burden and Unemployment', in: Francesco Forte, Ram Mudambi and Pietro Maria Navarra (eds), *A Handbook of Alternative Theories of Public Economics*, (Cheltenham: Edward Elgar Publishing, 2014), pp 116–140.

[40] See www.giuliosapelli.it.

Giulio Sapelli is an economist who has worked both as a historian of Southern European economies, as a business historian, and as an economic anthropologist (he is an expert in the cultural transformations behind economic change). He belongs to the political culture of Italian socialism which has 'turned right', choosing the 'Atlantic' side of the battlefield. He has been quite critical of the centre-left governments of the 1990s and 2000s. He has always been critical with the myopic European politics, the loss of national autonomy, and the built-in deflationary pressures of the European treaties. His position is at odds with ordoliberalism, as he is favourable to contextual policy able to expand demand, smooth tensions and assure a viable path with minimum costs and losses for the industrial structure. His contributions on the crisis have been collected in Sapelli's blog,[41] while his attitude towards German-Italian economic relationships is best expressed in Festa and Sapelli, *Italia. Se la Merkel è Carlo V*.[42]

Sapelli accuses the architecture of the ECB monetary policies of having asymmetric effects on different countries and being driven mainly by the interests of the core of Europe with little care for (or understanding of) the periphery. The enduring surplus of the German balance of payments is a further hot topic showing the lack of viability of the present institutional arrangement.[43]

Sapelli is appalled by the policies that are leading to the dismantling of Italian industry (-25% of value from the introduction of the euro).[44] He adopts both voluntaristic and Keynesian arguments to support his critics to European policies because demand management can reduce the tensions that are stifling Southern Europe. He accuses European constraints through fiscal policies of causing severe deflation, which is inducing a stagnation characterised by a 'liquidity trap' situation akin to the *Japanese syndrome*, all attributed to the ordoliberal culture which has characterised the recent treaties. In his view, there is a connection between fiscal dominance and foreign dominance, and he is critical of the liberal-progressive parties which brought about this situation of national domination by a centralised bureaucracy.[45]

---

[41] Giulio Sapelli, *Il Sapelli. Blog di una Crisi 2004–2014*, (Milan: goWare, 2015).

[42] Lodovico Festa and Guilio Sapelli, *Italia. Se la Merkel è Carlo V*, (Milan: goWare, 2014).

[43] See 'J'ACCUSE/Sapelli: la Germania ci sta distruggendo', Ilsussidiario.net. last accessed 8 May 2016.

[44] In Sapelli, as in many scholars characterised by a structuralist perspective, the industrial structure is seen as a capital to be preserved and cultivated.

[45] «i protagonisti della vicenda, i più filo euro e quindi i più responsabili dell'*ordoliberalismus* dilagante, furono le forze socialiste e cristiano sociali europee. Da questo punto di vista la creazione dell'euro e l'adesione entusiasta di tutto l'Ulivo alla politica ordoliberista è stata il trionfo della considerazione teorica che è possibile dedurre in casi di scelte monetarie assunte in questo caso non da singole nazioni, ma da una burocrazia eurocratica dominante sui parlamenti nazionali che teneva e tiene sotto il suo controllo le nazioni. Ossia la considerazione che in presenza di creazione monetaria decisa dal mercato e quindi endogena, tali decisioni non sono mai libere, ma assunte nel contesto dell'equilibrio di potenza internazionale che quei mercati costituisce». 'PRODI & L'ULIVO/ Sapelli: ecco chi ha svenduto l'Italia a Germania ed eurocrati', Ilsussidiario.net, 28 February 2016.

Translation: 'Here's who has undersold Italy to Germany and the eurocrats':

'The protagonists in the story, the most philo euro and therefore the most responsible of the rampant *ordo-liberalismus* were the socialist and social Christian European forces. From this point of view, the creation of the Euro and the enthusiastic adhesion of all the *Ulivo* to an ordoliberal policy was the triumph of the theoretical consideration that it is possible to deduce in cases of monetary choices taken in this case not by single nations, but by the Eurocratic bureaucracy which dominated the national parliaments and held and holds the nations under its control. Or rather, the consideration that, in the presence

Therefore, he accuses Christian social scholars (and politicians) as well as social-ists to have totally misconceived the consequence of the euro. Adopting the ordo view at European level re-inforces the German political dominance. In particular, the accusation is that this arrangement under-evaluates politics and relies too much on the spontaneous adjustment of markets. He is also critical of the quantitative eas-ing performed by the BCE,[46] because it is more dangerous than useful as it is being performed in the same badly conceived institutional architecture. Such an increase in the monetary supply does not enhance trust in the European economy. Thus, the kind of deflation from which we are suffering is more the result of the institutional structure than of the actual monetary supply. In general, his conception of ordolib-eralism is limited to a few points of this theory.

The critics of Paolo Savona are quite important, as he has—by and large—been included in the group of Italian scholars close to social market economy. Piero Bini defined him as a 'scholar who is inspired by social market economy and its ethical values. His view is characterised by the attempt to combine conditions of free initia-tive and competition in the marketplace with "an increased level of civil society, not only of material wellbeing"'.[47] Savona has always been very critical of irresponsi-ble Italian fiscal policies. At the same time, he citicises the European treaties, from Maastricht to the Fiscal Compact, as they give priority to the rigid ties and they for-get or postpone any measure useful to balance markets with the social dimension.[48] However, following the 'prudence' and the 'practical' attitude of Italian liberalism, his concern is with finding viable solutions to the present crisis. In this way, he has endorsed the creation of a European fund for investments proposed by Italian economists of the Christian-social group.

However, Savona has been quite severe about European deflationary policies. Growth is the urgency, he wrote. He urged German friends:

> to show greater commitment to prevent another tragedy in Europe—that of some nations returning to poverty with the resulting hatred and conflicts—by acting in such a way as to guarantee continued growth in your country as well as in all the other countries through a collaborative effort ... A myth from the past is coming back with a vengeance: that of a balanced budget, which has now become a constitutional value and which we had thought to have rejected due to the gains in terms of knowledge of the economic science.[49]

of a monetary creation decided by the market and therefore endogenous, such decisions are never free, but are made in the context of the equilibrium of the international power that those markets constitute.' 'Prodi & the *Ulivo*—Sapelli: 'Here's who undersold Italy to Germany and the eurocrats', Ilsussidiario. net, 28 February 2016.

[46] Blog 'FINANZA E POLITICA/Sapelli: ecco come salvarci dopo il flop di Draghi'. Ilsussidiario.net., last accessed 11 March 2016.

[47] Piero Bini, 'How to Escape from the Crisis', in: Antonio Varsori and Monika Poettinger (eds), *Economic Crisis and New Nationalisms: German Political Economy as Perceived by European Partners*, (Brussels: Peter Lang, 2014), pp 111–146, at 117.

[48] Paolo Savona, *Dalla Fine del Laissez-Faire alla Fine della Liberal-Democrazia: L'attrazione fatale per la giustizia sociale e la molla di una nuova rivoluzione globale*, (Soveria Manelli: Rubettino, 2016), p 239.

[49] Poalo Savona, 'Letter to German and Italian Friends. How the European Economic Mechanism Works', in: Varsori and Poettinger (eds), n 47 above, pp 53–66, at 53.

He is more aggressive when he argues that the present policies represent an old plan (the 1936 *Funk* plan) of Germany to become the country that 'would put order in Europe'. The *Funk* plan projected that national currencies would converge into the area of the Deutschmark and also envisaged that industrial development only pertained to Germany, which would only be accompanied by France. The plan wanted other countries to devote themselves to agriculture and tourist services, something that would happen out of necessity or because of a natural 'calling'. Moreover, these countries would lend skilled labour to the German leadership project.[50] However, the distrust of Savona leads him to underline that:

> leadership, particularly at supranational level, entails duties in terms of security and wealth, something that, for instance, the if US have performed rather well during the post-war period. Therefore your policy is not nationalistic by nature, because it would then be out-dated and would also not take into account your interests in terms of exporting country, your ambition to be European leaders misses these two fundamental principles to support it.[51]

The US leadership is seen by Savona as being more responsible. He asks his German friends to allow everyone to pay their own debts by rationalising their economies so that they can continue along the same path of development. This is what the Americans did for Europe when they launched the Marshall Plan. His main message is an invitation to Europe, shaped by practical wisdom, to prevent further tragedies and the return of entire nations to poverty. A further point is that system competition is increasing—in a context in which some countries have been disarmed of their fundamental assets for competing.

Savona also poses the problem of total inefficacy and of the counter-productive effect of European policies causing a deepening dualism in the development of European regions. Austerity and the specific shape of European policies are removing the barriers to centripetal forces acting on the factors of production.[52] Thus, he demonstrates a pragmatic attitude, that is to say, he maintains that policies should be judged by what they actually deliver.

Lelio Demichelis criticised ordoliberalism, taking as a reference the idea of the inter-dependence of the economic and social spheres of life.[53] He considers ordoliberalism as the imposition of the economic form on the social, and such an imposition of pro-market discipline includes a paradoxically high degree of coercion and government control. In this way, the market becomes a teleological as well as eschatological and theological element in the policies oriented to create the pro-market order. Demichelis also complains about the specific meaning given to the word 'social' by German liberalism, as he rejects the idea of socialising the market.

---

[50] An attempt was effectively made in 1940 to introduce a single money into the regions occupied by the German army as well as in Spain and Italy. With regard to Italy, Galeazzo Ciano refused the German proposal because he was worried about the destruction of Italian industry, which was more fragile and fragmented than its German counterpart. We may affirm that contemporary Italian politicians are endowed with less economic common sense than Galeazzo Ciano.

[51] ibid, p 50.

[52] Francesca Gambarotto and Stefano Solari, 'The Peripheralization of Southern European Capitalism within the EMU', (2015) 22 *Review of International Political Economy*, pp 788–812.

[53] Lelio Demichelis, 'L'Ordoliberalismo 2.0', (2016), available at: http://ilrasoiodioccam-micromega. blogautore.espresso.repubblica.it/files/2016/07/Ordoliberalismo.pdf.

Alberto Bagnai is the most popular scholar who supports a structuralist view which induced him to demand the exit of Italy from the EMU. He argues that the decline experienced by the Italian economy in the last two decades depends on the slow-down of its labour productivity, starting in the mid-1990s. The supply-side explanations of this slowdown are inconsistent with the major stylised facts. Bagnai verified that the effect of a negative demand shock is the best explanation of productivity stagnation by adopting the acumulative growth model in the tradition of Kaldor-Dixon-Thirlwall.[54] In particular, he analyses Thirlwall's balance-of-payments-constrained growth model, which allows him to investigate the contribution of Italy's main trading partners to Italy's long-term growth from 1970 to 2010. The results show that Italy's long-term growth has been consistent with the balance of payments constraint.[55] Thus, the problem does not lie directly in the ordoliberal ideas, as in the specific pattern of the unification of the European economy based upon straight constraints on demand.

In a similar way, Forges Davanzati, Patalano and Traficante have studied the decline of productivity.[56] They argue that aggregate demand and credit supply significantly affect the path of labour productivity, consistently with Kaldor's second law. More economists of the progressive (non-liberal) orientation share this view, which nonetheless totally contradicts the choices of the left-wing governments in Italy since the beginning of the 1990s.

The group of Bocconi economists tended to back the adhesion to the euro and, more recently, the policy of internal devaluation. Some of them fiercely supported the idea of 'expansionary fiscal contraction', but, in the end, acknowledged that the fundamental problem was a lack of aggregate demand. However, the liberalism of this generation of scholars of the Bocconi (Giavazzi, Alesina, Perotti, Tabellini ...) has no connection at all with ordoliberalism, nor with Italian ethical liberalism, as it is simply an expression of the US-style mainstream and it is aligned with the liberal-progressive ideology that has attempted to reform Italy since the 1990s.

Other economists of the social-conservative school such as Quadrio Curzio and Francesco Forte have not expressed precise critiques towards ordoliberalism and German views on policy-making. Nonetheless, they have tried to work out some proposals that go in the direction of some European co-ordination of fiscal policies and the constitution of some European bond-issue to finance public investment on a European scale. Francesco Forte has also welcomed the recent BCE's expansionary policy and low interest rates. This approach opens a bit to the Keynesian view of the economic process, in view of the exceptional nature of this European depression.

---

[54] Alberto Bagnai, 'Italy's Decline and the Balance-of-payments Constraint: A Multicountry Analysis', (2015) 30 *International Review of Applied Economics*, pp 1–26.

[55] Relented growth can be explained by a progressive tightening of this constraint, that the sudden slowdown of labour productivity in the 1990s corresponds to a major shock to Italy's external constraint, and that the major contributions to this shock came through different channels of transmission, from the core Eurozone countries and from OPEC countries.

[56] Guglielmo Forges Davanzati, Rosario Patalano and Guido Traficante, 'The Italian Economic Decline in a Kaldorian Theoretical Perspective', Post-Keynesian Economic Study Group, working paper n.1606, March 2016.

However, Wilhelm Röpke would have never liked such a centralised structure as a European fund for fiscal policy.

VI. CONCLUSION: SAME LIBERALISM, DIFFERENT ETHICS AND INTERESTS

Traditional Italian liberalism did not develop positions far from ordoliberalism, particularly with Luigi Einaudi and Costantino Bresciani-Turroni. However, Italian liberalism is shaped by an ethical view which is only superficially comparable to the rule-based Kantian tradition of ordoliberalism. It is rather characterised by a peculiar *virtue ethic* that is tied to classical philosophy and to the Roman Catholic tradition that assumes a definition of 'the good' which is beyond any rule and looks at the substantive results of the economic order. This is not procedurally compatible with the strict Kantian approach of German neoliberalism even if Italians may usually converge with Germans on both ends and means. This leads Italian liberals to abandon the rigour of orthodoxy in the event of crisis. In any case, Italian liberals have always displayed a weak interest in anti-trust.

It remains quite questionable whether ordoliberalism is really the approach underlying European policies. Many commentators in Italy have pointed to German politics as being responsible for the present austerity policies and the inspirer of 'internal devaluation' policies. Nobody has considered that a single economic space, be it politically unified or not, would imply some unpleasant policies in some of its regions, particularly in the case of small regions or regions with chaotic political systems. Not one of the Italian critics has observed that Southern countries were accumulating huge foreign debt in order to finance the expansion of demand. Therefore, instead of considering Europe to be too big and differentiated to be manageable by a single monetary policy, most of the Italian commentators have pointed to the responsibilities of Germany in fostering suffocating rules. On the other hand, this deficit of communication had its reverse version in Germany where Southern countries have been painted as unreliable and irresponsive (not implementing sufficient reforms) without any serious understanding of what was going on.

A few commentators had heard of ordoliberalism and therefore only a few scholars have connected this theory to the policy style adopted by European institutions. In any case, the policies enacted in Italy from 2011 onwards have had some worsening consequences on the Italian economy, with some deeply and irreversibly negative effects on banks and credit. From this perspective, the problems that had to be amended by European policies have actually been worsened. The discontent generated by these irrational policies is channelled against Germany and Europe in different ways by the different media (all affected by US interests).

Those Italian scholars who are closer to ordoliberalism have been disillusioned. They are aware that such a policy style cannot be applied to Europe as a whole and that the architecture of the euro is flawed at its foundations. In particular, they do not share the idea that *system competition* works well in managing the Eurozone. Moreover, they perceive a political interest of the centre in policies oriented at depressing the periphery. Thus, they turned to the view that growth was the primary objective and, then slowly became aware that growth in the South cannot be achieved within the existing rules.

On the other hand, old ordoliberal ideas are selectively applied by contemporary German liberals. German post-war neoliberalism was worried about the creative finance of the Nazi regime. Today, European liberals have not complained sufficiently about the present 'creative finance', and they have not foreseen its dangers, either. Having a solid currency also means a sound financial system which is able to finance the economy without destructive speculative bubbles. The concern limited to inflation and to prudential capitalisation is probably a too narrow perspective compared to the original spirit of ordoliberalism.

Certainly, what divides the German from the American view of monetary policy is that the former is aware that monetary expansion is likely to lead to financial bubbles and they are against it. In the US, large-scale financial speculation is theorised as a constitutive property of markets and nobody really demands either its limitation or monetary repression. On the contrary, since 1997, the systematic expansion of monetary supply in the US was used to prevent the catastrophic implosion of various financial bubbles, helping, however, to shift them from one market to another, as well to other regions.

Therefore, for the present day German orthodoxy, complementary to the restrictive idea of *solid currency*, is the principle that both debt and asset deflation are a necessary step to recover from bad investment and from over-investment. Liberals overlook the fact that the macroeconomic repression of bubbles tends to have a larger impact on small- and medium-sized firms as well as on the periphery (via credit rationing and demand weakness) compared to the slight effect on speculative finance. Moreover, today, debt deflation is surely a necessary step, but European authorities have systematically downplayed the important role of demand-led growth to help debt-deflation. Actual austerity and deflationary policies appear as though they are simply driven by a political choice of centralisation, sincerely unfavourable to credit-driven financial bubbles but managed by a simple large-scale administrative proceduralism, oriented to redress balance-sheets with no concern for the dynamic and evolutionary consequences of demand reduction on small firms and peripheral economies.

5

Ordoliberalism as Tradition and as Ideology

KENNETH DYSON

ABSTRACT

This chapter examines the value of seeing ordoliberalism as a tradition. Addressing it in this way not only offers insights into its character, but also highlights a series of problems in trying to clarify its nature, distinctiveness and boundaries. In addition, the chapter argues that many of these problems in ordoliberalism stem from its particular ideological character and the role of this character as connector and mobiliser of the tradition. This ideological character helps explain why many economists, social and political theorists, politicians, and commentators are hostile to it as an 'irritating' idea. In pursuing these two interconnected aims, the chapter draws attention to key factors that have affected the reception and influence of ordoliberalism and conditioned the way in which it has evolved as a tradition.

I. ORDOLIBERALISM AS A TRADITION

THE VALUE OF seeing ordoliberalism as a tradition lies in questioning conventional views of it as just an abstract and coherent mental entity whose boundaries can be clearly delineated; as a particular school whose founders define the body of doctrine and whose followers defend this legacy; or as no more than a German 'fixed idea' that represents a *Sonderweg* in economic and political thought. Seeing ordoliberalism as a tradition opens up possibilities for a more nuanced debate on its strengths and weaknesses, and for rescuing neglected ideas from selective processes of historical memorising.

But what does it mean to speak of ordoliberalism as a tradition? It involves the claim that ordoliberalism represents a distinctive way of thinking about the economy. In its broadest sense, it is a way of thinking, consciously or unconsciously, that is normatively grounded in ethics, law, and the shaping role of the state in securing an orderly competitive market economy governed by rules that protect individual rights. In this way, it differs from the Austrian, Chicago, and Keynesian traditions. In its approach, it is fundamentally anti-positivist, non-utilitarian, and interdisciplinary. It shares a broadly Kantian and phenomenological philosophic imprint, a constructivist approach to designing the economic order. It also rests on a shared belief in the autonomy and the distinctiveness of public power, a belief that makes alien the ideas of the self-regulating market as a natural phenomenon and of the *laissez-faire* state.[1]

However, as with any tradition, ordoliberalism begs questions about the form that this distinctive way of thinking takes. In particular, three questions about the tradition emerge. What is the relationship between explicit and tacit knowledge, between ordoliberalism's existence in the form of certain 'foreground' ideas, and its role as 'background' ideas? Secondly, how is one to adjudicate claims that it represents a unitary tradition, with fixed meaning, against claims that it is an internally varied tradition, with open and fuzzy boundaries? Thirdly, to what extent is the ordoliberal tradition a historical given, an inheritance, or invented, evolving as it is adapted to new circumstances and challenges?

II. THE ORDOLIBERAL TRADITION AS EXPLICIT AND AS TACIT KNOWLEDGE

When we speak about an ordoliberal tradition, what kind of knowledge are we talking about? Conventionally, attempts to define ordoliberalism rest on highly intellectualised account of its nature and its scope, grounded in textual analysis of certain key thinkers, their biographies, and their contexts. However, in his famous Herbert Spencer lecture, the Cambridge philosopher William Sorley argued that tradition exists in two forms. It can be discovered in the narrower form of formalised knowledge.[2] Seen in this way, the ordoliberal tradition can be read, learned, debated, and transmitted. Its importance can be traced by examining the correspondence between its prescriptions and actual institutional and policy reforms and practices (though correspondence is not to be confused with causality). This way of thinking has typically focused on Walter Eucken's *Foundations of Economics* and *Principles of Economic Policy*. They have become the standard seminal references in offering a codified account of ordoliberalism, specifying a principle-based approach to designing an 'economic constitution' that would safeguard the competitive market order.

Historians of economic and political thought can further flesh out this intellectual narrative of the tradition and its distinctiveness by reference to the Lutheran social ethics and to the idealist and the phenomenological philosophy that underpin these principles. Sorley points to a particular aspect of tradition as formalised knowledge. It is bound together by a clear creation myth. A narrative evolves which centres on one or more unifying heroes who provide the tradition with a distinctive intellectual 'face'. They act as a doctrinal rallying-point.

However, according to Sorley, tradition also exists in a second, wider sense. It takes the form of ordoliberalism as 'common-sense', practical or experiential knowledge.

---

[1] See Kenneth Dyson, *The State Tradition in Western Europe*, ECPR Classics Series, (Colchester: the European Consortium for Political Science Research, 2010).
[2] William Sorley, *Tradition*, The Herbert Spencer Lecture, (Oxford: Oxford University Press, 1926).

This type of knowledge is institutionally and culturally embedded. The significance of ordoliberalism as a tradition does not rest on those who identify with it having read the 'creation texts'. In contrast to the proposition of the president of the *Bundesbank*, Jens Weidmann, it is not necessary that politicians go to bed with a copy of Walter Eucken's *Grundsätze der Wirtschaftspolitik* under their pillow.[3] More likely, it is only the speech-writers in German federal ministries and in the *Bundesbank* who are likely to have looked at these texts, and then very briefly and selectively. The basis of the appeal of ordoliberalism resides in embodying values that are already present in society, like belief in personal responsibility and the virtue of discipline as safeguarded through the primacy of law and a rule-based ordering of life.

Sorley reminds us that scholarly work on the glue that binds together and gives life to the ordoliberal tradition has to attend to *praxis* and implicit knowledge. This point was developed by the philosopher Michael Polanyi in stressing the paramount role of tacit knowledge and implied values.[4] The role of 'background' ideas, and the resilience of 'taken-for-granted' understandings, tends to be overlooked by the analyst, because of their more elusive nature than formalised, 'foreground' ideas.[5]

Mapping the relationship between explicit and implicit knowledge, between 'foreground' and 'background' ideas, can prove complex. This complexity is evident even in such supposed institutional guardians as the economic policy divisions of the German Federal Economics Ministry, the Federal Finance Ministry and *Bundesbank*. Their officials possess formalised knowledge. However, this knowledge reflects their academic economic training in 'mainstream' new Keynesian models of the economy, rather than in ordoliberalism. They do not enter their posts as 'ordoliberals' in any formed sense. Nevertheless, ordoliberalism is embedded in their institutional context, part of the heuristic baggage that has been accumulated over time. It continues to manifest itself in the specification of the nature of the policy problems that need to be addressed and in the revealed preferences of officials and policy-makers about what constitutes 'sound', sustainable policies when confronted with complex interest-based problems of political economy and trying to draw conclusions from modelling.

Ordoliberalism becomes part of the operational code of decision-makers.[6] In particular, the prevalence of a rule-based administrative culture in Germany, which was re-inforced by the constitutional order of the Federal Republic, provides fertile ground for the ready, tacit acceptance of ordoliberalism there. Notably, lawyers continued to occupy a large proportion of the most senior roles in the German Federal

---

[3] Jens Weidmann, 'Von Zahnärzte und Ökonomen—zur Bedeutung eines konsistenten wirtschaftspolitischen Ordnungsrahmen', Rede bei der Juristischen Studiengesellschaft, in Karlsruhe, in Auszüge aus Presseartikeln, 12 February 2014, pp 3–8.

[4] Michael Polanyi, *The Tacit Dimension*, (Chicagi IL: Chicago Unversity Press, 1996).

[5] See Emanuel Adler, *Communitarian International Relations: The Epistemic Foundation of International Relations*, (London: Routledge, 2005); and John R. Searle, *The Construction of Social Reality*, (New York: Free Press, 1995).

[6] See Alexander George, 'The "Operational Code": A Neglected Approach to the Study of Political Leaders and Decision-Making', (1969) 13 *International Studies Quarterly*, pp 190–222.

Finance Ministry. The conception of the European Economic Community (EEC) as a process of 'integration by law' proved fertile ground for helping to project ordoliberal ideas onto a wider stage in the 1950s and 1960s. Conversely, the existence of different types of administrative culture in Britain, France and Italy helps to explain why an ordoliberal tradition was much slower to take root. The consequence was that historical path dependency made for acute difficulties in transposing rdo-liberalism into EEC policies and across EEC Member States.

III. THE ORDOLIBERAL TRADITION AS IDEAL TYPE AND AS FAMILY RESEMBLANCE

When we speak about an ordoliberal tradition, we must recognise the problem that a tradition can be understood in varied ways. Reflecting its own philosophical roots, the ordoliberal tradition is typically characterised by its adherents in idealist terms. It is pictured as a coherent abstract mental entity whose essential features can be formally delineated around one or more specific shared, defining traits.

For lawyers, Franz Böhm and his concepts of the 'economic constitution' and the 'private-law society' provide the seminal references.[7] They underline the importance of the legal framework for a competitive market economy. For political economists, Walter Eucken's constitutive and regulative principles have a similar status. His morphological approach was the most influential attempt to fix the essential and timeless features of ordoliberalism in an ideal-type formulation.[8] In this kind of account, the ordoliberal tradition claims clear boundaries. It is set apart from the German historical tradition, the Austrian tradition, the Keynesian tradition, and the Chicago tradition. It reflects the philosophical conditioning from Kantian idealism and from phenomenology. In particular, ordoliberalism rests on a conceptualisation of the relationship between the state and the economy that differs from these other traditions. The competitive market is not understood to be a natural phenomenon. It requires constitution by a 'strong state' which must protect competition from the competitors who will seek protection for their privileged positions. In the absence of this 'strong state', asymmetries of power will develop, represented in Weimar Germany by the cartelisation of industry. Hence a defining feature is that ordoliberalism is as much focused on the problem of private as of public power. Its enemy is rent-seeking capitalists whose self-aggrandisement erodes social welfare and public morals.[9]

---

[7] Franz Böhm, *Wettbewerb und Monopolkampf*, (Berlin: Carl Heymann Verlag, 1933); idem, 'Privatrechtsgesellschaft und Marktwirtschaft', (1966) 17 *ORDO Jahrbuch für die Ordnung von Wirtschaft und Gesellschaft* (hereinafter *ORDO Jahrbuch*), pp 75–152; and idem, *Freiheit und Ordnung in der Marktwirtschaft*, (Baden-Baden: Nomos Verlag, 1980).

[8] Wilhelm Eucken, *Grundlagen der Nationalökonomie*, (Berlin: Springer Verlag, 1940); and idem, *Grundsätze der Wirtschaftspolitik*, (Tübingen: J.C.B. Mohr, 1952).

[9] Böhm, *Freiheit und Ordnung in der Marktwirtschaft*, n 7 above.

However, the philosopher Ludwig Wittgenstein became uncomfortable with this kind of idealist narrative.[10] He emphasised the ambiguity and variety in the way in which words—such as democracy, market, solidarity, and state—are actually used in every-day life. This heterogeneity is evident amongst those who associate themselves with, and are regularly associated by others with, ordoliberalism. In particular, they have contrasting views about the state, the market and solidarity. These contrasts are very evident when comparing the works of Wilhelm Röpke and Alexander Rüstow with that of Eucken.[11] Their 'sociological' liberalism argues that a competitive market order is not enough to ensure social solidarity, that the market can poison society. An ethically-grounded society must look 'beyond supply and demand'.[12]

Following Wittgenstein, traditions take on the looser form of 'family resemblance'. Those who belong to the ordoliberal tradition resemble each other not through a specific feature. Their resemblance takes the form of a variety of features that are shared by some, but not all—as with members of a conventional family. The tradition is held together by a general overlapping mesh of features, but with different features in specific cases. It is not necessary that one feature be found in all who belong to the ordoliberal tradition. The tradition comprises cross-cutting and criss-crossing features which bind it together.[13] As we shall see later, these features can be seen as blending conservative and liberal ideologies. However, the tradition lacks exactness.

Again, following Wittgenstein, the ordoliberal tradition has imperfect and open boundaries, both intellectually and geographically. This openness is apparent with respect to the German Historical, to the Austrian, and to the US-based 'old' and 'new' Chicago traditions. Just as conventional families intermarry, there are cross-cutting features—such as devotion to the competitive market, and primacy to the value of personal freedom—shared by these three traditions.

At the same time, the conception of the ordoliberal tradition as held together by family resemblance allows for differences of degree in belonging. Friedrich von Hayek seems to belong to a lesser degree than Eucken, not least because of his Austrian-tradition roots.[14] However, von Hayek's period in Freiburg University,

---

[10] Ludwig Wittgenstein, *Philosophical Investigations*. 4th edition, (Oxford: Wiley-Blackwell, [1953] 2009).

[11] Wilhelm Röpke, *Die Gesellschaftskrise der Gegenwart*, 4th edition. (Erlenbach bei Zürich: Eugen Rentsch, 1942); and idem, *Civitas Humana*, (Erlenbach bei Zürich: Eugen Rentsch, 1944); A. Rüstow, *Das Versagen des Wirtschaftsliberalismus als religions-geschichtliches Problem*, (Istanbul: Istanbuler Schriften, 1945), p 12; idem, *Ortsbestimmung der Gegenwart: Eine universalgeschichtliche Kulturkritik. Band 1: Ursprung der Herrschaft* (1950); *Band 11: Weg der Freiheit* (1952); *Band 111: Herrschaft oder Freiheit?* (1957). (Erlenbach-Zürich: Eugen Rentsch, 1950–57; and idem, 'Wirtschaftsethische Probleme der sozialen Marktwirtschaft', in: P. Boarman et al (eds), *Der Christ und die Soziale Marktwirtschaft*, (Stuttgart: Kohlhammer, 1955), pp 53–74.

[12] See Wilhelm Röpke, *Jenseits von Angebot und Nachfrage*, (Erlenbach bei Zürich: Eugen Rentsch, 1958).

[13] See Wittgenstein, n 10 above, p 61.

[14] See Viktor Vanberg, 'Friedrich Hayek und die Freiburger Schule', (2003) 54 *ORDO Jahrbuch*, pp 3–20; and idem, 'Hayek in Freiburg', Freiburg Discussion Papers on Constitutional Economics, 2012/1, Freiburg i. Br.: Albert-Ludwigs Universität.

nearly a decade after Eucken's death in 1950, served as a springboard for launching new reflections on the competitive market as an evolutionary phenomenon, a discovery procedure, and on the problem of knowledge in regulation. He nudged the Freiburg School in new directions.[15] Similarly, from the 1980s, US-based public choice theory and the new institutional economics, notably the work of James Buchanan, were to shift the Freiburg School into a new reflection on the political basis for the competitive market order.[16] This reflection sought to neutralise the critique of ordoliberalism as 'authoritarian liberalism', advocating the 'strong' state.[17] It stressed consensus and the centrality of 'citizen' sovereignty alongside 'consumer' sovereignty.

Seeing the ordoliberal tradition in Wittgenstein's terms of family resemblance begs some serious questions which go to the heart of historical study and of social science. Should these subjects limit themselves to the pursuit of analytical exactness and the establishment of clear, firm boundaries? This belief inspired Eucken's morphological method for uncovering economic orders. Can we speak of an essential common feature of the ordoliberal tradition? This position is taken by those who see the 'strong state/free market' as the essential common belief.[18] This understanding of historical study and social science underpins the search for causal connections. For instance, one can examine the causal relationship between the ordoliberal 'idea'—represented by, say, Eucken's constitutive and regulative principles—and the nature of, and changes to, the German and the Euro Area or EU economies. These economies can then be assessed as more or less ordoliberal.

Alternatively, one can argue that a tradition is more than an idea, theory or school. Tradition rests on affinity, correspondence, and similarity in the way of looking at the world, in how one thinks and behaves. Seen in this way, the ordoliberal tradition emerges as not just specific to Germany or, more narrowly still, to the Freiburg School. It finds parallels within other national contexts, parallels that do not necessarily rest on causal influences from particular German ideas or theories. These parallels bear witness to the role of ideology in connecting and in mobilising people.[19] The ordoliberal tradition was a common feature in a particular conservative-liberal form of centre-Right in various countries.

In the UK, for instance, the economists Edwin Cannan at the London School of Economics and Ralph Hawtrey foreshadowed key ordoliberal traits. Cannan, who

---

[15] See, eg, Erich Hoppmann, 'Wettbewerb als Norm der Wettbewerbspolitik', (1967) 18 *ORDO Jahrbuch*, pp 77–94; and idem, *Wirtschaftsordnung und Wettbewerb*, (Baden-Baden: Nomos Verlag, 1988).

[16] See Viktor Vanberg, 'Ordnungstheorie as Constitutional Economics—the German Conception of a "Social Market Economy"', (1988) 39 *ORDO Jahrbuch*, 17–31; and idem, 'Die normativen Grundlagen von Ordnungspolitik', (1997) 48 *ORDO Jahrbuch*, pp 707–26.

[17] See, notably, Dieter Haselbach, *Autoritärer Liberalismus und Soziale Marktwirtschaft: Gesellschaft und Politik im Ordoliberalismus*, (Baden-Baden: Nomos Verlag, 1991).

[18] See, eg, Werner Bonefeld, 'Freedom and the Strong State: On German Ordoliberalism', (2012) 17 *New Political Economy*, pp 633–56.

[19] See Michael Freeden, *Ideologies and Political Theory: A Conceptual Approach*, (Oxford: Clarendon Press, 1998); and Andrew Vincent, *Modern Political Ideologies*, (Oxford: Blackwell, 1992).

had a wide influence, criticised the belief in self-correcting markets and stressed the legal and institutional framework of the market economy. He focused on the family, property and the state as the essential pre-requisites of a properly functioning market economy. Competitive markets required cultivation, they were not natural phenomena.[20] His position owed more to ordoliberalism than to the Austrian tradition.

Similarly, family resemblance with ordoliberalism is discernible both in the published works of, and even more so in the later private papers of, Hawtrey.[21] He was the key economist in the UK Treasury, the architect of the 'Treasury View' in the 1920s, and a major figure at the Genoa Conference in 1922. There is no evidence of a causal connection to German thinking, indeed Hawtrey acknowledged few sources. A major exception was G.E. Moore, the Cambridge philosopher. Like Hawtrey, Moore was a fellow Cambridge Apostle. His ethics led Hawtrey to develop a critique of utilitarianism, of the concept of 'economic man', and of consumer culture on both aesthetic and intellectual grounds. Hawtrey focused on the problem of how to bridge the gap between market values and intrinsic ethical values. He looked to the structure of rule—to law and the political system—to serve as gardener, ensuring that true ends prevailed. In his insistence that economic welfare was not enough, he echoed the later thinking of Röpke and Rüstow. His metaphor of the competitive market economy as requiring careful cultivation for its maintenance and proper functioning appeared frequently in ordoliberal literature.

Even more noticeably, family resemblance with ordoliberalism is to be found in the works of the French economist and arch-opponent of planning, Jacques Rueff, who was a leading French Treasury official in the 1930s and later architect of the radical liberalising economic reforms under President Charles De Gaulle in 1958–59. Rueff's *L'ordre social* went even further than Eucken in sketching a rules-based market order and in anticipating the design features of the successive EMU.[22] In particular, he sketched out in more detail fiscal policy rules and the institutional framework to govern them in terms that corresponded closely to the subsequent EU Stability and Growth Pact. Like Cannan and Hawtrey, Rueff was a conservative-liberal in ideology, and a zealous opponent of fiscal deficits. Though his views were rooted in the positivist philosophy of the *École Polytechnique*, he shifted towards a more phenomenological and constructivist conception of science. This conception of science reflected the strong influence of Immanuel Kant on twentieth-century French philosophy.

---

[20] See Edwin Cannan, 'The Incompatibility of Socialism and Nationalism', in: idem, *Collected Works, Volume 4, The Economic Outlook*, (London: Routledge and Thoemmes, [1909] 1997), pp 281–97, and idem, 'Introduction', in: idem, *Collected Works*, (London: Routledge and Thoemmes, [1912] 1997), pp 24–25.

[21] See Ralph Hawtrey, *The Economic Problem*, (London: Longmans, Green & Co, 1926); idem, 'Right Policy: The Place of Value Judgements in Politics', Hawtrey Papers 12/2, Churchill College, Cambridge University 1943–1973; and idem, 'Thought and Things', Hawtrey Papers 12/1, Churchill College, Cambridge University, 1946–1973.

[22] See Jacques Rueff, *L'ordre social*, 2 vols, (Paris: Sirey, 1945).

Similarly, ordoliberal traits were foreshadowed in the US, above all amongst opponents to President Roosevelt's New Deal interventionist policies in the 1930s. These traits were visible in the 'old' Chicago tradition, associated with Frank Knight, Henry Simons,[23] and Jacob Viner. The Chicago economists looked for an automatic stabiliser in monetary policy, echoing Eucken's concern.[24] Simons and his colleagues shared Hawtrey's monetary theory of the business cycle and emphasis on the role of monetary policy in correcting the instability of credit. They also stressed principles of anti-cartel policy and economic stability that bore a strong family resemblance to ordoliberalism. The 'old' Chicago School stressed a long-term, rule-oriented approach, grounded in the rule of law and enforced by the state.

A more direct inspiration to continental European ordoliberals came from the eminent US public intellectual and journalist, Walter Lippmann, whose *The Good Society* condemned 'reckless experimenters and intellectual adventurers' who pursued 'transient popular majorities'.[25] He called for strong, independent, non-partisan institutions, including universities and the judiciary, to provide the necessary restraint. His book heaped effusive praise on Knight, Simons, Röpke, and Louis Rougier. Lippmann's call to stem the rising tide of collectivism—represented for him by the New Deal—stimulated Rougier, a French philosopher, to convene the international Lippmann Colloquium in Paris in August 1938. It served as a milestone in the evolution of ordoliberalism as a cross-national tradition. Twelve of the 26 participants were later to be members of the Mont Pèlerin Society, which was similarly dedicated to the renewal of liberalism, including von Hayek, Ludwig von Mises, Röpke, Rougier, Rueff and Rüstow. Liberalism's crisis was attributed not just to Keynes and to fascism and Marxism, but also to its own self-inflicted wounds in the form of the *laissez-faire* state. In particular, the presentations of Röpke and Rüstow at this Colloquium had a significant influence on Rueff. They highlighted the importance not just of a rule-based economy, but also of attention to the interdependence of the economic with the social order.

Lippmann was to shift towards Keynesianism in the 1950s, terminating his membership in the Mont Pèlerin Society. However, he continued to argue for a public philosophy which, by the nature of its insistence on the principles of right conduct, was not designed to be popular. He remained a staunch critic of ideologues and sectarian interests which subverted government, as well as of economists who ignored philosophy, history and political science.[26] Again, these views of the importance, autonomy and distinctiveness of public power reflected an intellectual position on the state that had strong family resemblance to ordoliberal writing.

---

[23] See Henry Simons, *A Positive Program for Laissez Faire*, (Chicago IL: Chicago University Press, 1934).
[24] idem, 'Rules versus Authorities in Monetary Policy', (1936) 44 *Journal of Political Economy*, pp 1–30.
[25] Walter Lippmann, *The Good Society*, (New York: Grosset and Dunlap, 1937), p 224.
[26] idem, *Essays in the Public Philosophy*, (Boston MA: Little Brown, 1955).

IV. ORDOLIBERALISM AS AUTHENTIC AND AS INVENTED TRADITION—MEMORISING AND FORGETTING

Speaking of ordoliberalism as a tradition poses a third problem. Are we dealing with an authentic tradition, or with one that has been invented? An authentic tradition is understood as an historical given, as handed down as a set of understandings and practices. It is honoured, mythologised and defended, for instance, by those who seek to guard the integrity of the Freiburg School as the embodiment and interpreter of ordoliberalism. This task involves going back repeatedly to the seminal texts.

However, one can also see the role of the analyst as to uncover and to puncture the mythology that creeps into contemporary accounts of ordoliberalism. In particular, it is important to identify the element of institutional, intellectual and expert self-interest at work in constructing an 'authentic' tradition. As Eric Hobsbawm reminds us, traditions are not just original and authentic historical givens,[27] they are invented, institutionalised, and guarded by their initiates.

Looking at ordoliberalism as invented tradition is important in two ways. First, it draws attention to its institutional, intellectual and expert appropriation and usage, and the interests that inform this appropriation and usage. It highlights the selective and utilitarian process of 'cherry-picking' of old ideas and past experiences at work in constructing tradition. This process of 'cherry-picking' begs the question of just how authentic the commitment of, for instance, the *Bundesbank* and German federal ministry economists to ordoliberalism is. Ordoliberalism can be seen, above all, as an ideology of convenience. It helps, for instance, to buttress the case for central bank independence and monetary stability, and to protect the powerful interests behind the German model of export-led growth.

However, in the absence of an authentic commitment to the tradition, the process of 'cherry-picking' begs the further question about the relative significance of ordoliberalism even for these supposed embodiments of the tradition. Making the case of central bank independence and monetary stability or for market structures that support the model of export-led growth may be just as likely to involve the appropriation of ideas outside the ordoliberal tradition. Thus, the ideas of the 'new' Chicago School about oligopolistic competition practices accorded better with the interests of large German export-oriented companies in creating critical mass in a fast-changing market context of globalisation, Europeanisation, and technological change. Similarly, the *Bundesbank* case for central bank independence and for change in monetary policy goals and instruments, in the changed context of the collapse of the Bretton Woods system in 1971–73, drew more heavily on the Chicago School ideas of monetarism than on ordoliberal thinking about an automatic monetary stabiliser. Milton Friedman trumped Eucken.

Secondly, seeing ordoliberalism as invented tradition offers insight into its heterogeneity and into its processes of adaptation and change. These processes were

---

[27] Eric Hobsbawn, 'Introduction: Inventing Tradition', in: Eric Hobsbawm and Terence Ranger (eds), *The Invention of Tradition*, (Cambridge: Cambridge University Press, 1983), pp 1–14.

evident by the 1940s as Röpke and Rüstow developed their sociological form of ordoliberalism. They focused on what Eucken did not develop before his death in 1950, namely, the analysis of the social and the political order and their interdependence with the economic order.

Similarly, Alfred Müller-Armack linked his concept of the social market economy to the ordoliberal theorising of Eucken and the Freiburg School.[28] However, he gave greater attention to the questions of the social and political acceptability of the competitive market order than Eucken had. Böhm proved more prescient than his colleague, questioning the value of having a perfect system of order, only for the public to reject it.[29] Once an elected member of the German *Bundestag*, his concern for the social and political dimension increased.[30] Müller-Armack's attempt from the mid-1950s to develop a second phase of the social market economy illustrated the even greater flexibility and pragmatism of his thinking.[31] He differed from Eucken in being a 'statesman' economist, rather than a pure 'philosopher' economist. Social balance and peace became the guiding principles of his approach to economic policy, which entailed a greater concern with outcomes, rather than with just process, with avoiding deflation and with combating inequality.

In terms of political symbolism, the social market economy came to represent the politically popular and successful face of the ordoliberal tradition. But, for many in the tradition, above all those attached to the Freiburg School, Müller-Armack was not an authentic ordoliberal. His view of the 'social' was seen by them as a Trojan horse for interventionist policies and for mounting fiscal deficits and public debt. However, it could also be seen as better suited to developing a more inclusive and sustainable polity, one which took account of capabilities as well as abstract rights, and which better accorded with the preferences of citizens.

Moreover, the processes of adaptation and change have been as much a feature of the Freiburg School variant of ordoliberalism as a feature of the tradition as a whole. One can discern a Freiburg 2 and a Freiburg 3. Freiburg 2 involved the appropriation of von Hayek's evolutionary thinking about markets, represented internally by Erich Hoppmann. Freiburg 3 was linked to the influence of Buchanan's thinking about 'constitutional economics', mediated through Viktor Vanberg. The Freiburg School sought to adapt to von Hayek's general critique of economic 'scientism' as founded on the pretence of knowledge. It also sought to counter the broader critique of its 'authoritarian' liberalism by a new concern with the question of consent. In short, the Freiburg School underwent its own difficult process of re-inventing

---

[28] Alfred Müller-Armack, *Wirtschaftslenkung und Marktwirtschaft*, (Hamburg: Verlag für Wirtschaft und Sozialpolitik, 1946); and idem, 'Die Wirtschaftsordnung sozial gesehen', in: Alfred Müller-Armack, *Genealogie der Sozialen Marktwirtschaft*, (Bern: Haupt, [1947] 1974), pp 73–89.

[29] See Franz Böhm, *Die Ordnung der Wirtschaft als geschichtliche Aufgabe und rechtsschöpferische Leistung. Heft 1: Ordnung der Wirtschaft. Schriftenreihe herausgegeben von Franz Böhm, Walter Eucken and Hans Grossmann-Doerth*, (Stuttgart: Kohlhammer, 1937).

[30] idem, 'Der Rechtsstaat und der soziale Wohlfahrtsstaat', in: F. Böhm, *Reden und Schriften*, (Karlsruhe: C.F. Müller, [1953] 1960), pp 82–150; and idem, 'Marktwirtschaft von links und von rechts', in: ibid, pp 151–57. Originally, an article in the *Frankfurter Allgemeine Zeitung*, 24 October 1953.

[31] See Alfred Müller-Armack, 'Das gesellschaftliche Leitbild der Sozialen Marktwirtschaft', in: idem, *Genealogie der Sozialen Marktwirtschaft*, (Bern: Haupt, [1962] 1974).

the ordoliberal tradition. The open question was whether ordoliberalism had been hollowed out of its distinctive content in the process.

The historical selectivity that goes along with the claim to represent the authentic tradition of ordoliberalism goes along with the marginalisation and the neglect of the contributions of once-central figures. This fate has befallen Müller-Armack, Röpke, Rueff, and Rüstow. Memorising is also a process of forgetting.

Both Müller-Armack's, and, above all, Röpke's, writings were more widely read than those of Eucken in the 1940s and 1950s. Müller-Armack was close to the heart of economic and European policy-making under Ludwig Erhard as successively his head of the economic policy division and state secretary for European affairs in the Federal Economics Ministry. His proposals for a more pro-active European economic governance in 1958–59 included a European counter-cyclical capacity, including to ward off deflationary threats as well as inflationary threats.[32]

Röpke was generally regarded in the interwar period as the more outstanding economist. He served on the Brauns Commission on the unemployment question in 1931, and, along with Karl Lautenbach, was a key figure in generating radical proposals to counter German descent into a 'secondary' deflation in 1931.[33] Not least, he and Rüstow focused on the limits of the competitive market economy in their writings of the 1940s–50s. Though they shared the ordoliberal aversion to the welfare state, they were strong advocates of policies that would actively promote social solidarity. These policies included measures to encourage less inequality in wealth and income, including, in the case of Rüstow, a stringent attitude to inheritance taxation. The writings of Müller-Armack, Röpke and Rüstow attempted to build on ordoliberal ideas in order to generate a vision of an inclusive social as well as economic system.

The challenge facing the scholar of ordoliberalism is whether to limit oneself to the role of chronicler of the tradition's emergence and to contribute to this chronicle. The notion of traditions as invented opens up the possibility of encouraging a more self-reflexive process of critiquing 'tradition-construction'. It helps in the historical task of rescuing lost ideas and the figures with whom these ideas were associated. Examples include Müller-Armack on European economic governance and on social balance, as well as Müller-Armack and Röpke on deflationary as well as inflationary risks.

V. ORDOLIBERALISM AS IDEOLOGY

The question of what connects the ordoliberal tradition, whether as 'foreground' and 'background' ideas, as family resemblance, or as memorising and forgetting,

---

[32] See Kenneth Dyson, 'Hans Tietmeyer, Ethical Ordo-liberalism, and the Architecture of EMU: Getting the Fundamentals Right', in: Kenneth Dyson and Ivo Maes (eds), *Architects of the Euro: Intellectuals in the Making of European Monetary Union*, (Oxford: Oxford University Press, 2016), pp 138–69; and idem, *The Ordo-liberal Tradition*, forthcoming.

[33] idem, *The Ordo-liberal Tradition*, n 32 above.

draws attention to ideology. Ideology represents a broad world view that both connects and mobilises people.[34] In the case of ordoliberalism, the connector and mobiliser is a hybrid of conservative and liberal ideologies. This hybrid character helps us to understand why it exhibits a great deal of internal variety as well as an open-textured character. It also makes ordoliberalism difficult to pin down. For instance, it is difficult to tie it down in shared traits to a single conception of justice, with controversy focusing on whether distributive justice should be its concern.[35]

The appeal of ordoliberalism rests on its underlying model of the free, but, at the same time, 'solid' and responsible citizen. This model serves as a code for the interests of both savers and creditors. Specifically, ordoliberalism finds support amongst the institutions, intellectuals and experts who identify themselves with this citizenship model and its associated economic and social interests. They coalesce around a definition of the problem as feckless and irresponsible debtors and the collective as well as individual costs that their presumed profligacy generates. The answer to this problem is sought in basing policy on sound principles and on a clear and firm framework of rules that constrain both political rule and individual and corporate conduct. It means embedding policy in a holistic medium- to long-term perspective and examining the compatibility of individual measures with the whole system. The emphasis is on limiting discretion to do harm through opportunistic and inconsistent policies, associated with the worst excesses of authoritarian or of democratic rule. Ordoliberalism celebrates the traditional *bourgeois* values of 'solid' citizenship, exemplified in prudence, thrift, discipline, and respect for the traditional social order and for its institutions—such as the family and the churches—that support this order.

Conversely, the opponents of ordoliberalism are to be found amongst social-liberals and the Marxist Left. However, they are also present nearer to their ideological home. Fellow conservatives, such as the Italian philosopher Benedetto Croce in his debate with the economist Luigi Einaudi, distrust some of its features of liberalism as being corrosive of the organic unity of society and the eternal values that hold it together. Conversely, many fellow liberals, particularly American libertarians, are suspicious of its conservative traits as threatening to market freedom. This suspicion surfaced in the Mont Pèlerin Society during the 1950s and 1960s, and led to the marginalisation of the sociological ordoliberalism of Röpke and Rüstow.[36]

As a tradition and ideology that enshrines the interests of savers and creditors, ordoliberalism is inherently politically controversial. An important aspect of this controversy hovers around the question of the respective roles of individual culpability and of misfortune in debt. Critiques of ordoliberalism from the centre-Left typically identify the problem as one involving the plight of misled, misused, and ill-fated debtors. It produced collective as well as individual costs that follow from

---

[34] Freeden, n 19 above; Vincent, n 19 above.
[35] Manuel Wörsdörfer, 'Von Hayek and Ordoliberalism on Justice', (2013) 35 *Journal of the History of Economic Thought*, pp 291–317.
[36] Philip Plickert, *Wandlungen des Neoliberalismus. Eine Studie zu Entwicklung und Ausstrahlung der 'Mont Pèlerin Society'*, (Stuttgart: Lucius and Lucius, 2008), pp 178–93.

pursuing them in an 'Old Testament' vindictive fashion. These critiques point to ordoliberalism as a morality play about market successes and failures, rewarding the good fortune of some and punishing others.

Bringing in ideology also helps us to address the question of whether ordoliberalism is 'an irritating German idea', and, if so, irritating to whom? Answering this question requires a recognition of the particular ideological character of ordoliberalism in fusing together, in various hybrid ways, conservative and liberal values. On the one hand, ordoliberalism emphasises order, discipline, duty and family, based upon respect for a hierarchical social order. This conservative face reveals itself in an emphasis on religion and/or on metaphysical guidance as key pillars of order and as a source of ethical values. On the other hand, Ordoliberalism is inseparable from the legal safeguarding of individual rights, in particular, property rights, the central characteristic of liberal ideology. The fusing of these two sets of values is evident in the emphasis on the interdependence of orders: ethical, social, legal, political, economic, and monetary. Ordoliberalism's ideological character ensures that, as a tradition, it remains deeply unsympathetic to the centre-Left, above all, to the Marxist Left.

Section II

The Political Liberalism of Ordoliberalism

6

Ordoliberalism as a Variety of Neoliberalism

THOMAS BIEBRICHER

ABSTRACT

This chapter addresses the question whether there is a specific variety of neoliberal thought called ordoliberalism, and if so, what its distinguishing features are. Conventionally, ordoliberalism is identified with the notion of markets needing a robust and enforceable juridical framework, or, what ordoliberals called the 'competitive order'. However, I argue that, at least in early neoliberal thought, this was by no means a demand exclusively formulated by ordoliberals but one that was espoused even by Milton Friedman and Friedrich August von Hayek. Instead, the differentia specifica of ordoliberalism is to be found in its political dimension that seeks to remedy the alleged defects of pluralist democracy and its negative impact on the government of markets through a 'strong state', the 'de-pluralisation' of democracy and technocratic forms of rule. It is this combination of views regarding the state, democracy and the role of science that is unique to ordoliberalism. The chapter closes with a look at the modernisation of ordoliberal thought over the last two decades and concludes that what is now referred to as Ordnungsökonomik has abandoned most of these positions. While characteristics of the political theory of ordoliberalism in its original sense continue to be on display in the world of actually existing neoliberalism, ie the restructuring of the European Union in response to the debt crisis, as a distinct intellectual tradition it has become increasingly unrecognisable.

I. INTRODUCTION

IS THERE A specific variety of neoliberal thought called ordoliberalism? This is the question that the following remarks aim to address, albeit in a far from conclusive way. My argument is of a very preliminary nature and should not be considered to be more than a mere first attempt at a more thorough and encompassing research endeavour which lies beyond the scope of this chapter. I will proceed in three steps. First, I will provide a definition of neoliberalism that has the possibility of differentiating between varieties of neoliberalism (and I am only interested in neoliberal thought, not in 'actually existing neoliberalism', for the purposes of this chapter) built into it. In a second step, I will identify some aspects of ordoliberal thought that set it apart from other varieties of neoliberalism, at least for a certain period of time. Finally, I will examine some efforts to modernise the ordoliberal agenda, not least in response to some prominent and trenchant criticisms, and conclude that ordoliberalism, as a specific contemporary theoretical agenda, has vanished to a considerable degree, or, rather, has dissolved into *Ordnungsökonomik*, which is a mixture of the assumptions regarding the state and democracy held by constitutional economics and the views on science that can be found in von Hayek. Surprisingly, classical ordoliberal tenets are more present in the actual politics of European crisis management than in the thought of ordoliberalism's contemporary intellectual heirs.

II. WHAT IS NEOLIBERALISM?

As is well known, there are simply no self-avowed neoliberals to be found anywhere anymore. The term has acquired such toxic connotations that nobody concerned about their public reputation would identify with it, and even the critics of neoliberalism think twice before using it, because referring to neoliberalism or calling others neoliberals is tantamount to disqualifying oneself as someone more interested in polemics than reasoned argument.

   Given the inconveniences associated with the term and its negative connotations, a good starting-point to develop a somewhat more meaningful definition is the time when neoliberalism was actually used as a self-identifying marker by a group of intellectuals, albeit only for a fairly short period of time. This, of course is the 1930s and 1940s during which thinkers such as von Hayek, Röpke, Rüstow, Eucken and several others called for a concerted intellectual response to the multi-faceted crisis of liberalism that they were witnessing, which was to be the intellectual and political project of neoliberalism. Liberal ideas would have to assert themselves against the illiberal *zeitgeist* and is various manifestations from European Fascism to the New Deal. However, among the participants of the famous *Colloque Walter Lippmann* in 1938, where the term was 'born', albeit under curious circumstances, or the meetings of the *Mont Pèlerin Society* (MPS) which was founded in 1947, there was also widespread agreement that liberalism had not been put on the defence strictly due to external factors but also due to internal aberrations that needed correction. However, what precisely these aberrations were, and how severe they had been, proved to be controversial from the very inception of neoliberalism, and one of the reasons why neoliberalism, even in its most united moments, has never been 'one'. Even Friedrich von Hayek famously denounced simplistic 'classical' liberal notions such as '*laissez-faire*' as having done much harm to the liberal cause, and almost everybody except for Ludwig von Mises agreed that the neoliberal formula would have to include both, the positive component of a re-vitalisation of liberal ideas but also the more critical component of a revision of the classical liberal agenda that would be the crucial pre-condition for the development of a modern liberalism capable of contending with Keynesian, Fascist and Communist ideas. But even beyond this very thin and formal definition of neoliberalism, it is possible to identify not so much a shared basic consensus or a set of substantive core tenets, but rather a common *problématique* that can be sketched out in the following way. Neoliberals both obviously and trivially assume that functioning markets are of fundamental societal importance. Less trivial is the question that contains their shared *problématique*, namely, what the conditions of possibility of such functioning markets are. Given the widespread reservation regarding the option of laissez faire, this question or *problématique* naturally broadened the agenda of neoliberals in order to scrutinise the political, social and legal pre-conditions of functioning markets, and this goes for the ordoliberals and their mantra of the 'interdependence of orders' as much as for someone such as von Hayek. In this sense, neoliberalism is not an economistic perspective, but one which engages in political economy, to put it in somewhat old-fashioned terms. In the light of this re-construction of the neoliberal *problématique*, it is easy to see how the intellectual project experienced, from its very inception, strong centrifugal tendencies, as widely varying answers to the core question of neoliberalism persisted or developed. Neoliberal thought, accordingly, has always exhibited a range of positions depending on how its core question is addressed in its many different aspects, and whenever positions concurred on at least some of the respective answers it may be justified to refer to varieties of neoliberalism. Ordoliberalism has long been considered to be the most clearly distinguishable of these varieties, especially in juxtaposition with the Chicago-School variant, the two varieties thus arguably marking the opposite ends of the neoliberal spectrum.

III. THE SPECIFICITY OF ORDOLIBERALISM

A reading of ordoliberalism that has acquired some popularity beyond the usual circles who are interested in political economy and the history of economic thought is that of Michel Foucault in his lectures on the history of governmentality, in which he discusses ordoliberalism as a distinct 'governing rationality' and also sets it apart from 'American neoliberalism' represented first and foremost by Gary Becker. Foucault identifies competition as the crucial value of ordoliberalism, and describes its representatives as thorough anti-naturalist thinkers: market competition is an artificial phenomenon to be produced and maintained through some kind of order, namely, the so-called competitive order that was to be developed in a collaborative effort between jurisprudence and economics, as envisaged in what, in English, is referred to as the 'Ordo Manifesto of 1936' co-authored by Hand Grossmann-Doerth, Franz Böhm and Walter Eucken. The insistence on some kind of legal framework for markets, designed to expose market actors to the utmost competition, is often presented as the key difference between ordoliberalism and other neoliberal strands, a point that has been brought back to the public's attention in the aftermath of the financial crisis, when contemporary ordoliberals made it a point that they had never given in to the fantasies of self-regulating (financial) markets, supposedly espoused by other more radical varieties of contemporary neoliberalism. It would be implausible to dismiss this way of distinguishing ordoliberalism from other neoliberal persuasions entirely. There is a reason why the ordoliberals are called *ordo*liberals. In fact, their strict coupling of order and freedom sometimes appears as if the priority actually lay with the former rather than with the latter. But we must be careful not to overstate the originality of this stance, at least during the early days of neoliberalism, especially given the widely-shared sentiment that *laissez-faire* and the minimal state offered no viable alternative to 'collectivist' ideas. Early neoliberalism, all of its conflicts and heterogeneities notwithstanding, spoke the language of ordoliberalism—to a surprising degree. Two examples must suffice to illustrate this: first, consider von Hayek's presentation at the inaugural MPS meeting in 1947, in a session on 'Free Enterprise and Competitive Order':

> It is this fact which I have wished to emphasize when I called the subject of this discussion "Free Enterprise and Competitive Order". The two names do not necessarily designate the same system, and it is the system described by the second which we want.

Furthermore,

> It is the first general thesis which we shall have to consider that competition can be made more effective and more beneficent by certain activities of government than it would be without them.[1]

He continues by showing that the thesis can, indeed, be upheld, and makes reference to typical ordoliberal themes such as the problem of monopolies and the significance of patent law, licences, etc. The other piece of textual evidence comes from Milton Friedman and his article *Neo-liberalism and its Prospects* written in 1951:

> ... in place of the nineteenth century understanding that *laissez-faire* is the means to achieve [the goal of individual freedom], neoliberalism proposes that it is competition that will lead the way ... The state will police the system, it will establish the conditions favourable to *competition* and prevent monopoly, it will provide a stable monetary framework, and relieve acute poverty and distress.[2]

Hence, I will argue that, rather than the idea of some kind of (competitive) order itself, it is the unique *combination* of ordoliberal views on the defects of the democratic state as the guarantor of the competitive order and how they ought to be overcome that makes for its specificity as a variety of neoliberalism.

Although it is certainly possible to distinguish between the thought of various representatives of the first generation of ordoliberalism, such as Walter Eucken, Wilhelm Röpke, Alexander Rüstow and Franz Böhm, I will present a synthesised or rather stylised account of '*the*' ordoliberal position to emphasise what I think is unique about the strand of ordoliberalism, rather than what is unique about the individual authors. In short, I take the ordoliberal diagnosis regarding the problems of contemporary societies at its core to be a critique of pluralist mass democracy.[3]

---

[1] F.A. von Hayek, '"Free Enterprise" and Competitive Order', in: idem, *Individualism and Economic Order*, (Chicago IL: University of Chicago Press, [1948] 1980), pp 107–118, 111 and 110.

[2] Milton Friedman, 'Neo-liberalism and its Prospects' (1951) *Farmand*, February 17, pp 91–93, at 92, (translated from Norwegian by Anette Nyqvist and Jamie Peck).

[3] For discussion of the general relation between neoliberalism and democracy, see Thomas Biebricher, 'Neoliberalism and Democracy', (2015) 22 *Constellations*, pp 255–266.

The stylised argument proceeds in the following steps. Contemporary societies are mass societies with all of the problems and pathologies that accompany this macro-development.[4] Inspired by thinkers ranging from Gustave Le Bon to José Ortega Y Gasset, the ordoliberals view this as a process of cultural levelling and a trend that also makes for the increased receptiveness of the population for demagogues spreading ideologies. The gravity of this development is intensified by its coupling with the secular trend towards democratisation:

> First and foremost the simultaneous democratization grants political parties and the masses and interest groups organized by them a massively increased influence on the government of the state and thus on economic policy as well.[5]

The masses are easily swayed by ideologies that veil particularistic interests and political parties serve as the relay through which these demands from the masses and the interest groups are programmed into the state's agenda. The state 'falls prey' to these interest groups, and, rather than serving the common good, its actions dissolve into incoherence as it grants privileges, exemptions, subsidies, etc, to whoever is most resourceful in lobbying the state. What is the 'positive foil' for this critique, ie in the name of what alternative arrangement is this critique formulated? It seems as if the ordoliberal scepticism regarding mass democracy requires the circumscription of democratic processes and institutions as a positive vision. In other words, the most charitable reading of the transformations that the ordoliberals envision would be that of a 'de-pluralisation' of democracy. If societal demands directed at the state are interpreted as 'rent-seeking', then it would seem that these demands are per se considered as illegitimate, and, in this sense, an ordoliberal democracy is bound to be a non-pluralist one, at least when it comes to issues related to economic policy broadly speaking, ie whenever the competitive order has to be defended against the eroding effects of privileges, exemptions, etc. Possibly, democratic structures could still be maintained in other policy domains, but this is unclear as the 'interdependence of orders' makes any neat compartmentalisation of policy areas difficult. From here, it is not a long conceptual-analytical way to the implications for an ordoliberal state. The ordoliberals have repeatedly stated the demand for a 'strong state' as a guardian of the competitive order,[6] and, although this call has been defended tirelessly to this very day as a call for a state that restrains its scope of actions and gains strength through the prudent abstinence from socio-economic activism, this will not suffice as a defence against the charge of authoritarian tendencies in the ordoliberal view of the state. The point is that the ordoliberals demand a state that is no longer traversed by countervailing forces imported from civil society and the economy, either through transparent democratic channels or the oblique links of backroom lobbying. Eucken bemoans the fact that 'the power of the state today no longer serves its own will but

---

[4] See Wilhelm Röpke, *A Humane Society*, (Chicago IL: Gateway, [1958] 1971), pp 36–89.

[5] Walter Eucken, 'Staatliche Strukturwandlungen und die Krisis des Kapitalismus', (1932) 36 *Weltwirtschaftliches Archiv*, pp 297–321, at 306. All translations from German are mine.

[6] See Alexander Rüstow, 'Die staatspolitischen Voraussetzungen des wirtschaftspolitischen Liberalismus', in: idem, *Rede und Antwort*, (Ludwigsburg: Hoch, [1932] 1963), pp 249–258.

to a considerable degree the will of the interested parties', and concludes that 'the real independence of its will is missing'.[7] Röpke seconds this assessment, as can be inferred from this rhetorical question:

> What happens if governments [...] fail to take independent decisions based on objective assessment of all relevant facts and designed to serve the common interest?

He describes the process of decline in the following terms:

> Thus, the monistic state of democratic doctrine has developed into the pluralistic state of democratic practice.

And adds that:

> ... any responsible government must examine carefully all the possible means of resisting this pluralistic disintegration of the state.[8]

Röpke is right on target with his choice of terms because it is the monistic structure of the state that turns it into a semi-authoritarian one—while it is also clear that Röpke and the others have no totalitarian aspirations of the state controlling all parts of society. It is simply a state that has 'its own will', one which is formed independently from that of societal influence. But what is the will of the state aside from its own survival? The ordoliberals, it seems, equate the will of the state with the common good, as is already intimated by Röpke's rhetorical question quoted above. And the common good in its most parsimonious and formal meaning arguably coincides with the competitive order, ie a societal order that at least approximates the idea of 'ordo' in the normative sense as an order that is attuned to the human nature and the nature of things, to paraphrase a formulation by Eucken. However, the ordoliberals must have been suspicious of the possibility of a state run by politicians and bureaucrats to implement the common good. Their hope, it seems, lay partly (at least in the case of Röpke) in a class of citizens that would rise to such high levels of morality that they could be entrusted with this task, a *nobilitas naturalis*.

> The conviction is rightly gaining ground that the important thing is that every society should have a small but influential group of leaders who feel themselves to be the whole community's guardians of inviolable norms and values and who strictly live up to this guardianship. What we need is a true *nobilitas naturalis*.[9]

So, importantly, the twofold assumption is that neither can rules by themselves solve the problem, because an ethos is required to introduce, apply and enforce these rules; nor is human nature modelled in such a way that this is theoretically ruled out. We must sidestep the further considerations of Röpke regarding these 'aristocrats of the public spirit'[10] and immediately move on to the final ingredient in the ordoliberal formula.

---

[7] Eucken, n 5 above, pp 307–308.
[8] Röpke, n 4 above, p 141, 142 and 143.
[9] ibid, p 130.
[10] ibid, p 131.

These aristocrats may be of unassailable public spirit but the sheer willingness to strive for the common good is not enough to realise it in practice. This is due to the complexities of highly specialised societies, the socio-economic arrangements of which are not easily grasped by the untrained eye. This is where ordoliberalism's view of science comes into play, the clearest articulation of which is arguably found in the *The Ordo Manifesto of 1936*. Here, Böhm, Grossmann-Doerth and Eucken present themselves as the alternative to the pluralist system, as it was sketched out above. Rather than taking their directions from the societal actors through more or less democratic channels, decision-makers ought to consult with scientists and rely on their expertise.

> If men of science relinquish this role or are deprived of it, then other less competent advisers take over—the interested parties.[11]

The result is the already described incoherence of economic policy, broadly speaking, and, ultimately, the disintegration of the state. The ordoliberals claim a privileged knowledge, the superiority of which is based upon three factors. First of all, it is only the scientist who can grasp socio-economic complexities in their *totality*; in contrast, the private lobbyist only sees the aspects of this totality that is of interest to his or her cause. Furthermore, scientists can legitimately harbour aspirations of objectivity because of the unique 'class position' of an intelligentsia without any immediate and concrete interests that would taint its judgement. Interested parties make self-serving ideological claims, while scientists speak in the name of disinterested truth. Finally, science can rely on methods that yield reliable and robust knowledge about the socio-economic world. It generates a truth that is not just constructed and subjective, but one which is encapsulated in the objective world itself—at least, this is a plausible interpretation of Eucken's development of a science of political economy designed to overcome the 'great antinomy' of historicist and formal-theoretical schools exemplified by Gustav von Schmoller, on the one hand, and Carl Menger, on the other. Consider the following quotations for illustrative purposes:

> Men of science, by virtue of the profession and position being independent of economic interests, are the only objective, independent advisers capable of providing true insight into the intricate inter-relationships of economic activity and therefore also providing the basis upon which economic judgements can be made.

Towards the end of the Manifesto, the authors are clear about their desire to act as scientific political consultants—if not more:

> ... we wish to bring scientific reasoning, as displayed in jurisprudence and political economy, into effect for the purpose of constructing and re-organising the economic system. [...] The treatment of all practical politico-legal and politico-economic questions must be keyed to the idea of the economic constitution.[12]

---

[11] Franz Böhm, Walter Eucken and Hans Grossmann-Doerth, 'The Ordo Manifesto of 1936', in: Alan Peacock and Hans Willgerodt (eds), *Germany's Social Market Economy: Origins and Evolution*, (London: Palgrave Macmillan, 1989), pp 15–26, at 15.
[12] ibid, p 15 and 23.

Overcoming the defects of pluralist democracy through will formation by the state insulated from societal pressures under the direction of committed servants of the common good who are, in turn, guided by the expertise of economist and lawyers; this is the specific ordoliberal way of addressing the *problématique* of neoliberalism more generally and this is, to a large degree, what sets it apart from other varieties of neoliberal thought.[13]

IV. ORDOLIBERALISM AND *ORDNUNGSÖKONOMIK*

What happened to the traditional agenda of ordoliberalism that contained this vision of technocratic government with all of its anti-democratic, quasi-authoritarian and scientistic undertones? The trajectory of the evolution of ordoliberal thought is, of course, far from one-dimensional and linear, so it is impossible to do it justice here. Instead, I will simply take a look at what I take to be the crucial turning-point in this trajectory, which is to be found in the work of Viktor Vanberg. With Vanberg and others, such as Jens Voigt, the normatively questionable aspects of the ordoliberal theories of state and democracy were abandoned, and what increasingly became called '*Ordnungsökonomik*' was transferred to, and subsumed under, the paradigm of constitutional economics.[14] The crucial systematic screw that Vanberg turned for this operation was to shift the normative foundation of the entire framework to the single basis of normative individualism. In other words, it is solely the unforced agreement to whatever order in question that there might be by the individuals subjected to it that can provide the normative justification for this arrangement. This normative individualism and its methodological equivalent make a lot of the lingering organism in the ordoliberal view of the state that would treat it almost as a macro-subject with its own will, but also the deep scepticism regarding popular sovereignty, simply untenable.[15] The same goes for the hopes for a natural nobility to run the state, because, if there is anything that constitutional economics combined with public choice theory as exemplified in the works of James Buchanan rules out, it is a well-meaning class of politicians and bureaucrats. Applying the assumptions of *homo oeconomicus* to the realm of democratic and bureaucratic politics leads to the conclusion that the self-interest of political actors will vary, often lead

---

[13] This, of course, is a rather preliminary claim. It could be argued that another unique aspect of ordoliberal thought is the normative notion of *Vitalpolitik* that was particularly strongly articulated by Rüstow, and also echoed by Röpke.

[14] See, eg, Viktor Vanberg, *Rules and Choice in Economics*, (London: Routledge, 1994); idem, 'The Freiburg School: Walter Eucken and Ordoliberalism', 2011, Freiburger Diskussionspapiere für Ordnungsökonomik 04/11.

[15] Still, it must not be forgotten that Buchanan himself has retreated from a radical public choice perspective on government, which tends to dissolve the latter into interpersonal interactions, in his later works based on the paradigm of 'Leviathan'. Here, the state is still not conceived of in 'organic' terms but, for heuristic purposes, as a monolithic actor. See Geoffrey Brennan and James M. Buchanan, *The Power to Tax: Analytical Foundations of a Fiscal Constitution*, (Indianapolis IN: Liberty Fund, 1980).

to sub-optimal results for the general welfare, ie it will hurt the (constitutional) interests of citizens. Vanberg consequently shifts the focus of *Ordnungsökonomik* from hazy hopes for civic-minded public officials to rules that, at least, ensure that the aggregated self-interest of decision-makers will not do too much damage—and thus emulates the focus of constitutional economics in this regard as well.[16] As Lars Feld and Ekkehard Köhler in their assessment of the current condition of *Ordnung- sökonomik* agree, what used to be ordoliberalism is now, to a significant degree, a somewhat special compartment of constitutional economics.[17] *Ordnungsökonomik* continues to pursue both a positive and a normative programme, but, as already indicated, the latter has been purged of any obvious remnants of the natural law thinking that still animated much of the normative elements in Röpke's and Eucken's work. Instead, the sole normative criterion is the constitutional interests upon which all citizens can agree unanimously, or, in Vanberg's terms, whatever increases the sovereignty of consumers in markets and the sovereignty of citizens in polities. Needless to say that this operation—for better or worse—modernised *Ordnung- sökonomik* significantly, and made it look less like the 'odd man out' in contempo- rary economics, but it also imported into its own agenda the problems that haunt public choice/constitutional economics and its specific answer to the *problématique* of neoliberalism. The utility-maximising democratic entrepreneurs in ministries and agencies can only be reined in by strict rules, *pace* constitutional economics, but which clear-thinking utility maximisers would ever impose such rules upon them- selves? There is no need to dwell on this, it simply serves as a reminder that each 'answer' to the neoliberal problem comes with its own difficulties.

Finally, what about the remarkable faith of early ordoliberalism in the powers of science? Here, the re-programming of Vanberg is less clearly fashioned after the model of constitutional economics, maybe not least because the views on a science of economics and/or political economy by a representative of this tradition such as James Buchanan are ambiguous and complex. Buchanan was highly critical of many aspects of contemporary economics, and even suggested that half of the pro- fession had misunderstood the 'economic problem'.[18] He was also deeply sceptical when it came to the role of economists as political advisors.[19] But, despite all the

---

[16] Viktor Vanberg, 'Ordnungspolitik, The Freiburg School and the Reason of Rules', 2014, Freiburger Diskussionspapiere für Ordnungsökonomik 14/1.

[17] Lars Feld and Ekkehard Köhler, 'Ist die Ordnungsökonomik zukunftsfähig?', (2011) 12 *Zeitschrift für Wirtschafts- und Unternehmensethik*, pp 173–195, at 182. For a similar view from a more critical perspective, see Ralf Ptak, 'Das Staatsverständnisim Ordoliberalismus. Eine theoriegeschichtliche Analyse mit aktuellem Ausblick', in: Thomas Biebricher (ed), *Der Staat des Neoliberalismus*, (Baden-Baden: Nomos Verlag, 2016), pp 31–73.

[18] James Buchanan, *Economics from the Outside in: 'Better than Plowing' and Beyond*, (Chicago IL: University of Chicago Press, 1992), p 17.

[19] See, eg, 'The Chicago economist does not project an image of becoming an adviser to governments.' In: James M. Buchanan and Richard Musgrave, *Public Finance and Public Choice: Two Contrasting Visions of the State*, (Cambridge MA: The MIT Press, 1999), pp 16–17, and '"Economic Science" is not to be conceived as offering assistance to selected agents who seek to use scientific knowledge to control others.' In: James M. Buchanan, *Liberty, Market and State: Political Economy in the 1980s*, (Sussex: Harvester Press, 1986), p 38.

reservations that he had with regard to a potential scientism in economics, he still assumed that there could be a 'pure theory of politics or a genuinely scientific politics', and he discussed at length the possibilities—but also the limits—of a scientific theory of 'choice'.[20] As far as I can tell, with regard to the aspirations and limits of economics as a scientific discipline, Vanberg has aligned *Ordnungsökonomik* not so much with Buchanan, but, with von Hayek instead, who, as is well known, always cautioned vehemently against any pretence of knowledge by scientists or others. His unique way of outlining the possibilities and limitations of a science of economics is modelled on any science of complex systems. In unclosed systems like economies, but also in the ecosystem and others that exhibit a certain degree of complexity, it is impossible to reach the same kind of precision with regard to statements about cause and effect, let alone the prediction of events. All there is to be achieved in such a science is the identification of certain patterns at a fairly high level of generality, ie not much that is specific about the characteristics of the pattern will be known.[21] Vanberg seems to agree with this if we base our assessment on one of his contributions to the latest controversy surrounding the contemporary *Ordnungsökonomik* that began after the onset of the Financial Crisis in 2008. Here, Vanberg argues for an economics that is—and must be—content with such pattern predictions, and thus precludes any charges of scientistic megalomania; notwithstanding this, he leaves the door open for *Ordnungsökonomik* to play a special role: since this is the science that deals with the patterned effects of certain shifts in the politico-economic framework, it could, supposedly, claim a special significance for economic policy.[22]

To sum up, the ordoliberal triad of views on state, democracy and science has been broken up over the last decades, and what remains of it, to a large degree,[23] is an *Ordnungsökonomik* that is a mix of constitutional economics' view on state and democracy, on the one hand, and a Hayekian view of science, on the other.

This leaves us with an almost paradoxical situation. Traditional ordoliberalism with its semi-authoritarian democracy scepticism and technocratic aspirations is hardly to be found anywhere anymore in its contemporary representatives who, instead, claim the label of *Ordnungsökonomik*. However, in the realm of actual politics, not least in the politics of crisis management in response to the European Sovereign Debt Crisis, we can see all of these elements—the many other countervailing tendencies notwithstanding. Greece and the reign of the *Troika* is the most extreme example of this kind of rule, but the reformed governance structures of the EU more generally point us in the direction of decision-making structures at the

---

[20] James Buchanan, *What Should Economists Do?* (Indianapolis IN: Liberty Press, 1979), p 159 and 46.

[21] F.A. von Hayek, *Studies on the Abuse and Decline of Reason*, (Chicago IL: University of Chicago Press, 2010), pp 105–107.

[22] See, on this, Viktor Vanberg, 'Die Ökonomik ist keine zweite Physik', *Frankfurter Allgemeine Zeitung*, 13 April 2009.

[23] There is also the work of Nils Goldschmidt, who has been working on a modernisation of the concept of *Vitalpolitik* mentioned in n 13 above.

supranational level that are fairly well insulated from democratic influence and rely heavily on technical expertise, not the least from economists.[24] The theoretical heirs of ordoliberalism may have sworn off the 'lure of technocracy'[25] that its earlier instantiation stood for, but, in the real world of the re-structuring of European political economies, authoritarian liberalism[26] which closely resembles its ordoliberal sibling, arguably, continues to gain ground.

[24] See Thomas Biebricher, 'Europe and the Political Philosophy of Neoliberalism', (2013) 12 *Contemporary Political Theory*, pp 338–375.
[25] Jürgen Habermas, *The Lure of Technocracy*, (London: Polity, 2015).
[26] Wolfgang Streeck, 'Heller, Schmitt and the Euro', (2015) 21 *European Law Journal*, pp 361–370.

7

Breaking the 'Caging' Mentality: Ordoliberalism, Responsibility and Solidarity in the EU

MAURIZIO FERRERA*

ABSTRACT

Ordoliberalism has played a key role in shaping the management of the crisis as well as the institutional reforms of the Stability and Growth Pact. The burdens of structural adjustment have been entirely shifted onto national governments, under a disciplinarian and rule-based framework of top-down surveillance. Cross-national solidaristic transfers are not contemplated in the ordoliberal conception of integration, which remains suspicious even regarding the initiatives aimed at promoting upward convergence among systems. The competition, monetary and fiscal regimes should serve as bulwarks against interest group politics within the Member States and moral hazard and rent-seeking strategies on the part of their governments, while forcing them to act responsibly and to do 'their homework'. This ordoliberal 'caging mentality' has proved to be not only functionally ineffective, but also politically self-defeating. It undermines the legitimacy of the EU and provokes a spiral of Eurosceptic centrifugations at national level, which are now endangering the very survival of the euro.

I. INTRODUCTION

IN THE COURSE of the last decade, European integration has fallen prey to an 'econocratic' project—a dystopian vision which has corroded the EU's constitutional integrity, its legitimation basis, its very point and purpose. This project—imbued by ordoliberal assumptions, principles and recipes—needs to be brought to an end through an effective, but laborious, intellectual and political investment.[1]

---

* Professor of Political Science and Principal Investigator of the REScEU project. (Reconciling Economic and Social Europe, www.resceu.eu), funded by the European Research Council (grant no 340534).
    [1] I fully share in this sense the overall diagnosis and message of the editors and contributors of *The End of the Eurocrats Dream: Adjusting to Diversity*, edited by Damian Chalmers, Markus Jachtenfuchs and Christian Joerges, (Cambridge: Cambridge University Press, 2016).

The econocratic goal is to achieve market efficiency, monetary and fiscal stability through a mode of integration controlled by non-majoritarian institutions, operating through strict economic surveillance, discipline and sanctions, and aiming at 'caging' from above the standards and practices of Member States. This project rests on deep-seated (and mostly implicit) cultural predispositions of both descriptive and normative nature. In essence, the 'Econocrats' believe that budgetary stability and market efficiency are supreme goods, that there is a 'right way' of guaranteeing them (and, more generally, of solving all collective problems), that economics (as a discipline and as a sphere of activity), supported by law, must prevail over politics, especially agonistic politics. In so thinking, the Econocrats ignore both Friedrich von Hayek's reminder that economic science *is not* (and cannot pretend to be) 'omnicompetent about the problems of society', and Max Weber's warnings about the risks of 'organized irresponsibility', a combination of economic dogmatism and bureaucratic rule.

The failings of the econocratic project are now evident and can be summarised in a series of disastrous deficits: of justice, compliance, prosperity, democracy, and, of course, legitimacy. Instead of prompting a virtuous circle of upward convergence *cum* stability and greater closeness among the Member States, the institutional setting put in place during the crisis promotes and amplifies divergence as well as a moral economy which juxtaposes 'good' *versus* 'bad' pupils, encourages beggar-thy-neighbour policies, nurtures the (internally contradictory) illusion that domestic political economies can be coerced into adopting a single template for growth and competitiveness. This approach has not only proved ineffective in terms of outcomes, but has also been eroding the necessary conditions for polity maintenance (the EU polity), let alone its further 'building'. Obsessed with taming interest group pluralism (an evil beast for ordoliberal doctrines), the econocratic regime has unleashed the demons of anti-politics and populism, and has pushed them into attacking the EU as such. Historically, European integration has always been guided by a mixture of logics, reflecting, on the one hand, the heterogeneity of its constitutive components, but aimed, on the other, at encouraging joint action in order to achieve common goods. Econocracy has disrupted this delicate mixture or balance, with the result that 'existing trajectories and structures of European integration have become badly misaligned'.[2]

There is now a wide discussion about how to repair the damage and about how the Union should develop in the future. The reforms which are put forward range from the quite radical idea of dismantling the common currency and the return to flexible monetary regime to more or less incisive re-designs of the institutional/constitutional set-up, aimed at redressing the democratic, justice, stability and prosperity deficits of the EU in its present form. In this chapter, I will present some reflections on how to re-align 'Economic Europe' with 'Democratic' and 'Social' Europe. I will, of course, take issue with the Econocrat's vision and most of its ordoliberal underpinnings, but at the same time I will challenge some of the most radical counter-visions which have started to circulate in the debate. My general worry is, in fact, that the much-needed

---

[2] ibid, p 18.

critique of the econocratic project may inadvertently overshoot, thereby incurring the risk of throwing away some of the proverbial 'babies together with the bathwater'. I will first focus on issues of democracy and citizenship and then address a thorny question, but one which is key for Southern Europe: in the light of the Econocratic failings, should the euro be maintained or scrapped? I will then close with a brief discussion of ordoliberal views on solidarity and how to reconcile the latter with European integration.

II. THE EU, DEMOCRATIC RESPONSIBILITY AND SOCIAL CITIZENSHIP

Contemporary democracies share a political culture which assumes that the government does 'what citizens want', responding to their preferences. Sovereignty belongs to the people, legitimacy hinges on the latter's consent, free elections hold representatives closely accountable to the voters. This view offers comforting reassurances that we live in an ethically defensible system. But it reflects only part of the story. Elected officials are not mere translators of demands from below into public policies. However important, responsiveness and accountability do not exhaust the representation nexus. The third dimension is *responsibility*—often neglected or collapsed into accountability. By responsibility, I mean the duty of leaders to face up to collective challenges—often difficult to interpret, with no easy solutions—in the best interest of their own political community, considering the web of interrelationships with other relevant communities. As famously recommended by Weber, democratic responsibility requires some distance from electoral contingencies, a farsighted capacity to balance principled and consequentialist considerations when coping with a constant flow of substantive problems that can never be fully anticipated, but nonetheless demand relentless attention and tending. In grappling with problem flows, democratic leaders are still constrained by their electoral mandate and must be ready to justify their decisions. In other words, *responsibility* remains ultimately coupled with *responsiveness* and *accountability*. But it involves different logics and capacities, which require some degree of institutional nurturing.

In the present European context, democratic responsibility is faced by two major challenges. The first has to do with increased integration and the incessant creation of cross-national externalities. Very often, domestic leaders have to solve problems for their own *demos* which are the direct and recognisable consequence not only of the EU as such, but also of other EU *demoi* (how they behave, what they decide, etc); in turn, the solutions which domestic leaders adopt are very likely to generate cross-border effects.[3] There is, however, a second challenge, which has to do with the growing difficulty for domestic leaders to address policy problems in a long-term perspective. Most of the reforms which are today needed to recalibrate national socio-economic models imply explicit and extended inter-temporal trade-offs.

---

[3] Kalypso Nicolaïdis and Max Watson, 'Sharing the Eurocrats' Dream: A Demoicratic Approach to EMU Governance in the Post-crisis Era', in: Chalmers, Jachtenfuchs and Joerges (eds), *The End of the Eurocrats' Dream*, n 1 above, pp 50–77.

These reforms require up-front costs, in return for incremental and delayed benefits: for instance, let us think of the expansion of education and training today in order to enhance the human capital of tomorrow. Such 'policy investments' are difficult to undertake: the logic of partisan competition places a high premium on the short term.[4] Imposing losses to current voters with a promise of distant benefits is not the most effective strategy to win elections.

In theory, the EU should facilitate the search for the responses to both these challenges. Precisely because they operate 'at a distance', EU arenas and institutions can provide political leaders with the appropriate occasions, incentives and resources for the exercising of responsibility both vis-à-vis cross-national interdependences *and* the imperatives of the long-term. The econocratic project has, however, failed even to recognise these problems. In fact, as already mentioned, it has aggravated them by putting in place a system of 'organised irresponsibility' led by a small circle of authorities taking 'one-size-fit-all' unidimensional decisions inspired by a narrow and short-sighted economic orthodoxy.[5] This system is characterised by a total neglect for the cross-national, cross-sectoral or cross-domain consequences of policy decisions. Despite its rhetoric on long term 'sustainability', the rigid and rule-based austerity paradigm established during the crisis has created additional obstacles for policy investments. In debtor countries, it has eroded all margins of fiscal manoeuvre, while, in creditor countries, it has amplified the fetish of *schwarze Null*, ie the categorical imperative of zero-deficit, even in the presence of visible gaps in economic and social infrastructures.

It would be incorrect to reduce the econocratic regime to an exclusive offspring of ordoliberalism. But it is also hard to ignore, or to fail to recognise, the copious ordoliberal influences on such regime. This is especially true for its institutional choices and their underlying assumptions. The Stability and Growth Pact—as amended by the Six Pack, the Two Pack and the Fiscal Compact—is, in fact, imbued with a 'caging' mentality, which assumes that political and social actors are typically moved by predatory motivations. This caging mentality is not really in line with the tenets of economic (let alone, political or social) liberalism. It is a distinctive element of ordoliberalism. As highlighted by other contributions to this volume, ordoliberals are obsessed by the instincts of the 'special interests' which pervade social and political arenas and exchanges. They see society and democratic politics as sources of pathologies: organised groups ceaselessly attempt to distort competition by forming monopolies, by exercising pressures to obtain material advantages, by transforming their own private objectives into a matter of public policy and by looting the public budget. For the sake of economic liberty and efficiency, the state (and today the EU) has to keep social groups at arm's length through legal protections and formal

---

[4] Alan M. Jacobs, *Governing for the Long Term: Democracy and the Politics of Investment*, (Cambridge; Cambridge University Press, 2011); Maurizio Ferrera, 'Impatient Politics and Social Investment: the EU as "policy facilitator"', (2016) *Journal of European Public Policy*, published online on 19 September 2016.

[5] Maurizio Ferrera, 'Mission impossible? Reconciling Economic and Social Europe after the Euro-crisis and Brexit', (2017) 56 *European Journal of Political Research*, pp 3–22.

rules that guard market freedoms, undistorted competition, monetary stability, and fiscal restraint.

The market-making dogmatism and the caging mentality of the econocratic regime is the bathwater that needs to be thrown away, the sooner, the better. On this I cannot but fully concur with the anti-technocratic (-econocratic, -eurocratic) and anti-austerity critics. There are, however, various elements in the 'governing from a distance' mode, which it may be wise and reasonable to retain, and even enhance. It is important to stress this point openly in the debate. Let us think of the main pillar of current economic governance, ie the European Semester. Freed from the excessive rigidity of the reformed Stability and Growth Pact and adequately re-balanced towards growth and social objectives, this governance framework could serve as a key anchor for the long-term perspective (broadly understood) and the institutional encouragement of policy investments, as a precious instrument for the joint elaboration of functionally effective and normatively desirable objectives and—most importantly—as a transparent arena for identifying those externalities and risks which may require common management. Surely, there are ways to bring the Semester closer to the circuits of electoral representation, to enhance its throughput legitimacy via inclusion and accountability constraints—as currently advocated by many critical commentators. But the unique contribution (ie the 'baby') which a re-balanced Semester would produce has to do with *responsibility*. The relative insulation from domestic electoral contingencies and from the dynamics of partisan responsiveness would activate a logic of choice that was sensitive to fine-grained instrumental and normative considerations and open to reflexive learning—a logic that tends to be stifled in domestic contexts. Ordoliberalism is guilty of an excess of élitism and paternalism in its conviction that economists and experts know best—since their position is predicated on knowledge and competence, not on sympathy with any type of special interest(s). But it must be acknowledged that effective democracy does require an appropriate balance between popular demands and élite expertise. Governing from a distance remains, indeed, exposed to the risk of 'technocratisation' and even econocratisation. But it can also be made to work at the service of political responsibility, without necessarily violating the democratic standard.

Let me now briefly turn to citizenship. The anti-technocratic and anti-austerian critiques often argue that the advent of Econocracy has markedly exacerbated the de-stabilising effects of integration on national 'social contracts' and social citizenship regimes. The reformed Stability and Growth Pact and especially the conditionality regime of the Memoranda of Understanding (imbued with the ordoliberal caging mentality) have definitely contributed to pushing through painful social reforms, to the detriment of long established re-distributive arrangements and their supporting coalitions, laboriously built through domestic political channels and resting on territorially-bounded balances of power. In general terms, the worry about such developments is justified and well grounded. But, again, we must distinguish between the baby and the bathwater.

Historically, the institutionalisation of solidarity through social rights has effectively contrasted the dis-integrative tendency of the nineteenth century's greatest social utopia: that of a market entirely capable of self-regulation. Societies mobilised in search of protection; states responded with the production of rights. But not all the buffers against market expansionism have served their declared 'emancipatory' objectives, and some buffers have gone too far. In some moments and in some contexts, the noble instrument of democratic citizenship has been hijacked by petty interests, sectional lobbies, and circumscribed groups defending their privileges. Measures of social closure have been used to serve 'usurpative', rather than emancipatory, objectives. Handled with care and stripped from their dogmatic and moralistic overtones, some ordoliberal insights about politics and society are not completely unwarranted. The extensive literature on the insider/outsider cleavage has highlighted the distributive distortions resulting from the many forms of employment regulation and social protection inherited from the Golden Age.[6] The awareness and the preoccupation with such dynamics were already clearly present in the early and classical debates about social citizenship. Commenting on the rise of unofficial strikes at the time when he was writing his famous essay, Marshall lamented that an attempt had been made 'to claim the rights of both status and contract while repudiating the duties under both these heads'.[7] In his turn, Reinhard Bendix warned that a fundamental civil right and pre-condition of democratic participation, the freedom of association or the 'right to combine', can be used 'to enforce claims to a share of income and benefits at the expense of the unorganised and the consumers'.[8]

Economically inefficient and normatively unjustifiable forms of right-based closure must be singled out with care and precision, context by context. But, to the extent that EU pressures are (or can be) targeted at such forms of closure, then 'de-stabilisation' might serve such functionally-useful and normatively-desirable purposes. Among non-economists, there is sometimes the tendency to collapse the principled justification of the welfare state and of market-correcting policies into an acritical defence of the social status quo, whatever its characteristics and distributive implications. In contrast, I believe that it is important to combine the loyalty to abstract normative standards with a factually grounded acknowledgement and critique of real-world deviations from such standards. The challenge on the 'de-stabilisation' front is, of course, how to single out dysfunctional and inequitable forms of regulation and protection, and how to target them correctly when designing reforms.

III. HEAVEN OR HELL? THE EURO AND ITS POSSIBLE BREAK-UP

The Southern European countries (in particular, Italy and Greece) offer a good illustration of the dynamics just described. During the last couple of decades, EU membership and the so-called external constraint has provided these countries with precious incentives for stabilising public finances, modernising the state apparatus, re-calibrating the welfare state and the labour market, and re-balancing traditional

---

[6] Patrick Emmenegger, Silja Häusermann, Bruno Palier and Martin Seeleib-Kaiser (eds), *The Age of Dualization: The Changing Face of Inequality in Deindustrializing Societies*, (New York: Oxford University Press, 2012).

[7] Thomas Humphrey Marshall, 'Citizenship and Social Class', in: Thomas Humphrey Marshall and Tom Bottomore (eds), *Citizenship and Social Class and Other Essays*, (London: Pluto Press, 1950), p 42.

[8] Reinhard Bendix, *Nation-building and Citizenship*, (New York: Wiley, 1964), p 105.

distributive distortions. In other words, EU-induced 'de-stabilisation' has brought about positive effects, and not just painful sacrifices.

In my own work on the Italian case, I have often used the metaphor of a rescue by Europe:[9] during the 1990s, the Maastricht process prompted a real quantum leap in terms of institutional capabilities and *risanamento* (the restoring to health) of public finances in the name of equity and sustainability. A rather impressive sequence of reforms was implemented, with a view to correcting the 'original sins' of Italy's economic and social model. Admission into the Euro-zone was perceived as a hard-won achievement by the vast majority of Italians. The prize was a significant decline in the cost of debt service, from 9% in 1996 to 4% in 2006. Unfortunately, this bonanza was mostly squandered: savings mainly went into pensions (calculated with the extremely generous formulas). The reform process stalled, much needed public investments were not made. The weakening of the external constraint (the EMU's dysfunctionalities were not so evident then) removed one of the most effective incentives for policy innovation. Since the early 2000s, the country's economic performance has been less than satisfactory and the crisis—in combination with fiscal austerity—has pushed Italy into a very deep recession. It is no surprise that popular support for the euro has been markedly declining in recent years. With the demise of Berlusconi, the centre-right has become increasingly critical of the common currency, while *Il Movimento Cinque Stelle* (the new Five Star Movement) and the *Lega Nord* (the Northern League) are vocally asking for an exit referendum.

The idea of a euro break-up is now openly circulating in the expert EU debate as well. An orderly, negotiated and consensual break-up of the Eurozone would give back to peripheral countries—so the argument goes—the option of external devaluations, allowing them to recuperate competitiveness and thereby relaunch growth. The 'benevolent' version of this argument is that a euro-exit would benefit Italy's workers, who would avoid the painful social costs of internal devaluations. A more 'malevolent' version is that an exit would forestall the risk for core countries (Germany) to be somehow damaged by Italy's huge debt and the chronic 'unwillingness to reform' of both the Italian governments and the voters. This latter version is now explicitly voiced by prominent German economists of ordoliberal leanings, and is increasingly shared by this country's top financial authorities.[10]

The ordoliberal reading of the Italian crisis is analytically poor and programmatically unable to consider a series of important aspects. The first has to do with the very diagnosis of Italian problems and prospects. Italy's economic decline is linked to a wide range of factors, including a (still) defective state, a massive public debt, badly regulated and highly protected private services and product markets,

---

[9] Maurizio Ferrera and Elisabetta Gualmini, *Rescued by Europe?; Social and Labour Market Reforms in Italy from Maastricht to Berlusconi*, (Amsterdam: Amsterdam University Press, 2004).

[10] Maurizio Ferrera and Michael Best, 'Family, Neighbourhood Community or a Partnership among Strangers? A Conversation on the EU', (2016) *EuVisions*, available at: www.euvisions.eu/family-neighbourhood-community-or-a-partnership-among-strangers-a-conversation-on-the-eu. Federico Fubini, 'Se l'Italia non cresce, valuti l'uscita dall'euro. Berlino è preoccupata', *Il Corriera della Sera*, 16 December 2016, available at: www.euvisions.eu/family-neighbourhood-community-or-a-partnership-among-strangers-a-conversation-on-the-eu.

an old-fashioned system of industrial relations and the persisting socio-economic backwardness of the *Mezzogiorno* or South, still plagued by criminal organisations. The constraints of the euro have aggravated these problems, but did not cause them, and, thus, leaving the euro would not solve them. The key question, however, is: Does Italy have an internal springboard to remain competitive among the big export-oriented economic powers, hopefully within the euro? What is often overlooked or inadequately appreciated by foreign observers is that, beneath Italy's malaise, there is a resilient pounding heart. The country still has a wide and robust industrial base and is the seat of Europe's second largest manufacturing sector. Despite the dramatic drop of 2008–2009, this sector grew by 15.6% between 2004 and 2015. In medium-sized firms, productivity grew more than in Germany during the crisis. The recession led to the loss of many (small) firms, but, overall, it enhanced allocative efficiencies which were able to sustain export levels. Italy's 'growth model' rests on a big export-oriented industrial engine (the 'baby').[11] To (re-)gain momentum, such an engine needs incisive internal maintenance and re-adaptation. But, above all, it needs to be complemented by a much more efficient service sector (which should—itself—become a second engine for growth and employment) and to be supported by a more favourable institutional environment—including a modernised welfare state. A lot of dirty bathwater must be thrown away, especially in terms of bad regulations, rent-subsidising protection, and clientelistic distributions. It is misleading to disparage such an agenda as 'internal devaluation'. Instead of cutting wages, Italy's growth engine would (and hopefully will) benefit much more from liberalising professions and local public services, stirring up public administration, rationalising and re-calibrating inequitable and inefficient tax/transfers schemes, investing in human capital. A (reasonable) *vincolo esterno* remains key for moving in this direction. Net of the perverse consequences of the econocratic regime, developments during the crisis do lend support this view. After Berlusconi's departure from the scene (2011), important policy changes have been adopted, including much needed reforms in the field of pensions, labour market, public administration, education, and industrial relations. And, since 2014, growth and jobs have started to pick up again. It does not seem too late, or impossible, to revive the springboard.

I am not arguing that Italy is out of trouble: far from it. But let us sketch a counterfactual based upon the break-up hypothesis. A currency devaluation during the crisis would initially have boosted industrial competitiveness, but it would also have neutralised 'modernisation' incentives for all the relevant actors, granting new respite to many of the undesirable, efficiency-thwarting and inequitable dynamics of the past. There is a shared agreement among Italian economists that the pre-euro competitive devaluations bear a large responsibility for the adjustment delays of Italy's productive structure to the new trends of the European and global economy. A weaker lira gave exporting producers temporary relief for their losses in competitiveness. But it also discouraged investments and innovations on the side of firms, crippled incentives for reforming the state apparatus and for opening protected

---

[11] For the data and discussion, see Banca d'Italia. 2016. Bollettino Economico, n 4.

sectors, and caused a number of perverse distributional consequences, not to mention the activation of several vicious circles, such as inflationary spirals.[12]

There is a second, wider aspect to consider. From a symbolic and political point of view, an exit from the monetary union would seal the failure of one of the few broadly shared 'projects' of post-war Italy as a nation (*entrare in Europa*, or entry into Europe). It would thus de-legitimise entire generations of pro-integration leaders, including the younger ones who have gained office during the crisis. Prompted, as it would inevitably be, by mainstream political forces, such a move would not unarm Eurosceptic radicalism, but would instead inflame social and political arenas, providing additional fuel to all the populist, protectionist, parochialist and nativist actors and interests which have emerged in the last decade. It must also be noted that the mere starting of the break-up process (for example, negotiating the birth of a new currency regime and its bands of oscillation) may trigger off unintended and hard to predict consequences. Italy is not Greece; a European bailout would be impossible. Should financial markets come to believe that Italy might exit from the euro as it is, they would have enough weapons to force this outcome on their own, very unorderly, terms.

Some Italian analysts have recently offered rough estimates of the consequences of such a scenario.[13] I report some of them here just to give an idea of the numbers which are being seriously discussed in the domestic debate. Under fierce market pressures, a new lira would have to devalue by 50/60%, almost double compared to the current 30% loss of Italy's competitiveness vis-à-vis Germany. The immediate consequence would be a rise of inflation to around 15%. This would trigger off a price-wage-exchange rate spiral resulting in even higher inflation and huge losses for workers in terms of purchasing power, increased inequalities in the distribution of income and wealth between employees and self-employed, and between domestic creditors and debtors. A devaluation of 50% would raise extremely delicate problems with regard to the value of the public debt in the hands of foreign investors (more than 35% of the total), with a flight of capital and a likely default of the Italian state, which would be unable to meet redemption requests. In five years, the real value of domestic debt would be halved, with a loss for bondholding families of approximately 11% of their disposable income. For banks and financial institutions, which own about half of the debt, the impact on budgets would be tragic, especially for those which have foreign currency liabilities. In addition to the need for recapitalisation by the state, it would be necessary to prevent runs on banks by depositors. Interest rates would skyrocket in the wake of higher inflation, the currency and banking crisis, and the government default. Exporting firms would do business, but those producing for the domestic market would all be affected by the contraction of consumption and investment, as well as the banking crisis. It is true, as Baccaro

---

[12] Lorenzo Bordogna, 'Is Leaving the Euro a Solution for Italy?', (2016) *Euvisions*, available at: www.euvisions.eu/leaving-realistic-solution.

[13] Carluccio Bianchi, 'Storia breve dell'economia italiana dal secondo dopoguerra a oggi', (2014), available at: www.lincei.it/files/documenti/Bianchi%20Lincei-MI-marzo2014.pdf; Salvatore Biasco, 'Perché non uscire dall'euro?', (2015), *Il Mulino*, 1/15, pp 18–28. For a more recent critical evaluation of the exit scenario, see L. Bini Smaghi, *La tentazione di andarsene* (Bologna, Il Mulino, 2017).

argued, that the last big devaluation of the lira, in 1992, did not produce all these dramatic effects and that—to the contrary—it turned out to be beneficial for growth and jobs,[14] but that devaluation took place in the context of the Maastricht process: the Italian government was determined to enter into the forthcoming single currency. This created an incentive constellation for domestic and foreign actors, which is very different from the constellation that is likely to result from a euro-exit today (or the mere prospect thereof). In the light of all such elements, a well-known (left wing) Italian economist, Giorgio Lunghini, has recently concluded that abandoning the euro would have 'an enormous cost, which would generate civil unrest and popular uprisings; European history teaches that from crises of this magnitude one can exit only to the right ... The European Economic and Monetary Union is like the "Hotel California" in the Eagles' song'. For those who have forgotten or are too young to remember, the Hotel California was a one-way only establishment. As the lyrics went, it was 'programmed to receive. You can check-out any time you like, but you can never leave'.[15]

A Doomsday scenario? Perhaps. The pro-status quo camp tends to ignore or mini-mise the costs of non-disintegration. But—having personally experienced the dramas of some past devaluations of the lira—I believe that responsible politicians should be wary of playing with the fire of disintegration. The path of a smooth, agreed-upon, well-planned dismantling of the common currency is extremely narrow and very unsafe.

Needless to say, this does not mean that things should remain as they are: far from it. Italy must continue on the path of structural reforms. But the ordoliberal reading of the crisis starts with the assumption that the responsibility should exclusively fall on Italy's shoulders in a context of 'right' rules. This reading does not consider the other side of the coin: the econocratic regime is too constraining, rigid and dogmatic for the type of economic and institutional modernisation that befits Italy—and, *a fortiori*, the other Southern European countries. Maintaining the single currency is compatible with different modes of economic and fiscal governance. There is now a wide consensus on the idea that the EMU's institutional architecture needs to be reformed, for example, through the promotion of productive investments and aggre-gate demand management. It is true that all such paths would imply a higher degree of interstate redistribution—an obstacle which is very hard to bypass. For ordoliber-als, a *Transfer Union* is public enemy number one. But the issue of re-distribution should be put in a more correct perspective. For example, in the Greek bailout, Italy was one of the main paymasters, contributing (per capita) almost as much as Germany, despite the fact that its banks had an almost negligible exposure vis-à-vis Greece. But neither the Italian nor the German average taxpayer is aware of this. And in the ordoliberal narrative the former is perceived or labelled as a typical exam-ple of a 'guilty' grasshopper, the latter as a virtuous and exploited ant. It is obvious

[14] Lucio Baccaro, 'Salvati o rovinati dall'Europa?', *Convegno Nazionale Ais-Elo 2015*, Cagliari, 15–17 October 2015, Available at: https://fad.unich.it/mod/resource/view.php?id=2612.
[15] Giorgio Lunghini, 'Le conseguenze di un'uscita dall'euro', *Il Manifesto*, 22 September 2016, available at: http://ilmanifesto.info/le-conseguenze-di-unuscita-dalleuro.

that, in such a symbolic context, the idea of a *Transfer Union* remains a non-starter in the core countries, and that preserving the common currency is likely to turn EU politics into an 'ugly tug of war' between the North and the South.[16] But we know that the way in which problems are framed and solutions designed is key for political feasibility. The outlook of a nasty and self-defeating spiral of national juxtapositions is not inevitable, and there are ways of making the monetary union more viable, equipping it with a functionally decent degree of re-distribution—which does not need to flow through a scheme of direct and explicit interstate transfers. Here, we return to the remarks on responsibility made above. The euro could and should have been designed much better from the start. But we cannot wish away 20 years of fits and starts.[17] There are more margins for the exercise of political craftsmanship in reforming the euro than the current executive élites (and obviously ordoliberals) are ready or capable to acknowledge. In the famous song by the Eagles, those who enter Hotel California immediately realise that 'it could be Heaven or could be Hell'. Since there are no safe exit options, for the time being, it is wise not to check out from the euro, and commit our energies to ensuring that this it does not become a living hell for its participants, especially the weaker ones.

IV. THE SEARCH FOR EUROPEAN SOLIDARITY: THREE PRIORITIES

The econocratic regime does not consider the issue of European solidarity. As mentioned above, cross-national transfers are not contemplated in the ordoliberal conception of integration, which remains suspicious even with regard to the initiatives aimed at promoting upward convergence among systems. For ordoliberals, the EU should limit itself to providing the *Ordnungspolitik* which allows for institutional (or 'jurisdictional') competition. As highlighted by other contributors of this book, ordoliberalism is very critical of *any* form of re-distribution, even at national level. Far from being a justification of public welfare policies, the ordoliberal notion of the 'social market economy' was aimed at promoting the entrepreneurial society and at caging (again) individual forms of behaviour within 'psycho-moral forces' capable of restraining 'greedy self-seekers', containing the proletarianisation of workers and ingraining the discipline of the self-responsible enterprise into the moral fabric of society. According to ordoliberals, a similar logic should operate at EU level. The competition, monetary and fiscal regimes should serve as bulwarks against interest group politics within the Member States and against moral hazard and rent-seeking strategies on the part of their governments, while forcing them to act responsibly and to do 'their homework'.

A number of factors militate, however, against such restricted and narrow-minded views, and in favour of a more proactive role for the Union. First, increased integration generates a constant flow of cross-national externalities, as already highlighted.

---

[16] Wolfgang Streeck and Lea Elaässer, 'Monetary Disunion: The Domestic Politics of Euroland', MPIfG Discussion Paper 2014/17, Max-Planck-Institut für Gesellschaftsforschung, Cologne.
[17] Nicolaïdis and Watson, n 3 above.

Second, unbridled policy competition based upon the ordoliberal logic of comparative advantages may lead to suboptimal and inefficient mutual adjustments, generating a growing dualisation between core and peripheral Member States. Another shortcoming of the ordoliberal view and narrative is its (often implicit) moral charge, which is highly skewed in favour of creditor countries. If we want to avoid the self-defeating and ugly tug of war among Member States, we have to open a frank debate and squarely address the issue of pan-European solidarity.

The first priority of a debate on pan-European solidarity is to challenge the dominant narrative on factual grounds. The idea that there are good and bad pupils, that the euro-crisis originated because of Southern financial profligacy is neither in line with empirical evidence nor with the accurate reconstructions of economic and institutional developments. There is now a growing agreement on this diagnosis even among leading mainstream economists.[18] Why the ordoliberal narrative is impermeable to both counter-evidence and counter-arguments is a good research question for the sociology of knowledge. But it is also a fact which has serious implications for the life of millions of Europeans and for the future of the EU as such. In order to enhance the persuasiveness of criticisms, we need more detailed and articulated evidence about the negative consequences of the EMU's dysfunctionality, including the asymmetric gains implicitly or deliberately enjoyed by the core countries since the establishment of EMU itself. We also need to know more about the concrete externalities linked to the policy choices and actual behaviour of each *demos*, in order to sensitise its government and public opinion about the unperceived or misperceived implications of interdependence.

The second priority is to unveil the moral roots of the prevailing narrative and their disturbing implications. In his masterful book *States, Debt, and Power*, Kenneth Dyson has shown that, inspired as it was by the creditor narrative and moral perspective, the management of the euro-crisis has given rise to a 'politics of humiliation', based upon paternalistic and hierarchical chastisement, instead of fraternal encouragement.[19] In his vibrant *j'accuse* against Merkel and the Eurocrats published in *Die Süddeutsche Zeitung*, Habermas noted, in his turn, that, during the bailout negotiations, Greek authorities (ie the elected representatives of the Hellenic people) were often treated like 'zombies', in blunt violation of the principle of political equality of Member States enshrined in the EU covenant.[20] To quote his words:

> this transformation into zombies [was] intended to give the protracted insolvency of a state the appearance of a non-political, civil court proceeding.

Fritz Scharpf has recently argued, in his turn, that, in the borrower-lender constellation of the crisis, borrowers were not even considered as 'deserving poor.'

---

[18] Richard Baldwin, Thorsten Beck, Agnès Bénassy-Quéré, Olivier Blanchard, Giancarlo Corsetti, Paul de Grauwe, Wouter den Haan, Francesco Giavazzi, Daniel Gros, Sebnem Kalemli-Ozcan, Stefano Micossi, Elias Papaioannou, Paolo Pesenti, Christopher Pissarides, Guido Tabellini and Beatrice Weder di Mauro, 'Rebooting the Eurozone: Step 1—Agreeing a Crisis Narrative', *Vox-EU* 20 November 2015, available at: http://voxeu.org/article/ez-crisis-consensus-narrative.

[19] Kenneth Dyson, *States, Debt and Power*, (Oxford: Oxford University Press, 2014).

[20] Jürgen Habermas, 'Habermas: Warum Merkels Griechenland-Politik ein Fehler ist', *Süddeutsche Zeitung*, 22 June 2015, available at: www.sueddeutsche.de/wirtschaft/europa-sand-im-getriebe-1.2532119.

Humiliation has returned on a grand scale during the crisis. It will take time for the scar to heal, but the first step is a clear re-affirmation of the principles and practices of equal membership—which means, first of all, equal dignity and autonomy of each Member State, with no risk of unilateral demotion or forced deprivation of group membership.

The third priority is that of elaborating normative frames which are appropriate to the new social 'ontology' which has emerged in the wake of economic and monetary unification. The hardest challenge is to identify possible standards of pan-European solidarity: among EU citizens (in particular, mobile citizens) and among Member States, particularly within the eurozone. Such reflection must go hand in hand with empirical analysis, and it should build on factual evidence and sound reasoning about the causal impact of integration, as such, and about the matrix of cross-*demoi* externalities and payoffs. There is by now enough reasoning and evidence about a general fact: The EMU has an autonomous causal impact, and cross-national externalities do take place. We thus urgently need normative compasses to establish what the European *demoi* 'owe' to each other. We need *demoicratic* 'social theodicies'—to put it in Weberian terms: conceptions of distributive justice among increasingly integrated but still autonomous states and peoples. Elaborating such conceptions is inevitably going to be a balancing act between the minimalist, sufficientarian options typically tailored on the broader international system (solidarity as humanitarian aid) and the maximalist egalitarian options tailored on federal systems (solidarity as far reaching cross-regional fiscal re-distribution).[21]

Considering both historical experience and the tenets of contemporary (nation-based) theories of justice, the obvious starting-point for elaborating a 'third way' should be the analysis of the risk constellation of the institutional status quo. Which Member State is vulnerable to what and why is it vulnerable? To answer this question it may be useful to distinguish between *similar* and *common* risks. The first are the result of analogous dynamics (for example, demographic ageing) that have no significant link with either integration or externalities. Here, open co-ordination and mutual learning are important and useful, but there is no need for joint action, not to speak of transfers. Common risks are instead directly produced by integration and/or externalities: for example, the adverse consequence of an asymmetric shock in the presence of the EMU's constraints; or the cross-national implications of trade deficits or surpluses, or the negative impact of sudden surges in worker mobility or external immigration. For such types of risks, joint action (for example under the form of risk pooling or re-insurance schemes) is the appropriate solution, on both functional and normative grounds.

Andrea Sangiovanni has recently outlined a brilliant, reciprocity-based conception of inter-state solidarity, based upon a persuasive account of the point and purpose of the EU.[22] Another interesting debate has recently taken shape around the idea of a European Social Union (ESU): not a supranational welfare state, but a genuine union

---

[21] Vandenbroucke et al, n 4 above.

[22] Andrea Sangiovanni, 'Solidarity in the European Union', (2013) 33 *Oxford Journal of Legal Studies*, pp 213–241, available at: http://ojls.oxfordjournals.org/content/early/2013/01/21/ojls.gqs033.

of national systems, an effective 'hosting' (and hospitable) institutional framework supporting the effective and smooth functioning of domestic welfare schemes.[23] The ESU would help the latter to respond better to similar (as well as country-specific) risks, while putting in place new instruments for the mutualisation of common risks.

It will not be easy to move in this direction. As aptly put by Christian Joerges in a recent book, 'European citizens will have to distinguish between domestic and inter-state justice, between the solidarity in its various societies and the solidarity among its *demoi*'.[24] Admittedly, translating this distinction and its implications into a trans-national political agenda is a daunting task. Even if we were to come up with well-argued and articulated conceptions of *demoicratic* distributive justice, they may well prove to be incapable to defeat the biases and caging mentality of ordoliberals—not to speak of proving feasible in the present post-Brexit context. But without an ambitious and effective intellectual re-framing, such apolitical agenda cannot even be imagined in the first place.

---

[23] Vandenbroucke et al, n 4 above.

[24] Christian Joerges, 'Integration through Law and the Crisis of Law in Europe's Emergency', in: Chalmers, Jachtenfuchs and Joerges (eds), n 1 above, p 329.

8

What is Neoliberal in Germany's and Europe's Crisis Politics?

BRIGITTE YOUNG

ABSTRACT

The intent of this chapter is to analyse what is neoliberal in Germany's and Europe's politics. Much has been written in Anglo-Saxon political economic circles and the media about Germany's insistence on an outdated and conservative school of ordo-liberalism. As this chapter tries to show, Germany followed ordoliberal principles far less than has been advocated, first in the setting up the Bundesbank in 1957, and later in transferring supposedly ordoliberal constitutional principles to the European Central Bank. On closer inspection of the Eurozone crisis management and its rejection of Eurobonds, it can be seen that Germany pursued a policy of pragmatism and even national egoism. Neither the distinct set-up of the EMU, nor the logic of the Eurozone monetary union, are the outcome of specifically ordoliberal principles that are commonly assumed in the debate on the 'ordoliberalisation' of Europe. The design of the monetary union owed more to the New Institutional Economics taught at virtually all Anglo-Saxon economic departments as well as prominent economics and business school studies curricula in Europe. The chapter further argues that the most recent neoliberalism of radical market fundamentalism politically in vogue since the tenure of Margaret Thatcher in the UK and Ronald Reagan in the US with its negative liberty of ridding the economy of regulatory constraints differs fundamentally from the older concept of neoliberalism of the 1930s. The older concept of neoliberalism (and the then ordoliberalism) is concerned with both the negative and positive freedom in creating a constitutional framework that serves the common interests of its citizens.

I. INTRODUCTION

THE OUTCOME OF the Brexit referendum of the UK on 23 June 2016 to leave the EU has increased the already shaky foundation of the European Union (EU). The EU crisis mode has gone into top gear as crisis after crisis erupted. It all started with the US-American financial crisis in the sub-prime markets in 2007–2008, which triggered worldwide financial panic and staggering declines in global growth rates, which have not recovered even after eight years, despite unconventional monetary policy interventions by the largest central banks. In the Eurozone, the financial crisis manifested itself as a sovereign debt crisis in 2010, demonstrating the fragility of the European banking sector. On top of these economic and financial crises, geopolitical turmoil in the Middle East resulted in one of the biggest refugee exoduses, which began in 2014, and saw numbers rise as the crisis over Ukraine and the annexation of the Crimea precipitated a *Cold-war* climate between the East and West. None of these crises have been resolved, although some of them may have disappeared temporarily from the media headlines, only to re-emerge, as the present travail of the *Deutsche Bank* so clearly demonstrates.[1] The Brexit vote is just the newest challenge to the 60-year history of European integration.

Is the Eurozone doomed to fail and, if so, what role do economic ideas play? Do EU political leaders have a reform plan to boost economic performance to stem the swelling frustration of people expressed in euro-scepticism and the drift to populist and right-wing movements? Does the past fragmented crisis mode among EU Member States signal the 'new normal' of how to resolve the various interdependent crises? The post-Brexit mood has already led to disagreements about whether to proceed with European integration. Some warn that, in times of great uncertainty, more integration would lead to further euro-scepticism, as do some members of the German Economic Council of Economic Experts,[2] while others advocate that European governments should step in now and build a stronger Europe in order to avoid further anti-Euro sentiments.[3]

There is even more uncertainty and even irritation about the role that particular economic ideas may be playing in the crisis management, as Germany's ordoliberalism is assumed to have influenced the hardline austerity policy against the indebted peripheral countries of the Eurozone. The renaissance of ordoliberalism as a research topic mainly by Anglo-Saxon political scientists and political economists has sparked an ideational battle based upon the assumption that the Eurozone policy has followed the script of the ordoliberal ideas of fiscal austerity and competitiveness.[4] Largely unintended by Eurozone political actors, the Eurozone crisis has thus become the battleground which pits the supposedly 'German iron cage'[5] of ordoliberalism against post-Keynesianism.[6] It is for this reason that the University of Freiburg organised a Colloquium entitled *Ordoliberalism: A Chance or Danger for*

---

[1] See Martin Wolf, 'Deutsche Bank offers a tough lesson in risk', *Financial Times*, 5 October 2016.

[2] See Lars Feld, Christian Schmidt, Isabel Schnabel and Volker Wieland, 'Den Zugang zum Sozialsystem bremsen', *Frankfurter Allgemeine Zeitung*, 29 August 2016.

[3] See Henrik Enderlein, Enrico Letta, Jörg Asmussen, Laurence Boone, Aart de Geus, Pascal Lamy, Philippe Maystadt, Mario João Rodrigues, Gertrude Tumpel-Gugerell and Antonio Vitórino, 'Repair and Prepare: Growth and the Euro after Brexit', (Gütersloh-Berlin-Paris: Bertelsmann Stiftung, 2016), Jacques Delors Institut in Berlin and Jacques Delors Institute in Paris.

[4] See Mark Blyth, *Austerity: The History of a Dangerous Idea*, (Oxford: Oxford University Press, 2013).

[5] See François Denord, Rachel Knaebel and Pierre Rimbert, 'Germany's iron cage', *Le Monde diplomatique*, August 2015.

[6] See Brigitte Young, 'The Battle of Ideas in the Eurozone Crisis Management: German Ordoliberalism versus post-Keynesianism', in: Sebastiano Fadda and Pasquale Tridico (eds), *The Economic Crisis in Social and Institutional Context*, (London-New York: Routledge, 2015), pp 78–90.

Europe? on 14 September 2016. The purpose was to inquire into the existing ideational conundrum of whether ordoliberal ideas have provided a coherent paradigm and subsequent blueprint for the rule-based austerity governance of the Eurozone, as many Anglo-Saxon political economists and media pundits seem to maintain.

Problematical, in this ideational debate, is the lack of clarity of *who* the ordoliberals actually are, given that there are different branches of ordoliberalism, of which the Freiburg School is but one branch, and *what*, specifically, is ordoliberal in the shaping of the German Euro crisis management. A fundamental dispute and cause of confusion surrounds the meaning of the term 'neoliberalism', which was first coined in Paris in 1938 at a *Colloque* Walter Lippmann (successively becoming ordoliberalism in the 1950s) and the later usage of neoliberalism starting in the 1970s with a meaning completely different to that of the earlier one.[7] Is the recent convergence between the German neoliberal or ordoliberalism and the Anglo-Saxon neoliberalism justified on epistemological and ontological grounds?

The general purpose of this chapter is to engage with the different meanings of neoliberalism from a historical perspective, to describe the grounds on which German ordoliberalism has become a dangerous idea for critics of the Eurozone crisis management, and, finally, to answer the question of to what extent ordoliberalism has played a role in the German domination of EU macroeconomic policy. The structure of this chapter is as follows. First, it engages with the puzzling assumption that neoliberalism or ordoliberalism, as coined in the 1930s, is synonymous with neoliberalism, a term associated with the radical market fundamentalism of the *Chicago School* and politically in vogue since the tenure of Margaret Thatcher in Great Britain and Ronald Reagan in the US in the late 1970s/early 1980s. This involves delving into the historical roots of European neoliberalism and the re-emergence of neoliberalism in the 1970s, which the latter emphasising mainly the negative liberty of ridding the economy of regulatory constraints. Next, the discussion shifts to the critics of ordoliberalism and discusses their main negative contentions about the Freiburg School, pursuing a macroeconomic strategy based upon austerity, rather than stimulating growth. This discussion sets the stage to ascertain, in the next section, whether the economic policies of the German government are informed by the ordoliberal tradition.

II. FORMS OF NEOLIBERALISM: GERMAN NEOLIBERALISM AND ANGLO-SAXON NEOLIBERALISM

Defining neoliberalism is all the more difficult because the concept, as it emerged in the 1930s, differs fundamentally from the form in which it re-emerged in the 1970s. The old concept re-appeared as a policy response to the Keynesian crisis of stagflation and was made popular by the political ascendance of Margaret Thatcher in Great Britain and Ronald Reagan in the US. The new neoliberalism has become a

---

[7] Alessandro Vercelli, *Crisis and Sustainability: The Delusion of Free Markets*, (London: Palgrave Macmillan, 2016, forthcoming); and Young, n 6 above.

central concept in the social sciences, describing the structural changes in the global economy since the 1970s, implying the triumph of market forces and individual autonomy over state power. At a fundamental level, there is a normative difference in neoliberal ideas between negative and positive liberty. Drawing on Isaiah Berlin's discussion[8] on the dichotomy between negative liberty as *freedom from specific constraints* and *positive freedom to facilitate the self-determination of individuals*, the most recent neoliberalism of market fundamentalism focuses solely on the concept of negative liberty and rejects the relevance of positive freedom to facilitate individual liberty through state intervention.[9] In contrast, the older concept of neoliberalism (and the then ordoliberals) is concerned with both the negative and positive liberty of citizens. Negative liberty plays a role in constraining private and public monopoly power to prevent the negative dynamics of privilege seeking and privilege granting, while, positive freedom simultaneously involves the role of the state in creating a *constitutional framework* that serves the common interests of its citizens (*Ordnungspolitik*).[10]

III. HISTORICAL ORIGIN OF CONTINENTAL EUROPEAN NEOLIBERALISM

Historically, the European concept of neoliberalism originated in the 1930s, in opposition to the Anglo-Saxon *laissez-faire* liberalism of self-regulating markets. The best account of such a *laissez-faire* economic system is found in Karl Polanyi's *The Great Transformation*,[11] in which he argues that the collapse of the international economic system in the 1930s was a direct consequence of the attempt to organise the economy upon the basis of *laissez-faire* principles influenced by the British and Austrian schools of liberal economics. According to the German economist Wilhelm Röpke, the term 'neoliberalism' was coined at a symposium in honour of Walter Lippmann in Paris in 1938, the aforementioned *Colloque* Water Lippmann. The participants selected the term neoliberalism to signal the start of a new liberal movement against the *laissez-faire* liberalism of the nineteenth century. While not all members endorsed the term neoliberalism, it nevertheless became an umbrella designation for different strands of liberalism which developed under its roof with the economist Walter Eucken, the jurists Franz Böhm and Großmann-Doerthas as its most renowned representatives. The Faculty of Law and Economics of Freiburg University provided a conducive environment to integrate the legal and economic perspectives that are the trademark of the Freiburg School tradition, subsumed under the term of ordoliberalism.[12]

---

[8] See Isiah Berlin, 'Two Concepts of Liberty', in: idem, *Four Essays on Liberty*, (London: Oxford University Press, 1969).

[9] Vercelli, n 7 above.

[10] See Viktor Vanberg, 'Ordoliberalism, Ordnungspolitik, and the Reason of Rules', (2015) 2 *European Review of International Studies*, pp 27–36.

[11] Karl Polanyi, The Great Transformation: The Political and Economic Origins of our Time, (Boston MA, Beacon Press, [1944] 2001).

[12] Vanberg, n 10 above.

The exponents of this neoliberal circle united in rejecting the economic reductionism which they perceived as central to the ideas of nineteenth century *laissez-faire* liberalism. Instead, they emphasised a normative-ethical foundation of economics, delineating an important role for the state to set the constitutional framework for economic competition in order to serve the larger interests of society. The intellectual proponents of neoliberalism combined economic efficiency with human decency to achieve a just and stable social order. As suggested by the term *social market economy*, which developed from the earlier neoliberal circles and is still used today to describe some of the continental European (German) economic model, the belief in the self-regulatory capacity of the market was rejected. In contrast, *laissez-faire* intellectuals such as David Ricardo, Thomas Malthus, Edmund Burke, and, from the Austrian economic school, Ludwig von Mises, developed the theoretical foundation for claiming the superiority of negative freedom over public intervention (positive liberty). These intellectuals postulated that unfettered economic competition was superior to any form of state guidance in coordinating human efforts. A belief in the naturalness of the market and the self-regulating power of markets forces were the key concepts of *laissez-faire*. In rejecting the *laissez-faire* liberalism with its sole emphasis on the defence of negative liberty, the proponents of neoliberalism challenged the separation between the political and economic spheres. They envisioned the state to provide a constitutional economic framework to enhance positive freedom for citizens while at the same time constraining the power of private and public monopoly power that hinder citizens' autonomy.[13]

It is a puzzle how the term neoliberalism as an ethical concept has turned into the exact opposite becoming synonymous with a radical-market oriented system rejecting state intervention in the economy since the late 1970s. Intellectuals most closely identified with the norms of market fundamentalism are found in the so-called Chicago School, but only the political rejection of the post-war Keynesian consensus in Great Britain and the US in the late 1970s made the spread of anti-state rhetoric of *laissez-faire* neoliberalism globally possible. A central element of this new neoliberalism is the removal of regulatory and social constraints through such measures as liberalisation, de-regulation, and privatisation to unleash the productive forces of capitalism. Twenty-five years later, there is still no shared consensus on the meanings of neoliberalism as it emerged at the end of the 1970s except for its negative connotation. The term has become synonymous with human and natural resource exploitation, the dismantling of the welfare state, increasing global inequality, and even oppression in the name of freedom.[14] It is those negative effects resulting from a belief in unrestrained and self-regulating market forces ordoliberal economists and lawyers of the 1930s tried to mitigate.

It should not come as a surprise that I strongly reject the interchangeability of the meaning of continental neoliberalism of the 1930s with the Anglo-Saxon

---

[13] Brigitte Young, 'Neoliberalism', in: Bertrand Badie, Dirk Berg-Schlosser and Leonardo Morlino (eds), *International Encyclopedia of Political Science*, (Thousand Oaks CA: SAGE, 2011), pp 1677–80.

[14] Christian Müller, 'Neoliberalism und Freiheit—Zum sozialethischen Anliegen der Ordo-Schule', (2007) 58 *ORDO Jahrbuch*, pp 97–106.

neoliberalism coming into vogue in the 1970s. It neither does justice to the origin of the term and its further development of ordoliberalism after WWII. However, this differentiation between the two neoliberalisms does not answer the question on what grounds ordoliberalism has come to be seen as the 'danger for Europe' and whether this school of thought has been the major influence in German management of the Eurozone crisis.

IV. ORDOLIBERALISM AS DEFINED BY ITS CRITICS AS A DANGER FOR EUROPE

There are two contentious points dominating the discussion against ordoliberalism. The first deals with the austerity politics against the highly indebted Eurozone countries where the *Bundesbank* is seen as the epitome of the ordoliberal tradition. Second, there is much confusion about the phrase 'strong state' bringing to the fore the German tradition of state-centrism and authoritarianism.

In terms of the much demonised policy of austerity, it was Mark Blyth with his catching book title: *Austerity: The History of a Dangerous Idea* (2013)[15] who made the link between ordoliberalism and rule-based austerity. Essentially, the idea is that indebted peripheral countries have lived beyond their means and debt[16] reduction must result in cutting domestic wages and declining prices in order to restore competitiveness. This calls for drastic budget reductions, a dead economic idea, which has led to low growth along with tremendous increases in inequality. While the Republican government under George W. Bush argued for Keynesianism to stimulate the economy following the onset of the financial crisis of 2007–2008, the German government insisted on monetary stability plus strict rules on debt and deficit controls. That Germany was able to take this lead in managing the Eurozone crisis, has, according to Blyth, to do with the fact that German ideas have been at the very heart of both the EU and the euro since its inception by banning Keynesian demand management and insisting on running budgetary surpluses during economic slumps.

The central player in this game of austerity and thus preventing any Keynesian stimulus is the German *Bundesbank*, which supposedly is the main embodiment of ordoliberal values of monetary stability.[17] The specific German approach to monetary stability was then transferred to the European level with the introduction of the European Monetary Union (EMU) and the formation of the European Central Bank (ECB) in 1999. Whether the link between the ordoliberal *Bundesbank* and an ordoliberal mandate of the ECB did, in fact, shape the monetary economic

---

[15] See n 4 above.

[16] Debt is translated in German as '*Schuld*', which implies a personal normative guilt, and not just a material debt.

[17] See Kenneth Dyson, 'The Ordo-liberal Tradition: Germany and the Paradox of Creditor-State Power in the Euro Area', Presentation at the Conference 'Ordoliberalism as an Irritating German Idea', Hertie School of Governance, 13–14 May 2016. See also, idem, 'Ordoliberalism as Tradition and as Ideology', Ch 5 in this book.

constitution in the *Bundesbank* Act of 1957 has undergone little scrutiny. According to Lars Feld, Ekkehard Köhler and Daniel Nientiedt, there were several floating ideas among ordoliberals in the 1949s about 'how a monetary constitution of greater stability can be integrated into the competitive order'.[18] In the end, the various ordoliberal proposals for monetary constitution were not adopted in the *Bundesbank* Act of 1957. Eucken championed for a 'rational automatism' to guide monetary policy, but this was rejected in favour of the discretionary power of the German *Bundesbank*. Nor was the much cited independence of the *Bundesbank* ever a central feature for the monetary concepts of ordoliberalism.

It may come as a surprise to many critics that Keynesianism played a crucial role in the 1960s and that German monetary policy was seen as part of an integrated concept of employment policy. To stabilise the business cycle after the first recession in 1967, the *Bundesbank* deviated from the goal of price stability and introduced monetary measures to boost aggregate demand. A notable shift emerged in the wake of the Bretton Woods collapse when the *Bundesbank* endorsed Milton Friedman's quantitative theory of money as a target for monetary policy in 1974. The *Bundesbank* followed the monetarist policy rule into the 1990s. Feld et al,[19] conclude that, while price stability had emerged as the sole objective of German monetary policy by the time of the Treaty of Maastricht in 1992, German monetary development should be understood in the context of the international debate between Keynesianism and Monetarism. This debate owes much more to the dominance of New Institutional Economics (NIE) taught at virtually all Anglo-Saxon economic departments as well as prominent economics and business studies curricula in Europe.[20] The ordoliberal impact of the Freiburg School 'was far less important than commonly assumed in the debate on the "ordoliberalization" of Europe'.[21]

In terms of the second contentious issue, the phrase 'strong state' used by Eucken supposedly signals 'a vision of the state as a monolithic structure, insulated from societal influence, and willing and powerful enough to force other actors into compliance with its decision'.[22] This interpretation has led to view European governance as authoritarian, undemocratic and technocratic. Walter Eucken did use the phrase 'strong state' to 'indicate the importance of extending the logic of *Ordnungspolitik* from the realm of the economic constitution to that of the political constitution'.[23] Due to Eucken's early death in 1950, the concept of the 'strong state' remained largely vague. Werner Bonefeld, focusing mostly on Wilhelm Röpke and Alfred

---

[18] See Lars Feld, Ekkehard Köhler and Daniel Nientiedt, 'Ordoliberalism, Pragmatism and the Eurozone Crisis: How the German Tradition shaped Economic Policy in Europe', (2015) 2 *European Review of International Studies*, pp 48–61, at 53.

[19] Feld et al, n 18 above.

[20] See Malte Dold and Tim Krieger, 'Ordoliberalism is not Responsible for Jihadist Terrorism in Europe—A Reply to Van der Walt', (2016) *New Perspectives*, Vol. 25, No. 2/2017, pp 2–12.

[21] Feld et al, n 18 above, p 55.

[22] See Thomas Biebricher, 'Europe and the Political Philosophy of Neoliberalism, *Contemporary Political Theory*, 12(4), (2013), pp 338–375, at 340.

[23] See Viktor Vanberg, 'The Freiburg School of Law and Economics: Predecessor of Constitutional Economics', in: Peter Newman (ed), *The New Palgrave Dictionary of Economics and the Law*, Vol 2, (London: Macmillan, 1998), pp 171–79.

Müller-Armack's writings of the 1930s, asserts that a free economy amounts to a political practice of the strong state. In the ordoliberal account, a free economy and a strong state constitute an interdependent relationship, in which the state is the concentrated force of the system of liberty. As a result:

> the study of ordoliberalism brings to the fore a tradition of a state-centric neoliberalism, one that says that economic freedom is ordered freedom, one that argues that the strong state is the political form of free markets, and one that conceives of competition and enterprise as a political task.[24]

Much of the academic literature draws on the writings of the German ordoliberals of the 1930s and do not take into account the transformation and the distance that ordoliberals took from their initial sympathy with a 'strong state' authority. Thinkers of the different ordoliberal branches integrated the lessons that they had learned from the traumatic experience of the Nazi dictatorship and, after 1945, were intent on creating a constitutional order. The notion of the 'strong state' was replaced with a much more muted role for the state in providing a constitutional framework to guarantee both economic stability and freedom within this framework.[25] As Vanberg points out, the phrase 'strong state', if read in isolation, may sound undemocratic or even anti-democratic.[26] Rather than advocating an authoritarian concept of politics, the Freiburg scholars were intent on weakening the influence of special interests for the benefit of the common interests of citizens. Undoubtedly, a discussion about the role of the state and the 'democratic deficit' in the Eurozone is a much-needed research topic. Isaiah Berlin's discussion on the dichotomy between negative liberty as *freedom from specific constraints* and *positive freedom to facilitate the self-determination of individuals* could facilitate a more nuanced discussion. Rather than a 'strong state', the notion of a 'light state' may come closer to the ordoliberal concept of the *economic constitutional order* (the rules of the game) both in the economic arena and in politics.

The next section will 'look on the ground' and analyse the extent to which the ordoliberal tradition has informed the economic policies of the German government in the Eurozone crisis, and the extent to which it has pursued a strategy of political pragmatism and even one of national egoism during the crisis.

V. HAS ORDOLIBERALISM SHAPED THE EURO CRISIS MANAGEMENT?

The inquiry may be facilitated if we follow Dyson's recommendation to think of ordoliberalism not as a specific School with strict 'golden rules', but as an epistemic tradition, instead.[27] Tradition implies a more open way of interrogating the

---

[24] See Werner Bonefeld, 'Freedom and the Strong State: On German Ordoliberalism', (2012) 17 *New Political Economy*, pp 633–656, at 633.

[25] See Volker Berghahn and Brigitte Young, 'Reflections on Werner Bonefeld's 'Freedom and the Strong State: On German Ordoliberalism' and the Continuing Importance of the Ideas of Ordoliberalism to Understand Germany's (Contested) Role in Resolving the Eurozone Crisis', (2013) 18 *New Political Economy*, pp 768–778.

[26] Vanberg, n 10 above.

[27] Dyson, n 17 above.

characteristics of the ordoliberal way of viewing society, economics, the state, and ethics. Rather than formal intellectual knowledge that can be delineated according to a set of criteria, the concept tradition suggests a more practical and implicit form of knowledge. This type of knowledge is best seen as being institutionally and culturally embedded, and resembles a kind of 'common sense' which is not reducible to certain immutable rules.[28] Viewing ordoliberalism as a tradition, however, does not imply that there are no identifiable characteristics pertaining to this tradition. One of these is the long-standing tradition of a rule-oriented *Ordnungspolitik*, rather than an interventionist policy-making mode. This implies that 'the principle means by which economic policy can seek to improve "the economy" is by improving the institutional framework within which economic activities take place'.[29]

If we analyse the impact of ordoliberalism on the Eurozone crisis management, two characteristics should answer the question of whether a link exists between the two levels: the rule-based Eurozone Monetary Union (EMU), and the German rejection of joint liability (*Haftung und Kontrolle*). In terms of the EMU, the rule-based union reflects an attempt to create a framework of rules aimed to ensure a sound fiscal policy and sound money. In creating the euro as a de-nationalised currency with no links to the individual Member States, meaning that Member States had to pay their debt in a currency which they could not create, the Maastricht Treaty and the Stability and Growth Pact functioned to counteract fiscal profligacy by the Member States. Setting standards for fiscal discipline (which turned out to be insufficient) was an attempt to ensure sound fiscal policy and sound money. With the introduction of the single currency, the Member States of the Eurozone entered a regime of fixed exchange rates. This meant that countries could not devaluate in order to improve their competitiveness, as countries can do with national currencies. Since the nominal exchange rate is fixed, all they can do, to become more competitive, is to adjust wages and prices accordingly.

It is here that the critique sets in against the supposedly ordoliberal logic of the monetary union. However, as Feld et al,[30] point out, the design of the monetary union owes more to the New Institutional Economics (NIE), and not to any particular ordoliberal principles. Monetary economists from NIE suggest that any devaluation is short-lived, since it does not address the underlying causes of the prevailing economic conditions. To wit, as long as devaluations are ruled out as a policy option, the relative competitiveness of a country can only be adjusted through wages and prices, as is presently demanded of the indebted countries in the Eurozone.

> Notably, the need for such adjustment cannot be attributed to any specific type of ordo-liberal heritage or anything else specifically "German".[31]

Germany can be critiqued for following the tenets of applied monetary economics, which can be found in all mainstream economic textbooks, an economic doctrine

---

[28] ibid.

[29] According to Ludwig von Mises, a member of the Austrian economic school, ordoliberalism is 'ordo-interventionists' whereby von Mises tried to differentiate the Austrian and the Freiburg School of Economics (see Dold and Krieger, n 20 above forthcoming). See, also, Viktor Vanberg, 'Ordnungspolitik, the Freiburg School and the Reason of Rules', (2014), *i-lex* 21, pp 205–220.

[30] Feld et al, n 17 above.

[31] idem.

which is referred to as neoliberalism in the social sciences. In fact, ordoliberalism, or the 'Freiburg School economics', is no longer taught in German economics or business schools, and certainly not in any prestigious Anglo-Saxon programmes which are completely unfamiliar with ordoliberal ideas.[32]

If commentators criticise the German decision-makers for rejecting fiscal transfers among the Member States of the currency union, and accuse Germany of a lack of solidarity, the culprit is not ordoliberalism thinking, but rather the existing monetary economics of the NIE. Undoubtedly, there are grounds to criticise Germany for not showing more solidarity in the Eurozone crisis management. However, this position can also be explained by referring to national egoism, in that Germany was unwilling to support Eurobonds since this would have increased its interest rates and thus reduced its competitiveness. But what is most important for our argument, is that neither the distinct set-up of the EMU, nor the logic of the Eurozone monetary union, are the outcome of specifically ordoliberal principles.

Turning to the second tenet of whether the German rejection of Eurobonds is based upon ordoliberal thinking which signalled to indebted Eurozone countries that Germany was unwilling to share the debt burden with the Eurozone Member States in financial need. The rejection of joint liability is one of Eucken's seven principles for an economic and humane constitution.[33] In terms of the EMU, the primacy of currency policy (price stability) and the principle of liability are particularly central. Eucken's insistence on both liability and control stem from his reasoning that individual liability changes the parameters of costs and risk. As such, Eurozone countries which accumulated debts within the monetary union have to be held accountable for their decisions, and cannot impose the costs on others. Germany rejected the EU-Commission's proposal in 2011 to issue government bonds jointly in order to reduce the financing costs of the highly indebted peripheral countries. At the same time, the German government supported the European Stability Mechanism (ESM) as a rescue mechanism for the indebted countries, despite the fact that it also violated the joint liability principle, as Jens Weidmann, president of the German *Bundesbank*, testified before the Budget Committee of the German *Bundestag* in 2011.

Given the existential crisis of the Euro in 2012, the rejection of Eurobonds by Germany brought the ECB into the picture with the announcement of the Outright Monetary Transactions Policy (OMT) aimed at purchasing bonds from Member States of the Eurozone. The German government did not openly endorse the measure, but neither did it reject it. It clearly violated the ordoliberal principle of liability and resulted in a flood of lawsuits at the Constitutional Court in Karlsruhe from irate German politicians across the party spectrum and from citizens. Ordoliberals criticised the OMT programme, since the ECB was combining monetary with fiscal policy measures. More to the point, the European Stability Mechanism and the OMT programme seem, according to Feld et al,[34] to be driven by German

[32] Dold and Krieger, n 20 above.
[33] Eucken's seven constitutive principles are: functioning of the price system, the primacy of currency policy, open markets, private property, freedom of contract, liability, and the constancy of economic policy.
[34] Feld et al, n 18 above.

pragmatism at the time of the existential crisis, rather than adherence to an ordo liberal doctrine. In fact, 'Germany may have followed ordoliberal thinking rather too little than too much'.[35] It would have been more effective to agree to a 'partial (legacy) debt mutualisation against the preservation of independence of the ECB and national debt brakes'.[36]

During the height of the crisis in 2012, ordoliberals proposed to reform and construct a more rule-based EMU with a credible no-bailout clause (rejection of joint liability). The Council of the Economic Experts[37] in a Special Report advocated EMU reforms which focused on fiscal policy reforms (fiscal integration), a crisis mechanism in the form of a debt-restructuring regime, and financial market regulation. In fact, just recently some members of the Council reiterated their call for a Eurozone orderly debt restructuring mechanism with a creditor participation clause.[38] Their reflection rests on the fact that the likelihood of a new sovereign debt crisis cannot be ruled out, and thus an orderly process of debt re-structuring has advantages over the present status quo. In addition, 'the genie of sovereign debt restructuring in the Eurozone is already out of the bottle and cannot be put back',[39] and Greek and Cyprus debt re-structuring signalled that private creditors were no longer shielded from a bail-in. The authors Jochen Andritzky et al, suggest a reform of the European Stability Mechanism (ESM). This body was created during the sovereign debt crisis to provide liquidity assistance in cases where access to capital markets was no longer feasible ('loans against reforms'). A re-structuring would mean strict conditionality, but, at the same time, it would reduce uncertainty and ad hoc re-structuring, as was the practice with the privately held debt in Greece and Cyprus.

The idea is to differentiate between a mere funding crisis and a full-blown solvency crisis. Since this cannot be ascertained with any certainty at the start of a crisis, the proposal is divided into a sequential two-stage mechanism. In the first stage of the debt operation, a simple decision triggers a maturity extension in the following cases: (1) if the debt exceeds 60–90% of GDP; (2) if the funding requirement for the debt exceeds 15–20% of GDP; or (3) if there have been two to three or more violations of fiscal rules in the last five years. If such a mechanism were in place now, France, Portugal, Spain and Italy would have access to receive maturity extension and interim funding reducing the great uncertainty plaguing the financial stability of these countries. If the debt operation subsequently turns out to be more serious and the debt sustainability is in danger, then the ESM would conduct an analysis of deeper re-structuring and even consider debt relief.

---

[35] ibid, p 61.

[36] ibid.

[37] The Council is mandated by German law to support all decision-makers in the economic and political sphere, as well as the general public in Germany, to form views about economic policy and its potential risks. To this end, every November it presents an annual report to the German federal government and the general public. Invariably, the Report results in wide-spread, often quite contested, discussions among economists and political leaders.

[38] See Jochen Andritzky, Lars Feld, Christian Schmidt, Isabel Schnabel and Volker Wieland, 'Creditor Participation Clauses: Making Orderly Sovereign Debt Restructuring Feasible in the Eurozone', *voxeu.org* CEPR's Policy Portal (21 July 2016), available at: http://voxeu.org/article/mechanism-proposal-eurozone-sovereign-debt-restructuring.

[39] ibid.

Against the often-cited belief that German ordoliberalism is only about adhering to strict rules, the Council suggests some discretion with fiscal rules to policy-makers during the debt programme while nevertheless advocating compliance in accordance with their economic and political capacity. An advantage of this debt re-structuring programme is that it builds on the existing ESM Treaty, which demands that private sector involvement be considered. Only an amendment to the ESM guidelines is needed that makes ESM lending conditional on the new two-tier sequential mechanism.

VI. CONCLUSION

The intent of this chapter was to analyse what is neoliberal in Germany's and Europe's crisis politics. Much has been written in Anglo-Saxon political economic circles and the media about Germany's insistence on an outdated and conservative school of ordoliberalism.[40] As this chapter has tried to show, Germany followed ordoliberal principles far less than has been advocated, first in the setting up the *Bundesbank* in 1957, and later in transferring supposedly ordoliberal constitutional principles to the European Central Bank. In the early stages of the *Bundesbank*, it followed the international accepted practice of Keynesianism under Karl Schiller, Economics and Finance Minister, and, in the aftermath of the collapse of the Bretton Woods system, it followed monetarism of Milton Friedman until the middle of the 1990s. Monetarism has little to do with ordoliberalism; its intellectual roots lie in the mainstream of New Institutional Economics.

On closer inspection of the Eurozone crisis management, it can be seen that the dominant German influence has much more to do with the ascendancy of the so-called mainstream Anglo-Saxon New Institutional Economics and the New Consensus Macroeconomics. These ideas became the basis for economic teaching in Anglo-Saxon graduate programmes and influenced European economics curricula. The same is true for austerity, which, according to Mark Blyth, is linked to the ordoliberal school. However, the idea for austerity originated first in Great Britain under Margaret Thatcher and in the US under Ronald Reagan, both of whom advocated a 'lean and mean' state. More important than ordoliberal thinking which advocated both positive and negative liberty, libertarian economists such as Friedrich August von Hayek, Milton Friedman and Murray Rothbard, all emphasised the negative freedom to reduce constraints and permit the unfettered workings of capitalist forces.[41] It should be recalled that it was Wilhelm Röpke, an ordoliberal, who argued for fiscal stimuli in the 1929 Brauns-Commission at the time of the Great Depression. The German Chancellor, Heinrich Brüning, advocated a politics of deflation to overcome the world economic depression by strict household consolidation and mandated wage and price reductions to increase German export competitiveness on the world markets. This policy strongly resembles what the German finance minister, Wolfgang Schäuble, has advocated for the indebted Eurozone countries.

---

[40]   Young, n 6 above.
[41]   Dold and Krieger, n 20 above.

Critics are right to take Germany's handling of the Eurozone crisis management to task, but it is simply incorrect to hold that ordoliberal ideas are responsible for this. Rather, Germany used the crisis to act in a pragmatic manner, and, in many cases, pursued its national interest(s) at the expense of European solidarity.

After the worst financial crisis since the Great Depression, it should be evident even to die-hard free-marketeers that the present Anglo-Saxon neoliberalism based upon the self-regulating market and anti-state rhetoric is unsustainable. In these times of great uncertainty, increasing inequality, feelings of alienation from political élites, and the centrifugal tendencies within the European Union, it may behove us to return to the writing of the early ordoliberals and consider their writings on the need to include a strong welfare element in the EU reform programme. Not only did Walter Eucken in his *Grundsätze der Wirtschaftspolitik* (1952) acknowledge the state's role in social policies for those suffering from social misfortune, he was also acutely aware that the competitive market order might lead to an undesirable income distribution and that it might be necessary to use progressive income tax to correct such market distorting cases. Today's scholars, civil society, policymakers, and politicians may gain valuable insights from these older ordoliberal anti-laissez-faire advocates, and could use these ideas to reform the present 'turbo capitalism' which is only beholden to negative liberty at the expense of positive freedom.

9

The Success Story of Ordoliberalism as the Guiding Principle of German Economic Policy

STEPHAN PÜHRINGER*

ABSTRACT

Even after the financial crisis, which resulted in mass criticism against economics, economists still exert influence on politics and society in general on several levels and thus can still be interpreted as a discipline of power. Particularly in Germany, there is a long tradition of institutionalised economic policy advice, which offers economists a channel of direct and indirect impact on governmental politics. During the European crisis, many scholars stressed that there would be a 'comeback', 'revival' or 'return' of ordoliberalism, the German variety of neoliberalism. In this chapter I will highlight how economists involved in the 'German neoliberal thought collective' since the end of WWII built up a strong institutional power structure, which had a continuous impact on German economic policies over many decades. It can be shown that in several turning points in German economic history, German neoliberalism and its core concept of 'Social market economy' served as a guiding principle of economic policy. Hence, what was observed during the European crisis policies as a 'comeback of ordoliberalism' should rather be interpreted as the consequence of a persistent influence of German neoliberal networks on German economic politics.

*   Johannes Kepler University Linz, Institute for Comprehensive Analysis of Economy. The empirical parts of this chapter are partly built on joint work with Walter Ötsch and Katrin Hirte (see Walter Ötsch, Stephan Pühringer and Katrin Hirte, *Netzwerke des Marktes. Ordoliberalismus als Politische Ökonomie* (Wiesbaden: Springer VS, 2017) and Stephan Pühringer, 'Think Tank networks of German neoliberalism.' (ICAE Working Paper Series 53, University of Linz, Austria, 2015) and will partly also be published in the volume *The Roads from Mont Pélerin 2. Scales, Shifts and Drift in Knowledge/Power Structures* edited by Philip Mirowski, Dieter Plehwe and Quinn Slobodian (forthcoming). This research was supported by funds of the German Böckler-Foundation (Project number: 2012-575-1).

I. INTRODUCTION

IN SPITE OF the manifold critique about the state of economics in the aftermath of the crisis, an ever increasing presence of economists and economic experts can be observed in the public sphere during the last years.[1] Economists continue to exert influence on the public opinion about economic issues (for example, Hans-Werner Sinn in Germany or Carmen Reinhart and Kenneth Rogoff for the European austerity policy) and on economic policies. Due to the fact that economics is the only social science dominated by one dominant paradigm—neoclassical economic thought—the theoretical assumption and political support for 'free markets' over the years had a formative impact on the hegemonic academic and political discourse about the economy and formed the 'economic imaginary'[2] of a 'functioning market mechanism'.

At the level of economic policy, against the political background of the Cold War and, then, especially after the breakdown of Keynesian economics in the 1970s, the reference to the economic imaginaries of free markets and the free market mechanism simultaneously served as the theoretical background to promote neoliberal policies of de-regulation, privatisation and austerity. Although the financial crisis could have induced a paradigm shift in the field of economic policy, the dominance of neoliberal policies does not really seem to be contested and thus paved the way for austerity policies in the aftermath of the crisis. Whereas Colin Crouch denoted the persistence of neoliberalism as the 'strange non-death of neoliberalism',[3] Mark Blyth went on to warn of the severe social and societal consequences of austerity policies.[4]

In the context of European crisis policies, special attention was paid to the role of Germany in these debates. On the one hand, some scholars focused on the (new) hegemonic position of Germany as a central actor in European economic crisis policies, for example, the Fiscal Compact, the Eurozone crisis or the European Stability Mechanism (ESM) due to its economic power and its status as principal creditor.[5] On the other hand, the question was raised as to whether the European post-crisis economic policies reflect a 'return of ordoliberalism'[6] or even an 'ordoliberal

[1] Christopher. Johnston and Andrew Ballard, 'Economists and Public Opinion: Expert Consensus and Economic Policy Judgments', (2014), available at: SSRN: http://ssrn.com/abstract=2479439.

[2] Bob Jessop, 'Cultural Political Economy and Critical Policy Studies', (2010) 3 *Critical Policy Studies*, pp 336–356.

[3] Colin Crouch, *The Strange Non-death of Neoliberalism*, (Cambridge: Polity Press, 2011).

[4] Mark Blyth, *Austerity: The History of a Dangerous Idea*, (Oxford: Oxford University Press, 2013).

[5] Erhard Crome, 'Deutschland in Europa: eine neue Hegemonie debatte', (2012) 86 *Welttrends: Zeitschrift für Internationale Politik*, pp 59–68; Hans Kundnani, 'Germany as Geo-political Power', (2011) 34 *The Washington Quarterly*, pp 31–45; and Simon Bulmer and William Paterson, 'Germany as the EU's Reluctant Hegemon? Of the Economic Strength and Political Constraints', (2013) 20 *Journal of European Public Policies*, pp 1387–1405.

[6] Thomas Biebricher, 'The Return of Ordoliberalism in Europe—Notes on a Research Agenda', (2014) 9 *i-lex*, pp 1–24; Brigitte Young, 'German Ordoliberalism as Agenda Setter for the Euro Crisis: Myth Trumps Reality', (2014) 22 *Journal of Contemporary European Studies*, pp 276–287.

transformation'[7] or 'ordoliberalisation of Europe'.[8] Dullien and Guerot, however, report a 'long shadow of ordoliberalism' in German economic policies, claiming that, especially in the field of macroeconomic policy, ordoliberalism can be perceived as the 'basis of German economic thinking',[9] which also manifests itself in the power balances of German economists in media discourses after the crisis.[10]

Against this backdrop, in this chapter, I will show that German neoliberal thought had a persistent and formative impact on German economic policy over the post-war period up to the financial and economic crisis policies of 2008 and after. I will further argue that much of this influence can be attributed to an ideological bias of German economists, tightly organised in networks of German neoliberal think tanks and institutions with close personal and institutional links to core actors in German political institutions, such as the *Bundesbank* or the Ministries of Economics or Finance. The remainder of the chapter is structured as follows. Section II offers a theoretical reflection of ordoliberalism or German neoliberalism as a central part of the common neoliberal thought collective. In the main part of the chapter in Section III, I analyse the close connections of ordoliberal economists with politics (and media) in three important phases of German politico-economic history (the foundation of the German Federal Republic in the late 1940s, the 'monetarist turn' of the *Bundesbank* in the late 1960s and the 'neoliberal turn' induced by the *Lambsdorff-paper* in 1982). Section IV offers some concluding remarks and provides empirical evidence for the persistent discursive dominance of German neoliberal economists even in the financial crisis discourse.

II. ORDOLIBERALISM, NEOLIBERALISM, GERMAN NEOLIBERALISM

In the debate on a possible revival of ordoliberalism after the crisis, the question of the definition of the theoretical economic concept of ordoliberalism arises. This debate often revolves around theoretical similarities and disparities of ordoliberalism with 'American neoliberalism', that is with Milton Friedman's or Gary Becker's works, arguing in opposition to big-government. Michel Foucault, in his lectures on governmentality, distinguished between ordoliberalism and the American *neoliberalism*, and stresses a distinct 'political rationality' of ordoliberalism.[11] According to Foucault, American neoliberalism, which is associated with today's mainstream economic approach of Chicago-style neoclassics, was derived from German

---

[7] Thomas Biebricher, 'Europe and the Political Philosophy of Neoliberalism', (2013) 12 *Contemporary Political Theory*, pp 338–375.

[8] Blyth, n 4 above, p 142.

[9] Sebastian Dullien and Ulrike Guerot, 'The Long Shadow of Ordoliberalism: Germany's Approach to the Euro Crisis', (2012) Policy Brief, European Council on Foreign Relations, p 2.

[10] Stephan Pühringer, 'Still the Queens of Social Sciences? (Post-) Crisis Power Balances of 'Public Economists' in Germany', (2016) ICCONSS Electronic Conference Proceedings. Issue 5: Theoretical Debates in Social Sciences, No. 5.4.

[11] Michel Foucault, *The Birth of Biopolitics. Lectures at the Collège de France 1978–79*, (New York: Palgrave, 2008); Biebricher, n 6 above.

ordoliberalism and shares the common conviction of a de-regulatory free-market ideology, in which the functionality of the free market mechanism depends on processes of political engineering.[12] Yet in 1982, Wilfried VerEecke used the term 'neoliberalism' to describe German ordoliberalism and American Monetarism because of the similar preference for a strong state, whose central, but exclusive, task is the establishment and re-establishment of market mechanisms or the market economy.[13]

The ambivalent role of the state in the ordoliberal conception can be dated back to Walter Eucken's definition of the principles of economic policy. In the first principle, Eucken claims that 'the policy of the state should be focused on dissolving power groups or at limiting their functioning'.[14] The second principle requests that 'the politico-economic activity of the state should focus on the regulation of the economy, not on the guidance of the economic process'.[15] Whereas the first principle stresses the need for a strong state for political engineering (*Ordnungspolitik*), the second principle (*Prozesspolitik*) should avoid interventionist policies against the market mechanism.

Although there are some differences between ordoliberalism or German neoliberalism and American neoliberalism, particularly in terms of their policy implications,[16] from the perspective of the history of science, both conceptions can be assigned to a common neoliberal thought collective.[17] Philip Mirowski argues that, in the initial era of the neoliberal thought collective in the 1940s, ordoliberalism was one of the three important strands (he uses the terms 'sects or sub-guilds'), alongside Hayekian Austrian legal theory and Chicago School neoclassical economics. He further argues that the neoliberal thought collective can be understood in analogy to a Russian doll, with the *Mont Pèlerin Society* (MPS) founded in 1947 at its centre and a set of heterogeneous institutions and think tanks around it. Furthermore, the MPS and its annual meetings also offered a 'protected' place for the intellectual exchange and confrontation of the various scholars from

---

[12] Werner Bonefeld, 'Freedom and the Strong State: On German Ordoliberalism', (2012) 17 *Political Economy*, pp 633–656.

[13] Wilfried VerEecke, 'Ethics in Economics: From Classical Economics to Neo-Liberalism', (1982) 9 *Philosophy and Social Criticism*, pp 145–168.

[14] Walter Eucken, *Grundsätze der Wirtschaftspolitik*, (Bern-Tübingen: Francke und Mohr (Siebeck), [1952] 2004), p 334 et seq.

[15] Translation in Blyth, n 4 above, p 143.

[16] Ordoliberal scholars (for example, Lars Feld et al, 2015, Nils Goldschmidt and Michael Wohlgemuth 2008) often argue that ordoliberalism and especially the political concept of German Social Market Economy, which has become a catch phrase attributed to the German economic miracle of the 1950s and 1960s, represents a third way between capitalism and socialism and also laid the foundations for the German welfare state. See, eg, Lars Feld, Ekkehard Köhler and Daniel Nientiedt, 'Ordoliberalism, Pragmatism and the Eurozone Crisis: How the German Tradition Shaped Economic Policy in Europe', (2015) [Freiburger Diskussionspapiere zur Ordnungsökonomik, Nr. 04]; and Nils Goldschmidt and Michael Wohlgemuth, *Grundtexte zur Freiburger Tradition der Ordnungsökonomik*, (Tübingen: Mohr Siebeck, 2008).

[17] I will use the definition of neoliberal thought collective offered by Mirowski, 'to refer to this multilevel, multiphase, multisector approach to the building of political capacity to incubate, critique and promulgate ideas'; see Philip Mirowski, *Never Let a Serious Crisis Go to Waste: How Neoliberalism Survived the Financial Meltdown*, (London-New York: Verso Books, 2013), p 44.

these different strands of neoliberal reasoning. Likewise, Joachim Starbatty, one central actor in German neoliberal networks, head of the think tank entitled *Aktionsgemeinschaft Soziale Marktwirtschaft,* and member of the MPS defined the MPS as the 'organisational expression of neoliberalism' ('*der organisatorische Ausdruck*').[18] He further states that ordoliberalism should be seen as the 'German variety of neoliberalism'. Referring to this self-declaration of one of the most prominent ordoliberal economists in Germany, it is safe to define a 'network of German neoliberalism' organised in think tanks and institutions around the MPS in this chapter. Hence I define the 'German neoliberal network' as think tanks or institutions, in which at least one of the founding or leading members is also member of the MPS.[19]

The second main argument to interpret ordoliberalism as an integral part of the neoliberal thought collective is based upon very strong personal connections of the main ordoliberal scholars with other leading neoliberal protagonists, and, even more explicitly, with the twofold role of Friedrich von Hayek as main proponent in the two strands of neoliberalism. On the one hand, von Hayek was the leading scholar of the third generation of the Austrian School of Economics, and, together with MPS member Lionel Robbins, the main opponent of John Maynard Keynes at the London School of Economics. On the other hand, von Hayek had close connections with ordoliberals (and later also with MPS members) such as Walter Eucken, Wilhelm Röpke and Alexander Rüstow even in the 1930s.[20] In the 1960s, von Hayek was appointed professor of economics at the University of Freiburg, and head of the Walter Eucken Institute in Freiburg. Furthermore, he continuously contributed to ordoliberal publications and was even editor of the ordoliberal journal *ORDO Jahrbuch.* Henry Oliver, in the *Quarterly Journal of Economics,* thus stated, that 'in a sense he (von Hayek) serves as their (ordoliberals) leading political theorist'.[21] In a similar vein, Knut Borchardt stressed the similarities between ordoliberal scholars and von Hayek, especially in their common political will to establish and preserve capitalism.[22]

---

[18] Joachim Starbatty, 'Ordoliberalismus', in: Otmar Issing (ed), *Geschichte der Nationalökonomie,* (Munich: Vahlen, 2001), pp 251–269, at 251.

[19] Dieter Plehwe and Bernhard Walpen, 'Between Network and Complex Organization: The Making of Neoliberal Knowledge and Hegemony', in: Bernhard Walpen, Dieter Plehwe and Gisela Neunhöffer (eds), *Neoliberal Hegemony: A Global Critique,* (London: Routledge, 2006), pp 27–70.

[20] Ralf Ptak, *Vom Ordoliberalismus zur Sozialen Marktwirtschaft. Stationen des Neoliberalismus in Deutschland,* (Opladen: Springer, 2004).

[21] Henry Oliver, 'German Neoliberalism', (1969) 74 *The Quarterly Journal of Economics,* pp 117–149, at 119.

[22] Borchardt further argues that von Hayek also assumed that the stronger focus on social policy in the German Social Market Economy was a lesser evil to preserve a capitalist economy in German Federal Republic after the Second World War; see Knut Borchardt, 'Die Konzeption der Sozialen Marktwirtschaft in heutiger Sicht', in: Otmar Issing (ed), *Zukunftsprobleme der Sozialen Marktwirtschaft. Schriften des Vereins für Socialpolitik,* (Berlin: Duncker & Humblodt, 1981), pp 33–53. The position of members of the 'sociological strand' of German neoliberalism is ambivalent on this issue; see Josef Hein, 'The Ordoliberalism that Never was', (2013) 12 *Contemporary Political Theory,* pp 349–358. Rüstow, for instance, states that 'social policy has in the 80 years of its existence developed through uncontrolled growth'; see Alexander Rüstow, 'Sozialpolitik diesseits und jenseits des Klassenkampfes', in: Aktionsgemeinschaft Soziale Marktwirtschaft (eds), *Sinnvolle und Sinnwidrige Sozialpolitik,* (Ludwigsburg: Martin Hoch Druckerei und Verlagsgesellschaft, 1959), p 20, translated by Hien, this note, p 353.

Not least Alfred Müller-Armack, one of the politically most influential ordolib-
eral scholars in Germany from the 1950s to the 1970s, who also coined the term
'Social Market Economy', proclaims von Hayek, together with Walter Eucken,
Franz Böhm, Wilhelm Röpke and Alexander Rüstow, as a pioneer of the ordoliberal
'*Wirtschaftsordnungstheorie*'.[23]

Nevertheless, there seems to be a rather strong reluctance on the part of ordoliberal scholars to assign ordoliberalism to the neoliberal thought collective, which
can, perhaps, be explained by the rather negative image of American neoliberalism
in European political debates. Although many of the European crisis policies reflect
ordoliberal conceptions,[24] Feld et al stress that the influence of ordoliberal thought
is often over-estimated and the policies implemented in the aftermath of the crisis
should, instead, be characterised as 'pragmatic'.[25]

To sum up, first, the protagonists of neoliberal thought in the German ordoliberal
or the Chicago School American neoliberal strand often refuse to call themselves
'neoliberals' and therefore seem to remain 'The Political Movement that dared not
speak its own name'.[26] Second, after the crisis, one can observe a kind of metamorphosis of hegemonic neoliberal economic imaginaries in the European crisis policies which indicates a shift inside the neoliberal thought collective from American
de-regulatory neoliberalism, especially in the context of financial markets, to more
restrained markets within an ordoliberal framework.[27] Or as Jamie Peck put it, the
ordoliberal political project seems to be 'back in favour'.[28]

While the evaluation of a revival or a comeback of ordoliberalism or German
neoliberalism in economic policy might hold in the European, or maybe even in the
international context, in the next section, I will argue that it is misleading to claim
such a 'return-thesis' for Germany. Quite to the contrary, German neoliberal thought
had a formative impact on the course of German economic policy as well as, albeit
to a lesser extent, also on the history of economics in Germany over many decades.
Although ordoliberalism as an independent economic theory might, in fact, have
been 'marginalised and thus forgotten',[29] the infrastructures of German neoliberalism, such as politico-economic think tanks, political institutions, economic advisory bodies and economic research institutes remained an influential vehicle for the
German neoliberal power structure in German economic policies.

---

[23] Ptak, n 20 above.
[24] Blyth, n 4 above; Stephan Pühringer, 'The Strange Non-crisis of Economics.Economic Crisis and
the Crisis Policies in Economic and Political Discourses', Dissertation, 2015, Johannes Kepler Universität
Linz.
[25] Feld et al, n 16 above.
[26] Philip Mirowski, 'The Political Movement that Dared not Speak its own Name: The Neoliberal
Thought Collective Under Erasure', (2014), INET Working Paper 23.
[27] Biebricher, n 7 above, p 12; Bob Jessop, 'Recovered Imaginaries, Imagined Recoveries: A Cultural
Political Economy of Crisis Construals and Crisis-management in the North Atlantic Financial Crisis',
in: Mats Benner (ed), *Before and Beyond the Global Economic Crisis: Economics, Politics, Settlement*,
(Cheltenham: Edward Elgar Publishing, 2013), pp 234–54; and Stephan Pühringer, 'Markets as
'Ultimate Judges' of Economic Policies—Angela Merkel's Discourse Profile during the Economic Crisis
and the European Crisis Policies', (2015) 23 *On the Horizon* (special issue on Language and Economics),
pp 246–259.
[28] Jamie Peck, *Constructions of Neoliberal Reason*, (Oxford: Oxford University Press, 2010), p 275.
[29] Biebricher, n 7 above.

III. THE HISTORY OF GERMAN NEOLIBERALISM IN ECONOMIC THINK TANK NETWORKS

The roots of German neoliberalism can be dated back to the Freiburg School, built around Walter Eucken, Franz Böhm[30] and Leonhard Miksch in the 1920s and 1930s, and Alexander Rüstow and Wilhelm Röpke, two German economists in close personal contact especially with Walter Eucken,[31] respectively. At an economic theoretical level, the central aim of these early ordoliberal scholars was an attack on the 'ruins of the German Historical School',[32] which manifested in the idea of the foundation of a 'Theoretical Club of Ricardians'. Rüstow suggested also inviting Austrian economists such as von Hayek, Haberler Machlup or von Mises to this club.[33] Beside the personal contacts of ordoliberals with von Hayek and later proponents of the Chicago School, Ekkehard Köhler and Stefan Kolev also stress the similarities in the research agendas concerning monetary policy in Freiburg and Chicago even in the 1930s, particularly in the work of Eucken's pupils Friedrich Lutz and Henry Simons.[34] Eucken, furthermore, played a central role in the foundation of the MPS, which was manifested in the fact that von Hayek delegated the right to suggest German members for the MPS to Eucken.[35]

A. Networks of German Neoliberalism during the Foundation of the German Federal Republic

Although this academic exchange was interrupted in 1933 with the takeover of the Nazi regime, which forced Röpke and Rüstow to emigrate to Turkey, both the university of Freiburg and Walter Eucken, in particular, remained one of the core centres of economic research in Germany.[36]

---

[30] In contrast to the other early neoliberal scholars, denoted in this section, Böhm was a legal scholar. For the legal impact of ordoliberalism in Germany and Europe, see, for instance, Christian Joerges, 'Europa nach dem Ordoliberalismus: Eine Philippika', (2010) 43 *Kritische Justiz*, pp 394–406. The focus in this chapter is on ordoliberal economists and their political and societal impact via networks of German neoliberalism.

[31] Hauke Janssen, *Milton Friedman und die 'monetaristische Revolution' in Deutschland*, (Marburg: Metropolis, 2006). Jan-Otmar Hesse, *Wirtschaft als Wissenschaft. Die Volkswirtschaftslehre in der frühen Bundesrepublik*, (Frankfurt aM: Campus Verlag, 2010).

[32] Rüstow in a letter to Eucken in 1927, Janssen, n 31 above, p 32.

[33] F. von Hayek retrospectively remarked that this group of Ricardians was the only active and influential circle of economists fighting for a 'free economy' before 1933; see von Hayek, 'Die Wiederentdeckung der Freiheit—Persönliche Erinnerungen', VDMA (ed), *Produktivität, Eigenverantwortung, Beschäftigung. Für eine wirtschaftspolitische Vorwärtsstrategie*, (Cologne: Deutscher Institut Verlag, 1983), pp 9–22.

[34] Ekkehard Köhler and Stefan Kolev, 'The conjoint quest for a liberal positive programme: "Old Chicago", Freiburg and Hayek', (2011) HWWI Research Paper No. 109.

[35] Stefan Kolev, Nils Goldschmidt and Jan-Otmar Hesse, 'Walter Eucken's Role in the Early History of the Mont Pèlerin Society', (2014) Freiburger Diskussionspapiere zur Ordnungsökonomik 14(2), p 6.

[36] Walter Ötsch and Stephan Pühringer, 'Marktradikalismus als Politische Ökonomie. Wirtschaftswissenschaften und ihre Netzwerke in Deutschland ab 1945', (2015) ICAE Working Paper Series 38, University of Linz, Austria.

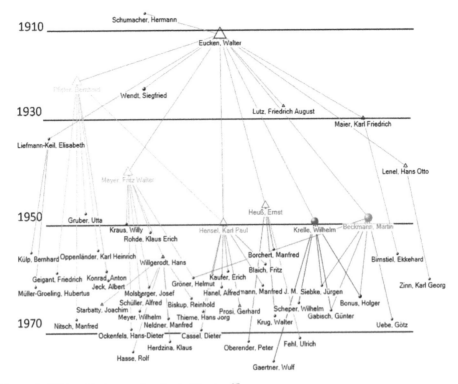

Figure 1: Walter Eucken as Academic Teacher[37]

The strong academic influence was, for instance, manifested in the very success-ful academic reproduction of the Freiburg School and Walter Eucken, respectively. Figure 1 shows German professors of economics, whose doctoral theses and/or habilitation theses were supervised by Walter Eucken (first generation). Although Eucken died rather young at the age of 59 during a research visit at the London School of Economics (to which he had been invited by von Hayek), he was one of the most successful 'academic teachers' in the history of German economics.[38] After the successful reproduction of the first generation of the Freiburg School (Eucken supervised at least eleven pupils who were later to become professors of economics at German universities), Eucken's pupils (in particular, Bernhard Pfister, Karl Paul Hensel and Fritz Walter Meyer, all of whom later became members of the MPS) proved to be very successful academic teachers, too. Beside this academic influ-ence on the course of German economic history both in and immediately after the

---

[37] Members of the MPS are plotted as triangles.
[38] Ötsch and Pühringer, n 36 above.

Second World War, ordoliberal economists were continuously engaged in policy advice partly for the Nazi regime and partly,[39] especially in the 1940s, in contact with the 'conservative opposition' to the Nazi regime.[40] During the early 1940s the *'Arbeitsgemeinschaft Erwin von Beckerath'* served ordoliberals as a meeting-point, with the main objective being to discuss and develop the economic order for post-war Germany. The engagement of ordoliberal economists in providing economic advice continued after the capitulation of Germany in 1945 and resulted in a strong dominance of ordoliberal economists in the two very influential scientific advisory boards of the Ministries of Finance and Economics (Figure 2) as well as in the central role of especially Ludwig Erhard in the adoption of the German 'currency reform', which was later discursively framed as the starting-point for the German economic miracle.

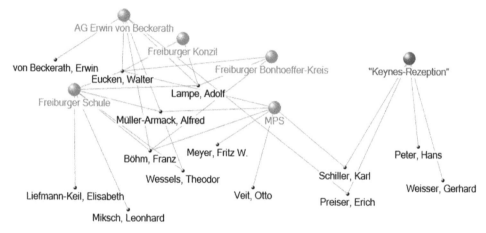

Figure 2: The Continuity of German Neoliberal Networks After Second World War

In addition to the direct influence on German post-war politics, ordoliberal economists were closely connected to international networks of the neoliberal thought collective. Four of Eucken's 'pupils' were also very early members of the MPS (Pfister, Maier, Hensel and Lutz) and seven of Eucken's eleven 'pupils' indicated in Figure 1 with a triangle, later became members of the MPS. Moreover, up to the third and fourth generation of Eucken's pupils, one can find core proponents of the German neoliberal network, for example, Hans Willgerodt, Manfred J.M. Neumann, Joachim Starbatty and Peter Oberender.

---

[39] Ptak, n 20 above.
[40] Daniela Rüther, 'Freiburger Nationalökonomen auf dem Weg in den Widerstand: Neue Erkenntnisseüber die Rolle des "Professorenausschusses" von 1939', (2013) 10 *Historisch-Politische Mitteilungen*, pp 75–94; Nils Goldschmidt, 'Die Rolle Walter Euckens im Widerstand', in: Nils Goldschmidt (ed), *Wirtschaft, Politik und Freiheit*, (Tübingen: Mohr Siebeck, 2005), pp 289–314.

To sum up, ordoliberalism, according to Ralf Ptak, developed in the interaction of three different strands of thought with a shared political will:[41] first, the Freiburg School with Eucken, Böhm and Miksch. Second, the 'sociological wing' of ordoliberalism with Rüstow and Röpke. And third, a group of practitioners, consisting of Ludwig Erhard and the long-standing editor of the newspaper *Frankfurter Allgemeine Zeitung*, Erich Welter. Alfred Müller-Armack, according to Ptak, could be ascribed to the second and third strand of ordoliberalism.[42]

B. Networks of German Neoliberalism during the 'Monetarist Turn'

A second episode in German economic history which indicates the continuous political influence of the economists organised around the infrastructure of German neoliberalism, was the period of the 'monetarist turn' in Germany in the early 1970s after a short period of 'German Keynesianism' in the late 1960s.[43] Janssen analysed the 'counter revolution in the German money theory', ie the theoretical debate of German economists on Milton Friedman's monetarist theory, and showed who had introduced monetarism into German economics.[44] Janssen concludes that 15 mainly young German economists ('the revolt of the 30-year olds'), particularly from 1970 to 1976, initiated the monetarist anti-Keynesian revolution in German economics.[45] This initiative resulted in the monetarist turn of the German *Bundesbank*, which, as first central bank worldwide, introduced the monetarist money supply target as suggested by Milton Friedman.[46] Figure 3 shows the group of economists active in the monetarist revolution, with their connections to the 'German neoliberal thought collective'.[47]

[41] Ptak, n 20 above.

[42] ibid, p 17. Jan-Otmar Hesse, in contrast, doubts that there is one homogeneous ordoliberal school at all; see Jan-Otmar Hesse, 'Der Mensch des Unternehmens und der Produktion. Foucaults Sicht auf den Ordoliberalismus und die 'Soziale Marktwirtschaft'', (2006) 2 *Zeithistorische Forschungen/Studies in Contemporary History*, available at: www.zeithistorische-forschungen.de/16126041-Hesse-2-2006. Stefan Kolev distinguishes between the ordoliberalism of the Freiburg School, and Rüstow and Röpke and the 'German neoliberalism' of Müller-Armack and Erhard; see Stefan Kolev, 'F.A. Hayek as an ordo-liberal', (2010), HWWI Research Paper, No. 5–11.

[43] The term 'German Keynesianism' indicates that Keynesianism in Germany was based upon a specific interpretation of Keynes' work. See H. Hagemann, 'Zur frühen Keynes-Rezeption der General Theory durch deutschsprachige Wirtschaftswissenschaftler', in: Harald Hagemann, Gustav Horn and Hans-Jürgen Krupp (eds), *Aus gesamtwirtschaftlicher Sicht*, (Marburg: Metropolis, 2008), pp 71–104; see, also, Pühringer, n 10 above; Arne Heise and Sebastian Thieme, 'What Happened to Heterodox Economics in Germany after the 1970s', (2015) Discussion Papers, Zentrum für Ökonomische und Soziologische Studien, No. 49.

[44] Janssen, n 31 above, p 83.

[45] ibid, p 93, See, eg, Manfred Neumann, 'Bank Liquidity and the Extended Monetary Base as Indicators of German Monetary Policy', in: Karl Brunner (ed), *Proceedings of the First KonstanzerSeminar on Monetary Theory and Monetary Policy*, (Berlin: Duncker & Humblot, 1972), pp 165–217.

[46] Herbert Giersch, Karl-Heinz Paque and Holger Schmieding, *The Fading Miracle: Four Decades of Market Economy in Germany*, (Cambridge: Cambridge University Press, 1994); Rudolf Richter, *Deutsche Geldpolitik 1948-1998*, (Tübingen: Mohr Siebeck, 1999); Feld et al, n 16 above.

[47] The seven actors not plotted in Fig 3 are Volbert Alexander, Emil-Maria Claassen, Ernst Dürr, Werner Ehrlicher, Hans-Edi Loef, Jürgen Siebke and Manfred Willms.

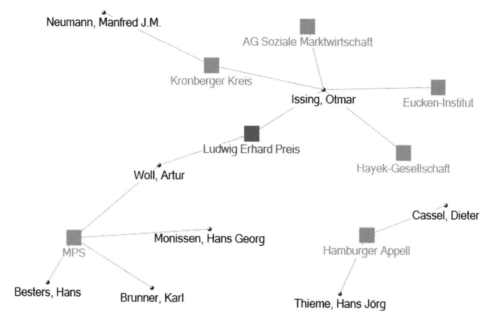

Figure 3: **Economists in German Neoliberal Networks During the Monetarist Turn in Germany**

This empirical result partly contradicts Feld et al,[48] who claim that there is no common ground of monetarism and ordoliberalism at all. At least in the common infrastructure of German neoliberalism, there are connections at a personal and institutional level.

The persistence of the influence of the economists organised around the infra-structure of German neoliberalism can, furthermore, be empirically shown as academic teacher-pupil-relationships. As indicated in Figure 4, there is a rather strong connection between the protagonists of the monetarist turn (as pupils) and the core early German neoliberal economists (as academic teachers), such as Eucken, Hensel, Welter and Müller-Armack.

Beside the group of 15 'monetarist rebels',[49] the monetarist turn of the German *Bundesbank* was also supported by the German Council of Economic Experts (GCEE), which argued in favour of a Friedman-oriented money supply target in its annual economic report (GCEE 1973).[50] It is not surprising that, in the early 1970s, after a paradigm shift in the GCEE from a Keynesian to a somewhat supply-oriented policy,[51] initiated mainly by Herbert Giersch and later his pupil Gerhard Fels in

---

[48] Feld et al, n 16 above.

[49] Janssen, n 31 above.

[50] GCEE 1973, available at: www.sachverstaendigenrat-wirtschaft.de/fileadmin/dateiablage/download/gutachten/jg72_73.pdf.

[51] Matthias Schmelzer even doubts whether there has ever been a Keynesian dominance in the GCEE; see Matthias Schmelzer, *Freiheit für die Wechselkurse. Die Ursprünge der neoliberalen Währungspolitik und die Mont Pèlerin Society*, (Marburg: Metropolis, 2010), p 164.

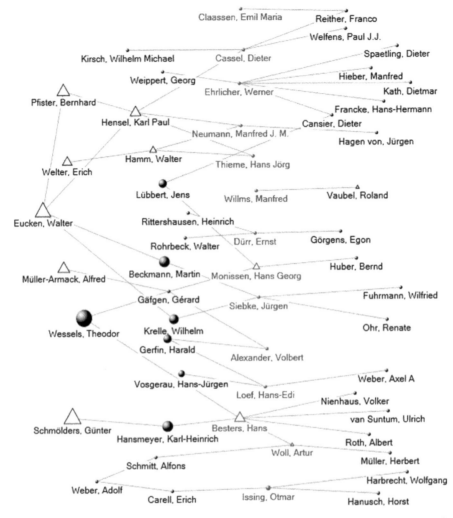

Figure 4: The Academic Roots of the Proponents of the Monetarist Turn in Germany. The 'Monetarist Rebels' are Printed in Blue, the Triangles Indicate MPS Membership

the run-up of the monetarist turn of the *Bundesbank*, a majority of at least three out of five members of the GCEE were organised in German neoliberal networks (Norbert Kloten, Olaf Sievert and Armin Gutowski).[52] The influence of German neoliberalism in the German *Bundesbank*, and later also in the ECB, manifests itself at both a theoretical and a personal level during the last decades.[53] Alberto

---

[52] Olaf Sievert, 'Vom Keynesianismus zur Angebotspolitik', in: GCEE (ed), *Vierzig Jahre Sachverständigenrat. 1963–2003*, (Wiesbaden: Mohr, 2003), pp 34–46; Rudolf Hickel, '40 Jahre Rat der 'Fünf Weisen'. Ungelöste gesamtwirtschaftliche Probleme trotz oder wegen der Sachverständigen zur Begutachtung der gesamtwirtschaftlichen Entwicklung', (2003), available at: www.memo.uni-bremen.de/docs/m2003c.pdf, last accessed 12 June 2016).

[53] Richter, n 46 above.

Alesina and Vittorio Grilli, for instance, stress that 'the institutional design of the ECB is more similar to that of the *Bundesbank* than to any other central bank of the Eurozone'.[54] Furthermore, central actors in the *Bundesbank*, for example, Othmar Issing, Hans Tietmeyer, Axel Weber and Jens Weidmann, are linked to the network of German neoliberalism via their academic background as well as via their membership in German neoliberal think tanks. At a speech at the Euro Finance Week in Frankfurt, Jürgen Stark,[55] the former president of the *Bundesbank* and an ECB Executive Board member, stressed that the work of Walter Eucken had been 'a constant source of inspiration throughout my career'. To sum up Feld et al[56] stress that the *Bundesbank*, alongside to the *Kronberger Kreis*, the GCEE, or at a personal level, Hans Werner Sinn, is coined by 'economists who argue in favour of Ordnungspolitik'. The *Kronberger Kreis* serves as one of the central nodes for the connection of the economists in German neoliberal networks, and has very close ties to economic advice institutions in Germany. Yet, the foundation of the *Kronberger Kreis* in the early 1980s reflects its political impact, because the history of this think tank is closely connected to the political upheaval, which was later called the 'neoliberal turn' in Germany.[57]

C. Networks of German Neoliberalism during the 'Neoliberal Turn'

A third important episode in German economic history, where the political impact of economists organised around the infrastructures of German neoliberalism becomes obvious is the period of the 'neoliberal turn' in Germany in the early 1980s. Jeremy Leaman,[58] for instance, argues that, although there are also several indicators of continuity,

> 1982 can still be seen as a very significant marker in the history of Germany's political economy (...) because it ushered in a period in which there was a gradual but inexorable shift in the quality of economic policy decisions, the ideological paradigm within which they were consistently framed and the global context within which nation, regional and global institutions operated.

In 1981, the Minister of Economics Otto Graf Lambsdorff (Free Democratic Party, FDP) published a seminal paper entitled 'Manifesto for market economy: concept for a policy to overcome weak growth performance and reduce unemployment'—the so-called *Lambsdorff-paper*, in which he stressed that the government interfered too

---

[54] Alberto Alesina and Vittorio Grilli, 'The European Central Bank: Reshaping Monetary Politics in Europe', (1991) NBER Working Paper no 3860.

[55] Jürgen Stark, 'Monetary, fiscal and financial stability in Europe, speech at the 11th Euro Finance Week in Frankfurt, 18 November 2008', available at: www.ecb.europa.eu/press/key/date/2008/html/sp081118_1.en.html.

[56] Feld et al, n 16 above, p 11.

[57] Mark Werding, 'Gab es eine neoliberale Wende? Wirtschaft und Wirtschaftspolitik in der Bundesrepublik Deutschland ab Mitte der 1970er Jahre', (2008) 56 *Vierteljahreshefte für Zeitgeschichte*, pp 303–321, at 312.

[58] Jeremy Leaman, *The Political Economy of Germany under Chancellors Kohl and Schröder. Decline of the German Model?*, (Oxford: Berghahn, 2009), p 5.

much in the free market and suggested radical labour market reforms, strict budget consolidation and de-regulation policies. Beside Lambsdorff, it were Otto Schlecht in particular, who was already in the Ministry of Economics under Ludwig Erhard, and Hans Tietmeyer, later president of the *Bundesbank* and one of the main initiators of the neoliberal advocacy think tank entitled 'Initiative for New Social Market Economy' (INSM) in 2000,[59] who were responsible for the content of the paper. The 'Lambsdorff-paper' marked the end of the social-liberal coalition in Germany and particularly the (Keynesian) economic concept of macroeconomic management (*'Globalsteuerung'*) and can therefore be interpreted as a politico-economic paradigm shift.[60] From the perspective of economic policy advice, the paper can be seen in the tradition of the GCCE annual report 1973–74, indicating a monetarist turn and the GCEE annual report of 1976–77, arguing for a supply-side-orientation of economic policy.[61]

The common politico-economic objective of these reform documents is also reflected in the institutional and personal connections of the members of the *Kronberger Kreis*. The *Kronberger Kreis* was founded in December 1981 as scientific advisory board to the *Frankfurter Institut* (later, *Stiftung Marktwirtschaft*) by the economist and editor of the magazine *Wirtschaftswoche*, Wolfram Engels and the entrepreneur Ludwig Eckes. The *Kronberger Kreis* was organised based upon the model of a modern American think tank, with the immediate objective of exerting influence on public opinion and the politico-economic discourse via 'organized events, publications, individual policy advice, concrete actions as well as formulated legislative texts'.[62] The initial goal of the *Kronberger Kreis* was to develop a market-oriented politico-economic programme for the forthcoming *Bundestag* elections in 1984. After the publication of the *Lambsdorff-paper* and the end of the social-liberal coalition—which was later termed as the 'ordo-political awakening of Germany' by Michael Eilfort,[63] an executive board member of the *Stiftung Marktwirtschaft*, the *Stiftung Marktwirtschaft* and the *Kronberger Kreis* successfully tried to influence the public debate with position papers and short statements. Over the next decades, during the chancellorship of Helmut Kohl and later also Gerhard Schröder, members of the *Kronberger Kreis*[64] held core positions in or close ties to central German economic policy institutions, for example, the German Ministry of Economics

[59] Christoph Butterwegge, 'Rechfertigung, Maßnahmen und Folgeneinerneoliberalen (Sozial-)Politik', in: Christoph Butterwegge, Bettina Lösch and Ralf Ptak (eds), *Kritik des Neoliberalismus*, (Wiesbaden: VS Verlag für Sozialwissenschaften, 2007), pp 135–213, Rudolf Speth, 'Advokatorische Think Tanks und die Politisierung des Marktplatzes der Ideen', (2006), *Friedrich Ebert Stiftung, betrifft: Bürgergesellschaft 24*.

[60] Leaman, n 58 above.

[61] Sievert, n 52 above; Feld et al, n 16 above.

[62] Stiftung Marktwirtschaft 2015, 'Mehr Mut zum Markt ...', available at: www.stiftung-marktwirtschaft.de/wirtschaft/kronberger-kreis.html.

[63] Michael Eilfort, 'Begrüßung', in: Stiftung Marktwirtschaft (ed), *25 Jahre Stiftung Marktwirtschaft und Kronberger Kreis*, (Berlin: Bloch & Co, 2007), pp 6–9.

[64] Most members of the *Kronberger Kreis* are economists; some are also legal scholars, which is another similarity to the early Freiburg School.

(Eekhoff), the *Bundesbank* (Issing, Neumann), governmental commissions (Möschel, Donges, Raffelhüschen) and the monopoly commission (Möschel, von Weizsäcker, Hellwig, Haucap). Moreover, members of the *Kronberger Kreis* were very active in economic policy advice in the GCEE as well as in the Scientific Advisory Boards of the German Ministries of Finance and Economics, and thus in a central position in the networks of German neoliberalism (Figure 5). Referring to the multi-dimensional political and partly public influence of economists of the *Kronberger Kreis*, as well as their dense connections in a network of German neoliberalism, Ralf Ptak denotes the *Kronberger Kreis* as 'an influential market-radical elite network'.[65]

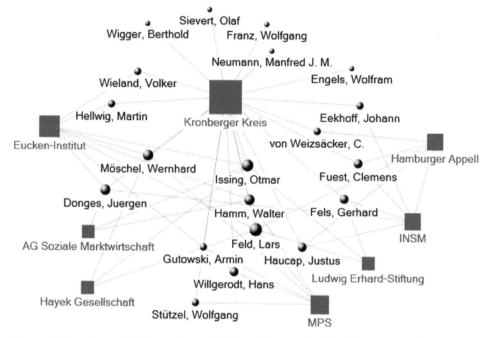

Figure 5: 'Kronberger Kreis' as a Central Node in German Neoliberal Networks of Economists

The immediate influence of the *Kronberger Kreis*, which also indicates the close ideological connection between the intention of the Lambsdorff-paper and the foundation of the think tank, is reflected in the following quotation from a speech by Otto Lambsdorff on the occasion of the 25th anniversary of the foundation of the *Kronberger Kreis*: 'I think, I simply copied from the *Kronberger Kreis*; this was the easiest way, because it was always right.'[66]

[65] Ralf Ptak, 'Grundlagen des Neoliberalismus', in: Butterwegge, Lösch and Ptak (eds), *Kritik des Neoliberalismus*, n 59 above, pp 13–86, at 79.
[66] Otto Graf Lambsdorff, 'Rückenwind für Reformen nutzen', in: Stiftung Marktwirtschaft (ed), *25 Jahre Stiftung Marktwirtschaft und Kronberger Kreis*, (Berlin: Bloch & Co, 2007), pp 37–45, at 39.

IV. CONCLUSIONS

The central contribution of this chapter is an empirical analysis of the role of ordo-liberal economists, organised in networks of German neoliberalism in the course of German economic policy during WWII. Using the conception of a German neoliberal thought collective, organised around the Mont Pèlerin Society, I have demonstrated the theoretical similarities between ordoliberalism as a German variety of neoliberal-ism and (American) neoliberalism and the interconnections of German economists to a neoliberal thought collective at a personal as well as at an institutional level in three important historical episodes.

Building on this twofold theoretical and methodological approach, this chapter shows that ordoliberal economists had a central position in the German politico-economic power structure. As early as with the foundation of the German Federal Republic in the late 1940s, and later during the 'monetarist turn' of the German *Bundesbank* in the 1970s and the 'neoliberal turn' in German economic politics in the early 1980s, economists connected via the infrastructures of German neoliberal-ism held key political positions, which allowed them to (re-) establish the economic imaginary of Social Market Economy in its German neoliberal interpretation.

Hence, the final conclusion of this chapter is that a densely connected infrastruc-ture of German neoliberalism, organised around German neoliberal economists, think tanks, policy advice institutions and economic research institutes over many decades were able to build up a formative influence on German economic policies. The continuity of German neoliberalism as a guiding principle for German economic policy, in turn, also explains the importance of ordoliberal-oriented policies in the aftermath of the global financial crisis of 2007–8 in Germany and Europe.

Section III

The Ordering Functions of Law in the Ordoliberal Tradition

10

Debunking the Myth of the Ordoliberal Influence on Post-war European Integration

ANGELA WIGGER

ABSTRACT

References to ordoliberal influence in the context of German and European Community/Union economic regulations, and competition rules in particular, are frequently made by scholars and politicians alike. Moreover, ordoliberalism is often conflated with the German postwar social market economy, and hence portrayed as distinctively different from neoliberalism. This chapter argues that the role of ordo-liberals and ordoliberal thinking tends to be exaggerated: ordoliberalism should not be mistaken with the notion of social market economy, nor seen as dissimilar from neoliberalism. Moreover, the chapter demonstrates that the role of ordoliberals in the formulation and subsequent enforcement of competition rules both in Germany and at European Community level has been marginal at best.

I. INTRODUCTION

CAPITALIST COMPETITION IS often praised as a stimulus for economic growth and for increasing the overall well-being of humanity. The rationale that competition functions as a welfare enhancer for society at large has a longstanding legacy within the trajectory of European integration. Rules on competition were first included in the 1951 Treaty of Paris, establishing the European Coal and Steel Community (ECSC). In the subsequent 1957 Treaty of Rome, which led to the European Economic Community (EEC), the efficacy of competition was highlighted in the preambles. Accordingly, the establishment of 'a system ensuring that competition in the internal market is not distorted' (Article 3(f)) received an almost constitutional status. The centrality of capitalist competition and competition rules since the beginning of the European integration project is often linked to the influence of ordoliberals from the Freiburg School in Germany, a group of economists and lawyers who developed a theory of 'comprehensive' competition control in the 1930s. Ordoliberals are also often portrayed as the intellectual founding fathers of the German post-war social order of *Soziale Marktwirtschaft*, the social market economy.

In the absence of English translations, ordoliberalism has long been discussed exclusively by German-speaking scholars. In the literature on Community competition rules, scholars talked about 'the Germans' being 'obsessed with reproducing the German model and the German virtues of competition policy at European level'.[1] References to ordoliberalism underwent a revival with David Gerber's (1998) seminal book *Law and Competition in Twentieth Century Europe: Protecting Prometheus*, which assigned a central role to ordoliberal doctrines when explaining why European competition provisions eventually looked so distinct from US antitrust rules—despite the marked presence of US legal experts in the immediate aftermath of the Second World War. The alleged influence of ordoliberal thinking on EU competition rules has been reiterated.[2] Or, as Christian Joerges has correctly observed, ordoliberalism is *'en vogue'*.[3] Scholars tend to portray ordoliberalism as a moderate and pragmatic school of thought, particularly when compared to the 'market fundamentalism often associated with neoliberalism today'.[4] Discussions about ordoliberalism being distinct from neoliberalism particularly flared up with the heyday of Third Way politics in the 1990s, evoking the image of a capitalism with a human face where capitalist competition is 'fair' and society harmoniously embedded in the economy. It is also in this vein that ordoliberalism has been equated

---

[1] See Stephen Wilks and Lee McGowan, 'Competition Policy in the European Union: Creating a Federal Agency?', in: Bruce Doern and Stephen Wilks (eds), *Comparative Competition Policy: National Institutions in a Global Market*, (Oxford: Clarendon Press, 1996).

[2] See, eg, Oliver Budzinski, 'Pluralism of Competition Policy Paradigms and the Call for Regulatory Diversity', Volkswirtschaftliche Beiträge Philipps-Universität Marburg, 14/2003, idem, 'Monoculture versus Diversity in Competition Economics', (2008) *Cambridge Journal of Economics*, pp 295–324; Hannah L. Buxbaum, 'German Legal Culture and the Globalization of Competition Law: A Historical Perspective on the Expansion of Private Antitrust Enforcement', (2006) 23 *Berkeley Journal of International Law*, pp 474–95; Nicola Giocoli, 'Competition versus Property Rights: American Antitrust Law, the Freiburg School, and the Early Years of European Competition Policy', (2009) 5 *Journal of Competition Law and Economics*, pp 747–86; Doris Hildebrand, 'The European School in EC Competition Law, (2002) 25 *World Competition*, pp 3–23; Jens Hölscher and Johannes Stephan, 'Competition Policy in Central and Eastern Europe in the Light of EU Accession', (2004) 42 *Journal of Common Market Studies*, pp 321–45; Bruce Lyons, 'An Economic Assessment of European Commission Merger Control: 1958–2007', in: Xavier Vives (ed), *Competition Policy in the EU Fifty Years on from the Treaty of Rome*, (Oxford: Oxford University Press, 2009), pp 1–17; Imelda Maher, 'Re-imagining the Story of European Competition Law', (2000) 20 *Oxford Journal of Legal Studies*, pp 155–66; Wernhard Möschel, 'The Proper Scope of Government Viewed from an Ordoliberal Perspective: The Example of Competition Policy', (2001) 157 *Journal of Institutional and Theoretical Economics*, pp 3–13; Okeoghene Odudu, *The Boundaries of EC Competition Law: The Scope of Article 81*, (Oxford: Oxford University Press, 2006); Magnus Ryner, 'Europe's Ordoliberal Iron Cage: Critical Political Economy from Germany, (2015) 1 *New Political Economy*, pp 233–257; and Conor C. Talbot, 'Ordoliberalism and Balancing Competition Goals in the Development of the European Union', (2016) 61 *Antitrust Bulletin*, pp 264–89.

[3] See Christian Joerges, 'What is Left of the European Economic Constitution II?', (2013) Paper presented at the conference entitled European Crises from Weimar until Today: History—Economy—Politics—Law, 11–12 December 2013, Copenhagen Business School; also published as 'What is Left of the European Constitution II? From Pyrrhic Victory to Cannae Defeat', in: Poul F. Kjaer and Niklas Olsen, *Critical Theories of Crisis in Europe: From Weimar to the Euro*, (Lanham MD: Rowman & Littlefield, 2016), pp 143–160.

[4] See Taylor C. Boas and Jordan Gans-Morse, 'Neoliberalism: From New Liberal Philosophy to Anti-liberal Slogan', (2008) 44 *Studies in Comparative International Development*, pp 137–61.

with the elusive German social market economy.[5] However, studies that bluntly cat-egorise EC/EU competition rules as an artefact of ordoliberal influence often fail to substantiate this claim. Moreover, studies that interpret the German social market economy as an ordoliberal contribution to the creation of a myth—a myth that cor-roborates an idealised vision of the past and that validates a particular historical understanding of the present. The alleged influence of German ordoliberals after the Second World War (WWII) in the field of German and Community-level institution-building tends to be exaggerated, while the social dimension within ordoliberalism has been misconstrued by ordoliberals and scholarly accounts alike. This chapter seeks to debunk these myths and to offer a more nuanced understanding by tracing the role of ordoliberals first in the context of Germany's social market economy and second in the adoption of competition rules both in Germany and at Community level. Certainly, the ideological positions and theories of the Freiburg scholars may have influenced a range of politicians in Germany, as well as German politicians involved in the trajectory of European integration; however, a diligent translation of ordoliberal templates into regulatory arrangements never happened. In particular, the substantive content of EC/EU competition rules reflects, at best, a very much watered-down version of ordoliberal notions. Ordoliberals envisaged a market with relatively small and equally-matched players, and strongly advocated the contain-ment of economic power. Had ordoliberalism been taken seriously in the aftermath of the WWII, there would be no large corporations in Europe today.

The chapter is organised as follows: Section II discusses and historicises the central premises of ordoliberalism and the utopia of ordered capitalist competition. Section III offers a critique of the ordoliberal notion of capitalist competition being a generic wealth enhancer for society at large, and shows that ordoliberals had a rather primitive understanding of social welfare provision. Section IV debunks the myth of ordoliberalism being distinct from neoliberalism, while Section V debunks the myth of ordoliberal influence on German and Community-level competition rules in the post-war era. The conclusions summarise the main findings and elaborate further on the alleged influence of ordoliberals.

II. THE ORDOLIBERAL UTOPIA OF AN ORDERED CAPITALIST COMPETITION

The group of economists and lawyers that met at the University of Freiburg in Breisgau in the 1920s and early 1930s, most notably, the economist Walter Eucken (1891–1950) and the lawyers Franz Böhm (1895–1977) and Hans Grossman-Dörth (1894–1944), as well as their assistants, Alexander Rüstow (1885–1963) and Wilhelm Röpke (1899–1966), shared the vocation to establish *Ordnung* (order) after years of political turmoil and hyperinflation during the Weimar Republic, and the successive mass unemployment and pauperisation of large parts of society during

---

[5] See, eg, Razeen Sally, 'Ordoliberalism and the Social Market: Classical Political Economy from Germany', (1996) 1 *New Political Economy*, pp 233–257, and Brigitte Young, 'Introduction: The Hijack-ing of German Ordoliberalism', (2015) 2 *European Review of International Studies*, pp 7–15.

the Great Depression.[6] In a political climate of creeping protectionism already in the years prior to the Great Depression, ordoliberals were convinced that free-market principles would lead to a just and harmonious socio-economic order and enhance the economic well-being of society in its entirety. Their ideas evolved at a time when unrestrained liberalism was almost universally rejected. Ordoliberals also criticised the *laissez-faire* liberalism of classical and neoclassical economists in the tradition of Adam Smith (1776), who had assigned almost a metaphysical status to the 'invisible hand' of the market. In marked contrast, ordoliberals reserved a strong role for the state in creating order. As Franz Böhm wrote, a market free from state intervention may be free, but is not ordered.[7] To establish order, ordoliberals suggested an economic constitution in parallel to a political constitution. Upon this basis, more fundamental economic institutional choices and substantive market-ordering principles had to be derived. Somewhat paradoxically to the notion of a strong state, the role of the state as a stage-manager also had to be contained. The state had to act according to the rule of law without interfering with decisions about supply and demand, producer and consumer choice, price mechanisms and resource allocation. In the view of Walter Eucken, 'the nature of state activity should influence the form of the economy, but not amount to state planning and control of the economic process'.[8] The state, instead, had to provide basic institutions, such as a monetarist policy conducted by an independent national bank, private property rights, contractual freedom and free trade, and, most importantly, the state had to guarantee a competitive economic environment.

The state had to be omnipresent in securing capitalist competition. Ordoliberals were convinced that competition did not evolve naturally, but had to be carefully cultivated and policed by the state as the *Hüter der Wettbewerbsordnung*, the guardian of the competitive market order. In no domain other than competition was the state to be equipped with more discretionary powers. The state had to ensure the proviso of *vollständiger Wettbewerb*—complete competition, a hypothetical state of affairs in which no corporate entity has the power to coerce the conduct of others.[9] The ordoliberal ideal of complete competition closely resembles the stylised neoclassical imaginary state of perfect competition in which allegedly powerless capitalists cannot achieve further welfare gains, as if capitalist markets can be stationary. The envisaged ordered competitive structure consisted of equally-matched companies that would engage in economic exchange with each other and with consumers upon a voluntary basis, while driving down prices to marginal production costs.[10] Economic concentration in the form of large corporations was deemed a major distortion to the economic order. According to Walter Eucken, all the relevant

---

[6] See, also, Angela Wigger, 'Competition for Competitiveness: The Politics of Transformation of the EU Competition Regime', Dissertation, 2008, Department of Political Science, Vrije Universiteit, Amsterdam.

[7] See Franz Böhm, *Die Ordnung der Wirtschaft als geschichtliche Aufgabe und rechtsschöpferische Leistung*, (Stuttgart: W. Kohlhammer, 1937), p 107.

[8] Walter Eucken, *The Unsuccessful Age or the Pains of Economic Progress*, (London: William Hodge and Company, 1951), p 95.

[9] Walter Eucken, *Wozu Nationalökonomie?*, (Leipzig: Felix MeinerVerlag, 1938), Ch III.

[10] Böhm, n 7 above, p 105.

fields of economic law, ranging from patent to corporate law, shareholder rights and liability schemes, tax and trade policy, needed to be subordinated to the maintenance of minimised economic power.[11] To achieve this, Eucken considered the monopoly office as indispensable as the highest court.[12] The monopoly office had to be equipped with the power to prosecute price-fixing and market-allocating cartels, and, importantly, have the right to de-concentrate excessive private economic power and to split up oligopolies or monopolies into smaller components. Importantly, the monopoly office had to be independent, and hence insulated from partisan interests and political opponents, as well as rent-seeking market players trying to get hold of state power and change the rules to their benefit. According to ordoliberal Franz Böhm, 'a government is constantly faced with a considerable temptation to meet the contradictory demands of pressure groups' which, in the pursuit of their narrow objectives, would ignore the common welfare of society.[13]

The ordoliberal aversion to economic concentration was not unique at that time. The Harvard School in the US also propagated a 'polypolistic' market structure in which firms have small market shares and thus little market power.[14] Louis Brandeis, author of *The Curse of Bigness* (1934),[15] and one of the key Harvard School protagonists, was a fervent advocate of diluted market power, promoting 'a society of small, independent, decentralised businesses' and keeping 'economic power dispersed'.[16] Both the Freiburg and the Harvard School developed their theories in response to a long-lasting phase of monopoly capitalism. In the US, capitalists had formed giant trusts or other collusive ties to supersede competitive pressures arising from the lingering overproduction in a time of rapid industrialisation. Similarly, in Germany, cartels and economic concentrations started to emerge in the capital intensive, large-scale heavy industries of steel, iron, and coal during the Second Industrial Revolution, lasting from 1870 to 1913.[17] In 1905, there were 400 cartels in Germany encompassing 12,000 companies, and five years later, the number of cartels had almost doubled.[18] In the 1920s and 1930s, cartel formation in Germany, but also in other parts of Europe, had its heyday, encompassing virtually every sector of industry. As part of the liberal trade regime at that time, many of these

[11] Walter Eucken, *Grundlagen der Nationalökonomie*, 9, (Berlin: Springer Verlag, [1940] 1989), in: V.J. Vanberg, 'The Freiburg School: Walter Eucken and Ordoliberalism', Freiburg Discussion Papers on Constitutional Economics 2004/11, p 14.

[12] David J. Gerber, *Law and Competition in Twentieth Century Europe: Protecting Prometheus*, (Oxford: Oxford University Press, 1998), p 254.

[13] Franz Böhm, *Rule of Law in a Market Economy*, (London: Macmillan, 1989), in: Alan T. Peacock and Hans Willgerodt (eds), *Germany's Social Market Economy: Origins and Evolution*, (London: Palgrave Macmillan, 1989), pp 46–67, at 66.

[14] John M. Clark, 'Toward a Concept of Workable Competition', (1940) 30 *The American Economic Review*, pp 241–56, at 241.

[15] Louis Brandeis, *The Curse of Bigness*, (New York, Viking Press, 1934).

[16] Eleanor M. Fox and Robert Pitofsky, 'United States', in: E.M. Graham and J.D. Richardson (eds), *Global Competition Policy*, (Washington D.C.: Institute for International Economics, 1997), p 236.

[17] Marie-Laure Djelic, 'Does Europe Mean Americanization? The Case of Competition', (2002) 6 *Competition and Change*, pp 233–250.

[18] Harm G. Schröter, 'Cartelization and Decartelization in Europe, 1870–1995: Rise and Decline of an Economic Institution', (1996) 25 *The Journal of European Economic History*, pp 129–153.

cartels exhibited a strong international dimension, transgressing national borders. At the outbreak of the Second World War, about 40% of world trade was controlled by cartels. Thus, ordoliberals sought to break with the centralised economic and political power of the Weimar Republic and later the Nazis, in which cartels and monopolies formed an integral part of the totalitarian state apparatus. The Nazi government had secured the industrial élite with the necessary profits through guaranteed procurement contracts and the re-distribution of allocated Jewish industries and the industries of the annexed territories. Industrial élites, in turn, provided the indispensable production of military equipment, financial and political support. The closed market structures of the Third Reich eliminated outside competition and the industrial élite administered cartels in an authoritarian fashion, marginalising the position of the German *Mittelstand*. After the war, Walter Eucken wrote a declaration entitled *Über die Gesamtrichtung der Wirtschaftspolitik* (1946) in which he strongly recommend *Konzernentflechtung*, the immediate dissolution of large corporations, and the overall break-up of the cartels and syndicates.[19]

Ordoliberals did not, however, hold identical views with regard to the stringency of competition and the interventionist role of the state in correcting uncompetitive conduct. While Hans Grossmann-Dörth fiercely condemned the way in which large corporations and cartels created their own legal rules,[20] Wilhelm Röpke saw room for exceptions, particularly if intercompany collaboration served the rationalisation, specialisation or diffusion of technology and research.[21] Nevertheless, ordoliberals shared the conviction that competitive market structures were a cultural masterpiece. As will be argued in the next section, the persuasion that a competitive market is key to economic freedom, and a variety of other socio-economic goals, including societal cohesion, is utterly naïve and flawed.

III. DEBUNKING THE MYTH OF THE ORDOLIBERAL COMPETITIVE MARKET ORDER AND THE SOCIAL MARKET ECONOMY

The ordoliberal understanding of competition as a welfare enhancing mechanism and as a motor for societal cohesion completely ignores the contradictory logics of capital accumulation. Ordoliberals did not ask *for whom* welfare would increase as a result of competition, and simply assumed *some* general abstract welfare *somewhere* in the system—without distinguishing between capital owners and those that have to sell their labour. Rather than facilitating social cohesion, capitalist competition disunites more than it unites. As a social relation that is essentially antagonising, capitalist competition erects hierarchies in wealth and power, and pits not only capital against capital and capital against labour, but also labour against labour. Ordoliberals somewhat blindly associated the freedom to compete with broader

---

[19] See, also, Walter Eucken and Paul Hensel, *Grundsätze der Wirtschaftspolitik*, (Tübingen: Mohr und Siebeck, 1952), p 334.
[20] See Hans Grossmann-Dörth, *Selbstgeschaffenes Recht der Wirtschaft und staatliches Recht*, (Tübingen: Walter Eucken Institut/Mohr Siebeck, 1933).
[21] Wilhelm Röpke, *Economics of a Free Society*, (Grove City PA: Libertarian Press, 1994), p 172.

notions of political freedom and individual self-determination. As Marx wrote in *Grundrisse*:

> [i]t is not individuals that are set free by free competition; it is, rather, capital which is set free.[22]

Capitalist competition 'is nothing more than the way in which many capitals force the inherent determinants of capital upon one another and upon themselves'.[23] Through the coercive laws of competition, capitalists are compelled to re-invest accumulated surplus capital to create even more surplus. As not to compete means to perish, capitalists that accumulate more quickly tend to drive those out of business that accumulate at a slower rate, while the elimination of laggards inevitably strengthens the 'winners' and re-enforces their advantages, notably those able to set the (price) standards of competition for others. Ordoliberalism, like all forms of neoliberalism, was premised on a supply side oriented view, perceiving labour merely as a cost factor. The fact that capitalist competition deflates labour has been disregarded. As Marx noted,

> [t]he battle of competition is fought by cheapening of commodities. The cheapness of commodities depends, all other circumstances remaining the same, on the productiveness of labour [...].[24]

Thus, to remain profitable and stay in production, capitalists constantly have to enhance the productivity of labour and to cheapen labour as a way to undercut the prices of competitors.[25]

Ordoliberalism also reached beyond economic spheres. Based upon the notion of the *Interdependenz der Ordnungen*, the interdependency of orders, ordoliberals also assigned an important role to churches, schools and the media, as additional ordering institutions next to the state; however, the hierarchy of the different orders was unequivocal: all social spheres had to give way to the pre-eminence of the state-ordered competitive market. Ordoliberals believed that the state-controlled order of complete competition would reduce social inequality automatically, and that supplementary social provisions were not necessary. Thus, despite envisaging a strong role for the state, ordoliberals foresaw no re-distributive role for the state, and paid scant attention to realms *other* than the economy. Nonetheless, ordoliberalism is sometimes mistaken with the political programme of *Soziale Marktwirtschaft*, the social market economy of post-war Germany.[26] Even Foucault relegated

---

[22] Karl Marx, *Grundrisse*, (London: Penguin Classics, [1939] 1973), p 651.

[23] ibid, p 650.

[24] Karl Marx, *Capital*, Vol 1, (Moscow: Progress Publishers, [1887] 1965), p 626.

[25] Angela Wigger and Hubert Buch-Hansen, 'Competition, the Global Crisis and Alternatives to Neoliberal Capitalism. A Critical Engagement with Anarchism', (2013) 35 *A Journal of Politics and Culture*, pp 604–626.

[26] Ralf Ptak, 'Neoliberalism in Germany: Revisiting the Ordoliberal Foundations of the Social Market Economy', in: Philip Mirowski and Dieter Plewhe (eds), *The Road from Mont Pèlerin: The Making of the Neoliberal Thought*, (Harvard MA: Harvard University Press, 1989); Viktor J. Vanberg, 'The Freiburg School: Walter Eucken and Ordoliberalism', Freiburg Discussion Papers on Constitutional Economics, 2004/11; N. Goldschmidt, 'Alfred Müller-Armack and Ludwig Erhard: Social Market Liberalism', Freiburg Discussion Papers on Constitutional Economics, 12; Nils Goldschmidt and Herman

German ordoliberalism to the notion of social market economy in his lecture series on neoliberalism.[27] The term 'social market economy' was coined by Alfred Müller-Armack (1901–1978), Professor of Economics and Cultural Sociology at the University of Münster, member of the *Nationalsozialistische Deutsche Arbeiterpartei* (NSDAP), and later State Secretary in the Ministry of Economic Affairs, to denote a strong role of the state as a guarantor of social justice and the human functioning of the market. Müller-Armack's conception of social market economy came to form part of the political programme of the conservative Christian Democratic Union (CDU), the political party of the middle class. With the support of the Liberals (FDP), the CDU pushed for a free market with a social welfare tint in the hope of generating similar political support to that of the political left (see *Düsseldorfer Leitsätze*, 15 July 1949). A key figure in this was Ludwig Erhard (1897–1977), Minister of Economics from 1949 to 1963 under Chancellor Konrad Adenauer, and Chancellor himself from 1963 to 1966. The title of his book *Wohlstand für Alle* (1957)—'Prosperity for All'—became his political slogan. Erhard, however, never considered himself an exponent of the Freiburg School or as the executor of their ideas. According to his logic, welfare and economic growth stemmed from large corporations being able to reap the benefits of economies of scale and scope production, and consequently higher wages.[28] 'Prosperity for All' thus had to be realised through Fordist accumulation structures.

Ordoliberals were very active in disseminating their ideas to a broader public and had a clear programmatic vision: they signed the *Ordo Manifesto* of 1936; launched the journal *ORDO*, which became the main outlet for ordoliberal ideas; they wrote books, pamphlets, and newspaper articles, particular in the *Frankfurter Allgemeine Zeitung* until the Nazis banned the newspaper in 1943. Despite their public presence, ordoliberal views were far from hegemonic in post-war Germany. Yet, a range of ordoliberals reproduced and supported the discourse of social market economy, which seemed far more suited to appeasing antagonistic forces with strong anti-capitalist convictions and aligning them with the workings of a capitalist market economy than the notion of an ordered market economy. Alexander Rüstow, for example, was the chair of the *Aktionsgemeinschaft Soziale Marktwirtschaft* in Tübingen, the Action Group for Social Market Economy from 1955 to 1961; and Walter Eucken proclaimed, in 1952, that social security and social justice were the

Rauchenschwandtner, 'The Philosophy of Social Market Economy: Michel Foucault's Analysis of Ordoliberalism', Freiburg Discussion Papers on Constitutional Economics 2007/4; Joachim Zweynert, 'Shared Mental Models, Catch-up Development and Economic Policy-making: The Case of Germany after World War II and its Significance for Contemporary Russia', Hamburgisches Welt-Wirtschafts-Archiv (HWWA) Discussion Papers 2004, p 288; Keith Tribe, 'Ordoliberalism and the Social Market Economy', (2007) 49 *The Society for the History of Economic Thought*, pp 155–160; Oliver M. Hartwich, 'Neoliberalism: The Genesis of a Political Swearword', CIS Occasional Paper 114, 2009.

[27] Thomas Lemke, 'The Birth of Bio-bolitics: Michel Foucault's Lecture at the Collège De France on Neoliberal Governmentality', (2001) 30 *Economy and Society*, pp 190–207: 197; Goldschmidt and Rauchenschwandtner, n 26 above.

[28] Patrizia Commun, 'Erhards Bekehrungzum Ordoliberalismus: Die grundlegende Bedeutung des wirtschaftspolitischen Diskurses in Umbruchszeiten', Freiburg Discussion Papers on Constitutional Economics 2004/4.

greatest concerns of the time.[29] However, prior to that, Eucken had considered the semantic linkage of the 'social' and 'market economy' to be a hybrid compromise that was contradictory and unstable, 'as if two conductors with two orchestras play in the same concert hall, until one gives way to the other'.[30] This view was also echoed by Friedrich August von Hayek,[31] one of the most famous proponents of neoliberalism, who considered 'social market economy' to be a 'weasel word'—referring to the characteristic skill of the weasel to 'empty an egg without leaving a visible sign'. He argued, alongside ordoliberals, that *any* form of state-led social intervention would result in an unproductive economy. Although some ordoliberals—in contrast to von Hayek—had accounted for some minimal standards of social welfare schemes to alleviate acute poverty and misfortunes, the fact remains that ordoliberals had painstakingly little to say about social welfare policies.[32] According to Philip Manow,[33] ordoliberals were even among the most vigorous opponents of the re-construction of the Bismarckian welfare state. Hence, ordoliberals, at best, merely adopted the notion of the social market economy as part of a foundational myth.[34]

IV. DEBUNKING THE MYTH OF ORDOLIBERALISM BEING DISTINCT FROM NEOLIBERALISM

Walter Eucken, one of the main ordoliberal protagonists, vehemently refused to be called a neoliberal, and claimed that ordoliberalism was equally far away from the free market economy as it was from the planned economy.[35] Likewise, Alexander Rüstow published an article entitled 'Between capitalism and communism' in *ORDO* in 1949, where he positioned ordoliberalism in the middle ground between liberalism and socialism. Ordoliberalism, however, is not distinct from neoliberalism. To the contrary, ordoliberals belong to many early architects of neoliberalism.[36] Neoliberalism did not emanate from a single source, but consists of a plural set of ideas that have unfolded over time through polycentric controversies from within its ideological realm as well as from outside critiques.[37] Neoliberalism, rather than being static, evolved and changed over time, both in terms of theory and in its actual manifestation. Neoliberalism has never become manifest in a pure, prototypical form, as it is unattainable in reality. As Jamie Peck poignantly put it,

---

[29] Gerber, n 12 above, p 37.

[30] Eucken, n 11 above.

[31] Friedrich August von Hayek, *The Fatal Conceit: The Errors of Socialism*, (Chicago IL: University of Chicago Press, 1988), pp 116–17.

[32] See, also, Christian Joerges, 'Sozialstaatlichkeit in Europe? A Conflict-of-laws Approach to the Law of the EU and the Proceduralization of Constitutionalisation', (2009) 10 *German Law Journal*, pp 335–360, and idem, n 3 above.

[33] See, also, Philip Manow, Ch 19 in this volume.

[34] See Josef Hien, Ch 16 in this volume, and Sally, n 5 above.

[35] Gerber, n 12 above, p 236.

[36] See, also, Thomas Biebricher, Ch 6 in this volume.

[37] Dieter Plewhe, 'Introduction' in: Philip Mirowski and Dieter Plewhe (eds), *The Road from Mont Pèlerin: The Making of the Neoliberal Thought Collective*, (Harvard MA: Harvard University Press, 2006), pp 1–43.

the very impossibility of realising a free market repeatedly energises the neoliberal political project,[38] neoliberalism works as a frontal ideological programme that is unfinished and that always collides antagonistically with the existing institutional regulatory landscapes and other ideologies. In the words of Peck,[39] neoliberalism is an 'ideological parasite' that 'both occupies and draws energy from its various host organisms'.

Neoliberalism was never about *laissez-faire*, but always reserved a very active role for the state in the provision of extensive regulatory regimes that ensure the reproduction of capitalism; and yet, at the same time, the state is continuously blamed for distorting the assumed market equilibrium. In ordoliberalism, we find the selfsame tension between the role of the state as the creator of order and its role as the guarantor of economic freedom. As the label 'ordo'-liberalism suggests, establishing order enjoyed clear primacy above economic freedom, which is why ordoliberalism is sometimes considered liberal 'only in the very limited sense'.[40] However, as Karl Polanyi reminds us, a self-regulating liberal capitalist economy without a state is a stark utopia.[41] The continued accumulation of capital relies upon coercive state practices to succumb anti-capitalist oppositional social forces. Ordoliberalism is hence as liberal as any other type of liberalism can be. The type of liberalism promoted by ordoliberalism needs, instead, to be seen as a particular form of authoritarian neoliberalism.[42] The economic constitution envisaged by ordoliberals had to delineate the economic realm, and thus limit political interference into how the economy was governed, ultimately rendering a democratic choice on how to organise the economy impossible. The ordoliberal conception of the state was premised on a technocratic and rule-bound executive state that would preserve a de-politicised economy in which the free play of the capitalist market is the main driver and allocator of wealth in society, and in which the economic realm would be shielded from popular opposition.

Ordoliberals were actively involved in neoliberal circles and formed part of the neoliberal think tank, entitled the *Mont Pèlerin Society*, founded by Friedrich von Hayek in 1947, and named after the Swiss mountain of Mont Pèlerin. The *Mont Pèlerin Society* was devoted to the diffusion and development of Hayekian ideas.[43] Even though von Hayek had also worked at the Freiburg University, he and his disciples never supported the ordoliberal idea of strong state institutions that would correct the workings of the market and curb the concentration of economic power.[44] The *Walter Eucken Institute* founded by Ludwig Erhard in 1954 and sponsored

---

[38] Jamie Peck, 'Remaking *laissez-faire*', (2008) 32 *Progress in Human Geography*, pp 3–43, at 33.

[39] idem, 'Explaining (with) neoliberalism', (2013) 1 *Territory, Politics, Governance*, pp 132–157, at 144.

[40] See Tribe, n 26 above, pp 155–160, at 158.

[41] Karl Polanyi, *The Great Transformation: The Political and Economic Origins of our Time*, (Boston MA: Beacon Press, [1944] 1992).

[42] Ian Bruff, 'Neoliberalism and Authoritarianism', in: Simon Springer, Kean Birch and Julie MacLeavy (eds), *The Handbook of Neoliberalism*, (Abingdon: Routledge, 2016), pp 107–17; see, also, Niklas Poulantzas, *State, Power, Socialism*, (London: Verso, [1978] 2014).

[43] Plewhe, n 37 above.

[44] Vanberg, n 26 above.

by the *Commerzbank*, nonetheless came to form part of the *Mont Pèlerin Society*'s institutional machinery. Ironically, the *Walter Eucken Institute* is foremost devoted to the work of Friedrich August von Hayek, while Eucken's legacy of books and unpublished works has been left to his family, who founded the *Walter-Eucken-Archive*.[45] Rumour has it that there is not a single monograph by or on Walter Eucken in the Institute, while contributions both by von Hayek or on von Hayek's work are countless.[46] The subordinate position of Walter Eucken is also reflected by the fact that, until recently, the Institute's entry hall only displayed a portrait of von Hayek.[47]

V. DEBUNKING THE MYTH OF ORDOLIBERAL INFLUENCE ON GERMAN AND EC/EU COMPETITION RULES

As part of the de-nazification by the US and its allies after the war, a range of eminent ordoliberals successfully ascended from their enclave in Freiburg and assumed leadership positions or became consultants, advising on the economic policy-planning of post-war West Germany. For example, Walter Eucken gave a range of advisory opinions to the Allied Forces on the economic transition in 1946 and 1947; and Franz Böhm became a Member of the *Bundestag* during the period 1951–1961. Under Böhm's auspices, the *Wissenschaflicher Beirat*, the Academic Advisory Council, was established in 1947 and was entrusted with the task of advising the government on the development of economic policies. Notwithstanding this, ordoliberal ideas were neither codified in the competition rules of post-war Germany, nor, as will be shown below, in the emerging European integration project.[48]

The US Occupation Forces commissioned Böhm to advise on the adoption of competition rules in post-war Germany. Under the leadership of Paul Josten and a team from the Ministry of Economic Affairs, the Josten Draft was worked out in 1949, which foresaw a strong monopoly commission equipped with the right to de-concentrate large conglomerates and prosecute anti-competitive horizontal and vertical agreements under criminal law. The proposal was, however, vehemently boycotted by representatives of the German bureaucracy, the US Occupation Forces, and, importantly, by the industrial élite of the Ruhr and the *Bundesverband der Deutschen Industrie* (BDI), the Federal Association of German Industry. The way in which the Josten Draft problematised economic power concentration was deemed far too radical by industry, while the US authorities saw no evil in large corporations. As a result of fierce controversies, the draft ended up being shelved without

---

[45] *Süddeutsche Zeitung*, 'Das umstrittene Erbe Walter Euckens', *Süddeutsche Zeitung* 1994, p 34.

[46] Sybille Tönnies, 'Die Wissenschaft in der Familienpflege. Gegen das Misstrauenmachensich die Nachkommen der Vordenker des Ordoliberalismus um das Erbe verdient', *Tagesanzeiger* (TAZ), 12 September 2000, p 14.

[47] Walter Oswalt, 'Machtfreie Marktwirtschaft', *Tagesanzeiger* (TAZ), 20 June 1995, p 10.

[48] See Hubert Buch-Hansen and Angela Wigger, The Politics of European Competition Regulation: A Critical Political Economy Perspective, (New York: Routledge, 2011).

a further parliamentary debate.[49] Ludwig Erhard, then Minister of Economics and, as outlined above, a staunch supporter of stimulating large Fordist corporations, committed an ad hoc commission to come up with competition rules in 1953. More than 20 draft versions followed until the *Gesetzgegen Wettbewerbsbeschränkungen* was finally adopted in 1957.[50] The German industry and its partisan allies, the FDP and the CDU, successfully pushed for a 'less prohibitive approach to cartels' and for abandoning the idea of a merger control law.[51] Thus, the 1957 German competition rules did not include merger provisions, and allowed for generous exemptions in the area of cartels. The view that 'many German firms had not yet reached their optimal size' prevailed, and cartel formation was believed to evoke rationalisation, standardisation and specialisation. In particular, cartels were considered to be the 'functional equivalents' of the large corporations that could be found in the US.[52] The *Bundeskartellamt*, the cartel authority, in every sense of the word, was an authority that could authorise cartels. Contrary to ordoliberal prescriptions, the *Bundeskartellamt* was not independent, either. The Ministry of Economic Affairs appointed the president and was entitled to give general or individual directions and could overturn decisions upon the basis of Germany's general national economic interest. When, in 1973, merger control rules were adopted and the *Monopolkommission*, the Federal Monopoly Commission, was established to monitor economic concentration, it was only given an advisory task. Thus, the ordoliberal political project had failed dramatically in post-war Germany.

When, in 1951, the Treaty of Paris established the European Coal and Steel Community, US political pressure was pivotal for the inclusion of competition rules. The initial Schuman Declaration contained only a vague provision to rule out cartel practices.[53] In the course of the negotiations among the six governments of France, Germany, the Benelux and Italy, Jean Monnet, head of the French delegation, noted that 'substantive differences' existed, and that 'the provisions on cartels and industrial concentrations' affected 'the very substance of the Schuman Plan'.[54] The French negotiators, supported by the Italian delegation, initially envisaged price regulations in which prices would be fixed by national governments in collaboration with producers' associations.[55] However, the prospect of supranational price controls

[49] Norbert Eickhof and Kathrin Isele, 'Eine Politökonomische Analyse des Einflusseswettbewerbspolitischer Leitbilder auf die Europäische Fusionskontrolle', Volkswirtschaftliche Diskussionsbeiträge, Potsdam: Universität Potsdam 2005, p 93.

[50] Tony A. Freyer, *Antitrust and Global Capitalism, 1930–2004*, (Cambridge: Cambridge University Press, 2006), p 264.

[51] Sebastian Eyre and Martin Lodge, 'National Tunes and a European Melody? Competition Law Reform in the UK and Germany', (2000) 7 *Journal of European Public Policy*, pp 63–79, at 66.

[52] Marie-Laure Djelic, *Exporting the American Model: The Postwar Transformation of European Business*, (Oxford: Oxford University Press, 1998), p 232; Gerber note 12 above, p 302.

[53] Robert Schuman, The Schuman Declaration of 9 May 1950, available at: https://europa.eu/european-union/about-eu/symbols/europe-day/schuman-declaration_en.

[54] Jean Monnet, Memorandum to Robert Schuman. Paris, 30 November 1950. Available at: www.cvce.eu/en/obj/memorandum_from_jean_monnet_to_robert_schuman_16_september_1950-en-259c61d1-8fee-488a-bf0d-6e0958e0d222.html.

[55] Tobias Witschke, 'The First Antitrust Law in Europe—Success or Failure? Origins and Application of the Merger Control Policy of the High Authority of the European Coal and Steel Community 1950–1963', Working Paper, European University Institute, Florence, 2001, p 7.

within the framework of the ECSC raised immediate concerns in the US. When US Secretary of State Dean Acheson was confronted with the draft treaty on 7 May 1950, he called it 'a clever cover for a gigantic European cartel for coal and steel producers'[56] The US government subsequently threatened that, without the inclusion of competition rules, it could not support 'in good faith that the general idea is a single market characterised by competition'.[57] Against the backdrop of the long-standing cartel tradition in Europe, and particularly in Germany as one of the most cartelised countries, the inclusion of competition rules was regarded as a pivotal first step in the establishment for the same US Fordist-type production and consumer structures in Europe. As US industries were eager to expand across the Atlantic and to gain a foothold in the newly emerging common market, the prospect of high prices for steel worried US industries, particularly in a context of rapidly rising demand for raw materials during the Korean War.[58] Although US officials did not directly participate in the ECSC Treaty negotiations, a range of leading US industrial capitalists and US decision-makers kept themselves briefed about the proceedings during the drafting phase. To counteract the influence of cartel-minded Europe, the US government transferred US High Commissioner for Germany, John McCloy, and two US antitrust experts, Robert Bowie and George Ball, to assist the drafting process in Paris. The overall idea was to (re-) create an open world economy along capitalist logics. The Marshall Plan provided the US government with the necessary leverage in the promotion of competition rules and in buttressing capitalist logics in post-war Europe.[59]

The US government found a loyal ally in Jean Monnet and his staff, who assured it that the Schuman Plan would be the exact opposite of a cartel.[60] The French delegation eventually proposed to prohibit cartels on a per se basis, declaring all cartels categorically illegal, similar to the antitrust provisions of the US Sherman Act.[61] The German representatives, including Ludwig Erhard and Walter Hallstein, the principal negotiator on behalf of Germany, did not considered every cartel to be evil, and also contested the inclusion of supranational merger control rules. The German delegation, which was surrounded by a group of experienced and cartel-minded industrialists, which included Max Boden, CEO of AEG Electrics, as well as Max C. Müller, CEO of the *Vereinigte Stahlwerke*, all feared that the suggested competition rules would lead to a downsizing of the German coal and steel industry.[62] They suggested competition rules based upon the abuse principle, instead—a far more lenient approach according to which cartel practices and the like would be legal in

---

[56] See Dean Acheson, *Present at the Creation: My Years in the State Department*, 1987 edn, (New York: Norton, 1990), pp 383–4.

[57] Witschke, n 55 above, p 17.

[58] Viktor R. Berghahn, *The Americanisation of West German Industry 1945–1973*, (New York, Berg, 1986), p 136.

[59] Wigger, n 6 above.

[60] Buxbaum, n 2 above, p 4.

[61] Thomas Hoeren, 'Europäisches Kartellrechtzwischen Verbots- und Mißbrauchsprinzip—Überlegungenzur Entstehungsgeschichte des Art. 85 EGV', in: Ulrich Hübner and Werner F. Ebke (eds), *Festschrift für Bernhard Großfeld zum 65. Geburtstag*, (Heidelberg: Recht und Wirtschaft GmbH, 1999), p 414; Jean Monnet, *Memoirs*, (New York: Doubleday & Company, Inc., 1978).

[62] Hoeren, n 61 above, pp 412–3.

principle, and only be prosecuted in cases of abuse.[63] The controversies between the French and Germans about the substantive nature of competition rules threatened the ratification of the entire ECSC Treaty.[64] The Germans eventually lost the battle. The substantive differences with the US antitrust rules turned out to be negligible—with exception that the Treaty's provisions were rewritten 'in a European idiom'.[65]

While the Treaty of Rome, which established the European Economic Community (EEC), was being negotiated, the direct US influence in Western Europe had decreased significantly; but the idea of competition rules was here to stay. The opposition of industry had waned considerably as the ECSC provisions on competition had been hardly enforced. Moreover, the German Adenauer government saw clear benefits in free competition and, hence, in free market access in the common market, and thus emerged as a strong proponent of competition rules. After all, the German export-oriented industry in manufactured goods depended on free market access. Walter Hallstein was again the negotiator on behalf of the German government, and subsequently became the first President of the European Commission, which he headed for nine years. His friend Hans von der Gröben, a lawyer by origin, who became the first Competition Commissioner, played a pivotal role in the detailed formulation of competition rules. He was later also called the 'Jean Monnet of Germany', as he drafted much of the Spaak Report.[66] The concept of competition came to occupy a central position in the EEC Treaty, which exposed almost all economic sectors to the need to compete. The rationale of supranational competition rules was to break down both public and private market barriers, in addition to the abolition of trade-related quotas and tariffs among the six Member States, and to re-configure several national markets into one giant single market.

Whereas the ECSC Treaty was a *traité-loi*, specifying, to a large extent, the regulatory substance, the EC Treaty was a *traité-cadre*, which merely set out a broader legal framework that needed secondary legislation or jurisprudence from the Court in order to have any effect.[67] This meant that EEC competition provisions were formulated in vague and ambiguous terms, including notions such as violating 'Community-interest' or 'if trade between the Member States is affected', all concepts that left ample room for interpretation. Moreover, merger control rules were not included. Whereas Article 66 of the ECSC Treaty on mergers and the prohibition of restrictive business practices was the longest article in the entire Treaty, in the EEC Treaty, mergers were not even mentioned.[68] Instead, Article 82 had been included,

---

[63] Berghahn, n 58 above, pp 120–1.
[64] ibid, p 120.
[65] Gerber, n 12 above, pp 338–9.
[66] Hans von der Gröben, 'Competition Policy as a Part of Economic Policy in the Common Market'. Address to the European Parliament, Strasbourg, 16 June 1965, (Brussels: Historical Archives of the European Commission); Michael Gehler and Hans von der Gröben, 'Europäische Integration aus historischer Erfahrung. Ein Zeitzeugenge spräch mit Michael Gehler/Hans von der Gröben', Zentrum für Europäische Integrations forschung Discussion Paper, Bonn: RheinischeFriedrich-Wilhelms-Universität, 2002, p 8.
[67] See Simon Bulmer, 'Institutions and Policy Change in the European Union: The Case of Merger Control', (1994) 72 *Public Administration*, pp 423–44, at 427.
[68] See Buch-Hansen and Wigger, n 48 above, p 53.

prohibiting 'any abuse by one or more enterprises of a dominant position within the common market or in a substantial part of it in so far as it may affect trade between Member States'. Article 82 is often referred to as an anti-monopoly law with strong ordoliberal tenets.[69] This, however, is misleading, as holding a dominant market position was not prohibited—only the abuse of such a position. There were, hence, no legal pre-requisites that allowed the Commission to fight monopolies or oligopolies. Combined with the absence of merger-control rules in the Treaty of Rome, this implies that the ordoliberal notion of a competition authority entrusted with the right to de-concentrated the economy also did not materialise at EC level.

The actual enforcement provisions were spelled out in Regulation 17/62, which provided the procedural framework for the application of Articles 81 and 82 (TEU), and the procedural and interpretative framework for their application for the next 40 years (see Council Regulation No. 17/1962). Regulation 17 entrusted the European Commission with the combined role of investigator, prosecutor, judge, jury and executioner in antitrust cases, which allowed it—in addition to a generous exemption regime—to make use of wide-ranging discretionary executive powers both in the interpretation and in the enforcement of the competition rules. The Commission could access all the relevant documentation of the company under investigation, search this documentation unannounced (dawn raids), interrogate employees, and sanction anti-competitive conduct with up to 10% of the company's annual turnover. Moreover, it allowed the Commission to intervene in the competition control of the Member States, both with regard to private and public companies, and, most notably, Regulation 17 allowed the Commission to formulate its policy without the Council and the European Parliament having a say. To recapitulate, although the Commission may, indeed, have reflected the ordoliberal ideal of an independent competition authority, with regard to the idea of curbing economic concentration and the degree of discretionary powers, ordoliberal logics materialised, at best, in a much watered-down fashion.

The actual enforcement of Community competition rules in the post-war decades deviated considerably from the ordoliberal ideal. Until the late 1970s, the enforcement of competition rules reflected the broader post-war hegemonic order of state-organised capitalism known as 'embedded liberalism'[70]—a socio-economic order characterised by a broad-based commitment to an open and competitive world economy, accommodated domestically by state-organised capitalism in the form of active state interventions and industrial policies, mixed economies and Keynesian-type domestic welfare states. The increasing openness of national markets to foreign trade was sustained through the elimination of trade barriers by the General Agreement of Trade and Tariffs (GATT) in the late 1950s and early 1960s, and the stepwise liberalisation of capital controls supported by the Bretton Woods system of fixed exchange rates. Competition rule enforcement, alongside industrial policies, formed part of the 'embedding' domestic institutional nexus, and exemplified strong

---

[69] See Maher, n 2 above, p 164.
[70] John G. Ruggie, 'International Regimes, Transactions, and Change: Embedded Liberalism in the Postwar Economic Order', (1982) 36 *International Organization*, pp 379–415.

neo-mercantilist and protectionist traits, allowing for significant distortions of competition, whenever justified for general reasons of industrial and social policy.[71] The protectionist stance at Community-level was rooted in the exposure of European industries to US competitive challenges, as US corporations enjoyed a structural advantage over European corporations. The large homogenous home market, supported by a single currency, one language and a rather business-friendly competition unit of regulation, allowed US companies to reap the benefits of economies of scale and scope production, and expand through mergers and compete in global markets. In 1960s, 27 of the 30 largest industrial companies worldwide originated from the US,[72] while the largest US companies located more than half of their total assets abroad and generated most of their profits across the Atlantic.[73] Compared to their US counterparts, European companies were rather small in size, and the European marketplace continued to be highly fragmented along national borders. The dominance and technological superiority of US industrial capital in the market for high-value goods was captured in the bestselling and widely-discussed book, *Le defi américain*, the American Challenge, by the French journalist Jean-Jacques Servan-Schreiber,[74] warning that Europe was about to 'become an annex of the United States'.

The protectionist orientation strengthened throughout the great stagflation crisis of the 1970s, which brought the long wave of the post-war economic growth of Fordism to a halt. Markets in the advanced economies were saturated, and production grew faster than demand, leading to overcapacity in manufacturing sectors, and eventually a major profit squeeze and sharp decreases in output and exports. To alleviate declining aggregate demand, the Commission permitted so-called crisis or emergency cartels in a range of industrial sectors, making use of exemption rulings, while national governments adopted other protectionist measures to cushion their industries from global competition. Once inflation-based Keynesian interventions proved unsuccessful, policy-makers in the Western industrialised world adopted neoliberal policies in the hope of restoring corporate profits. However, with regard to the post-war era of embedded liberalism, ordoliberal logics were neither reflected in the substantive Community competition rules, nor in their enforcement.

VI. CONCLUSION

The myth that both German and Community-level competition rules were inspired by ordoliberalism is quite entrenched among scholars and competition practitioners alike. As a matter of fact, a range of German officials nurtured in the German

---

[71] Wigger, n 6 above, and Buch-Hansen and Wigger, n 48 above.

[72] Walter Adams and James W. Brock, 'Mergers and Economic Performance: The Experience Abroad', (1990) 5 *Review of Industrial Organization*, pp 175–88, at 175.

[73] Ngaire Woods, 'International Political Economy in an Age of Globalization', in: John Baylis and Steve Smith (eds), *The Globalization of World Politics: An Introduction to International Relations*, (Oxford: Oxford University Press, 2001), p 284.

[74] Jean-Jacques Servan-Schreiber, *Le défi américain*, (Paris: Livre de Poche, 1968), p 139.

competition law occupied strategic positions in the Commission's DG Competition until far into the 1980s. In particular, the Commission's Cabinets formed enclaves for Germans, as Commissioners in charge could hire and fire advisors and experts according to their own discretion. For example, Ernst Albrecht, was *Chef de Cabinet* under Hans von der Gröben from 1958–1967, and ascended to become Director General from 1967 to 1969. Manfred Caspari, Director General, was in office from 1980 to 1990, and his successors, Claus-Dieter Ehlermann, and Alexander Schaub, held this post from 1990 to 1995, and 1995 to 2002, respectively. Assistant Director General Götz Drauz was appointed in 1999 and remained in office until 2009. However, the vast presence of Germans should not be equalled with the presence of ordoliberals. Notwithstanding this, references to ordoliberalism have been made not only by scholars but also by practitioners over and over again. For example, Competition Commissioner Karel van Miert (1989–1994) once stated 'to have developed an interest in the writings of Ludwig Erhard very early on both privately and professionally'.[75] In 1998, when he was awarded the Ludwig Erhard Prize, he acknowledged that 'ordoliberalism had lost nothing of its relevance' and that 'again and again German politicians and competition specialists have taken a leading role in the shaping and practical development of the European competition rules'.[76] Such references should not, however, be taken at face value. Arguably, there is always a discrepancy between an ideology and its actual implementation, as ideologies or theories are, by definition, incomplete and riddled with contradictions. Moreover, the foundational texts of ordoliberals were far from monolithic or static, while ordoliberal thinking did not survive the course of history unchanged. One could thus argue that ordoliberal self-representations cannot be taken as a yardstick to assess regulatory content and enforcement practices. However, the ordoliberal utopia of a de-concentrated economy was a central pre-requisite of ordoliberalism as a variant of neoliberalism. Despite the presence of ordoliberal debates in the 1940s and 1950s, a de-concentrated economy with equally matched players did not generate the political support required, and hence, never materialised. In fact, to the contrary. Both in Germany and at Community-level, there has been at the outset a permissive approach towards economic concentration to sustain Fordist accumulation structures by means of large corporations that could exploit economies of scale and scope production. Thus, ordoliberalism as a form of neoliberalism was rather insignificant at the time. With the neoliberal turn in the mid-1980s little changed. Since the adoption of the supranational merger rules in 1989, the vast majority of notified mergers were approved.[77] Thus, to date, there is nothing distinctively ordoliberal either in the substantive outlook of competition rules or in their enforcement.

---

[75] Karel van Miert, The Future of European competition policy. Paper for Ludwig Erhard Prize Award, Bonn, Germany, 17 September 1998, available at: http://ec.europa.eu/competition/speeches/text/sp1998_042_en.html, pp 1–2.

[76] ibid, p 3.

[77] Angela Wigger and Hubert Buch-Hansen, 'Explaining (Missing) Regulatory Paradigm Shifts: EU Competition Regulation in Times of Economic Crisis', (2014) 19 *New Political Economy*, pp 113–37.

11

The Overburdening of Law by Ordoliberalism and the Integration Project

CHRISTIAN JOERGES

ABSTRACT

The focus of this contribution will be a re-construction of the impact of the ordoliberal concept of an economic constitution on the legal configuration of the integration project throughout its various phases. The formative years of the EEC were dominated by the integration-through-law agenda, which corresponded essentially to the ordoliberal idea of a European economic constitution. After the regulatory turn in the mid-1980s, the prospects for a further realisation of that vision started to erode. Contrary to widely-held views, the establishment of the EMU by the Maastricht Treaty of 1992 was, at best, a pyrrhic victory of ordoliberalism. The design failures of Maastricht form the background of the concern of this chapter with the responses to the financial crisis. It will be submitted that these are—a widespread rhetoric notwithstanding—anything but ordoliberal. They must instead be characterised as a post-liberal authoritarian mode of governance which is irreconcilable with the European commitments to the rule of law and democracy. Is this unruly state of the integration project provisional and invertible? A cure through a return to the provisions of the EMU of 1992–1997 or their strengthening is inconceivable. The recent legalisation of the transformation of Europe's constitutional constellation by the CJEU has 'bought time' for the management of the crisis by the ECB, but it has deepened the Europe's constitutional malaise.

I. INTRODUCTION

MY WORK ON this chapter is set out with four complaints: the first complaint is about non-lawyers not taking the legal dimension of ordoliberalism seriously enough, or simply to belittle it as an odd and old rule fetishism; the second complaint concerns the conceptual decoupling of the ordoliberal *Ordnungstheorie* and *Ordnungspolitik* from socio-political contextual conditions, and its failure to take the impact of the societal change on its original premises seriously; my third complaint is about the, by now, so-widely shared perception of the ordoliberal tradition as an ideational superpower which would dominate and orient German policy-making, and the failure to explore the embeddedness of ordoliberalism in what is left of the German variety of capitalism; my fourth complaint concerns the all too superficial and erroneous equations of ordoliberal theorems with the Schmittian imprint of Europe's crisis politics.[1]

My reading of the ordoliberal tradition which informs my queries is, to a large degree, inspired by an author whose name never shows up in the by now so intense debates and intense critiques, but who has delivered the most insightful re-constructions of this tradition of which I am aware: namely, Rudolf Wiethölter.[2] This is particularly true with respect to my first complaint. Wiethölter underlined—in all of his pertinent essays—that ordoliberalism is to be understood first and foremost as a *theory of law*, which assigns to law a constitutive function in the ordering of economy and society. The prime exponent of this vision was Franz Böhm, whose work Wiethölter has analysed subtly, critically and respectfully. My indebtedness to Wiethölter should be clear from the queries which I have listed. But I had, of course, to shift from Wiethölter's discussion of the accomplishments and failures of the 'Bonn Republic' to the integration project and our present concerns with the dreadful state of the EU. With this shift, I follow the move of the ordoliberal school from the national to the European context and depart from the all too wishful ordoliberal reading.[3] The proceedings in Berlin have convinced me, however, that I should re-conceptualise the discussion of my complaints in two respects. The first seems rather trivial. The ordoliberal reading of the European Treaties and the

---

[1] The term 'authoritarian liberalism' was coined by Carl Schmitt's great opponent Herman Heller in a short essay: 'Autoritärer Liberalismus' (1933) 44 *Die Neue Rundschau*, pp 289–298, now available in an English translation: Hermann Heller, 'Authoritarian Liberalism?', (2015) 13 *European Law Journal*, pp 295–301.

When I first became aware of Heller's piece, I suggested that Heller's critique was also addressed to ordoliberalism (see Christian Joerges, 'What is left of the European Economic Constitution? A Melancholic Eulogy', (2005) 30 *European Law Review*, pp 461–489, at 467). This equation is wrong, however. Heller dealt exclusively with Carl Schmitt's infamous speech 'Starker Staat und gesunde Wirtschaft. Ein Vortrag vor Wirtschaftsführern', held on 23 November 1932, published, eg, in (1933) *Volk und Reich. Politische Monatshefte*, pp 81–94; the text has become recently available in English: 'Strong State and Sound Economy: An Address to Business Leaders' (1932), in Renato Christi, *Carl Schmitt and Authoritarian Liberalism* (Cardiff: University of Wales Press 1998), Annex, pp 212–232. With respect to the European responses to the financials crisis the term 'authoritarian' is adequate, the term 'liberalism'—of whatever variety—much less so; see Section IV below and previously Christian Joerges and Maria Weimer, 'A Crisis of Executive Managerialism in the EU: No Alternative?, in: Gráinne de Búrca, Claire Kilpatrick and Joanne Scott (eds), *Critical Legal Perspectives on Global Governance: Liber Amicorum for David M Trubek*, (Oxford: Hart Publishing, 2014), pp 295–322.

[2] See, in particular, '*Die Position des Wirtschaftsrechts im sozialen Rechtsstaat*', (The Status of Economic Law in the Social *Rechtsstaat*) was the title of the inaugural lecture, which Wiethölter, who succeeded Franz Böhm in Frankfurt, delivered on 31 January 1964; the lecture was published in: Helmut Coing et al (eds), *Festschrift zum 70. Geburtstag von Franz Böhm*, (Karlsruhe: C.F. Müller, 1968), pp 41–62; 'Wirtschaftsrecht', in: Axel Görlitz (ed), *Handlexikon zur Rechtswissenschaft*, (Munich: Ehrenwirth, 1972), pp 531–538, and 'Franz Böhm (1895–1977)', in: Bernhard Diestelkamp and Michael Stolleis (eds), *Juristen an der Universität Frankfurt am Main*, (Baden-Baden: Nomos, 1989), pp 207–252; both pieces are reprinted in: Peer Zumbansen and Marc Amstutz (eds), *Recht in Recht-Fertigungen: Ausgewählte Schriften von Rudolf Wiethölter*, (Berlin: Berliner Wissenschaftsverlag, 2014), pp 321–331, ('Wirtschaftsrecht'), pp 67–109 ('Franz Böhm').

[3] See Section II, below.

rather seamless fit of ordoliberal theorems with the core provisions of European law is indicative of a well-considered ideational strategy, but must not be read as a proof of some deep practical impact.[4] The trivial distinction between impact and interpretation, however, has implications which are not so trivial. These concern my so far under-theorised assumptions on the potential of economic ordering 'through law'. I will hence differentiate more stringently between the elaboration of transdisciplinary theoretical concepts and the normative ideational components of the ordoliberal tradition which are so attractive for political leaders and influential in the public sphere even after, and in spite of, the erosion of the academic credentials of ordoliberal theorising.

The ensemble of these observations adds up to a counter-narrative to both the prevailing self-description of the protagonists and to the allegations of so many of the opponents of the ordoliberal tradition. My counter-narrative departs from both positions in that it questions the validity of the widespread belief in the impact of ordoliberal theorems. This is a differentiated departure, however. One should distinguish between three phases: (1) the conceptual affinities between the ordoliberal theorems and the European 'treaty constitutionalism' in the formative phase of the integration project;[5] (2) the adaptation of ordoliberal policies to the Anglo-Saxon neoliberalism which dominated the 1970s up to the Treaty of Maastricht—a move that can be understood as some kind of hijacking operation;[6] and (3) the marginalisation of ordoliberalism as a theoretical vision with constitutional precepts during the financial crisis. Implicit in this latter observation is the deepest discrepancy between my narrative and the argumentations of both the defenders and the critics of the ordoliberal tradition. The defenders insist on the validity of their concepts and prescriptions, but concede some '*Ohnmacht des Sollens*' (powerlessness of the ought) which had to cede to political resistance, while the critics argue that ordoliberal theorising is just a fair-weather philosophy camouflaging the authoritarian objectives which are pursued rigorously in times of crisis. The third part of my narrative is the most controversial. It will be elaborated in two separate steps, namely, an analysis of the Maastricht Treaty, which will argue that the EMU established by that Treaty marks the erosion, rather than a consummation, of the ordoliberal project of an economic constitution,[7] and an analysis of Europe's crisis politics as they are actually pursued.[8]

II. ECONOMIC CONSTITUTIONALISM: THE LEGAL FORM OF A PRE-EXISTING ORDO

In the present critical surveys of the ordoliberal tradition, the constitutive importance of law within the ordoliberal tradition has disappeared from view, although two of

---

[4] See again Section III.
[5] See Section A.
[6] See Section B.
[7] See Section IV A.
[8] Section IV B (crisis 'law') and Section IV C (the legalisation of emergency governance).

the three authors of the foundational manifesto of 1936[9] were lawyers, and the co-originality of law—the legal ordering of economy and society—and economics was of constitutive importance in the early years of the Federal Republic and many years thereafter. The erosion of this synthesis, which became apparent in the 1970s,[10] heralds the deep constitutional *malaise* which we are witnessing in the wake of the financial crisis. The present disregard of law in the neighbouring disciplines mirrors an erosion of the ordering functions of law; there is hence realism in the recent tendency not to take the law seriously. The implications of this de-juridification process for the legitimacy and governability of the European project seem equally real, albeit very difficult to measure with any precision.

A. The Private Law Society and its Ordo

The constitutive importance of law in the ordoliberal tradition has a name: Franz Böhm. Böhm's conceptualisation of societal relations, of the ordering of the economy, his understanding of the functions of the state, his equation of public rule ('*Staatsverfassung*') with economic constitutionalism ('*Wirtschaftsverfassung*')—each and every angle of his theoretical edifice is permeated with law.[11] In a nutshell, the system (*Ordnung*) of private law is an economic order, an order in which autonomous individuals pursue plans and organise their co-operation under legal rules as exchange relations. Market prices provide the signals in a competitive process. In this way, the private law society constitutes itself as a competitive order. The state is to ensure the proper functioning of this order through competition law. Competition law provides the institutional framework of this order, but does not steer economic processes. Because of this restraint, market processes are nothing less than the ongoing referenda of the market citizens—the most perfect democratic machinery conceivable.[12] The establishment of this order has to be understood as an irrevocable decision. '*Staatsverfassung*' and '*Wirtschaftsverfassung*' are dependent upon each other; the autonomy of economic actors and the commitment of the state to subject economic processes to a system of undistorted competition are, so-to-speak, two sides of the same coin—they realise and mirror the pre-existing ordo.[13]

---

[9] Franz Böhm, Walter Eucken and Hans Großmann-Doerth, 'Unsere Aufgabe. Vorwort', in: Franz Böhm, *Die Ordnung der Wirtschaft als geschichtliche Aufgabe und rechtsschöpferische Leistung*. No. 1 der Schriftenreihe 'Ordnung der Wirtschaft', (edited by Franz Böhm, Walter Eucken and Hans Großmann-Doerth), (Stuttgart-Berlin: Kohlhammer, 1937), pp VII–XXI. English Translation: 'The Ordo Manifesto of 1936', (signed by Franz Böhm, Walter Eucken and Hans Großmann-Doerth), in: Alan Peacock and Hans Willgerodt (eds), *Germany's Social Market Economy: Origins and Evolution*, (New York: St. Martin's Press, 1989), pp 15–25.

[10] See Section III B.

[11] Out of the writings of Franz Böhm, see, in particular: 'Die Idee des Ordo im Denken Walter Euckens', (1950); 'Wirtschaftsordnung und Staatsverfassung', (1950); 'Privarechtsgesellschaft und Marktwirtschaft', (1966) reprinted in Ernst-Joachim Mestmäcker's, *Freiheit und Ordnung in der Marktwirtschaft/Franz Böhm*, (Baden-Baden: Nomos, 1980), pp 11–168.

[12] '… die technisch idealste Erscheinungsform von Demokratie, die überhaupt existiert', (Böhm, *Wirtschaftsordnung und Staatsverfassung*, (Tübingen: Mohr/Siebeck, 1950), p 51).

[13] The impact of these ideas on politics, law and academic scholarship in the Federal Republic was considerable. Suffice it here to point again to the work of Wiethölter (n 2 above). Much more is avail-

It is easier to substantiate the specifics of this thinking negatively than to define its theoretical status. Ordoliberalism is *not* an economic theory in the conventional sense of this discipline, nor is it just a legal methodology or the kind of interdisciplinary exercise which the later 'law and economics' school has promoted. What keeps the school together, economic historian Alexander Nützenadel concludes, is an economic and political programme,[14] in particular the promise of a 'third way' beyond *laissez-faire* liberalism and all the versions of socialism,[15] the vision of a sustainable ordering of economic and political freedom under law. '*Ordnungspolitik*' is the notion which designates a framing of this programmatic which can be bound by and implemented through legal rules.[16] These are abstract formulae. But they capture what remained a characteristic feature of the ordoliberal tradition. They are discernible in von Hayek's political and economic liberalism, clearly visible in Mestmäcker's œuvre which has oriented the 'second generation' of ordo-liberal scholarship,[17] and it re-surfaces in the *Ordnungsökonomik* (constitutional economics) advocated in particular by Viktor Vanberg, Lars P. Feld and Ekkehard Köhler.[18]

B. Objections

The ordoliberal modelling of economy and society 'through legal rules' is not as unusual as the theological affinities of its core concept may make one believe. Franz Böhm was, in important respects, a particularly lucid and coherent forerunner of a

---

able of outstanding precision in Heinz-Dieter Assmann, *Wirtschaftsrecht in der Mixed Economy. Auf der Suche nach einem Sozialmodell für das Wirtschaftsrecht*, (Königstein/Ts.: Athenäum, 1980), pp 157–167, but not the type of sociological account delivered for the economic branch of ordoliberalism by Stephan Pühringer, 'The Success Story of Ordoliberalism as Guiding Principle of German Economic Policy', (Ch 10 in this volume, with pertinent references).

[14] Alexander Nützenadel, *Stunde der Ökonomen. Wissenschaft, Expertenkultur und Politik in der Bundesrepublik 1949–74*, (Göttingen: Vandenhoeck & Ruprecht, 2005), p 41; in the same vein much earlier, Wiethölter, 'Wirtschaftsrecht', n 2 above, p 326.

[15] *Nationalsozialismus* included; see Walter Eucken, 'Wettbewerb als Grundprinzip der Wirtschaftsordnung', (Competition as the Basic Principle of the Economic Constitution), Lecture before the *Akademie für Deutsches Recht* 3 November 1941, (*Schriften der Akademie für Deutsches Recht: Gruppe Wirtschaftswissenschaft*, Heft 6), pp 29–48; the economic order of the Third Reich is criticised as a *Zentralverwaltungswirtschaft*: for the quest for the 'third way', see p 37 et seq.

[16] Werner Abelshauser, *Kulturkampf. Der deutsche Weg in die Neue Wirtschaft und die amerikanische Herausforderung*, (Berlin: Kadmos Kulturverlag, 2003), p 153 et seq.

[17] Economic constitutionalism 'formuliert die politische Potenz des Ökonomischen. ... Nicht um der demokratischen Regierung in den Arm zu fallen, sondern um sie instand zu setzen, ihren rechtsstaatlichen und sozialstaatlichen Aufgaben in Unabhängigkeit gerecht werden zu können. Es handelt sich nicht um die Priorität des Ökonomischen, sondern es handelt sich darum, die Möglichkeit unabhängigen staatlichen Handelns mit den wirtschaftlichen und politischen Handlungsfreiheit der Bürger in Einklang zu bringen', Ernst-Joachim Mestmäcker, 'Wirtschaftsordnung und Staatsverfassung', in: Heinz Saubermann and Ernst-Joachim Mestmäcker (eds), *Festschrift zum 80. Geburtstag von Franz Böhm*, (Tübingen: Mohr/Siebeck, 1975), p 383 ff, and 419.

[18] Viktor Vanberg, '"Ordnungstheorie" as Constitutional Economics—The German Conception of a "Social Market Economy"', (1988) 39 ORDO Jahrbuch, pp 17–31; idem, 'Ordnungspolitik, the Freiburg School and the Reason of Rules', Freiburg Discussion Papers on Constitutional Economics 14/01; Lars P. Feld and Ekkehard A. Köhler, 'Ist die Ordnungsökonomik zukunftsfähig', (2011) 12 *Zeitschrift für Wirtschafts- und Unternehmensethik*, pp 173–195.

broad range of similar attempts to conceptualise the societal embeddedness of law and its social functions. The most famous and influential suggestion was submitted by the legal historian Franz Wieacker. In his lecture on the social model of the classical private-law legislature and the development of modern society,[19] he presented a re-construction of the ideational and economic pre-conditions for Germany's Pandect science (*Pandektenwissenschaft*) and the civil code of 1900. His key concept was the notion of the law's 'social model'. This model mediated the positively enacted law with social reality, culture and history. As a historian, Wieacker refrained from an assessment of the normative validity of his re-construction. But his social model is very akin to what Crawford B. Macpherson has characterised in his theory of 'possessive liberalism',[20] and Wieacker's understanding of the interdependence of law and society re-surfaces in Duncan Kennedy's work on 'classical legal consciousness'[21] as well as in Jürgen Habermas' paradigm of 'formal law'.[22]

I am less concerned at this point with the obvious substantive and political differences between these authors than with their methodology and the kind of critique which they advocate in their approaches. In Böhm's work, the status of a *critical* theory is particularly obvious. Suffice it here to mention his powerful critique of the infamous legalisation of cartels by Germany's *Reichsgericht*.[23] However, it is one thing to subject the state of Germany's organised capitalism of the late nineteenth century or the state of the law of the Weimar Republic and the Third Reich to ordoliberal scrutiny, it is another to defend the ordoliberal project in the context of post-war Germany's constitutional democracy. This is so for two interdependent reasons. For one, the need to examine the adequacy of the legal modelling of economy and society is irrefutable for any theory of economic law, and such reflections have to consider how social changes affect their premises.[24] This is not to say that the normative validity of an approach would be dependent on its factual or potential impact. In this respect, ordoliberalism, notwithstanding its dominance in Germany's law faculties, lost much ground in the 1960s in the arenas of economic policy with Germany's adoption of Keynesian paradigms,[25]

---

[19] Franz Wieacker, *Das Sozialmodell der klassischen Privatrechtsgesetzbücher und die Entwicklung der modernen Gesellschaft*, (Karlsruhe: C.F. Müller, 1953).

[20] Crawford B. Macpherson, *The Political Theory of Possessive Individualism: From Hobbes to Locke*, (Oxford: Oxford University Press, 1962).

[21] 'Toward an Historical Understanding of Legal Consciousness: The Case of Classical Legal Thought in America, 1850–1940', (1980) 3 *Research in Law and Sociology*, pp 3–24.

[22] 'Paradigms of Law', in: Michael Rosenfeld and Andrew Arato (eds), *Habermas on Law and Democracy*, (Berkeley CA: University of California Press, 1998), pp 13–25; idem, *Between Facts and Norms: Contributions to a Discourse Theory of Law and Democracy*, (Cambridge MA: The MIT Press, 1996), pp 396–401.

[23] 'Das Reichsgericht und die Kartelle: eine wirtschaftsverfassungsrechtliche Kritik an dem Urteil des RG. vom 4. Februar 1897', RGZ 38, 155, (1948) 1 *Ordo*, pp 197–213.

[24] See, for a systematic elaboration and critique, Klaus Günther; '"Ohne weiteres und ganz automatisch"? Zur Wiederentdeckung der "Privatrechtsgesellschaft"', (1992) 11 *Rechtshistorisches Journal*, pp 473–500; Thomas Vesting, 'Wiederkehr der bürgerlichen Gesellschaft und ihres Rechts? Zur neueren Diskussion über das Verhältnis von öffentlichem Recht und Privatrecht', in: Hans Schlosser (ed), *Bürgerliches Gesetzbuch 1896–1996*, (Heidelberg: Springer, 1997), pp 183–201.

[25] See Nützenadel, n 15 above, p 51 *et seq*.

with the revival of corporatist practices,[26] and last, but not least, in proceedings before the *Bundesverfassungsgericht*.[27]

With its rejection of the concept of economic constitutionalism, Germany's *Bundesverfassungsgericht* reiterated what Oliver W. Holmes had explained in his legendary dissent in the *Lochner* case: democratically-legitimated politics trump ordoliberal *Ordnungspolitk*.[28]

C. Economic Sociology

This constitutional objection is in line with what economic sociology keeps explaining about the social embeddedness of markets. To summarise some of the core messages briefly: markets are anything but mechanically-functioning entities. They are social institutions. This is a core message in particular of Karl Polanyi's seminal *Great Transformation*,[29] a work which has experienced a remarkable renaissance recently[30] after continuous elaboration.[31] It follows from this perception of markets that we have to understand 'the economy as a polity'.[32] Among the policy implications which Polanyi has addressed, one is particularly noteworthy in the present context:

> [G]overnments will find it possible to ... tolerate willingly that other nations shape their domestic institutions according to their inclinations, thus transcending the pernicious nineteenth century dogma of the necessary uniformity of domestic regimes within the orbit of world economy. Out of the ruins of the Old World, cornerstones of the New can be seen to emerge: economic collaboration of governments and the liberty to organize national life at will.[33]

With this remark, Polanyi underlined what the *praxis of* integration politics has so thoroughly neglected, namely, the structural diversity of the European economies

[26] See Werner Abelshauser, *Deutsche Wirtschaftsgeschhichte. Von 1945 bis zur Gegenwart*, 2nd ed., (Munich: C.H. Beck, 2011), p 163 *et seq.*

[27] See the famous *Investitionshilfe* judgment of 20 July 1954, BVerfGE 4, 7 and later the seminal *Mitbestimmungs-Urteil* of 1 March 1979, BVerfGE 50, 290.

[28] '... a Constitution is not intended to embody a particular economic theory, whether of paternalism and the organic relation of the citizen to the state or of laissez faire. It is made for people of fundamentally differing views, and the accident of our finding certain opinions natural and familiar, or novel, or even shocking, ought not to conclude our judgment upon the question whether statutes embodying them conflict with the Constitution of the United States', *Lochner v People of State of New York*, US Supreme Court, 198 US 45 (1905).

[29] Karl Polanyi, *The Great Transformation: The Political and Economic Origins of Our Time*, (Boston MA: Beacon Press, [1944] 2001) (with foreword by Joseph Stiglitz and introduction by Fred Block).

[30] Tellingly, Germany's leading economic sociologist observes: 'We are all Polanyians now', Jens Beckert, 'The Great Transformation of Embeddedness: Karl Polanyi and the New Economic Sociology', *MPIfG Discussion Paper* 07/1, Cologne, 2007, 7.

[31] See, eg, John G. Ruggie, 'International Regimes, Transactions, and Change: Embedded Liberalism in the Postwar Economic Order', (1982) 36 *International Organization*, pp 379–415, and the collected essays in: Fred Block and Margret R. Somers, *The Power of Market Fundamentalism: Karl Polanyi's Critique*, (Cambridge MA: Harvard University Press, 2004).

[32] Christian Joerges, Bo Stråth and Peter Wagner, *The Economy as a Polity: The Political Constitution of Contemporary Capitalism*, (London: UCL Press, 2005).

[33] Polanyi, n 29 above, pp 253–254.

which is not only constituted by formal positively enacted laws, but also by their continuous handling, by social norms, cultural traditions and experience.[34] It does not seem too far-fetched to read into Polanyi's remark an anticipation of the findings of the studies on the varieties of capitalism which were initiated by Peter Hall and David Soskice in 2001.[35] All the analyses undertaken in this tradition confirm and underline that the operation of market economies is not uniform because their institutional configurations vary significantly. The main reference and starting-point is 'the way in which firms resolve the coordination problems they face' in five spheres: industrial relations; vocational training and education; corporate governance; inter-firm relations; and employees.[36] Two implications of normative significance seem obvious: a transformation of one variety into another is hard to achieve, and selective insertions of elements of one variety into the fabric of the other can have counter-productive disintegrative effects.[37]

Against the background of this observation, we can turn to the process of European integration.

III. THE ORDOLIBERAL PROJECT OF A EUROPEAN ECONOMIC CONSTITUTION

In view of the current preoccupations with 'The Long Shadow of Ordoliberalism',[38] it may be worth recalling that this school's move to Europe, which implied a retraction from earlier, more global orientations, was anything but straight-lined.[39] The just mentioned signs in Adenauer's Federal Republic of a corporatist revival provide an explanation of this re-orientation which was apparently in line with Germany's national and business interests.[40] However, the arrival of ordoliberalism

---

[34] Werner Abelshauser's notion of 'Wirtschaftskulturen' (economic cultures) captures these configurations best; see, for a comprehensive, discussion Werner Abelshauser, David Gilgen and Andreas Leutzsch (eds), *Kulturen der Weltwirtschaft*, (Göttingen: Vandenhoek und Ruprecht, 2013), and, more recently, Werner Abelshauser and Christopher Kopper, 'Ordnungspolitik der sichtbaren Hand. Das Bundeswirtschaftsministerium und die Kunst der Wirtschaftspolitik', in: Werner Abelshauser (ed), *Das Bundeswirtschaftsministerium in der Ära der Sozialen Marktwirtschaft. Der deutsche Weg der Wirtschaftspolitik*, (Berlin-Boston MA: Walter de Gruyter, 2016), p 22 et seq.

[35] Peter A. Hall and David Soskice (eds), *Varieties of Capitalism: The Institutional Foundations of Comparative Advantage*, (Oxford: Oxford University Press, 2001).

[36] ibid, pp 6–8.

[37] Gunther Teubner, 'Legal Irritants: Good Faith in British Law or How Unifying Law Ends up in New Differences', (1998) 61 *Modern Law Review*, pp 11–32; Anke Hassel, 'The German Model in Transition', in: Brigitte Unger (ed), *The German Model Seen by its Neighbours*, (Düsseldorf: Hans-Böckler-Stiftung, 2015), pp 105–134.

[38] Much cited but over-valued: Sebastian Dullien and Ulrike Guérot, 'The Long Shadow of Ordoliberalism: Germany's Approach to the Euro Crisis', *European Council on Foreign Relations Policy Brief* 22/2012.

[39] The scepticism and resistance of leading ordo-liberals has been re-constructed meticulously by Milène Wegmann, *Früher Neoliberalismus und europaische Integration: Interdependenz der nationalen, supranationalen und internationalen Ordnung von Wirtschaft und Gesellschaft* (1932–1965), (Baden-Baden: Nomos, 2002), especially, p 351 et seq. See, also, the instructive passages in Pierre Dardot and Christian Laval, *The New Way of the World: On Neoliberal Society*, (London: Verso Books, 2013), p 205 et seq.

[40] Hagen Schulze-Forberg and Bo Stråth, *The Political History of European Integration. The Hypocracy of Democracy-through-market*, (London: Routledge, 2010), p 24 with references.

in European studies beyond the German borders is a recent phenomenon. In an instructive historical account of Germany's European law scholarship and a more recent history of the formative phase of European law, ordoliberalism is not even mentioned.[41] Europe's intense constitutional debates have dealt with the political dimension of the economy mostly only in passing. In Germany, the discussion 'the economic' was assigned primarily to ordoliberal scholars.[42] A recent British monograph on *The Economic Constitution* touches upon the ordoliberal understanding of this notion only in passing.[43] Competition law is an—unsurprising—exception.[44] The first thorough monograph that I am aware of which includes an intensive discussion of ordoliberalism has only recently been submitted at the University of Amsterdam—by an Austrian scholar.[45] Somewhat unsurprisingly in view of recent campaigning,[46] ordoliberalism has gained new prominence in the literature on the financial crisis[47]

Does ordoliberalism attract attention of the right kind? The above-mentioned Austrian author signals irritations—with good reasons in my view.[48] The focus of the following analyses is, as announced in the introductory remarks, on the *legal dimension* of the ordoliberal tradition, and, in particular, on the project of a European economic constitution. The narrative, however, is not about an 'ever longer shadow' but on the erosion of the law's ordering functions. This discrepancy between the once dominating role of law and the benign neglect of the legal dimension of law in the current critique of ordoliberalism may seem paradoxical. What seems paradoxical and irreconcilable becomes quite easily comprehensible if one understands the '*Ohnmacht des Sollens*' as a foundational characteristic and weakness of the ordoliberal project. Knut Wolfgang Nörr, a renowned legal historian whose partisanship with ordoliberalism is beyond any doubt, identifies two concepts in the (German)

---

[41] Billy Davies, 'The Constitutionalisation of the European Community: West Germany between legal sovereignty and European integration 1949–1974', PhD thesis, King's College London, 2007 (updated in *Resisting the ECJ: Germany's Confrontation with European Law, 1949–1979*, (Cambridge: Cambridge University Press, 2012); Antoine Vauchez, *L'Union par le droit. L'invention d'un programme institutionnel pour l'Europe*, (Paris: Presses de Sciences Po, 2013); Anne Boerger and Morten Rasmussen, 'Transforming European Law: The Establishment of the Constitutional Discourse from 1950 to 1993', (2014) 10 *European Constitutional Law Review*, pp 199–225. A bit more is to be found in the sociological account of Antoine Vauchez, *L'Union par le droit. L'invention d'un programme institutionnel pour l'Europe*, (Paris: Presses de Sciences Po, 2013).

[42] Two pertinent contributions leading work on European constitutionalism provide instructive illustration: Armin Hatje, 'The Economic Constitution within the Internal Market', in: *Armin v Bogdandy* and Jürgen Bast (eds), *Principles of European Law*, Munich-Oxford: C.H. Beck, 2nd ed. 2009, pp 589–622; J. Drexl, 'Competition Law as Part of the European Constitution', ibid, pp 659–697.

[43] Tony Prosser, *The Economic Constitution*, (Oxford: Oxford University Press, 2014), p 11.

[44] David J. Gerber, 'Constitutionalizing the Economy: German Neo-Liberalism, Competition Law and the "New" Europe', (1994) 42 *American Journal of Comparative Law*, pp 25–84; Angela Wigger, 'Competition for Competitiveness. The Politics of the Transformation of the EU', PhD Thesis, VA Amsterdam, 2008; Kiran Patel and Heike Schweitzer (eds), *The Historical Foundations of EU CompetitionLaw*, (Oxford: Oxford University Press, 2013).

[45] Clemens Kaupa, *The Pluralist Character of the European Economic Constitution*, (Oxford: Hart Publishing, 2016).

[46] See the Introduction to the present volume by Josef Hien and Christian Joerges, p 1 ff.

[47] See, in particular, Kaarlo Tuori and Klaus Tuori, *The Eurozone Crisis. A Constitutional Analysis*, (Cambridge: Cambridge University Press, 2014), p xi f, 12 ff.

[48] See Christian Joerges, '"Brother, can you Paradigm"?, Review Essay', (2014) 12 *International Journal of Constitutional Law*, pp 769–785, also at www.globallawbooks.org/reviews/detail.asp?id=819.

history of economic law: the 'organised economy' and the 'social market economy'. He downplays the tensions within the second camp, but rightly underlines that the co-existence of the 'organised economy' tradition, on the one hand, and ordoliberalism, on the other. His conclusion is that Germany has institutionalised a paradox: it cultivated both the ordoliberal *credo* and a *praxis* which took ordoliberal theorising lightly.[49] The recent re-construction of the '*Ordnungspolitilk der sichtbaren Hand*' by Werner Abelshauser and Christopher Kopper[50] confirms Nörr's insights. The ordoliberal project of a European Economic Constitution was flawed from the very beginning, in that it over-estimated the law's ordering potential very significantly. This self-delusion can be observed at all stages of the integration process, albeit to varying degrees. Three stages will be distinguished: the so-called formative period, the establishment of the Economic and Monetary Union (EMU) by the Treaty of Maastricht, and the financial crisis and its management since 2008.

A. The *de facto* Alliance Between Economic Constitutionalism and the Integration-through-Law Project

It means carrying coals to Newcastle both within and beyond legal quarters to underline that the foundational period of the integration process was dominated by the integration-through-law agenda, which built upon the authority of the European Court of Justice, its seminal judgments on 'direct effect',[51] 'supremacy',[52] the characterisation of the economic freedoms as basic rights of Europe's market citizens and the conceptualisation of the reference procedure as a means of empowering private parties and national courts to act jointly with the ECJ as supervisors of national legislatures. As Joseph H.H. Weiler has summarised this:

> in critical aspects the Community has evolved and behaves as if its founding instrument were not a Treaty governed by international law, but, to use the language of the European Court of Justice, a constitutional charter governed by a form of constitutional law.[53]

'Democracy', Weiler substantiated later, 'was not part of the DNA of European Integration.'[54] Nor was social justice between, let alone within, the Member States— and it seems obvious why all this was very much to the liking of ordoliberal scholars and like-minded officials: the freedoms guaranteed in the EEC Treaty, the opening up of national economies, the anti-discrimination rules, and the commitment to a system of undistorted competition, were interpreted as a principled and de facto irrevocable 'decision' for the establishment of a free market economy and its competitive

---

[49] Knut Wolfgang Nörr, *Die Republik der Wirtschaft. Teil I: Von der Besatzungszeit bis zur Großen Koalition*, (Tübingen: Mohr Siebeck, 1999), p 5 et seq.

[50] See n 34 above.

[51] Case 26/62, *Van Gend en Loos v Nederlandse Administratie der Belastingen* [1963] ECR 1.

[52] Case 6/64, *Flaminio Costa v E.N.E.L.* [1964] ECR 585.

[53] Joseph H.H. Weiler, 'The Reformation of European Constitutionalism', (1997) 35 *Journal of Common Market Studies*, pp 97–131, at 97.

[54] Joseph H.H. Weiler, 'Europe in Crisis—on "Political Messianism", "Legitimacy" and the "Rule of Law"', (2012) *Singapore Journal of Legal Studies*, pp 248–268.

ordering. The EEC Treaty promised to ensure what Germany's Federal Constitutional Court had refused to accept, namely, the assignment of constitutional validity to the core principles of an ordoliberal 'economic constitution' which claimed primacy over national law. Again, the alliance between economic constitutionalism and the core doctrines of the ECJ was hardly noticed even by the two allies, let alone elsewhere in European law scholarship. Equally noteworthy, ordoliberalism did, by no means, represent the majority of Germany's domestic professors of public law (*Staats- und Verfassungsrechts*) or European law scholarship. Germany's constitutional lawyers defended the primacy of the legislature even in instances in which its policies appeared to be opportunistic and unprincipled.[55]

It is worth noting that the ordoliberal reading provided a seemingly elegant response to the thorny legitimacy *problématique*. The validity of Europe's economic governance was not dependent upon some foundational political democratic act. Quite to the contrary, the EEC could be perceived as a non-majoritarian settlement *par excellence*; its competitive order was based upon law—and shielded against political influence.[56] All this contrasts markedly and positively with the ideational backing of the integration-through-law agenda. This agenda assumes that the establishment of a common order for the EEC/Union can rely on 'law as such'. Indeed, as late as 1990 Renaud Dehousse and Joseph Weiler presented law as 'the agent and the object of integration'. This occurred while the American law and society movement advocated the study of 'law in its context', and all sorts of interdisciplinary 'law and ...' explorations were *en vogue* on both sides of the Atlantic.

Both concepts, however, shared very similar flaws. On what grounds can one argue that an ever more uniform legal order deserves the same degree of recognition throughout the entire Community? And how could one expect that harmonised laws would be implemented everywhere in the same way? On what grounds could the proponents of economic constitutionalism claim that their project would overcome the varieties of Europe's forms of capitalism?

B. The Road to Maastricht: Between Freiburg and Chicago

Through and after the Single European Act of 1985 with its turn to majority-voting, the integration process gained new momentum—and deepened by the same token, as nobody else but Joseph Weiler noted, with the legitimacy deficit of the renewed Community.[57] Two moves which were expected to open new sustainable prospects followed: one was Jacques Delors' internal market programme. As the sociologist M. Rainer Lepsius observed,[58] this programme institutionalised 'economic rationality' as the *leitmotif* of the integration project. With this notion, Lepsius captures a

---

[55] BVerfGE 4, 7, n 27 above.

[56] Wigger, 'Competition for Competitiveness', n 44 above, p 131 et seq.

[57] Joseph H.H. Weiler, 'The Transformation of Europe', (1991) 100 *Yale Law Journal*, pp 2403–2483, at 2453 et seq.

[58] See M. Rainer Lepsius, 'Institutionalisierung und Deinstitutionalisierung von Rationalitätskriterien', in: Gerhard Göhler (ed), *Institutionenwandel*, (1996) 16 *Leviathan* (Special Issue), pp 57–69.

re-configuration of the relations between law, politics and the economy. A congenial transformative change was advocated by a new generation of ordoliberal scholars. This mutation had started at national level with the move of Friedrich August von Hayek from Chicago to Freiburg, where he soon found strong support for a change of paradigmatic dimensions in the ordoliberal conceptual edifice. His key concept, the understanding of 'competition as a discovery process' replaced the orthodox commitments to law-controlled competitive conditions and the taming of economic power. This shift led the 'second generation' of ordoliberal scholars to re-define the objectives and the methods of national and European competition law dramatically. From this time onward, their focus was on the critique of anti-competitive state activities and the promotion of entrepreneurial freedom, rather than the control of economic power. A further highly significant re-orientation was the adoption of the principle of mutual recognition which was to expose national laws to 'regulatory competition'. The reasons were explained in pertinent publications of officious ordoliberal institutions, such as the Advisory Board of the German Ministry of the Economics.[59]

Pierre Dardot and Christian Laval, in their analyses of the political meaning of the integration project, characterise this re-orientation as 'neo-ordo-liberalism' and rightly underline its affinities with the Austro-American neoliberalism.[60] What they take less seriously is the second compensatory move, namely, the proclamation of an 'ever closer Union' with meta-economic ambitions and powers in new policy fields; it was in particular the chapter on 'industrial policy', which provoked harsh ordoliberal critique,[61] quite understandably, so that it seems obvious that the establishment of this new objective is irreconcilable with the commitment to a 'system of undistorted competition'. Be that as it may, by now, we have experienced that all-important innovation which the Maastricht Treaty brought about was the Economic and Monetary Union (EMU). Our discussion of this move will take issue with the widely-shared perception of the EMU as an ordoliberal concept and the understanding of the institutional cornerstones of the EMU as essentially ordoliberal constructs. We will complement this dissent by a critique of the judgment of the *Bundesverfassungsgericht* on the Maastricht Treaty in which the German Court sought in vain to read an ordoliberal 'stability philosophy' into the Treaty, before we turn, against this background, to the impact of the new modes of economic governance which Europe developed after the financial crisis.

IV. THE EU AFTER MAASTRICHT

The Treaty of Maastricht was ambitious and multi-faceted. Our focus here is on the EMU and its infamous characteristic: monetary policy has become an exclusive

---

[59] Wissenschaftlicher Beirat beim Bundesministerium für Wirtschaft, *Stellungnahme zum Weißbuch der EG-Kommission über den Binnenmarkt*, Schriften-Reihe 51 (Bonn, 1986).

[60] Note 39 above, p 208 et seq.

[61] Suffice it here to name Manfred E. Streit and Werner Mussler, 'The Economic Constitution of the European Community. From "Rome" to "Maastricht"', (1995) 1 *European Law Journal*, pp 5–30.

competence of the Union (Article 3(1) c TFEU), while the Member States remained responsible for fiscal and economic policy. The resistance on the part of the Member States against a conferral of powers in these fields is unsurprising. Budgetary autonomy is a core institution of constitutional democracies and its exercise is directly linked to the mandate of the citizenry. Economic policy is exercised within a complex institutional infrastructure of formal rule and social norms. The implications have been outlined above in the passages on economic sociology.[62] Economic and fiscal policies will vary according to socio-economic constellations, political preferences, and historical experiences. At earlier stages of the integration project, it may have been plausible to count on increasing convergence under the impact of a common currency. In 1992, this was no longer the case. Socio-economic diversity with the Union and within the eurozone deepened continuously. European monetary policy was bound to conflict to various degrees and intensities with national policies. Such constellations are not vertical conflicts for which the supremacy doctrine would provide a response. They are 'diagonal conflicts': both the Union and the Member States are certainly interested in the functioning of their economies, but the powers required to accomplish this objective are attributed to two distinct levels of governance. One response foreseen in Article 119 TFEU was 'the adoption of an economic policy which is based on the close coordination of Member States' economic policies' as substantiated in Article 121 TFEU. The second response was the Stability and Growth Pact of 1997,[63] so famously 'breached' by Germany and France. Both responses are very soft—fortunately enough, observed Barry Eichengreen in *DIE ZEIT* of 20 November 2003 because the 3% ceiling foreseen in the Stability Pact is 'at best silly and at worst perverse'.

A. What is Ordo-liberal about the EMU?

The characterisation of the EMU as an ordoliberal accomplishment can certainly point to the language used by its advocates in Germany, and, more significantly, to core principles enshrined in the Treaty and the establishment of the ECB. On closer inspection, all of these indicators prove to be not so trustworthy. To be sure, an ordoliberal imprint is visible in the prohibition of monetary financing (Article 123(1) TFEU), the prohibition of bailouts (Article 125(1) TFEU), and the objectives of the Stability and Growth Pact. Lars P. Feld and Ekkehard Köhler, when underlining these features emphasise, however, that there were no credible means available to ensure compliance which these objectives. Feld has recently added that the disrespect of the no bailout-clause and of the prohibition of state financing was favoured by the German government, the continuous appeal to ordoliberal principles notwithstanding.[64]

---

[62] Section II C.
[63] OJ C 236, 02 August 1997, 1.
[64] See Feld and Köhler, n 18 above, pp 173–195.

Most persuasive seems the establishment of the independent ECB with its commitment to price stability. The delegation of monetary policy to a non-majoritarian institution is indeed an ordoliberal concern of *longue durée*. The underlying reasons cannot be discussed meaningfully in passing. What is certainly wrong, however, is the equating of the ECB with the *Bundesbank*. Suffice it here to underline that the autonomy of the latter rested on simple legislation and could hence be abolished by a simple majority in the *Bundestag*. Equally importantly, the *Bank* was concerned with just one economy and interacted with a broad spectre of stakeholders. Its autonomy, reputation and broad social acceptance had been acquired and shaped during the post-war history of the Federal Republic. Its powers did not enable it to take decisions with far-reaching distributional implications within and between states. It could not directly interfere with labour law legislation and social policy through the acquisition or non-acquisition of state bonds. Its autonomy was not subject to the kind of intergovernmentalism which governs in the European System of Central Banks (ESCB).

All this is not to say that the ECB has wilfully chosen to do what it feels by now entitled to do. The notion of 'diagonal conflicts' is again illuminating. Due to the enormous socio-economic and political diversity within the eurozone, the 'one-size-fits-no-one' dilemma established through the EMU cannot be subjected to general rules. The Maastricht Treaty failed to establish a political infrastructure and institutional frameworks within which democratic political contestation could address, and democratically-accountable actors deal with, the complex conflict constellations which the common currency generated. What we are witnessing is a *de-legalisation* of European rule. Anatole Kaletzky has praised President Mario Draghi for his 'transformation of the ECB into the world's most creative and proactive central bank'.[65] He has good reasons not to call this an ordoliberal approach.

B. The Maastricht-*Urteil* of 12 October 1993

Ordoliberal jurists[66] felt uncomfortable with the Maastricht Treaty and ordoliberal economists hesitated to identify themselves with the EMU.[67] But there is one important actor who sought, or thought, to promote the ordoliberal stability philosophy,

---

[65] 'Are we Heading Towards a Roman Europe?', *Social Europe Journal*, 27 April 2016, available at: www.socialeurope.eu/2016/04/heading-towards-roman-europe.

[66] See, for a prominent voice, Peter Behrens, 'Die Wirtschaftsverfassung der Europäischen Gemeinschaft', in Gert Brüggemeier (ed), *Verfassungen für ein ziviles Europa*, (Baden-Baden: Nomos, 1994), pp 73–90.

[67] See, eg, Werner Mussler, *Die Wirtschaftsverfassung der Europäischen Gemeinschaft im Wandel. Von Rom nach Maastricht*, (Baden-Baden: Nomos, 1998). At the time, it was not yet common that German authors would write in English. There were, of course, exceptions. Tellingly enough, however, the most prominent ordoliberal exception, namely, the critique of the Maastricht Treaty by Manfred E. Streit and Werner Mussler (cited in n 61 above) does not deal with the EMU. On the intense controversies in Germany over the common currency at the time of its introduction, see Friedrich Heinemann, 'Zwischen "Kernschmelze" und "Fass ohne Boden"—zum Dissens deutscher Ökonomen in der Schuldenkrise', (2013) 60 *Zeitschrift für Politikwissenschaft*, pp 207–219.

namely, the Second Senate of the German Constitutional Court (GCC) in its judgment on the Maastricht Treaty.[68]

What the Court had to say about the economy did not attract much attention at the time, but these passages were, in fact, the most irritating pronouncements in the lengthy judgment. The GCC found that it was precisely the substitution of politics and policies by legal rules and the independence of the ECB which ensured the compatibility of the EMU with the Basic Law. This pronouncement was the Court's response to the submission of the plaintiffs that the EU was about to acquire such wide-ranging competences that Member States could no longer act as the masters of their 'democratic statehood'. Economic integration, so the Court argued, was an autonomous and apolitical process, which might, and indeed should, operate beyond the reach of Member-State political influence. By virtue of a constitutional commitment to price stability and rules that guarded against inappropriate budgetary deficits, the EMU seemed, in its view, to be adequately designed. Accordingly, doubts about the democratic legitimacy of economic integration were diverted. To rephrase the argument slightly: yes, the Treaty is compatible with the Basic Law; but this is true only because it is inspired by Germany's stability philosophy and only as long as this stability commitment is actually respected.[69]

The Court had been explicitly warned:

> by important contributors to the debate that a currency union, especially between Member States which are oriented towards an active economic and social policy, can ultimately only be realised in common with a political union (embracing all essential economic functions), and cannot be realised independently thereof or as a mere preliminary stage on the way to it.[70]

It could hence not take the sustainability of the stability community for granted. And indeed, Ernst-Wolfgang Böckenförde, the most renowned judge of the deciding Second Senate, has recently underlined that the judges were, indeed, fully aware of the fragility of the *Stabilitätsgemeinschaft* (stability community) which they defended as a constitutional command.[71] Böckenförde refers to a passage in which the GCC seeks to distinguish its constitutional guardianship from essentially political decisions:

> The decision to agree on a monetary union and put it into operation without a simultaneous or immediately subsequent political union is a political one, for which the institutions with competence on the matter must take political responsibility.[72]

---

[68] *Brunner v The European Union Treaty* [1994] 1 CMLR 57.

[69] Para 90 of the judgment reads: 'This conception of the currency union as a community based on stability is the basis and subject-matter of the German Act of Accession. If the monetary union should not be able to develop on a continuing basis the stability present at the beginning of the third stage within the meaning of the agreed mandate for stabilisation, it would be abandoning the Treaty conception.'

[70] ibid, para 92 of the Brunner sentence; the President of the *Bundesbank* is mentioned here; already on p 12 the judgment underlined that two particularly 'qualified informants on questions of economic and monetary union' had been heard, namely 'the President of the Bundesbank, Prof. Helmut Schlesinger, and the Director of the Bundesbank, Dr. Wolfgang Rieke'.

[71] 'Kennt die europäische Not kein Gebot? Die Webfehler der EU und die Notwendigkeit einer neuen politischen Entscheidung' (Does necessity not know rules? Design flaws of the EU and the necessity of a new political decision), *Neue Züricher Zeitung*, 21 June 2010.

[72] Böckenförde is referring to para 93 of the judgment. The passage reads: 'This does not raise a question of constitutional law, however, but of politics. The decision to agree on a monetary union and

One remains perplexed. The judges must have known that it would be simply inconceivable to correct politically the deal among the many signatories of the Maastricht Treaty to which they had given their legal blessing. And they decided accordingly when they were confronted with the request to prevent Monetary Union from entering the third stage.[73] Under the common currency, the financial inter-dependencies in a socio-economically ever more heterogeneous Union were deepened, but the new exclusive European competence for monetary policy was too weak an instrument to govern the European economic sphere. It was strong enough, however, to deprive the Member States of former crucially important governmental powers. Europe continued to be a 'market without a state', while the former 'masters of the treaties' had become 'states without markets'.[74]

C. Europe's Responses to the Financial Crisis

As argued above in Section IV A, the fragility of the Maastricht arrangement was a birth defect that remained latent until the economic crisis began to unfold in 2008. Since then, we have witnessed a turbo-speed establishment of new modes of transnational economic governance and unprecedented regulatory techniques. Detailed descriptions are readily available[75] and need not be reproduced here. The following observations will instead comment first on methodological issues, then on substantive concerns, and finally on the role of the European judiciary.

i. New Economic Governance and the Rule of Law

A characterising feature of ordoliberalism was its insistence that economic policy should be guided by law and justiciable criteria.[76] What happened in the course of Europe's crisis management? Three features of the present European *praxis* seem particularly intriguing.

---

put it into operation without a simultaneous or immediately subsequent political union is a political one, for which the institutions with competence on the matter must take political responsibility. If it emerges that the desired monetary union cannot in reality be achieved without a (not yet desired) political union, a fresh political decision will be required as to how to proceed further. There is room for such a decision as a matter of law, because under the present Treaty the monetary union is no more able to give rise automatically to a political union than to an economic union; that would require an amendment of the Treaty, which could not happen without a decision of the national state institutions, including the German Bundestag. Whether that decision is taken is again—in the context of what is constitutionally permissible—a political matter.'

[73] 2 BvR 1877/97 und 2 BvR 50/98 *German Participation in EMU*, Judgment of 31 March 1998.

[74] See, in more detail, Christian Joerges, 'The Market without a State? States without Markets? Two Essays on the Law of the European Economy', n 3 above.

[75] See, comprehensively, Fernando Losada and Agustín José Menéndez (eds), *The Key Legal Texts of the European Crises Treaties, Regulations, Directives, Case Law*, ARENA Centre for European Studies, Oslo 2014.

[76] See Ernst-Joachim Mestmäcker, 'Power, Law and Economic Constitution', (1973) 2 *The German Economic Review*, pp 177–198.

The first: the supervision and control of macro-economic imbalances, which the two 'six-pack' regulations 1176/2011 and 1174/2011 mandate,[77] disregard the principle of enumerated powers, and, by the same token, the democratic legitimacy of national institutions, in particular the budgetary powers of the parliaments of the 'states receiving assistance'. *The second*: in its departure from the one-size-fits-all philosophy that orients European integration in general and monetary policy in particular, European crisis management nonetheless fails to achieve a variation, one which might be founded in democratically-legitimated choices; quite to the contrary, the individualised scrutiny of all Member States is geared to the objective of budgetary balances and seeks to impose the functionally, seemingly-necessary accompanying discipline; the 'receiving states' cannot but respond to pertinent requests through austerity measures: reductions of wage levels and of social entitlements. *The third*: the machinery of the new regime with its individualised measures which are oriented only by necessarily indeterminate general clauses is resorting to *Maßnahmen* (regulatory ad hoc interventions); it has established transnational executive machinery outside both the realm of democratic politics *and* the form of accountability which the rule-of-law used to guarantee; core concepts used by new economic governance cannot be defined with any precision, either by lawyers or by economists, and are therefore not justiciable; rule-of-law and legal protection requirements are being suspended. This type of de-legalisation is accompanied by assessments of Member State performance, which cannot be but highly discretionary. To characterise all this as 'ordoliberal' is to disregard the legal legacy of this tradition completely.

ii. Substantive Concerns with Europe's Crisis 'Law'

In the scholarly discussion of the legality of Europe's 'crisis law', complacency prevails. But it seems difficult not to be as irritated as Böckenförde in his comment in the *Neue Zuricher Zeitung*[78] by the treatment of so many seemingly very firmly established principles and rules by these practices.

Three points seem particularly embarrassing:[79]

The first can be illustrated by the treatment of Greece in the judgment of the *Bundesverfassungsgericht* of 12 September 2012. The German Court has, in this judgment, defended the budgetary powers of the *Bundestag*. But our Court failed to explain why the Parliament of Greece should not deserve the same respect.[80] To put the critique of the *praxis* of the 'memoranda of understanding' drastically:

> The Republic of Germany cannot, in its relations with the EU contract with "slaves". It cannot enter into partnership with anything other than fully sovereign states.[81]

---

[77] See Losada and Menéndez, n 75 above, p 443 et seq, and 449 et seq.

[78] See n 71 above.

[79] Very similar concerns have been underlined by a non-lawyer: Jonathan White, 'Authority after Emergency Rule', (2015) 78 *Modern Law Review*, pp 585–610.

[80] See Judgment of 12 September 2012 on the ESM and Fiscal Compact, 2 BvR 1390/12 for an early critique Christian Joerges, 'Der Berg kreißte—gebar er eine Maus? Europa vor dem Bundesverfassungsgericht', (2012) 65 *WSI-Mitteilungen*, p 560.

[81] Michelle Everson, 'An Exercise in Legal Honesty: Rewriting the Court of Justice and the *Bundesverfassungsgericht*', (2015) 21 *European Law Journal*, pp 474–499, at 497.

This kind of mutual recognition defines the Union as a Union.[82]

A *second query* concerns the prevailing complacency with the technocratic character of Europe's crisis management. Europe must not pervert democratic constitutionalism into technocratic rule. It has to justify and de-limit the resort to non-majoritarian institutions. The assumption that the ESCB, which is not legitimated by a democratic vote and cannot be held accountable by Europe's citizens, can be empowered to take far-reaching distributional decisions and intervene in all policy fields, is simply indefensible. To this point, we will return in the following section on the *Gauweiler* judgment.

The third irritant is the *praxis* of conditionality. This *praxis* has been legalised explicitly by the Council Decision of 25 March 2011 amending Article 136 TFEU. One should nevertheless ask: is this amendment reconcilable with the foundational principles of the European project? Can the principles of equality, mutual respect and co-operation be transformed into command-and-control relationships? I submit that 'conditionality' is an unacceptable intrusion into the practice of democratic political will-formation, an unconstitutional amendment of the TFEU.[83]

iii. The Legalisation of Emergency Governance by Europe's Judiciary

Over decades, the foundational jurisprudence of the ECJ has been praised and admired. Its much-venerated accomplishment was the so-called 'constitutionalisation' of the European Treaties. The recent controversy between the *Bundesverfassungsgericht* and the CJEU over the Outright Monetary Transactions (OMT) programme of the ECB builds on this legacy—and breaks with it dramatically.

The legal facet of the OMT saga took off from the German Court's 'first reference ever'. The reference was spectacular indeed also because the German Court made its views on the proper answer to its question clearly known, a gesture which was perceived as a provocation, in particular by German commentators.[84] How should one qualify the CJEU's response in its judgment of 16 June 2015?[85] The reader of this response feels drawn into the boring triviality of cases such as '*Molkereizentrale Westfalen-Lippe* v *Hauptzollamt Paderborn*'.[86] This impression contrasts sharply with the substance of the CJEU's reasoning.

---

[82] See Claire Kilpatrick, 'On the Rule of Law and Economic Emergency: The Degradation of Basic Legal Values in Europe's Bailouts', (2015) 35 *Oxford Journal of Legal Studies*, pp 1–29.

[83] See Anneli Albi, 'Erosion of Constitutional Rights in EU Law: A Call for "Substantive Co-operative Constitutionalism"', (2015) 9 *Vienna Journal of International Constitutional Law*, pp 151–185; Jonathan White, n 79 above, p 590 *et seq.*

[84] BVerfG, 2 BvR 2728/13 vom 14.01.2014, available at: www.bverfg.de/e/rs20140114_2bvr272813en. html. Suffice it to point to the pertinent special issue of the (2014) 15 *German Law Journal* with 16, mostly highly critical, contributions.

[85] Case C-62/14 *Gauweiler*, EU: C:2015: 400.

[86] Case 28/67, judgment of 3 April 1968, ECLI:EU:C:1968:17; I would like to thank Hauke Brunkhorst (Berlin/Flensburg) for making us aware of this paradoxical affinity.

This reasoning was prepared by the Opinion of the Court's Advocate General.[87] The AG observed, in his discussion of the notions of monetary and economic policy, that:

> The Treaties are silent ... when it comes to defining the exclusive competence of the Union in relation to monetary policy.[88]

> The division that EU law makes between those policies is a requirement imposed by the structure of the Treaties and by the horizontal and vertical distribution of powers within the Union, but in economic terms it may be stated that any monetary policy measure is ultimately encompassed by the broader category of general economic policy.[89]

> It follows that the delineation which the text of the Treaty expects us to make when characterising measures as monetary rather than economic policy has to rely on "the objectives ascribed to that policy".[90]

In contrast to facts, which can be ascertained when a decision is being taken, it is usually uncertain and controversial whether such objectives can be realised at all, and, if so, how. What *can* nevertheless be ascertained is whether a measure 'belongs to the category of instruments which the law provides for carrying out monetary policy'.[91]

But here the law's conditional programming ends. Independent expertise must step in. The ECB has explained that it *intended* to pursue a monetary policy objective and enjoys broad discretion in its framing and implementation.[92]

> The ECB must ... be afforded a broad discretion for the purpose of framing and implementing the Union's monetary policy. The Courts, when reviewing the ECB's activity, must therefore avoid the risk of supplanting the Bank, by venturing into a highly technical terrain in which it is necessary to have an expertise and experience which, according to the Treaties, devolves solely upon the ECB. Therefore, the intensity of judicial review of the ECB's activity, its mandatory nature aside, must be characterised by a considerable degree of caution.[93]

The CJEU, in its judgment of 16 June 2015, has endorsed this argumentation. Just like the AG, the Court underlines that the 'Treaty contains no precise definition of monetary policy but defines both the objectives of monetary policy and the instruments which are available to the ESCB'.[94] What the ECB decides to undertake is legal as long as 'it does not appear that that analysis of the economic situation of the euro area as at the date of the announcement of the programme in question is vitiated by a manifest error of assessment'.[95]

---

[87] Opinion of GA Cruz Villalón delivered on 14 January 2015.
[88] Cruz Villalón, ibid, para 127.
[89] ibid, para 129.
[90] ibid, para 127.
[91] ibid, para 130.
[92] ibid, paras 109–112.
[93] ibid, para 111.
[94] *Gauweiler*, n 85 above, para 41.
[95] ibid, para 74.

What, then, is left, one may ask, of the powers of the Member States in the sphere of economic policy? These powers depend, first of all, on how the ECB defines its mandate. The implementation of this mandate comprises and even requires the linking of the OMT programme to the conditionality of financial assistance.[96] The ECB is also entitled to proceed selectively in its buying activities and to focus on those Member States in which the monetary policy transmission channels do not work.[97] The ECJ follows suit. The conditionality of financing which the Court had qualified as a matter of *economic policy* in its *Pringle* judgment in view of their function 'to safeguard the stability of the euro area as a whole'[98] does not affect the qualification of the OMT programme as monetary policy, because the latter is meant 'to support the general economic policies in the Union' as provided for by Article 119(2) TFEU.[99]

The unruly conflict between European monetary policy and national economic policy has been settled through a novel regulatory arrangement, in which the ECB is an extremely powerful actor, albeit one which needs the support of the machinery ensuring the targeted conditionality of financial assistance. '[T]he Union today is governed by a set of principles relating both to its objectives and to its boundaries', so the AG assures us and does not hesitate to characterise this arrangement as a 'constitutional framework'.[100] This, however, is a framework beyond any constitutional, let alone democratic, credentials. The ordering of the entire economy of the eurozone is depicted as a non-political *epistemic* task. This task is delegated to a supranational bureaucracy which enjoys practically unlimited discretionary powers. The irony of this appeal to expertise is that this expertise must operate under high uncertainty and can only assert that its actions are for the common European good and all controversies in the quarters of monetary policy scholarship notwithstanding, are simply '*alternativlos*'. Furthermore, the appeal to 'excellence' and 'expertise' implies that the deep distributional implications of the ECB's actions both between and within the Member States of the EU are un-political and hence not in need of any kind of political legitimation. To put it slightly differently, Europe's 'economic constitution' and its entire constitutional configuration has been replaced by the discretionary decision-making powers of an unaccountable technocracy. What kind of ordoliberalism can this be? Europe's constitutional scholarship seems hardly irritated. The most insistent critique of the CJEU of which I am aware has been articulated by the *Kronberger Kreis*, a circle of renowned ordoliberal scholars.[101] As with European crisis politics in general, the critique is mitigated by pragmatic concerns. It is the reasoning, not the result of the CJEU, which is held to be unacceptable.

---

[96] ibid, para 145.

[97] ibid, para 153.

[98] Case C-370/12 *Pringle*, EU:C:2012:756, para 56.

[99] ibid, para 59.

[100] See n 68 above, para 215.

[101] But this seems not to be the case; see *Kronberger Kreis* (Lars P. Feld, Clemens Fuest, Justus Haucap, Heike Schweitzer, Volker Wieland, Berthold U. Wigger), 'Dismantling the Boundaries of the ECB's Monetary Policy Mandate: The CJEU's OMT Judgment and its Consequences', (Berlin: Stiftung Marktwirtschaft, 2016), available at: www.econbiz.de/Record/dismantling-the-boundaries-of-the-ecb-s-monetary-policy-mandate-the-cjeu-s-omt-judgement-and-its-consequences-feld-lars/10011445584.

At this point, we come close to the gist of the matter: facticity and political fiat replace both normativity and epistemic reason. Stefan Oeter, in a comment on the reference of the *Bundesverfassungsgericht* written prior to the CJEU's judgment, has hit the nail on the head: the German Court's concept of the rule of law, he submits, 'is impossible to match with the realities of European economic policy'. Since it is 'definitely impossible to know exactly what is right or wrong ... judges should accord the competent organs equipped with the necessary expertise and experience a strong dose of trust'.[102] This is where the law ends and the commitments to democracy and the rule-of-law are suspended. Will this type of legalisation of the a-legal save the European project? The integrity of constitutional law and the sustainability of the European projects would have been better served by a refusal of the judiciary to rubber-stamp un-justiciable practices. Judge Gertrude Lübbe-Wolff, in her dissent to the reference order of the Karlsruhe Court has listed many good reasons militating in favour of such restraint.[103] To name but a few: 'The more far-reaching, the more weighty, the more irreversible—legally and factually—the possible consequences of a judicial decision, the more judicial restraint is appropriate'.[104] 'Where for reasons of law the judges' courage must dwindle when it comes to the substance, they ought not to go into the substance at all'.[105] 'The democratic legitimacy which the decision of a national court may draw from the relevant standards of national law (if any) will not, or not without substantial detriment, extend beyond the national area'.[106]

In my view, the OMT litigation is 'undecidable' in a courtroom.[107] This is certainly not the kind of 'solution' lawyers are expected to deliver. It is one which exposes Europe's crisis 'law' to political contestation. This may be a risky move. The same holds true, however, for the establishment of an emergency regime of unlimited duration.[108]

---

[102] Stefan Oeter, Conflict at the Interface of Economic 'Policy and Law: Cognitive Dissonance in the German Constitutional Court OMT Case Reasoning', in: Tim Krieger, Diana Panke and Bernhard Neumärker (eds), *Europe's Crisis: The Conflict-Theoretic Perspective*, (Baden-Baden: Nomos, 2016), pp 197–220, at 217.

[103] BVerfG, 2 BvR 2728/13 vom 14.1.2014, §§1–105, available at: www.bverfg.de/entscheidungen/rs20140114_2bvr272813en.html.

[104] ibid, para 7.

[105] ibid, para 27.

[106] ibid, para 28.

[107] On this notion, see Jacques Lenoble, 'Law and Undecidability: on a New Vision of the Proceduralization of Law', (1995–96) 17 *Cardozo Law Review*, pp 935–1004.

[108] See Christian Joerges, '*Pereat iustitia, fiat mundus*: What is left of the European Economic Constitution after the OMT-litigation', (2016) 23 *Maastricht Journal of European & Comparative Law*, pp 99–118.

12

Ordoliberal Escape from Societas Economica: Re-establishing the Normative

MICHELLE EVERSON

ABSTRACT

Following Brexit and the election of Donald Trump, the global outlook has changed. Above all, the two-guiding universalism of the post-cold-war era, or the pursuit of human rights and global markets, are now increasingly being called into question. This chapter argues that the contemporary rejection of cosmopolitan values has its roots in a crisis of economic liberalism. It traces the roots of this crisis within the European integration project and counters that Europe might be better served by a more cautious approach, or a return to balance between ordo-liberal markets and social democratic principles. The chapter argues that globalisation processes must be guided by efforts to pursue two countervailing principles of order and security.

I. GLOBAL WEIMAR: LONGING FOR GLOBAL ORDER

FOLLOWING THE FINANCIAL crisis, the sovereign debt crisis, the border crisis and Brexit, Europe is in disarray. It is not alone. The global trend is one of deep uncertainty and intractable conflict. Above all, a populist movement, reacting to the two great movements of the post-Cold War era, is aggressively questioning the purpose and structures of large-scale migration and cross-border trade on both sides of the Atlantic. Importantly, however, consternation is not confined to a realm of political extremism. Instead, the contradictions and upheavals inherent to global integration by means of free human and economic movement are also straining our curiously-entrenched paradigms of political, social and cultural organisation in ways that were impossible to anticipate during the intensified pursuit of human rights and the heightened economic liberalisation that followed the fall of the Berlin Wall. Commenting on the not-so-slow evolution of a Fortress Europe within the Treaty of Lisbon's emphasis upon the then new concept of securitisation, Hans

Lindahl long ago reminded European lawyers of the enduring currency of Hannah Arendt's concept of 'spatiality' as:

> [N]ot merely a geographical term. It relates not so much, and not primarily, to a piece of land as to the space between individuals in a group whose members are bound to, and at the same time separated and protected from each other by all kinds of relationships, based on a common language, religion, a common history, customs, and laws.[1]

For lawyers, the complex of sociological and cultural artefacts that are called upon to instantiate spatial community may appear opaque, but they translate not simply into jurisdictional notions, or territorial instruments of nationality law and security policy, but rather into far more fundamental constitutional structures of political representation and democracy, as well as regulatory frameworks of national economic steering and social re-distribution. And it is here, in the unravelling of the nationally-bounded, majoritarian politics and policies of economic and social integration through intensified globalisation that political populism has found its niche, and that academic thought struggles to identify the new paradigms of political, social and economic organisation,[2] which might bridge the gap between a traditional, spatially-delineated world and a post-war globe of universalising aspirations and complex interdependencies.

Post Brexit, the (European) world, or at least our perception of it, is a very different place. Contrary to the comfortable intellectual certainties of the post-Cold War era, a significant segment of the population demonstrably does not perceive itself to have benefited from economic liberalisation or global free trade. Equally, to the degree that a similarly decisive section of UK popular opinion proved itself malleable during campaigning, or highly-receptive to press-driven concerns that immigration posed a threat to the social cohesion of the nation, the ascendancy of notions of a 'human rights'-based global community has also been checked. At the same time, however, Brexit would appear to have been a chronicle foretold, at least within the setting of the EU.

As long ago as 2008, the economic sociologist, Neil Fligstein, found a clear signal within Eurobarometer data warning of the increasing alienation of a number of Europeans, broadly-defined as a working class, from an integrationist project which they saw as further diminishing their already precarious social standing. More worryingly still, data similarly confirmed that a far larger and more comfortable middle class, though happy, especially when on holiday, to engage with and benefit from cultural and economic Europeanisation processes, retained a contingent outlook towards the Union, content to support it in good times, but ambivalent with regard to the bad.[3] Brexit explained, although Fligstein's work was largely unremarked

---

[1] Hans Lindahl, 'Finding a Place for Freedom, Security and Justice: The European Union's Claim to Territorial Unity', (2004) 29 *European Law Review*, p 461, at 466.

[2] Christian Joerges, 'Brother, can you Paradigm?', Review Essay of Kaarlo Turi and Klaus Tuori, *The Eurozone Crisis: A Constitutional Analysis*, (Cambridge: Cambridge University Press, 2014), (2014) 12 *International Journal of Constitutional Law*, pp 769–785.

[3] Neil Fligstein, *Euro-clash: The EU, European Identity and the Future of Europe*, (Oxford: Oxford University Press, 2008).

within the Europeanist canon, the emphatic vote of proud labour heartlands for Brexit, together with middle England's mistrustful rejection of a European Union which they also perceived to be in the grip of economic and border crises, underlines the fragility of our still predominantly-functionalist model of European integration, or the de-politicised creation of European community through establishment of a European economy which has demonstrably failed to create a European 'community of fate', or a sense of solidarity between European citizens.

However, Brexit is far more than Brexit: Where the Brexit vote may also be taken as the first popular response of a global public to global cosmopolitanism, albeit mediated through a UK and Europeanisation lens, a degree of light is also shed on the always vexed issue of economic opportunity, belonging and community, or the public perception of it, in a global age. As the months since the Brexit vote within the UK also demonstrate, a sad corollary of resistance through rejection of cosmo-politanism, can also be a parochialism that verges on, or descends into racism, a retrograde nationalistic recalibration, which similarly denigrates the cosmopolitan rights-bearer who has seized, either by virtue of want or by reason of outlook, on the opportunities presented by our modern universalisms. The worries of the final years of Weimar hang heavy over the juxtaposition of cosmopolitanism and commu-nity; over the now very tangible and seemingly intractable paradox of cosmopolitan opportunity *versus* national community.[4] We have now entered a worrying period of challenge to post-national orders.

Within this setting, any effort to address crisis within Europe accordingly also raises more global concerns. Our age of economic globalisation is urgently demand-ing our conceptual attention: What are its challenges, how can we tame economic powers that ignore national boundaries, is there a common good within this global world, and, if so, how might we defend it? For a present-day generation of European peoples, a generation long distanced from the absolute certainty of a post-war gen-eration determined never again to break the peace, and, in its youthful global out-look, even less inclined to commit to a culturally-foreclosing European federalism, there is only one possible ideational vision of the EU to which they might commit themselves: the search for an order in chaos, for a form of governing beyond closed national communities, an order which defies the inequalities created by uncon-strained markets and capital, and an order which seeks also to establish justice, democracy and solidarity outside once-comforting but now illusionary territorial (national) sovereignties. The European Union of 2016 is not the European Economic Communities of 1958, having morphed from an international community of market building into a supranational body of 'ever closer Union' between its peoples. Nor is the Union of 2016 a happy or uncontroversial one, as efforts to save the euro feed the pressure for 'more Europe', but simultaneously undermine the political and social values that must always be a part of the European project, a pressure that is only intensified by the migration crisis.

---

[4] See, only, the worrying speech made by Theresa May to the Conservative Party Conference in 2016, and her assertion (paraphrasing) that citizens of the world have no home. Press commentators have already noted the worrying similarities to the rhetoric of 1930s Germany, see www.theguardian.com/politics/2016/oct/09/theresa-may-rejection-of-enlightenment-values.

Yet, throughout its history and still today, the European project has been the drawing board for a sustainable ideal of civilised internationalism. That Europe is, and always will be, beset by its own contradictions of equalisation and boundary-drawing, or that it seems, currently, to be complicit within, rather than controlling of, the economic forces that are threatening globally to overwhelm all human (non-economic) self-determination, are happenings that cannot be denied. At the same time, however, Europe's current malaise cannot and should not be taken as reason to walk away from the best enunciated and most practised iteration of the search for order in chaos offered by any post-national organisation now operating on the global stage. Instead, we must learn from Europe's failures in order to fight *within* the EU for all of the advantages of order in chaos, for opportunities of human innovation, on the one hand (the rights of engagement within markets), and for the securities of self-determination, on the other (rights of control over markets).

II. LEARNING LESSONS FROM EUROPEAN MALAISE

2016 is a long way away from 1989. Given the gap, it is perhaps all too easy to forget the upheaval which followed the collapse of the Soviet Union and, above all, the immediate challenges faced by the then European Communities in the process of the reconstruction of its relationships with the nations of Eastern Europe. Yet, a perception that the latter-day surrender of the EU to economic utility rationalities was precipitated by the unforeseen geopolitical earthquake that followed the fall of the Berlin Wall, has much to recommend it. The final surrender of the *Deutschmark* to the long-resisted euro within the 1992 Treaty of Maastricht was simply the price that Germany had to pay for its reunification.[5] By the same token, the EU's decision to alter the rules of the game of accession to the Union by requiring the nations of Eastern Europe to adopt all European market regulation *prior* to beginning membership negotiations, might be argued to have cemented the enduring and troublesome paradigm, whereby Eastern Europe is required to compete itself to economic parity with the old Member States, thereby simultaneously undermining Western labour and welfare rates.[6] Failed efforts to re-constitute the European Union within a constitutional treaty notwithstanding, the geopolitical challenge was met with a shorthand rationale of economic efficiency: Europe was not to create its own (re-distributive) Marshall Plan.

Nevertheless, if the full truth be told, the destructive potentialities of economic rationality had already begun to afflict the EEC a decade earlier as the rhetorical dominance of Thatcherism and Reaganomics extended throughout the continent, colonising market integration logics to lever out distinct varieties of European capitalism from complex national patterns of sometimes corporatist, and sometimes

---

[5] Fritz W. Scharpf, 'Monetary Union, Fiscal Crisis and the Preemption of Democracy', (2011) 9 *Zeitschrift für Staats- und Europawissenschaften*, pp 163–198.

[6] Alain Supiot, 'A Legal Perspective on the Economic Crisis of 2008', (2010) 149 *International Labour Review*, pp 151–162.

welfarist economic-political organisation. Campaigners for Brexit were obsessed to the point of absurdity with the safeguarding of a national sovereignty that is a simple chimera in our contemporary world of global economic interdependence. They paid little, if any, attention to the historical paradox that, whilst the then European Court of Justice had established its legendary doctrine of the limitation of national sovereignty as early as the 1960s, a palpable loss of national territorial control only emerged with the success—originating at *national* level—of programmes of new economic liberalism in the 1980s. Far more than the introduction of majority voting in the Council of Ministers in the pursuit of Jacques Delors' programme to complete the Single Market by 1992, it was this new predominance of the liberalising economic-political mind that created a 'beginning of the end' of human self-determination (in politics), be that self-determination national, European or global.[7]

Markets are never simply markets: Karl Polanyi famously theorised his conception of the inherent embedding of economic exchange within social and cultural mores, or within the 'fictitious commodities' of land, labour and capital, with exemplary reference to nineteenth-century England. The process of European market-building in the 1980s, however, similarly underlined his thesis, if only in reverse, as the integration of European markets was matched by a process of disintegration at national level, or a disembedding of national economies from their sustaining framework of social and cultural norms of acceptance. For this author, in her field of study of European financial services markets, the integration as disintegration trend first became readily apparent in the 1980s with regard to the integration of private insurance and finance markets. In a comparison between German and UK provision, a happy coincidence between the demands for the capital-generating efficiency promised by a single European finance market and the concomitant integrative unravelling through legislation and case law of decades-old national regulatory schemes was highly disquieting; and especially so, as it precipitated the unravelling of underlying interest accommodations between consumers, industry and national economic policy. In this particular case, the already-liberal UK was not to be an immediate loser, as the axe fell instead upon a competition-dampening scheme of German financial regulation which had escaped the reformist zeal of the Federal Republic's economically-liberalising post-war Finance Minister, Ludwig Erhard, and which seemed, instead, to support a corrective corporatist strategy of controlled inward investment.[8] Yet, as the 1990s also brought with them a sea-change in European competition policy away from 'range of market offer' and towards economic efficiency, and Germany's local investment banks (*Landesbanken*) were also prised out of their state-supported role of structural financing,[9] we were all

---

[7] Wolfgang Streeck, 'Markets and Peoples: Democratic Capitalism and European Integration', (2012) 73 *New Left Review*, pp 63–71.

[8] Michelle Everson, 'Regulating the Insurance Sector', in: Niamh Moloney, Eilís Ferran and Jennifer Payne (eds), *The Oxford Handbook of Financial Regulation*, (Oxford: Oxford University Press, 2014), pp 409–52.

[9] Claus-Dieter Ehlermann and Michelle Everson (eds), *European Competition Law Annual 1999: Selected Issues in the Field of State Aids*, (Oxford: Hart Publishing, 2001).

very soon to pay a high price indeed for the rolling out of a level competitive field by means of the flattening of distinct, nationally-embedded economies, especially in the field of financial services.

In explanation: the example of insurance and finance may be a relatively small one, but it was replicated across the Single Market, and also gains in core significance when seen in the light of sovereign debt crisis and the EU's own austerity regime imposed in order to shore up the euro, and especially the role of the Federal Republic of Germany within it. A powerful analysis squarely lays the blame for the anti-democratic and economically self-defeating regime of new Eurozone economic governance on the shoulders of the German economic-constitutional organising ideal of 'ordoliberalism'.[10] Working with the powerful mantra of 'never again', ordoliberalism, it is said, seeks still, in an unfortunately-displaced act of memory politics, to fight the bogey of hyper-inflation experienced in Germany in the wake of the 1929 Wall Street crash, asserting its supreme goal of the constitutionalisation of monetary stability within the new technocratically-European crisis law.

Contrary to the explicit terms of the European treaties, financial succour may be given to the debtor nations of the Eurozone, but—with the full blessing of the Court of European Justice[11]—will now necessarily be subject to the imposed brutality of an economic conditionality which gives even the International Monetary Fund pause for thought. The hands of the European Central Bank are concomitantly tied, such that it cannot engage in the inflationary policies that might save the weakest members of the Eurozone from unbearably-austere pain. Finally, permanent austerity is cemented within and beyond a new European Fiscal Compact, as its members are required to constitutionalise a debt brake, and its non-members, or their politicians, seize on the rhetorical attractiveness of a financially self-restraining government to garner votes from a public bludgeoned into believing that there is simply no alternative. Germany reaps and Greece weeps: painful German remembrances dictate the rules of the Eurozone game such that all who dream of a different way of doing things are left bereft of political voice in their vain battering against a tight mesh of legal and technocratic inevitability.

So far, so German, but a slightly more nuanced tale may also be told: '*Zutiefst undeutsch*', this so very 'unGerman', is surely an appropriate response to the slow death of the once pervasive German guild and the corporatist tradition of co-ordinated economic steering.[12] All gone, or going, in the blink of an eye, or in the 30 years of an equalising and disembedding bastardisation of capitalism that has seen German financial institutions ejected from their drearily-constructive roles of fostering engineering enterprises from Dresden to Detmold only to be launched, ill-prepared, upon a global financial market ruled by a myth as insane as it is an

---

[10] The examples of this somewhat last thinking are so many that it would be unfair to highlight particular articles or books.

[11] See Case C-370/12, *Thomas Pringle*, [2012] ECR I-0.

[12] Note, importantly, that the corporatism of the post-War German state is strictly to be distinguished from the pre-war corporatism of the National Socialist state, calling on far older (though still authoritarian) roots of self-organising (guild) tradition and upon co-ordinating functions of steering state tradition. See, for a possible eccentric UK take upon German corporatism, Maurice Glasman, *Unnecessary Suffering; Managing Market Utopia*, (London: Verso Books, 1996).

opiate for those masses who have been ejected from their economic vocations into zero-hours contracts: Capital will beget Capital, world without end, Amen. Take a look at the destructive role played by *WestLB*, once a prince amongst the structurally-oriented *Landesbanken*, or the most stable of donators of venture capital to Wolfgang in Wuppertal, in the Irish housing, and ask yourself this: Did Germanness or unGermanness cause the financial crisis in the first place?

So what have we learned from Europe? That it is bad, or that it is good? In its ideological substance, it is neither, but it has been held captive for the past 30 years by an economic rationality that was born and nurtured at national level, is now dominant on a global stage, and is often seized upon by equalising institutions as a short cut to European integration. Yet, within the EU, we do at least have *institutions*—institutions that have betimes resisted bastardised capitalism, the doctrinally-measured 1980s European Court of Justice being a case in point.[13] It is this that distinguishes Europe from the still-uncivilised global stage. Meanwhile, European institutions provide us with the best framework within which we can begin the fight back. Brexit campaigners would have us believe that, with its sovereignty restored, the UK will bestride a global stage, operating autonomously and serenely within the World Trade Organisation here, and calmly concluding bilateral trade agreements there. The delusion is absolute: neither the WTO, nor international treaties possess ameliorating institutions; the Investor Protection principle— now being successfully resisted by the *institution* of the European Parliament within bilateral trade negotiations between the EU and the US (TTIP)—is not only the *sine qua non* of all existing bilateral trade agreements, but also the final bonfire of the vanity of national sovereignty, establishing the absolute primacy of all trade interests and requiring signatory states to compensate economic forces which have been so sadly inconvenienced by their (social as well as economic) regulatory protections.

A. The Crisis in Economic Liberalism: A Common Ground for the Fight?

One of the surprises of the Brexit campaign was the presence of the German-born MP for Birmingham Ladywood, Gisela Stewart, within the ranks of the outers. At first glance, Stewart would be expected to be a staunch pro-EU figure. Yet, as UK parliamentary delegate to the ill-fated European Convention, she nevertheless experienced a deep moment of cynicism towards the project. Far from producing a shiny Constitution for the Peoples of Europe, the Convention process and its subsequent denouement in the Treaty of Lisbon merely confirmed a non-democratic status quo of technocratic domination.[14] For many non-Federalist Europeans, the subsequently more functionalist approach taken by Commission and the Member States to EU governance within the Lisbon Treaty was an inevitability: Europeans were not and

---

[13] See, eg, its efforts to restrict the reach of its jurisprudence on the free movement of goods (C-267, 268-91, Keck and Mithouard [1993] ECR I-6097).

[14] See, eg, her views in the *Guardian* newspaper, www.theguardian.com/commentisfree/2016/jun/05/britain-better-off-in-or-out-of-europe.

are not ready to embrace a federalist European dream of shared competence and identity. Emotions remain local: in Puglia, Carla looks to the *Regione* when her vines fail, in Manchester, Martha collects plates of royal weddings, in Germany, Christian rejoices when Werder Bremen avoid relegation. The daily experience of the vast majority of European peoples is one of political, cultural and emotional attachment to the local, regional or national level. Although the visions of a democratically-federal Europe proposed, amongst others, by great minds such as Jürgen Habermas offer an immediate solution to problems of democratic deficit within Europe, precipitate federalisation would only de-legitimate itself. Bismarck and Garibaldi are long dead: today, the only sustainable European federalisation would be one that was felt in the soul as strongly as it was born in conviction.

Nevertheless, Gisela Stewart now makes a telling point. For the left, she argues, the EU is a lost cause.[15] The majority of European governments are formed by right-wing parties, the European Parliament voted to be led by Jean-Claude Juncker, not by Martin Schultz. *Fazit*: the left can never defeat the dominant economic rationality of the right within the Union. Now, this is all, perhaps, true, but vitally so, only in so far as the dominant economic rationality that now governs the EU, as it does the globe, is a natural appendage to the right. And here, returning slowly to our much-maligned German ordoliberals, we might state that all is not as it seems, or that Gisella Stewart is wrong to dismiss the potential for revolution within EU institutions. She is wrong because she has yet to understand the depth of a current crisis that is not simply a crisis of capitalism, but is rather a crisis that challenges the entire political-social edifice of economic liberalism. Seen in this light, the left might yet have common cause with the right within the EU.

Since the financial crisis, strange partnerships have formed in academic circles between small 'c' conservatives and a liberally-oriented left: the shared ground has been a desire to consign the rhetorical usage of the catch-all-hate-term 'neoliberalism' to the dustbin: blindly hating capitalism, or those facets of capitalism which we may feel are bad, does little to extricate us from economic malaise. Contemporary crisis has its roots in very many distinct movements, not just in the unbridled rent-seeking of private actors, but also—in a term coined by the political scientist, Colin Crouch—within a 'privatised Keynsianism' promoted by governments of the left and of the right that is predicated on the substitution of a putatively-endless supply of self-generating private capital for the fiscally-engendered revenues of the now economically-castrated nation state; a process which still continues, albeit now subject to Central Bank oversight of private money creation.[16] Neoliberalism, when used to denote a rampant state of market nature, first misses the immediate point that the *systemic* failure of capitalism is not only being overseen, but is also being promoted, within an exponential growth of regulatory oversight that is dedicated to the service of the chimera of efficiently-perfected competition. Secondly, and far more importantly however, it also misplaces the fatal underlying alienation of all of our dominant economic rationalities from our human condition.

---

[15] ibid.
[16] Colin Crouch, *The Strange Non-Death of Neoliberalism*, (London: Polity Press, 2011).

If one thing unites the disparate strands of bastardised capitalism, it is their social amorality, or a denuded worldview that is exhibited either in their belief that man is no more than an economic animal flourishing or failing as markets dictate, or in their contrary reification of 'scientifically-constructed' and market-fostering regulation, and concomitant denial of any (Hayekian) uncertainty in the affairs of the market or of man: 'if only we can identify the right logarithms, Capital will always beget more Capital, Amen.' This is all so very far from a first incarnation of the term neoliberalism in 1930s Paris as a *moral* response to the communist and fascist challenge then being made not only to free markets, but also to the liberal framework of *social constitution* within which classical economic liberalism had always suspended them.[17] It is also light years away from a first and enduring clarification of this defensive liberalism in the Berlin of 1938. It is a world away from the rebirth of a cornered but still battling economic liberalism within the ordoliberal work of lawyers and economists, steeped in Lutheran tradition, such Franz Böhm and Walter Eucken, the latter of whom, also bravely resisted Martin Heidegger's determined attempts to Nazify the University of Heidelberg.

Even a liberal left may be troubled by much ordoliberal writing. Nonetheless, it is not the individual precepts of ordoliberalism that are at issue here, but rather its *idealised* view of economy within society, a model more recently enunciated by one last living-link with the beginnings of the movement, the Hamburg Law Professor, Ernst-Joachim-Mestmäcker. The Economic Constitution of ordoliberalism:

> constitutes the political potency of the economic realm ... but not with an eye to offering up this realm to the democratic regime; instead, it does so in order to place the democratic regime in a position from which it might disinterestedly achieve its tasks of securing justice and social welfare. The role of the Economic Constitution is not one of securing the priority of the economic. Instead, its role is one of enabling the exercise of independent state action in a framework of respect for the economic and political autonomy of citizens.[18]

In his final *Collège de France* lectures, Michel Foucault distinguished ordoliberal thinkers from what he termed 'anarcho-liberals'. Ordoliberals, so he argued, had an abiding fear of social forces, and hence sought to suppress *all* revolution and reaction by means of their pre-emption within a constraining narrative of constitutionalised freedom.[19] And, indeed, for a collectivist left, this distinction must inevitably mutate into a critique of the forces of small 'c' conservatism who would deny socialist governments the full use of the political potency of the economic realm. Yet, today, in the face of alienating economic rationalities that have forgotten, or simply choose to ignore, the fact that the market exists *within* society, the painful irony of the left enjoining in a battle to overcome crisis *within* economic liberalism is perhaps ameliorated. In its ordoliberal form, the moral language of economic

---

[17] See Thomas Biebricher, Ch 6 in this volume.

[18] Ernst-Joachim Mestmäcker, 'Wirtschaftsordnung und Staatsverfassung', in: Heinz Saubermann and Ernst-Joachim Mestmäcker (eds), *Festschrift zum 80. Geburtstag von Franz Böhm*, (Tübingen: Mohr/Siebeck, 1975), p 383, at 419.

[19] Michel Foucault, *Birth of Biopolitics: Lectures at the Collège de France, 1978-79*, (Basingstoke: Palgrave MacMillan, 2008).

liberalism is one that we can recognise and engage with. More importantly, it is a moral language of political self-restraint which has proven itself accommodating to the demands of the counter-posing forces of social tradition and of the left. The success and stability of Germany's post war economy—*and social settlement*—was not the work of ordoliberals alone, but rather the joint graft of ordoliberals (Ludwig Erhard), Christian Democrat (Konrad Adenauer) and Social Democrats (Willy Brandt) in their shaping of a now sadly-unravelling composite variety of German capitalism—a sometimes frustrating, but always democratic, culturally-rooted and socially-embedded capitalism.[20]

B. More Order, but less Europe: The Normative Outlook

Today, a vote for Europe cannot be a vote for its current malaise of totalising economic rationalism, for its political abdication, or for its heedlessness for the dispossessed of Lisbon. It is a vote for the EU *qua* its status as institution, an institution unique within a global mass of bilateral trade agreements that is bestridden, at the point of its judicial application, by the equally-disembedded economic thinking of the WTO. However imperfectly, the EU, *qua* institution, is open to the voices of cultural and social self-determination *and* to those voices of economic value that are similarly traduced within dominant economic rationality. Hobbes is *very* long dead: in their rush to resurrect fairy tales of sovereignty, Brexit and other anti-EU campaigners would have us abdicate, at the global level, all potential for the re-establishment of political and social self-determination over the economy. We, by contrast, should take our fight for the soul of economic liberalism to Europe.

Mrs Thatcher's legendary axe-man, Norman Tebbit, tells an interesting tale of his own disenchantment with the European project.[21] As a pilot, working together with European colleagues to ensure airline safety, he was seized by their commonality, liberated by the ease of communication between pilot-experts solving shared technical problems. Only later did he worry that this enthusiastically-technocratic group had become divorced from the masses still locked in more generalist national cultural discourse. To this, we might answer, yes, you are right 'Norman', but only in so far as you are utterly wrong. In academic jargon, 'epistemic communities' of shared expertise are major culprits within democracy-denuding technocratisation processes, as well as within the near collapse of the global financial system. Yet, in the medium of Ryanair-facilitated movement around Europe, in the Europeanisation of media discourse and of consumer, environmentalist and economic pressure groups, the far broader conversation amongst European peoples can be heard, and is similarly exciting for its commonalities, rather than made discordant by its differences.

What do the peoples of Europe want? They want what we all want: economic and political autonomy, welfare, and an effective means of their realisation.

---

[20] Glasman, n 12 above.
[21] 'Reflections', BBC Radio 4 (Broadcast 13 November 2013), available at: www.bbc.co.uk/programmes/b0376x76.

In a globalised age that is as terrifying as it is exciting, people want an order of opportunity and of security; and therein lies the common 'European' cause for those of the left and of the right. The joint project for those with tradition and for those who wish to break free from their own cultural confines, the shared programme for those who wish to make use of their new opportunities and for those who prefer their own four stone walls. Yet, this want will never be satisfied, this order will never be created, where we continue to sacrifice ourselves to the totalising powers of a dominant economic rationality that is as socially-amoral as it is delusional. By contrast, *our* first sacrificial victim in the effort to save European economic liberalism and re-establish civilised EU order, must be the idea of economic efficiency, the founding myth of bastardised capitalism. Who on the streets of Athens believes that the unbearable pain of myriad ruined lives can be made good in the maybe never-to-be fulfilled promise of future riches? Also, and perhaps more significantly so, what price the economic opportunities of the farmer or the supplier forced out of business by the price-cutting imperatives of 'perfectly-efficient' competition between ever more fast concentrations of economic power? The second sacrifice follows from the first, and, for the foreseeable future at least, must be given in a commitment to *less* rather than more Europe.

In European economic constitutionalist mode, we can create circumscribed rights of cross-border economic opportunity and can reverse the surrender of a once-decentralising European competition policy to the efficiency demands of global markets. Yet, by the same ordered token, where the primary *locus* of political, cultural and emotional attachment remains local, regional or national, we must curtail European re-regulatory impulses, no matter how attractive. The complex of ordoliberal, corporatist and social-democratic interest that still, to a certain extent, defines life in Bochum would go down like a lead balloon in Birmingham. Vice versa, the National Health Service, the one major survivor of Britain's post-war universalist welfare tradition, is still met with as much incomprehension in Europe as it is in the US. It is certainly possible that, with time, Europe will find its own way to embed a European economy within a European society. In the meantime, however, this, like European federalism, is just a very pretty dream. The remnants of our national economic traditions left to us are sometimes irritatingly quaint, but they are still the greatest expression of 'independent state action in a framework of respect for the economic and political autonomy of citizens', and must be determinedly defended within the institutions of the Union.

Within this setting, as well as within a context of global rejection of cosmopolitanism and the concomitant need to recapture the normative heart of economic liberalism, the directions given to us by the ordoliberal movement are invaluable. First, their *liberal* outlook, or their insistence that the free movement of workers (*Freizügigkeit*) is not simply a tool of economic theory, but also a social good, which protects workers from being directed to the particularist goals of their leaders,[22] can

---

[22] Walter Eucken, 'Staatliche Strukturwandlungen und die Krisis des Kapitalismus', (1932) 36 *Weltwirtschaftliches Archiv*, pp 97–321 (Reprint: *ORDO Jahrbuch*, vol 48).

and must become a part of a defence of, and support for, a new cosmopolitanism, an ordered form of globalisation which rejects both retrograde or racist nationalism, *as well as* those theoretical chimeras of allocative efficiency or 'allocative justice',[23] which, at the political level, have been deployed to instrumentalise the free movement of workers to the dark ends, for example, of shoring up a fatally-flawed Economic and Monetary Union. But, secondly, and perhaps more importantly, Walter Eucken's core pragmatism, his recognition of the differential contexts and complexes of employer power and union might, of the always varied devices and desires of farmers, workers, consumers and small- and large-scale entrepreneurs, must serve as the starting-point of our efforts to globalise the economy: *Von diesen bekannten Erscheinungen des Alltags gehen wir aus*.[24] A new political liberalism for a new global age must never forget that it is there to order, or to constitutionalise, societies that pre-date it, rather than—as is currently the case—to impose a disembodied economically-driven revolution upon the increasingly unwilling populaces of the Globe—that way, disaster lies.

---

[23] See, eg, the opinion of AG Maduro in Case C-438/05, *International Transport Workers' Federation, Finnish Seamen's Union v Viking Line ABP, OÜ Viking Line Eesti*, 2007 ECR I-1079.
[24] Eucken, n 22 above, p 245.

Section IV

The Moral and Normative Dimension of 'the Economic' and the Ordoliberal Tradition

13

Ordoliberalism, Polanyi, and the Theodicy of Markets

DAVID M. WOODRUFF

ABSTRACT

Though they are seldom paired, there are important points of contact between the thought of ordoliberals like Eucken and Böhm and that of the idiosyncratic social democratic theorist Karl Polanyi. Like Polanyi, the ordoliberals recognised the crucial historical and contemporary role of the state in creating and sustaining market economies, and the consequent emptiness of the laissez-faire slogan. Some of Polanyi's inter-war analyses of the political use of state power to create monopolies show significant parallels with ordoliberal diagnoses. There were points of contact in moral perspectives as well: both Polanyi and the ordoliberals emphasised that inter-war markets were producing manifestly unjust outcomes, incompatible with any notion of desert. Their reactions, of course, were very different. To put it in Polanyi's terms, ordoliberals accepted that laissez-faire was planned, and argued it needed to be re-planned: more consistently, with the state mobilised to structure markets in ways that ensured market earnings reflected desert. Polanyi, for his part, felt that the state structures underpinning any market order made the very idea of individual desert unintelligible and a barrier to clear thought about how society ought to be organised. This chapter will analyse these parallels and distinctions, and discuss the ways in which Polanyi offers significant resources for analysing ordoliberal positions.

I. INTRODUCTION

S TARTING IN THE interwar period, ordoliberals sought both to diagnose the failings of classical market liberalism and draw conclusions about what should follow. At the same time, very similar issues preoccupied the idiosyncratic social democratic theorist Karl Polanyi. Both Polanyi and the ordoliberals recognised the crucial historical and contemporary role of the state in creating and sustaining market economies, and the consequent emptiness of the *laissez-faire* slogan. Their analyses of the political and economic origins of interwar upheavals likewise prove to have significant parallels. In moral perspectives, too, there were points of contact: both Polanyi and the ordoliberals emphasised that interwar markets were producing manifestly unjust outcomes. They agreed, in particular, that these outcomes were incompatible with any notion of desert (understood here and throughout as what people deserve as a matter of morality).

Their reactions to this morally unacceptable circumstance, however, were very different. Ordoliberals shared the ideas encapsulated in Polanyi's famous assertion that '[l]aissez-faire was planned'. Indeed, the burden of their programme was that *laissez-faire* needed to be re-planned: more consistently, with the state mobilised (and constrained) to structure markets in ways that ensured market earnings reflected desert. This sort of *morally* appropriate market order, I argue below, was the central aim of the reforms in society, economy, and polity that ordoliberals proposed. Polanyi, by contrast, rejected the notion of desert as a barrier to clear thought about how societies and economies ought to be organised. He argued that because state structures underpin any market order, the very idea of individually deserved distributional outcomes under such an order is unintelligible.

This chapter seeks to use the contrast between the two projects to bring into sharp relief both the enduring moralism of ordoliberalism, and the function of this moralism in the ordoliberal project of replanning *laissez-faire*. (The reader will already have noted that I permit myself to speak of 'ordoliberalism' as a coherent whole. I believe that there was enough overlap and consistency in ordoliberal thought in the period that I discuss, running from the 1930s to the 1950s, that such a collective reference is justified. In what follows, I draw particularly on Walter Eucken but also refer to Alexander Rüstow, Franz Böhm, and Wilhelm Röpke). The chapter is divided into two sections. In the first, I discuss how Polanyi and the ordoliberals analysed the rise and fall of *laissez-faire*. The second focuses on the ordoliberals' efforts to replan *laissez-faire* and how a 'theodicy of markets'—an account of how the outcomes of properly structured market competition have moral significance—became crucial to this effort.

II. STATE AND MARKET: TWO ACCOUNTS OF THE 'DOUBLE MOVEMENT'

The degree to which Polanyi and the ordoliberals can be seen as in implicit dialogue with one another is perhaps unsurprising. After all, Polanyi emphasises that his account of the rise and fall of what he terms the 'self-regulating market' differs from that of liberal writers more in interpretation than in historical content.[1] Polanyi defines the self-regulating market as one in which 'order in the production and distribution of goods is ensured by prices alone', which marked a radical departure from prior ways of organising the economy.[2] This price-governed market was not the

---

[1] Among liberals, he mentions, inter alia, Ludwig von Mises, whom Walter Eucken also cites in a similar context. Karl Polanyi, *The Great Transformation: The Political and Economic Origins of Our Time*, (Boston MA: Beacon Press, [1944] 2001), p 148; Walter Eucken, *Grundsätze der Wirtschaftspolitik*, (Tübingen: J.C.B. Mohr, 2004), p 28 n 1.

[2] Polanyi, n 1 above, p 147 and 71.

end-point of an evolutionary process of de-centralised exchange, Polanyi contends, but rather the product of a conscious design: an effort to mould an economy operating with the same sort of de-centralised, spontaneous mechanisms that balance populations of predators and prey. Polanyi sees Joseph Townsend's (1786) *Dissertation on the Poor Laws* as the crucial programmatic document of this transformation. Townsend's deployment of blood-drenched naturalistic metaphors to claim the prestige of science enabled indifference to the massive suffering involved in the move to a self-regulating market.[3]

The origins of this suffering lay in the irreversible damage that market price fluctuations could do to the 'human and natural components of the social fabric', comprising labourers and productive organisations on the human side and land on the natural one. The predictable result was 'an urge on the part of a great variety of people to press for some sort of protection' from the indiscriminate destruction wreaked by markets.[4] These protective efforts, he argued, arose spontaneously, in multiple contexts and under multiple political banners, prompted by the manifest arbitrariness with which the market economy gouged at the social fabric. Polanyi draws on liberal writers for his descriptions of the wave of restrictions on the operation of the price mechanism dating from the latter third of the nineteenth century. But whereas liberals, he suggests, saw these measures as deriving from the 'sinister interests of agrarians, manufacturers, and trade unionists', or a 'collectivist conspiracy', Polanyi insisted that they instead represented the 'realistic self-protection of society'.[5] By re-purposing von Hayek's absurdly polemical equation of all efforts to shape or tame markets with 'planning', Polanyi is able to sum up his distinctive interpretation in epigrammatic form: '*laissez-faire* was planned; planning was not'.[6]

Liberals' analytical failures, in Polanyi's view, were not limited to misunderstanding the motives underpinning the 'protective countermovement'.[7] Polanyi also zeroes in on what he sees as liberal hypocrisy regarding the role of the state. As a blueprint for constructing a new form of society, one comprehensively subordinated to the price mechanism, *laissez-faire* implied not 'legislative quietism', but state activity along a broad front.[8] A paradigm of such state activity was the 1834 Poor Law Amendment Act, which did not simply abolish the Speenhamland system of locally administered wage support, but created a new system of workhouses under 'dictatorial central supervision'.[9] Moreover, state activism in the era of the 'self-regulating market' did not cease with its inception. Polanyi suggests that 'the introduction of free markets, far from doing away with the need for control, regulation, and intervention, enormously increased their range. Administrators had to be constantly on the watch to ensure the free working of the system'.[10] To deny that this watchful

---

[3] ibid, pp 117–118 and 132.
[4] ibid, p 156 and 136–137.
[5] ibid, p 148 and 158.
[6] ibid, p 147.
[7] ibid, p 148 and 151.
[8] ibid, p 126 and 146–147.
[9] ibid, p 106 and 146.
[10] ibid, pp 146–147.

and active state was engaged in 'intervention' was nothing more than sloganeering. For instance, rather than interpreting '*laissez faire*' as implying that workers be left undisturbed to organise unions, and businesses to arrange cartels, liberals advocated forbidding both. 'The only principle economic liberals can maintain without inconsistency is that of the self-regulating market, whether it involves them in interventions or not'.[11]

Here was a conclusion with which ordoliberals could have fervently agreed. Indeed, their programme could almost be summarised as discovering and defending the precise state interventions required to maintain the self-regulating market.[12] Their reading of the rise and fall of *laissez-faire* served as both justification for this project and its evidentiary base. On the key turning-points and empirical developments, they were in broad agreement with Polanyi. Thus, even at the outset, according to Eucken, *laissez-faire* did not in the least involve a 'stateless economy'. Instead, it was 'in precisely this [*laissez-faire*] period [that] the state created strict laws governing property, contracts, corporations, and so on'.[13] They likewise see the latter part of the nineteenth century as dominated by a wave of policies that pushed back against the hegemony of the price mechanism.[14] Finally, the ordoliberals shared with Polanyi the view that features of classical market liberalism itself prompted the policies that undermined it. Imagining *laissez-faire* as a 'lost paradise' would hinder efforts to learn from it. The spiritual successors of classical liberals must seek to understand why 'the implementation of the principle of *laissez-faire* unleashes tendencies to its revocation [*Aufhebung*]'.[15]

Despite these parallels, the ordoliberals' analysis of precisely why *laissez-faire* contained the seeds of its own destruction naturally diverges sharply from Polanyi's. The divergence starts with their distinct readings of the key doctrinal origins of *laissez-faire*. Polanyi, as noted above, highlights the importance of Townsend, and dismisses the role of Adam Smith; Smith's 'broad optimism' that 'the laws governing the economic part of the universe are as consonant with man's destiny as are those that govern the rest', was not of the sort that could have justified the indifference to human suffering necessary to launch the self-regulating market.[16] For ordoliberals

[11] ibid, pp 155–156.

[12] Foucault, in fact, offers a summary of the ordoliberals' central principle very nearly in these terms: Michel Foucault, *The Birth of Biopolitics: Lectures at the Collège de France, 1978–1979*, (Basingstoke: Palgrave Macmillan, 2008), p 116. Compare Walter Eucken, 'A Policy for Establishing a System of Free Enterprise (1952),' in: Horst Frierich Wünsche (ed), *Standard Texts on the Social Market Economy: Two Centuries of Discussion*, trans. Derek Rutter, (Stuttgart-New York: Gustav Fischer, 1982), p 116: 'the inception of a viable system of unrestricted competition [should be] the essential criterion of every economic measure'.

[13] Eucken, n 1 above, p 27. Making similar points would have strengthened Polanyi's arguments, since beyond the Poor Law and the regularisation of the gold standard he is rather vague on the precise ways in which the functions of the state were expanded with the rise of *laissez-faire*.

[14] ibid, p 28 and 55; Alexander Rüstow, *Das Versagen Des Wirtschaftsliberalismus Als Religionsgeschichtliches Problem*, (Istanbul-Zürich-New York: Europaverlag, 1945), pp 68–69; Walter Eucken, 'Staatliche Strukturwandlungen und Die Krisis Des Kapitalismus', (1932) 36 *Weltwirtschaftliches Archiv*, pp 297–321.

[15] Eucken, n 1 above, p 28 and 55. While the Eucken makes the latter claim in a somewhat narrower context, I believe it to be a fair summary of the broader project in which he is engaged.

[16] Polanyi, n 1 above, p 117 and 131.

such as Eucken and Rüstow, however, Smith's influence was decisive—and that his theory was 'pronouncedly optimistic' was, in fact, a key weakness of classical market liberalism.[17] Smith's belief that the market was implicit in divinely ordained human nature meant that little thought needed to be devoted to the market's institutional pre-conditions and prevented him from giving a systematic account of these.[18]

The idea of freedom under the rule of law, which ordoliberals identified as a second ideological cornerstone of *laissez-faire*, likewise could not serve as a fighting creed when the self-regulating market was challenged.[19] The characteristic stance of classical liberalism was to assume that, having created the legal framework for a market economy, no further state action was necessary.

Thus, the ordoliberals held, when challenges to the price mechanism emerged, a legalistic and theologically inflected classical liberalism did not offer an ideological apparatus capable of justifying and organising a vigorous defence against them. As Rüstow put it:

> The social and political catastrophe of economic liberalism was, in essence, a result of the absolutism with which it implemented its maxim of '*laissez faire, laissez passer*', in which it had placed so much stock.[20]

Such passivism was insufficient, in particular, to deal with the efforts of interest groups to subvert market competition. These could happen either through taking advantage of the opportunities offered by liberal law—for instance, the use of freedom of contract to uphold cartels—or through pushes for anti-competitive legislation, which a democratic state could do little to resist.[21] Ordoliberals spared no passion in excoriating such attempts to escape the strictures of the market economy. Here is a representative example from Franz Böhm:

> What confronts us here is ... a general rebellion of the broadest sections of those engaged in the economy, whether they are supporters, or critics, or opponents of the market system, who, at least when it comes to their own personal interests, are prepared to demand that the market system can go to hell so that special rules of the game, and a special slice of the cake, shall be cooked up for them, contrary to market principles. The agents in this process of anarchic disintegration are countless: workers against entrepreneurs, consumers, and the owners of land and capital; entrepreneurs against workers, consumers, and those not remunerated through markets; bureaucrats for their own vested interests against all other vested interests; one sector against all others; agriculture against the rest of the economy; one trade against every other possible interest.[22]

---

[17] Eucken, n 1 above, pp 27–28; Rüstow, n 14 above, pp 15–28. For the quote, taken here out of context but hopefully not unfairly so, see ibid, 40. See Alexander Rüstow, 'Appendix', in: Wilhelm Röpke (ed), *International Economic Disintegration*, (London: William Hodge and Company, 1942), p 271.

[18] Rüstow, n 14 above, p 54 and 62–67; Rüstow, 'Appendix', n 17 above, p 268.

[19] Eucken, n 1 above, pp 49–50.

[20] Rüstow, n 14 above, p 1.

[21] Eucken, n 12 above, p 125; Ralf Ptak, 'Neoliberalism in Germany: Revisiting the Ordoliberal Foundations of the Social Market Economy', in: Philip Mirowski and Dieter Plehwe (eds), *The Road From Mont Pèlerin: The Making of the Neoliberal Thought Collective*, (Cambridge MA: Harvard University Press, 2009), p 1443.

[22] Franz Böhm, 'Left-wing and Right-wing Approaches to the Market Economy (1953)', in: Wünsche (ed), n 12 above, p 364.

Such rhetoric might seem little different from the invocations of the 'sinister interests of agrarians, manufacturers, and trade unionists' that Polanyi had ascribed to the broader liberal school. Yet, the ordoliberals were not entirely blind to the issues that prompted Polanyi to speak instead of the 'realistic self-protection of society'.[23] In a passage with deliberate echoes of Karl Marx, Walter Eucken writes:

> There were free contracts of employment, freedom of movement and guarantees for private property. But whereas people's freedom and equality of status appeared secure in political and legal terms, industrial workmen were not in fact free either economically or socially. In their dependence and search for an easily identifiable target, workers saw themselves as being at the mercy of the "omnipotence of capital".[24]

Workers' lack of practical freedom arose from a situation of monopsony on labour markets.[25] Anti-capitalist attitudes, then, stemmed in part not from capitalism itself, but from the congenital inability of *laissez-faire* doctrines to protect the kind of competitive circumstances whose consequences they extolled. Indeed, Polanyi himself could have served as an excellent example for this argument. In the 1920s, his justification for his advocacy of replacing capitalism with guild socialism included the complaint that, under capitalism, 'income from work does not necessarily correspond to the effort and burden of labor, nor to services and utility. Instead, work incomes are often determined by monopolies enjoyed by traditional social groups [*Stände*] or individuals, or those created by transient economic circumstances'.[26]

Whatever discontent workers, or, for that matter, businesses felt over their fortunes in the market economy, this could only be translated into political action if some ideas legitimated this action. This brings us to a final element of the ordoliberals' analysis of the downfall of *laissez-faire*. If it was an inconsistently implemented market economy that left workers disadvantaged, why would they not champion the restoration of market competition rather than state action curtailing it? Eucken claimed that, given that even the imperfect market of the late nineteenth century had improved workers' material situation, the roots of anti-capitalist sentiment needed to be sought elsewhere.[27] In fact, these roots lay in shifting moral and religious attitudes. In an argument with some distant echoes of Max Weber's 'Protestant Ethic' thesis, Eucken suggested religion's waning capacity 'to provide a meaningful context for life and thus economic action too' gave rise to 'faith ... in a total, all-controlling state' as a 'substitute for religion'. Where once 'man had accepted economic misfortune as fate', 'today the farmer, like the employee and the worker, is inclined to make the contemporary state responsible for [this misfortune] and to demand help from

---

[23] Polanyi, n 1 above, p 148 and 158.
[24] Walter Eucken, 'The Social Question (1948)', in: Wünsche (ed), n 12 above, p 267, a translation of Eucken, n 1 above, p 185.
[25] ibid.
[26] Karl Polanyi, 'Socialist Accounting', (2016) 45 *Theory and Society*, pp 398–427.
[27] Eucken, n 14 above, p 305.

it as a self-evident right'.[28] Rüstow highlighted the role of the doctrinal failings of *laissez-faire* in such a context:

> Instead of being frank about the fact that the extraordinary chances of gain which the game of the market economy offers for the good players are accompanied by chances of loss for those who are less capable or less fortunate, and that all those who want to participate in this game are obliged to take their chance, the [classical liberal] propaganda promised prosperity and happiness to all without exception. ... The result in this case was that a type of player was bred, particularly in countries where the hardening tradition of Calvinism was non-existent, who enjoys playing a game only as long as he wins, but who, the moment he begins to lose, runs off in a huff and refuses to continue playing. This behaviour of the bad loser could be observed in the attitude of many entrepreneurs who went begging to the government to protect them against even the smallest losses.[29]

What *laissez-faire* lacked, in this light, was some sort of functional substitute for Calvinism's 'hardening tradition'.

To recapitulate: the two crucial differences between Polanyi's and the ordoliberals' accounts of the rise and fall of the automatic price mechanism concerned, on the one hand, its doctrinal roots, and, on the other, the motivations of those who demanded its limitation. These distinctions were linked. For Polanyi, *laissez-faire* was an effort to institutionalise disregard for human suffering by aping Nature's vast indifference: an 'act of vivisection performed on the body of society by such steeled to their task by an assurance which only science can provide'.[30] Society's self-defence was only to be expected, and contribution to the repair of the social fabric was a crucial driver of the success of classes in political struggle.[31] For the ordoliberals, *laissez-faire* was an effort to implement Smith's vision of 'natural liberty' under the rule of law, but one which, because of its reliance on a divine dispensation, did not 'steel' its advocates to its defence. The emergence of self-interested enemies of market competition indicated not the essential viciousnesses of the doctrine, but challenges with which *laissez-faire* had failed to grapple.

III. REPLANNING *LAISSEZ-FAIRE*: THE THEODICY OF MARKETS

In sum, surveying the history of *laissez-faire*, the ordoliberals concluded that it had not been planned thoroughly enough: it needed to be planned again, this time focusing on the problem of how best to defend market competition and the price mechanism from the forces that could undermine them. The spirit of this endeavour emerges very clearly in the 1937 essay entitled 'Our tasks', a vigorous technocratic manifesto calling on lawyers and economists to take on the task of promoting free

---

[28] ibid, 306.
[29] Rüstow, 'Appendix', n 17 above, p 271.
[30] Polanyi, n 1 above, p 132.
[31] ibid, pp 158–170.

competition.[32] In this section of this chapter, I wish to defend the thesis that the ordoliberals' solution to the challenges that they set themselves relied crucially on notions of desert. What they sought to construct was a market economy in which commercial success would reflect praiseworthy qualities, so that those who flourished in the market would have deserved to do so. This idea of a morally satisfying market order—a market order of which it would be possible to give a theodicy in the Weberian sense, which I shall describe below—served to unify and motivate different parts of the ordoliberal agenda.

Polanyi, in fact, can offer us a powerful insight into why the ordoliberals' ambitions to design a heavily-armored version of Smithian liberalism drew them to ideas of desert. In the final chapter of *The Great Transformation*, he suggested that:

> Liberal economy gave a false direction to our ideals. It seemed to approximate the fulfillment of intrinsically utopian expectations. No society is possible in which power and compulsion are absent, nor a world in which force has no function. ... Yet this was the result of a market view of society which equated economics with contractual relationships, and contractual relations with freedom. ... Vision was limited by the market which "fragmentated" life into the producers' sector that ended when his product reached the market, and the sector of the consumer for whom all goods sprang from the market. The one derived his income "freely" from the market, the other spent it "freely" there. Society as a whole remained invisible. The power of the state was of no account, since the less its power, the smoother the market mechanism would function. Neither voters, nor owners, neither producers, nor consumers could be held responsible for such brutal restrictions of freedom as were involved in the occurrence of unemployment and destitution. Any decent individual could imagine himself free from all responsibility for acts of compulsion on the part of a state which he, personally, rejected; or for economic suffering in society from which he, personally, had not benefited. He was "paying his way", was in "nobody's debt", and was unentangled in the evil of power and economic value. His lack of responsibility for them seemed so evident that he denied their reality in the name of his freedom.[33]

Polanyi here proposes a relationship of mutual definition between the notion of morally praiseworthy market flourishing—the ideal of the individual 'paying his way' and being 'in nobody's debt'—and that of 'free' action on a market. Only if consumers and producers are free to choose their actions can they be held responsible for their consequences. American legal realists and institutional economists, on whom Polanyi certainly drew here, resoundingly demonstrated that contractual relationships can *not* be equated with a kind of freedom implying the absence of compulsion.[34] The crux of the legal realist/institutional economist argument is easy to illustrate: contracts involve the exchange of property rights, and property itself rests on the threat of state compulsion to protect assets from those who do not

---

[32] Franz Böhm, Walter Eucken and Hans Großmann-Doerth, 'Unsere Aufgabe', in: Jürgen Schneider and Wolfgang Harbrecht (eds), *Wirtschaftsordnung und Wirtschaftspolitik in Deutschland (1933 Bis 1993)*, (Stuttgart: Steiner im Kommission, 1996), pp 207–218.

[33] Polanyi, n 1 above, p 266.

[34] The syllabus for a university course that he taught while working on *The Great Transformation* includes John R. Commons' 1924 classic *The Legal Foundations of Capitalism*, (Madison WI: University of Wisconsin Press, 1957). The syllabus is available at: http://hdl.handle.net/10694/589.

own them.[35] Polanyi concluded, in effect, that in the light of the emptiness of the liberal ideal of freedom, both it and the associated notion of desert needed to be abandoned.

Ordoliberals, by contrast, placed the idea of economic freedom as non-compulsion at the very heart of the market liberal order that they hoped to construct, and found themselves mobilising notions of desert as a key buttress of this order.[36] Certainly, desert was not the sole defensive emplacement. To protect economic freedom from the processes that had undermined it in the nineteenth century, ordoliberals focused on both constraining the ability of the state to *supply* policies that would empower monopolists or otherwise undermine competition, and on reducing the inclination of businesses and individuals to *demand* them. The key 'supply' constraints were contained in the well-known notions of the 'economic constitution' and 'ordering policy' [*Ordnungspolitik*] which were intended to limit the state to establishing the legal framework for a competitive economy while preventing interference with its outcomes. The purpose of this approach was to insulate the state from the demands of both the masses and what Böhm had termed the 'exploiting gangs' seeking to force consumers to pay higher prices.[37] Polanyi had suggested that the 'crudest version' of the liberal interpretation of the double movement was 'an attack on political democracy, as the alleged mainspring of interventionism', and he might well have analysed the ordoliberal demand for a 'strong' state empowered to ignore calls to interfere with the price mechanism in this vein.[38] As for the 'demand' side, one tactic, ably discussed by Michel Foucault, was an effort to devise ways to diffuse the capacity for competition through society.[39]

Both the supply-side measures insulating the state and demand-side measures diffusing competitive capacities represented instances of the ordoliberals' determination to transcend the confusions and hypocrisies of the term 'interventionism' that Polanyi diagnosed by making the preservation of competitive markets, rather than *laissez-faire*, the principle from which state structure and policy were to be derived. As Eucken recognised, this focus on competition detached the ordoliberal legitimation of markets from 'natural law or the higher plane of dogmatic axioms'.[40] But if natural law or other moral postulates were to be set aside in favour of the competitive market as the ultimate yardstick of political morality, this forcefully posed the question of what guaranteed the legitimacy of such a market. Note that the question is not merely one of economic efficiency. The ordoliberals do not, for instance, make the common claim that, because competitive markets generate the most social wealth, they can be used to fund any distributive outcomes that society wishes to

---

[35] An outstanding survey can be found in Barbara Fried, *The Progressive Assault on Laissez Faire: Robert Hale and the First Law and Economics Movement*, (Cambridge MA: Harvard University Press, 1998).

[36] Eucken, n 1 above, pp 169–179.

[37] Böhm, n 22 above, p 364.

[38] Polanyi, n 1 above, p 151. On the anti-democratic thrust of Ordoliberalism, exemplified especially in Eucken, n 14 above, see, eg, Ptak, n 21 above.

[39] Foucault, n 12 above, p 160.

[40] Eucken, n 12 above, p 130.

achieve—an argument that explicitly views markets as a means to an end. Similarly, although ordoliberals do provide arguments for the efficiency of competitive markets compared to planned economies, these offer no grounds for affirming competitive markets' status as a moral axiom from which constitutional conclusions could be drawn.

To understand how the ordoliberals resolved the issue of the market's moral standing—which they probably grasped more intuitively than explicitly, but definitely grasped nonetheless—it is helpful to turn briefly to Max Weber. As noted above, the ordoliberal analysis of the degeneration of *laissez-faire* implicitly asserted a descendent of Weber's 'Protestant Ethic' thesis: with a state constitutionally incapable of defending the competitive market from the self-interested acts of those who would undermine it, the survival of competition depended on the willingness of competition's losers to accept this outcome as 'fate'. To the extent that a belief in predestination could facilitate such acquiescence to market outcomes, its waning would not only heighten 'demand side' pressures for a turn against self-regulating markets, but also deny the outcomes produced by such a market regarding any particular moral standing. In his later work, Weber situated the 'Protestant Ethic' analysis in the broader context of a 'very general [psychological] need' to regard one's fortune as justified. He argued:

> The fortunate is seldom satisfied with the fact of being fortunate. Beyond this, he needs to know that he has a *right* to his good fortune. He wants to be convinced that he "deserves" it, and above all, that he deserves it in comparison with others. He wishes to be allowed the belief that the less fortunate also merely experience[s] his due. Good fortune thus wants to be "legitimate" fortune.'[41]

More recent psychological research has supported Weber's claim. There is a widespread 'belief in a just world', summarised by Roland Bénabou and Jean Tirole as 'the nearly universal human tendency to want to believe that people generally get what they deserve'.[42]

For Weber, this desire to experience oneself as morally worthy is an example (indeed, the prime example) of an 'ideal interest'. To address this ideal interest, one needs what Weber terms an 'ethical interpretation of the "meaning" of the distribution of fortunes among men',[43] or, more compactly, a 'theodicy'.[44] He argues that this need imparts a powerful impulse to the development of religious doctrine, and that these doctrines in turn have important effects on action. 'Not ideas, but

[41] Max Weber, 'The Social Psychology of the World Religions', in: H.H. Gerth and C. Wright Mills (eds), *From Max Weber: Essays in Sociology*, (New York: Oxford University Press, 1946), p 271.
[42] Roland Bénabou and Jean Tirole, 'Belief in a Just World and Redistributive Politics', (2006) 121 *The Quarterly Journal of Economics*, pp 699–746. For more background on this literature, see John J.T. Jost and Aaron A.C. Kay, 'Social Justice: History, Theory, and Research', in: Susan T. Fiske, Daniel T. Gilbert and Gardner Lindzey (eds), *Handbook of Social Psychology*, volume 2, (Hoboken NJ: John Wiley & Sons, Inc., 2010), pp 1122–1165.
[43] Weber, n 41 above, p 275.
[44] In theological thought, theodicy refers to the problem of reconciling the existence of evil with the presence of an omnipotent and benevolent god. A good introduction can be found in James Wood, 'Holiday in Hellmouth', *New Yorker* 84, no 17 (2008), p 116. Weber uses the term somewhat more generally.

material and ideal interests, directly govern men's conduct. Yet very frequently the "world images" that have been created by "ideas" have, like switchmen, determined the tracks along which action has been pushed by the dynamic of [material and ideal] interest'.[45] The 'Protestant Ethic' thesis is an example of this dynamic. Calvinists' ideal interest in belief in their moral worth became, in their religious context, the need to achieve certainty of salvation, which set them on the track to vigorous worldly actions that they could interpret as evidence that they were among the elect.

Calvinism, then, offered in Weber's rendering a kind of 'theodicy of markets', a means of reconciling market outcomes with morality in an emotionally resonant way. For the ordoliberals, a successful theodicy of markets would offer two benefits. First, it might serve as a substitute for Calvinism's 'hardening tradition', blunting critiques of the outcomes of market competition and defending the price mechanism. Second, and more significantly, defending the moral standing of market competition would justify its elevation to the sort of principle around which one might legitimately structure a polity.

In this light, it is perhaps not surprising to find the ordoliberals repeatedly asserting that a competitive market economy would allocate rewards in line with moral desert. Some telling examples of this implicit legitimation strategy can be found in Eucken's discussion of macroeconomic issues, where moral claims serve to buttress tenuous assertions about the relationship between the microeconomic and macroeconomic levels of analysis. For instance, discussing inflation, Eucken seeks to establish that 'all efforts to translate a system for regulating competition into reality are fruitless until a certain stability in the value of money has been ensured'.[46] This is so, he argues, because inflation reduces liabilities while increasing sales, which 'results in profits from inflation instead of from *the skilful [zutreffenden] direction of the economic process* [emphasis added]'.[47] A parallel problem occurs with deflation. With stable prices, then, it is skill that drives profit, and without this there is no true competition. This should be regarded as an implicitly moralised definition of what competition is—its absence is recognised by *undeserved* profits. Note, in particular, that this argument relies on the moral standing of liabilities—without this implicit claim, one could equally make the argument that funding a business via debts subsequently made lighter by inflation could be regarded as a display of far-sighted business virtuousity.

A second area in which the ordoliberals' moralisation of the market is apparent is in their treatment of liability. Eucken asserts:

> Those who are accountable for the plans and measures adopted by businesses, factories and private families must be accountable in law (the liability principle).[48]

Certainly, some of the reasoning mobilised to defend this principle is detached from any direct moral considerations. Eucken argues that liability ensures that markets

[45] Weber, n 41 above, p 280.
[46] Eucken, n 12 above, p 116.
[47] ibid, p 117, translating Eucken, n 1 above, p 256.
[48] Eucken, n 12 above, p 127.

can promote 'natural selection of enterprises and of managers', in so far as it eliminates those who cannot compete. He also sees limited liability as a temptation to economic concentration, because it makes available larger profits without the corresponding risk. But his is not solely an ethically neutral, incentive-based argument. Consider, for instance, the following:

> As *Röpke* has pointed out, the competitive system presupposes "that the attainment of profitability will only be possible by means of an equivalent economic achievement [*Leistung*], while at the same time it must be ensured that a blunder [*Fehlleistung*] will find its inexorable atonement [*Sühne*] in losses and finally in exclusion via bankruptcy from the ranks of those responsible for production. Steps must be taken to prevent both the devious enjoyment of income without a corresponding achievement and the non-atonement for blunders by passing on the losses to others".[49]

Again, we have the link of profitability to achievement, and now the need to 'atone' for errors. Others should not suffer for mistakes not their own. The supposed functional pre-requisites of market competition are conveyed in a language saturated with moral overtones. A properly regulated market is thus figured as a *morally* meaningful universe, in which good fortune is legitimate good fortune.

The desire to see profits reflect praiseworthy behaviour can also be found in the ordoliberal analysis of the dangers of restricting competition, developed especially by Böhm. Non-competitive orders face a 'moral danger' because 'entrepreneurs are enabled to determine the size of their income and profit by means of price-setting'.[50] By contrast, 'competition forms the moral backbone of a free profit-based economy'.[51] The line between immoral and moral earnings is traced by the famous distinction between '*Leistungswettbewerb*, "achievement" or "performance competition" ... as opposed to *Behinderungswettbewerb*, "prevention competition", ie competition by means that are directed at preventing competition from other producers rather than improving one's own performance'.[52]

IV. CONCLUSION

A compact way of conveying the parallels and distinctions in the way Polanyi and the ordoliberals reacted to the rise and fall of the self-regulating market is to consider their analyses of Britain's abandonment of the gold standard in 1931. Eucken suggested that this occurred 'not due to an internal failure of the well-known classical gold-standard mechanism, but rather because the state-society setting [*Umgebung*] the gold-standard mechanism required had been destroyed'.[53] Polanyi would not

---

[49] Eucken, n 1 above, p 281. Translation modified from Eucken, n 12 above, p 127.
[50] Franz Böhm, 'The Non-state ("natural") Laws Inherent in a Competitive Economy (1933)', in: Wünsche (ed), n 12 above, p 108.
[51] ibid, p 110.
[52] Viktor J. Vanberg, *The Constitution of Markets: Essays in Political Economy*, (London-New York: Routledge, 2001), p 46.
[53] Eucken, n 14 above, p 315.

have disagreed in the least: both saw that democracy, re-inforcing workers' ability to defend their wages despite international trade deficits, meant that the gold-standard adjustment mechanism could not function.[54] The distinction lay in the lessons to be drawn. Eucken and the ordoliberals saw this as a failing of the 'state-society setting', which they proposed to re-construct to protect the market from political interference, limiting democracy while fostering a kind of society capable of sustaining competition. Polanyi, by contrast, saw the self-regulating market as a utopian and destructive ideal, and state and society's reaction to the market's 'disembedding' as inevitable.

This chapter has endeavoured to show that the comparison between Polanyi and the ordoliberals reveals how an effort to give market outcomes a moral standing was a crucial prop for the ordoliberal position. The present author finds Polanyi's rejection of the logical coherence of this project convincing. But it is worth considering the extent to which the ordoliberals' readiness to provide a theodicy of markets contributed to their long-term political success. Polanyi believed that it was simply the misconceptions of the classical liberals that gave 'a false direction to our ideals'.[55] But if Weber's view of the emotional power of the ideal interest in viewing one's economic fortunes as legitimate is correct, the roots of the dilemma go far deeper.

[54] For a discussion of Polanyi's reaction to this episode, see David M. Woodruff, 'Governing by Panic: The Politics of the Eurozone Crisis', (2016) 44 *Politics & Society*, pp 81–116.
[55] Polanyi, n 1 above, p 266.

14

Ordoliberalism Within and Outside Germany's Co-ordinated Market Economy

ALBERT WEALE*

A study of the history of opinion is a necessary preliminary to the emancipation of the mind. I do not know which makes a man more conservative—to know nothing but the present, or nothing but the past.[1]

ABSTRACT

Ordoliberalism has played an important intellectual role in the development to date of European economic and monetary union. However, with its constitutive bias against reflationary measures in the Eurozone economy, many doubt that it can play a constructive role in shaping its future. How far is this scepticism justified? To examine this question, this chapter examines some aspects of Eucken's thought. It focuses on one particular moment in his theoretical approach with questions raised about his opposition to the full employment policy of a sympathetic Keynesian contemporary. It also examines the extent to which the conditions under which the ordoliberal inspired social market economy developed were the conditions in which the theory itself suggested that economic policy-making would fail. This has implications for how EU institutions might be reformed.

* Revised version of a paper prepared for the conference on 'Ordoliberalism as an Irritating German Idea', Hertie School of Governance, Berlin, 13–14 May 2016. I thank the participants at the conference for comments on the original paper, Christian Joerges for giving me the incentive to think about ordoliberalism, and Martin Ricketts for his insight into the work of John Jewkes. Albert Weale is Emeritus Professor of Political Theory and Public Policy, School of Public Policy, University College London.
    [1] John Maynard Keynes, 'The End of Laissez-Faire', reprinted in idem, *The Collected Writings of John Maynard Keynes, Vol 11, Essays in Persuasion*, (London-Basingstoke: Macmillan, 1972), p 277.

I. INTRODUCTION

ORDOLIBERALISM IS COMMITTED to the idea of an economic order as a constitutional regime of rules. In relation to the domestic economy, one of its central implications is the establishment of rules, ideally with constitutional status, imposing limits on the scope of government borrowing. In the context of European monetary union, the corresponding implication is a political contract among the countries participating in the Eurozone to limit their borrowing to agreed limits.[2] The influence of these ideas was seen in the original terms of the Treaty of Maastricht and were re-inforced by the Stability and Growth Pact.[3] These rules have been further strengthened by the Fiscal Compact, which limits the ability of governments to borrow money, as well as by the European Semester and associated instruments to control the budget deficits of national governments.[4] It is these ideas that the critics of ordo-liberalism have seen as imposing an 'iron cage' on the conduct and development of European economic policy.[5] For some critics, a significant consequence of these measures is that they prevent governments from engaging in the sort of counter-cyclical deficit spending that is necessary to avoid deflation and the permanent loss of output in the Eurozone economies. From this point of view, the rules of the Fiscal Compact mean that European countries are behaving too much like the Swabian housewife and not enough like the modern firm, balancing the budget in the short term without considering the returns on possible investments, thereby exhibiting a form of 'deficit fetishism'.[6]

Keynesianism at the European level requires greater tax and re-distributive powers for the EU. The reason for this is simple. The countries that could most easily practise counter-cyclical Keynesianism through budgetary loosening are those, such as Germany, which are already in a good budgetary position. Countries such as Spain, Italy and Greece, which are in need of economic stimulus, are those where borrowing costs would be high. In consequence, arguments for budgetary stimulus imply some mutualisation of government debt or the expansion of the EU's own budget to finance public works or equivalent measures in countries where unemployment is high. In turn, this would imply greater powers of economic management and policy for the EU. Such a Europeanised Keynesianism has profound implications for the constitutional ordering of the EU. It is, of course, a central insight of ordoliberalism that the economic and political orders are closely inter-related, so there is no surprise

---

[2] See Albert Weale, 'Political Legitimacy, Credible Commitment, and Euro Governance', in: Mark Dawson, Henrik Enderlein and Christian Joerges (eds), *Beyond the Crisis: The Governance of Europe's Economic, Political, and Legal Transformation*, (Oxford: Oxford University Press, 2015), pp 185–202.

[3] See Kenneth Dyson and Kevin Featherstone, *The Road to Maastricht: Negotiating Economic and Monetary Union*, (Oxford: Oxford University Press, 1999), and Otmar Issing, *The Birth of the Euro*, (Cambridge: Cambridge University Press, 2008).

[4] See Demosthenes Ioannou, Patrick Leblond and Anne Niemann, 'European Integration and the Crisis: Practice and Theory', (2015) 22 *Journal of European Public Policy*, pp 156–64.

[5] See Magnus Ryner, 'Europe's Ordoliberal Iron Cage: Critical Political Economy, the Euro Area Crisis and its Management', (2015) 22 *Journal of European Public Policy*, pp 1275–94.

[6] See Joseph Stiglitz, *The Euro: And its Threat to the Future of Europe*, (London: Allen Lane, 2016), p 106 and 245.

that the advocacy of Keynesian economics has constitutional implications. Whatever else they might disagree on, Keynesians and ordoliberals agree on this.

These contrasting diagnoses and prescriptions represent a long-standing contrast between two policy paradigms.[7] So what is being played out today in contemporary debates about austerity is the latest act in a long-running battle of ideas. In this chapter, I aim to place this contemporary discussion at an earlier stage in this longer history, the only point, so far as I am aware, in which the proponents of the two views do not simply talk past one another. In particular, I shall return to some detailed arguments about the futility of counter-cyclical policy in the work of Walter Eucken,[8] and the reactions that such arguments prompted in the mind of one of his sympathetic and similarly liberal contemporaries, John Jewkes.[9] I focus on Eucken in part because it was his work that provoked Jewkes' reaction, and in part because of the central and decisive role that Eucken played in the construction of ordoliberal ideas. Eucken's current influence is diffuse, seen principally not only in his general concept of an economic order, but also in a re-iteration of his principle of liability in economic transactions, which has found echoes in the EU debate about government budgetary deficits, as well as, more surprisingly, in a left-wing invocation of the principles of the social market economy.[10]

II. EUCKEN ON FULL EMPLOYMENT POLICY

To understand Eucken's views on full employment policy, we need to set his claims in the context of his more general theory. Eucken's analysis of economic order is built upon his morphological method. This method is seen, by Eucken, as resolving what he thought of as the 'great antinomy' between an historical approach to the social sciences, on the one hand, and a theoretical approach, on the other. He acknowledges that economic problems need to be treated as historical problems, arguing that we are not able to understand economic interrelations 'simply by looking at contemporary economic reality'.[11] Yet, by contrast with war, diplomacy or internal political reforms, which can be understood purely historically, economic problems require some degree of abstract theoretical treatment. By contrast with the order of

[7] See Christopher S. Allen, 'The Underdevelopment of Keynesianism in the Federal Republic of Germany', in: Peter A. Hall (ed), *The Political Power of Economic Ideas*, (Princeton NJ: Princeton University Press, 1989), pp 263–89, and Harold James, 'What is Keynesian about Deficit Financing? The Case of Interwar Germany', in: Hall (ed), *The Political Power of Economic Ideas*, this note above.

[8] See Walter Eucken, *The Foundations of Economics: History and Theory in the Analysis of Economic Reality*, translated by T.W. Hutchinson, (London: William Hodge and Company Limited, 1950); idem, *This Unsuccessful Age or The Pains of Economic Progress, with an Introduction by John Jewkes*, (Edinburgh: William Hodge and Company Limited, 1951); and idem, *Grundsätze der Wirtschaftspolitik*, edited by Edith Eucken and K. Paul Hensel (Tübingen: Mohr Siebeck, [1952] 2004).

[9] See John Jewkes, Introduction to Walter Eucken, *This Unsuccessful Age or The Pains of Economic Progress*, (Edinburgh: William Hodge and Company Limited, 1951).

[10] See Sahra Wagenknecht, *Freiheit statt Kapitalismus*, (Munich: Deutscher Taschenbuch Verlag), p 53.

[11] Eucken, *The Foundations of Economics*, n 8 above, p 38.

nature, there is no single economic order: 'but there is an unlimited and constantly changing variety of economic "orders" or systems'.[12]

So, central to Eucken's analysis is the claim that no single order exists at a given historical period. Consequently, we cannot understand economies in terms of there being historical stages of economic development. Concepts like 'primitive independent economies', 'household economies' or 'city economies' are misleading. In part, his criticism turns on the fact that ancient economies were highly complex and, as they developed over time, they did not always become more complex. For example, a banking system existed in the third century BC in Egypt under the Ptolemi, which decayed during the following centuries, moving from a credit economy to a money economy and then to a barter economy. Complexity of organisation can also be seen in the way in which a medieval city economy such as that of Ulm was engaged in extensive trade, via Venice, with Syria and Cyprus, with its sources of wool.[13]

Eucken thus rejects a 'stages' approach, in favour of an 'orders' approach. As an example of an order, consider the tenant economy after the first century BC in Italy: tenants worked the land owned by the Emperor and a few other large landowners, replacing the independent peasants and the slaves. As this example illustrates, the core feature of an 'order' is that it involves particular sets of relations among actors. As such, an order can exhibit a variety of forms, as exemplified by the German medieval guilds. In Lübeck, for example, the guilds pursued a defensive policy, whereas, in Nüremberg, they followed a policy of freedom of production, immigration and competition. In Freiburg, the policy was different again, since the craftsmen had gained power in the city, with the monopoly policy of the guilds being pursued with more vigour.

In summary, for Eucken, an economic order is thought of as a structure made up of the constituent units joined together in specific patters of economic relations. A central organising idea in this context is the morphology of the forms of market that Eucken develops,[14] in which varying degrees of competition and monopoly in supply and demand form 25 types of economic order. The identity of an economic order does not, therefore, consist in its embodying particular, pure forms; rather, it consists in its containing a *selection* of pure forms. As an example, Eucken instances cartels in Germany: in 1930, they were associations of independent undertakings, whereas, by 1940, they had become instruments of the central administration.[15] In consequence:

> An economic system (or order) comprises the totality of forms through which the everyday economic process at any particular time or place, past or present, is actually controlled.[16]

Eucken's analytical framework, based upon the idea of an 'order', is a device for thinking about contrasting forms of economic organisation. In and of itself, it carries

---

[12] ibid, p 42.
[13] ibid, pp 71–4.
[14] Summarised in the table in Eucken, *The Foundations of Economics*, n 8 above, p 158, and idem, *Grundsätze der Wirtschaftspolitik*, n 8 above, p 22.
[15] idem, *The Foundations of Economics*, n 8 above, p 225.
[16] ibid, p 227.

no normative significance. An economic order may be liberal or authoritarian, as the economic history of Germany from the late nineteenth century shows.[17] The concept of 'order' itself functions solely to classify the underlying organisational principles of an economy and economic relationships. However, ordoliberalism is a form of *liberalism*. Ordoliberals accept the normative proposition that it should be liberal principles that define the economic order at which public policy is to aim. When we turn from the purely analytical question of how to classify different types of economy to the policy question of what types of economic ordering to prescribe or recommend, then the task is to find a way of linking liberal principles with economic forms. Eucken approaches this problem by saying that the problem of economic policy is to understand what order of an economy would be *funktionsfähig* and *menschenwürdig*, functionally efficient and worthy of humanity.[18]

Eucken's key argument is that only the use of a de-centralised price system will enable economic actors to calculate the costs of alternative uses of resources and thereby successfully co-ordinate their different plans. Pricing the marginal cost of the use of resources is not distinctively a capitalistic device but is necessary to bring supply and demand into equilibrium.[19] The centralised administrative control of production and supply, by contrast, fails to co-ordinate satisfactorily the plans of different agents, and thus does not 'steer' the economy in a way that is as efficient as the price mechanism. Eucken was aware of the von Hayek-von Mises view that the efficient allocation of resources was impossible in a centrally-planned economy since economic calculation was rendered impossible, and he seems to have endorsed this analysis. However, his principal arguments are typically empirical.[20] The experience of an administratively planned economy under Communism or national socialism showed that such a way of organising production led to shortages, administratively suppressed inflation and a failure of co-ordination among the plans of different economic agents.[21]

It is against this background that Eucken develops his scepticism about Keynesian counter-cyclical policies. He points out that, even in situations in which there is unemployment, individuals are still working. However, instead of working in positions that would produce their highest output, for example, in a workshop or a factory, individuals engage in such activities as growing vegetables in their own gardens.[22] Unemployment does not mean that people are doing nothing; it means that what they are doing is not the most productive thing that they could be doing. The policy problem raised by unemployment is to create the conditions under which

[17] idem, *This Unsuccessful Age*, n 8 above.
[18] ibid, pp 27–8, and idem, *Grundsätze der Wirtschaftspolitik*, n 8 above, p 14.
[19] idem, *Grundsätze der Wirtschaftspolitik*, n 8 above, pp 159–62.
[20] See Friedrich von Hayek, *Collectivist Economic Planning*, (London: Routledge & Kegan Paul, 1950).
[21] Eucken, *This Unsuccessful Age*, n 8 above.
[22] See Walter Eucken, 'What Kind of Economic and Social System?', in: Alan Peacock and Hans Willgerodt (eds), *German Neo-Liberals and the Social Market Economy*, (London: Palgrave Macmillan, 1989), pp 27–45, at 43–4, originally published in *Ordo*, 1 (1948). Eucken's examples reflect actual postwar German experience; see Henry C. Wallich, *Mainsprings of the German Revival*, (New Haven CT: Yale University Press, 1955), p 65.

human beings are able to work in their most productive way. Since this requires a de-centralised economic order in which the price system brings resources in line with their marginal cost(s), solving the problem of under-employment in the labour market is a matter of enabling the price system to equilibrate between supply and demand, ensuring that labour works most productively. Eucken acknowledged the seriousness of what, in Germany from the late nineteenth century onwards, was known as the 'social question', the dislocation brought about by poverty and unemployment. However, given the above logic, it is not hard to see why he thought that solving the economic problem of the mis-allocation of resources brought about by abandoning the price mechanism would also solve the social problem.[23]

Eucken carries over this general stress upon the centrality of the marginal cost principle, embodied in the price system, to a critique of credit expansion in order to boost employment. Such policies fail, according to Eucken, because they distort relative prices and thus create bottlenecks in the processes of production.[24] He had read Keynes' *General Theory* and was sceptical of its policy prescriptions as a third way between planning and the market.[25] He held that central plans and the plans of individual consumers are not co-ordinated when the market was compromised. Eucken's opposition to reflationary policies was thus built into the conceptual core of the theory, in which the marginal cost principle was central, through his argument that a functionally efficient economic order had to rest on the price mechanism as the only instrument that could value resources at their real marginal cost.

Moreover, Eucken was critical of what he saw as the corporatist dimension of Keynes' political economy, citing Keynes' preference for intermediate organisations, between the individual and the state, in 'The End of Laissez-Faire'.[26] For Eucken, group egoism prevents a corporatist system from achieving collective welfare. Giving groups power in an economic order creates conditions under which they can lobby for their own sectional interest at the expense of the collective interest.[27] In this, he anticipates a whole line of 'public choice' analysis by James Buchanan, Friedrich von Hayek and others, culminating in the *locus classicus* of Mancur Olson's *Rise and Decline of Nations*,[28] with its argument that it is the accumulation of special interests within a stable economy that slows down the rate of economic growth. Eucken seems to have thought that Keynes' position was at one with the form of corporatism that was established in Italy in the 1920s. Thus, his scepticism about Keynesian policy was re-inforced by his economic sociology and his general scepticism about the dangers of corporatism, and his view about the extent to which pressure-group influences would aim to distort the efficient functioning of the market.

---

[23] Eucken, *Grundsätze der Wirtschaftspolitik*, n 8 above, pp 312–24.
[24] ibid, pp 140–44.
[25] ibid, pp 140–49.
[26] Keynes, n 1 above.
[27] Eucken, *Grundsätze der Wirtschaftspolitik*, n 8 above, p 171 *et passim*.
[28] See Mancur Olson, *The Rise and Decline of Nations: Economic Growth, Stagflation, and Social Rigidities*, (New Haven CT-London: Yale University Press, 1982).

Not all ordoliberals were as sceptical of counter-cyclical policies.[29] Both Alfred Müller-Armack and Wilhelm Röpke advocated counter-cyclical measures. However, Eucken's position has been the one that has predominated in ordoliberal thinking, so that the long-standing conflict between Keynesianism and ordoliberalism has turned on this issue. In particular, for Keynesians, it is possible for an economy to be trapped in a sub-optimal equilibrium as far as employment is concerned, as a result of mutually re-inforcing deflationary expectations, and only deficit spending can re-balance the economy at a higher level of activity. Usually, as at the present time in respect of the European economy, this controversy is fought out as though the proponents of each side occupied parallel non-interconnecting universes. However, there was one interesting point in history, arising from the lectures that Eucken gave at the London School of Economics (LSE) in 1950, where the universes did touch in an interesting way.

III. WHEN PARALLEL UNIVERSES TOUCHED

Eucken's lectures at the LSE were posthumously published in the volume entitled *This Unsuccessful Age*.[30] In his Introduction to the book, John Jewkes provided a warm and sympathetic account of Eucken both as an individual and as an economist.[31] However, he questioned Eucken's distrust of full employment policy. Such questioning is particularly note-worthy. Although he was one of the wartime young Keynesians in government, supporting the Keynesian line of argument from the Cabinet Office's Economic Section against the Treasury in the preparation of the 1944 White Paper on *Employment Policy*, Jewkes was a staunch liberal.[32] Like Eucken, he was a founding member of the Mont Pèlerin Society and, later in his career, he became known for his opposition to economic planning, the monopoly structure of the National Health Service, and the nationalisation of industry.[33] So his questioning of Eucken's position on employment policy cannot be construed as the passing of ships in the night between statist Keynesianism, on the one hand, and ordoliberalism, on the other. It is as a liberal that Jewkes raises the issue of employment policy.

He begins by noting Eucken's opposition to planning, but says that the problem of unemployment has led English liberal economists to remain 'convinced that the state has a useful function to perform in the prevention of unemployment by accepting ideas and adopting methods which would go beyond those heretofore accepted as constituting the proper role of government'.[34] Here, he refers to Keynes' diagnosis

---

[29] Hans Willgerodt and Alan Peacock, 'German Liberalism and Economic Revival', in: Alan Peacock and Hans Willgerodt (eds), *German Neo-Liberals and the Social Market Economy*, (London: Palgrave Macmillan, 1989), pp 1–14.

[30] Eucken, *This Unsuccessful Age*, n 8 above.

[31] See Jewkes, n 9 above.

[32] See Peter Hennessy, *Never Again: Britain 1945–51*, (London: Jonathan Cape, 1992), pp 187–88.

[33] See Martin Ricketts, 'Jewkes, John 1902–1988', in: Donald Rutherford (ed), *Biographical Dictionary of British Economists*, (Bristol: Thoemmes Continuum, 2004), pp 600–607.

[34] Jewkes, n 9 above, p 18.

of unemployment brought about by a deficiency in general demand, saying that it is difficult to accept the view that, when competition is restored and money sound, 'full employment can be taken for granted'.

Jewkes then goes on to list the circumstances under which a boost in demand would work in a non-inflationary way.[35] These are captured in an elaborate list of conditions, which comprise: a government with strong liberal instincts and conscious of the evils of open inflation; a government that recognises that the price system only works if relative prices are allowed to change; a government that is not too ambitious in its employment policy, and so would not attempt to keep unemployment down below 5–6% through financial devices; a government that is sceptical of prediction and relies upon the speed of its measures rather than upon its power to anticipate; a government that is prepared to allow prices to rise and not impose price controls; and trades unions that 'recognize that caution in pressing for wage increases in a position of full employment is just as essential a part of the use of the full employment technique as is the adoption of non-conducting devices in the use of electricity'.[36]

Jewkes interprets these conditions as an element of the functioning of a mature political democracy. He writes:

> In brief, that the average citizen shows, in economic matters, the kind of common sense and communal wisdom revealed in the working of any mature political democracy: reluctance to press in full what may appear to him to be legitimate demands; sagacious understanding of the evil social consequences of apparently innocuous individual acts multiplied endlessly; sobriety in perceiving that there are always some inequities which can be remedied only at a cost quite out of proportion to the gain.[37]

Jewkes goes on to note that some people will say that such conditions are fanciful, and that, though Keynesianism might, in principle, work as a technique, it is a question of providing the proper institutional surroundings for that technique. To this scepticism, he offers a counter-example:

> Events in Great Britain since 1945 provide some relevant evidence on these matters. ... There is no doubt that Sir Stafford Cripps and his advisors accepted that diagnosis and pursued courageously a long-period policy of reducing inflation and that the public generally, despite the unpleasant effects for them, broadly supported that policy.[38]

In this context, the purpose of the anti-inflationary policy was not to make the controls work better, but to allow the price mechanism to work. The attempt to control inflation and keep the external value of sterling constant was bound to cause the devaluation that occurred in 1949: 'But this does not alter the fact that a Minister

---

[35] ibid, pp 20–22.
[36] ibid, p 21.
[37] ibid, pp 21–22.
[38] ibid, p 23. I note as a matter of historical observation that UK Labour governments in the twentieth century were more orthodox in their management of the public finances than the Conservatives: Philip Snowden in 1929; Stafford Cripps in 1947; Roy Jenkins in 1967; Denis Healy in 1976; and Gordon Brown in 1997. There is, I think, an interesting paper to be written about austerity economics in Labour Party thinking.

did take sound advice, did pursue unpleasant policies courageously, and that the public, whilst grumbling, understood generally what was on foot and co-operated', so that, in respect of wage restraint, '… it can be said that in this period communal common sense was in charge in a manner which many, perhaps most, people, thinking of these problems before 1945, would have thought inconceivable'.[39]

By the time that Jewkes had written these words, Eucken had already died. It can only be a matter of regret that he was unable to participate in the conversation as one liberal to another. It is hard to know how far Eucken's resistance to full employment measures was based upon the fact that he had little experience of economic policy-making within democracies. Most of his working examples, like his discussion of the Reich's Court judgment of 1897 or the attempts at the administrative suppression of inflation under national socialism, are taken from authoritarian systems, as is the appeal to the experience of pre-war Italian corporatism.[40] In the context of these conditions, it is easy to see the logic of an argument premised on the claim that only de-centralised decision-making could achieve marginal cost pricing, steering resources to where they would be most productive. Yet, evidence from such cases does not address conditions in which de-centralised wage bargaining has cumulative consequences that are self-defeating for those involved in the bargaining—the case that Jewkes has in mind.

In drawing attention to the differences between Jewkes and Eucken, I am not advancing the simple claim that Jewkes was right and Eucken wrong. Through force of circumstance, Eucken was not able to reflect upon the democratic political conditions that would make a liberal economic order possible. More importantly, however, although Jewkes' remarks are sketchy and tentative, they interestingly anticipate a line of argument that has emerged from the varieties of capitalism literature.[41] In particular, what is most notable is the emphasis that Jewkes places on the political conditions and collective understandings of the processes of wage negotiation that, in his view, created the right conditions for successful full employment policies. Much of the trajectory of the German experience in respect of wage bargaining since 1948 seems to have embodied the Jewkesian logic that successful non-inflationary full employment policy requires trades unions to recognise the need for caution in pressing for wage increases in a position of full employment.

IV. ORDOLIBERALISM AND GERMAN POLITICAL ECONOMY

The influence of ordoliberal ideas on the formation of the post-war German economic order is a much-discussed matter. It is well-known that the idea of the social market economy came from a leading figure of the 'Cologne School' of ordo-liberalism, Alfred Müller-Armack, and it is also well-known that Ludwig Erhard

---

[39] ibid, p 24.

[40] Eucken, *This Unsuccessful Age*, n 8 above.

[41] See David A. Hall and David Soskice (eds), *Varieties of Capitalism*, (Oxford: Oxford University Press, 2001), pp 1–68.

was influenced in his 1948 reforms by ordoliberal thinking, with Eucken serving on the Advisory Board of the Economics Ministry of the Federal Republic of Germany. It is not surprising, therefore, that a certain chain of reasoning has emerged, which runs something as follows. Ordoliberalism shaped the ideas of the social market economy, and the social market economy defines the form that the German economy took from 1948 onwards. The post-war German economy has been a success. *Therefore*, so the putative syllogism runs, it is the implementation of the theory of ordoliberalism that has led to the success of the German economy. The story takes on an almost mythical form when it is noted that there were contemporary Keynesian commentators on Erhard's price reforms, who were fiercely critical of the lack of attention given to planning for full employment. The social market economy worked, so it is said, precisely in those conditions that Keynesian critics said it could not.[42] Indeed, there is an anecdote sometimes cited to the effect that Erhard pushed through price de-regulation in the face of the opposition of the occupying military authorities.[43] For Keynesians, it is claimed by the non-Keynesians, the German economic miracle must—literally—be miraculous.

The truth seems to be a more prosaic matter, however. The crucial currency reform was announced by Robert Lochner, the speaker of the US military government on 19 June 1948, because currency matters were still under the authority of the occupying powers. There were good practical reasons why Germany could not have unilaterally acted to supply the Deutschmark: the only suitable printing presses were in East Berlin or Leipzig, both under the control of the Soviet Union, which would not allow their use. In the end, the new notes had to be printed in the US and transported secretly to Germany. Price de-control was Erhard's policy, but it was limited, excluding food and basic industrial materials. It was the Allied occupying powers that forbade government deficits.[44] German post-war economic growth is not so miraculous when placed in comparative context.[45] As the German economy developed, there were episodes of struggle between the *Bundesbank* and the Chancellor's office, particularly Konrad Adenauer and Helmut Schmidt.[46] And Adenauer's 1957 pension

[42] See Norman P. Barry, 'Political and Economic Thought of German Neo-Liberals', in: Alan Peacock and H. Willgerodt (eds), *German Neo-Liberals and the Social Market Economy*, (London: Palgrave Macmillan, 1989), pp 105–24; Terence W. Hutchinson, 'Notes on the Effects of Economic Ideas on Policy: the Example of the German Social Market Economy', (1979) 135 *Zeitschrift für die gesamteStaatswissenschaft/Journal of Institutional and Theoretical Economics*, pp 426–441; and Wilgerodt and Peacock, n 29 above.

[43] See Rudinger Dornbusch, 'The End of the German Miracle', (1993) 31 *Journal of Economic Literature*, pp 881–85.

[44] For these and other points, see Herbert G. Giersch, Karl-Heinz Paqué and Holger Schmieding, *The Fading Miracle: Four Decades of Market Economy in Germany*, (Cambridge: Cambridge University Press, 1992); Heinz Sauermann, 'On the Economic and Financial Rehabilitation of Western Germany (1945–1949)', (1979) 135 *Zeitschrift für die gesamte Staatswissenschaft/Journal of Institutional and Theoretical Economics*, pp 301–319; and Wallich, n 22 above, p 15.

[45] See Wolfgang F. Stolper and Karl W. Roskamp, 'Planning a Free Economy: Germany 1945–1960', (1979) 135 *Zeitschrift für die gesamte Staatswissenschaft/Journal of Institutional and Theoretical Economics*, pp 374–404.

[46] Dyson and Featherstone, n 3 above, p 276; see, also, E. Kennedy, *The Bundesbank: Germany's Central Bank in the International Monetary System*, (London: Pinter Publishers, The Royal Institute of International Affairs, 1991).

reforms, which shifted funding onto an inflation-proof pay-as-you-go basis, were at odds with the stability culture of ordoliberalism. None of this is to say that ordoliberalism was not a decisive influence on the German economic policy paradigm, but it is to say that the influence needs to be set in the context of political constraints and ideological contestation.

There is, however, one aspect of post-war German political economy that is significantly at odds with Eucken's scepticism about organised mediation between the state and individual citizens, which assumes particular importance in the light of Jewkes' argument, namely, the wage-negotiating strategies of German trade unions, which should be put in the context of Jewkes' observation on the need for trade unions to understand that caution in wage bargaining is 'just as essential a part of the use of the full employment technique as is the adoption of non-conducting devices in the use of electricity'.[47] The strategy of wage moderation on the part of German trade unions has been crucial at various times in the post-war period. For example, there was no union strike action in response to the currency reform in 1948 and labour moderation in the early years kept exports competitive and helped the financing of the investment boom, avoiding an inflationary spiral.[48] After exploring various possible explanations of these and similar examples, Herbert Giersch, Karl-Heinz Paqué and Holger Schmieding conclude that such moderation reflecting some form of social responsibility and 'the working of an element of group rationality'.[49]

Moreover, the moderate wage-bargaining to which Jewkes refers is part of what would come to be known as co-ordinated market economies.[50] In saying this, I am supposing that Jewkes anticipated the theory of the co-ordinated market economy. A number of the elements that he mentions find a counter-part in theories of the co-ordinated market economy, most notably the need for individual wage-bargaining to be placed in the context of a collective understanding of the cumulative consequences of individual level action ('the evil social consequences of apparently innocuous individual acts multiplied endlessly'[51]), that collective understanding being an element in the culture of a mature democracy. What matters is not just a set of policies or formal institutions, but how those policies and institutions are understood by social actors.

According to Hall and Soskice,[52] the distinguishing feature of co-ordinated market economies, by comparison with liberal market economies, is the way in which they supplement the institutions of hierarchies (firms) and markets, with non-market modes of co-ordination among economic actors, including employers' associations and trade unions. Such associational co-ordination is required to deal with problems of monitoring and incentive compatibility in respect of such matters as vocational training, corporate governance, inter-firm relations, relations with employees, and bargaining over pay and working conditions. Thus, in Germany for much of the

---

[47] Jewkes, n 9 above, p 21.
[48] Wallich, n 22 above, pp 74–5, 299–300 and 303.
[49] Giersch, Paqué and Schmieding, n 44 above, p 78.
[50] Hall and Soskice, n 41 above.
[51] Jewkes, n 9 above, pp 21–22.
[52] ibid, pp 8–9.

post-war period, pay was negotiated through industry-wide employers' associations and trade unions, with the 'leading settlement' occurring in the engineering industry where the unions were powerful enough to assure other unions that the rate of pay settlement represented a good deal. In this way, the high degree of concentration and co-ordination provided essential information to actors throughout the system.[53] Moreover, this concentrated bargaining explains something that would otherwise be inexplicable, namely, why the German *Bundesbank* addresses its pronouncements to wage-price bargaining, and threatens to respond aggressively to inflationary settlements.[54] In a simple neo-classical model of the economy, it is puzzling why unions should press for increases in nominal wages that cannot be sustained in real terms. In a co-ordinated market economy, however, central bank independence operates in a complementary way to central wage-bargaining, constraining wage settlements which are out of line with productivity improvements. These co-ordinating practices and institutions are not intended as a substitute for the price mechanism, but as the *framework* for the price mechanism. In Jewkes' words, the purpose of the anti-inflationary elements of full employment policy is to make the price-system work to better effect than planning. The particular function that they perform is to allow the representatives of economic interests to take notice of the aggregate consequences of their own behaviour.

To underscore the analysis, the contrasting case is that of wage-bargaining in the UK, which soon lost the co-ordinated element to which Jewkes referred. With the failure of the various attempts at co-ordination over wage-bargaining, the inflation history of the post-war British economy illustrates what happens in the absence of co-ordination. The relatively poor UK economic performance in years between 1945 and 1979 was a consequence of the mutually destructive leap-frogging of wage demands and the prisoner's dilemma that is created when powerful actors seek positional advantage through the rectification of 'anomalies' or the maintenance of relative wage positions or differentials.[55] When UK government accommodative monetary and fiscal policy underwrote such practices, the stage was set for the stagflation of the 1970s. The lesson was that price stability and growth could be maintained in the absence of co-ordination but only in the presence of relatively high levels of unemployment and the highly flexible labour markets that give managers high levels of discretionary power (and, typically, high levels of remuneration relative to their peers in other economies).

What is happening in these contrasting examples exhibits a difference in the role that the practice of interest-group intermediation plays in the two societies. Firstly, in Germany, co-ordinated wage-bargaining counteracted sectional wage-bargaining

---

[53] ibid, pp 24–5.

[54] See Robert J. Franzese Jr., 'Institutional and Sectoral Interactions in Monetary Policy and Wage/Price-Bargaining', in: Peter A. Hall and David Soskice (eds), *Varieties of Capitalism*, (Oxford: Oxford University Press, 2001), pp 104–44, at 111.

[55] See Samuel Brittan, 'Inflation and Democracy', in: Fred Hirsch and John H. Goldthorpe (eds), *The Political Economy of Inflation*, (Oxford: Martin Robertson, 1978), pp 161–85, at 173–6, and J.S. Flemming, 'The Economic Explanation of Inflation', in: Fred Hirsch and John H. Goldthorpe (eds), *The Political Economy of Inflation*, (Oxford: Martin Robertson, 1978), pp 13–36.

through an awareness of collective unintended outcomes, in line with the logic of what Jewkes called 'sagacious understanding of the evil social consequences of apparently innocuous individual acts multiplied endlessly'.[56] Secondly, interest-group intermediation provides a process by which acts of government policy and developments in the economy can be interpreted to citizens at large. This is a function of interest-groups for which no provision is made in an individualist theory of political economy such as that of ordoliberalism. The type of de-centralised economy that ordoliberals favour requires individuals to hold in their minds an understanding or model by which they can interpreted price movements and fluctuations, including fluctuations in the price of labour, otherwise they are not able to use the signalling function of the price system beyond the most elementary consumer choices. In the absence of such a model, individuals are unable to evaluate whether a seemingly low wage offer is an attempt to take advantage of bargaining power or a justified response to reduced profitability. In a world in which economic signals have to be interpreted in a purely individualistic way, workers and consumers face an insoluble identification problem. They cannot know to what the signal refers. Given that individuals are boundedly rational, only intermediate groups provide cues and heuristic frameworks within which developments can be understood. What seem, otherwise, random fluctuations in economic processes acquire a meaning.

This interpretative element to any satisfactory theory of the price system is also relevant to Eucken's claim about the sectional bias of interest-group corporatism. As I pointed out above, Eucken here anticipated a whole line of public choice analysis. However, the apotheosis of that work in Olson's *Rise and Decline of Nations* also shows its limitations. In particular, although Olson seemed to have a persuasive case for the adverse effects on economic growth of the sclerotic economies in which interest-groups had accumulated, he had difficulty with the Swedish economy, which met the conditions for a sclerotic system but which performed relatively well. His answer was that small and relatively homogeneous societies were more likely to have encompassing institutions in which there would be less opposition between special and general interests.[57] This may seem like a theoretical epicycle to deal with an otherwise anomalous observation, but, in fact, it points to a deeper and more permanent lesson, captured in Jewkes' line of argument that successful expansionary policies are possible given 'the common sense of a mature democracy'.[58] Once we recognise that the conditions of economic success may require the sort of interest-group intermediation of which ordoliberal theory is suspicious, achieving the goals of ordoliberalism will depend upon conditions that ordoliberal theory itself holds as inimical to its success. The central irony of post-1948 German policy-making is that success, in ordoliberal terms, has depended upon the sort of concertation at industrial and national level to which ordoliberal theory was hostile.

---

[56] Jewkes, n 9 above, pp 21–22.
[57] Olson, n 28 above, pp 89–92.
[58] Jewkes, n 9 above, pp 21–22.

V. A EUROPEAN CONSTITUTIONAL ECONOMIC ORDER?

So far, I have argued that the dispute between Keynesians and ordoliberals on full employment policy turns, at least in significant part, on a difference about the role of corporate agents within a modern political economy. But what does this mean for the role of ordoliberalism in the process of European integration?

Given the constellation of economic and political forces, it is not surprising that a German ordoliberal conception of the European economic constitution would pre-dominate.[59] However, as Kenneth Dyson and Kevin Featherstone have also shown, the translation of ordoliberal ideas to the EU level took place *despite* the long-standing theoretical understanding of ordoliberals, rather than because of it. In general, leading ordoliberal thinkers from Erhard onwards were sceptical about too hasty a rush to monetary union without the political institutions being in place. They generally held to a 'coronation theory' of monetary union, according to which monetary union would be the final stage of the process of European integration, crowning a convergence in economic policy orientation and underpinned by a political union in which there would be solidarity in budgetary policy with the Council responsible for economic policy.[60] The orientation of the ordoliberal coalition, in the *Bundesbank*, the Economics and Finance ministries and among academic economists, was opposed to premature monetary union, since the underlying performance of the different European economies was so divergent. What was translated into monetary union were the rules of an ordoliberal economy without the institutional pre-suppositions of an ordoliberal economy that could make those rules meaningful.

Moreover, if ordoliberal prescriptions benefited from conditions to which the trend of ordoliberal thinking was hostile, as happened in Germany, it is hardly likely that policy-makers would make a significant effort to recreate, at European level, the institutions and practices that were historically given at national level. In any case, it is fanciful to suppose that the institutions and organisations—principally political parties, trade unions and non-governmental organisations—that mediate an understanding of public policy measures and conditions at national level have found, or are likely to find in the near future, a functional equivalent at European level. To be sure, political parties campaign and vote as party-family-ideological groupings in the European Parliament, but they do so within a context in which turn-out is low, European Parliamentary elections have a second-order character, and party contests over policy are transparent to only very few. Even were such institutions to exist, they would need to display Jewkes' 'sagacious understanding', recognising that economic prudence requires the political context of a mature democracy, in which intermediating institutions are capable of providing cues to workers and citizens about the meaning and scope of the economies that need to be made, and the

---

[59] Dyson and Featherstone, n 3 above, pp 751–8, and Harold James, *Making the European Monetary Union: The Role of the Committee of Central Bank Governors and the Origins of the European Central Bank*, (Cambridge MA: The Belknap Press, 2012).
[60] Dyson and Featherstone, n 3 above, p 291 *et passim*.

advantages of taking the short-term pain for the long-term gain. This happens in few places and times at national level; there is no reason to suppose that it could occur at European level.

Moreover, the conditions of the fiscal compact among Eurozone Member States turns the basis of political difference into one that pitches national governments and ideological traditions against one another, so that the absence of European institutions that could aggregate cross-cutting cleavages is compounded by the form that political and policy differences take in the wake of the financial crisis, with its bailouts, recriminations and envies. This problem is made more acute in a monetary union, given the well-known fact that, in such a union, variations in economic performance have to be absorbed in the real economy, rather than being disguised in 'painless' exchange rate fluctuations. In other words, the money illusion is no longer to enable people to pretend that there are easy solutions. Finally, asymmetry of economic experience belies the claim that, because the rules take a general form, they function in the interests of all.

Some will say that the conditions of 'sagacious understanding' do not matter, because the burden of political legitimacy in the EU can be carried by improved output legitimacy, that is to say, legitimacy derived from the 'capacity to solve problems requiring collective solutions because they could not be solved through individual action, through market exchanges, or through voluntary cooperation in civil society'.[61] On this view, if European economic and monetary policy could be moved to an expansionary stance, increased economic activity will quieten political discontent. However, even output legitimacy needs mediation, as Scharpf observes, to secure the support of electors, policy experts, functional interest groups, and policy networks.[62] Problem-solving does not wear its success on its sleeve. The importance of this aspect of output legitimacy has been stressed by Erik Jones in relation to economic and monetary union. Jones points out that general consent among the electorates of Europe to monetary union is mediated through key groups and actors in the relevant policy system, including public officials, independent experts and the representatives of functional interests.[63] If voters take their cue from the signals given by such key groups and actors, then we should expect high levels of consent when those groups and actors are in accord, but find lower levels of conviction and consent when the groups and actors exhibit fundamental differences. Moreover, a mature democracy, in Jewkes' terms, is just what the EU does not have. To expect citizens to be able to make sense of economic developments in the EU without institutions to mediate understanding is like supposing that public policy decisions would be best taken at European level by direct plebiscite. Without the mediating institutions, ordoliberalism at EU level is a steering wheel without connections to the rudder.

---

[61] See Fritz W. Scharpf, *Governing in Europe: Effective and Democratic?*, (Oxford-New York: Oxford University Press, 1999), p 11.
[62] ibid, pp 14–21.
[63] See Erik Jones, 'Output Legitimacy and the Global Financial Crisis: Perceptions Matter', (2009) 47 *Journal of Common Market Studies*, pp 1085–110.

Ordoliberalism has become an irritating German idea because, although Europe has become German in one sense, in other senses, it has not.[64] Nor should it, for the contribution of German ordoliberalism is to stress, in a partial form, a few elementary, but essential, economic truths. If Jewkes was right, then to combine ordoliberalism with full employment requires a common political culture in which citizens mutually learn the importance of not pressing their demands to the full, in which they learn not to ignore the cumulative adverse consequences of seemingly innocuous acts, and in which they learn not to press for the rectification of inequities when this would jeopardise the common good. In short, Europe needs the true democrat to marry the Schwabian housewife.

---

[64] See Ulrich Beck, *German Europe*, (Cambridge: Polity Press, 2013).

15

Competition or Conflict? Beyond Traditional Ordoliberalism*

MALTE DOLD AND TIM KRIEGER

ABSTRACT

According to the traditional ordoliberal view of the Freiburg School, the central role of the state in economic affairs is to set up rules that create a competitive order within which private actors have sufficient incentives to coordinate their economic affairs efficiently. Underlying this view is the implicit assumption that, given the right institutional framework, competition within markets is mainly characterised by peaceful and conflict-free rivalry between actors that leads to an optimal allocation of resources. In such a setting, competition may be described as a 'record-type' game. This view, however, ignores the possibility that competition itself may very well trigger conflict rather than having an appeasing effect. In this case, competition appears to be a 'struggle-type' game in which competitors invest in conflict activities that are not efficiency enhancing but rather resource wasting. Against this background, ordoliberalism has yet to provide a clear-cut distinction between competition and conflict. In addition, it fails to identify—in a normative way—which institutional and regulatory framework could hamper conflict sensitivity of economic competition, given the harmful effect of conflict on the security of property rights. Our contribution investigates how the ordoliberal research program needs to be extended when introducing conflict.

> The efforts of men are utilized in two different ways:
> they are directed to the production or transformation
> of economic goods, or else to the appropriation
> of goods produced by others.
>
> *Vilfredo Pareto***

---

* The authors would like to thank Bernhard Neumärker whose lecture on 'Economic Policy and Public Choice' inspired this chapter.
** Vilfedo Pareto, *Manual of Political Economy*, (New York: A.M. Kelley, [original French publication 1927] 1971), p 341.

I. COMPETITION *v* CONFLICT

ECONOMISTS CONSIDER COMPETITION to be a highly effective mechanism to achieve an efficient allocation of resources and, thus, to maximise social welfare. The principles of scarcity, private property, freedom of contract and exchange between equal legal subjects are essential characteristics of free markets, in which each individual is pursuing his or her own self-interested ends.[1] Under these conditions, a well-functioning price mechanism allows voluntary and peaceful social co-operation between autonomous market actors to the benefit of the whole economy. In contrast to the classical libertarian idea of the nightwatchman state as the basis of fully functioning competition, the proponents of the *Ordoliberal School* have emphasised the necessity to protect the competitive order against the accumulation of private economic power through an appropriate institutional order.[2]

Only under the rules of this order, typically anti-trust legislation, may competition work as 'the most magnificent and most ingenious instrument of deprivation of power in history'.[3] In this context, Walter Eucken argues in favour of 'performance competition' (*Leistungswettbewerb*)[4] and against 'hand-to-hand combat' or 'prevention competition' (*Behinderungswettbewerb*), ie competition by means that are directed at preventing competition from other producers.[5] His approach, which also lies at the heart of the concept of a social-market economy, combines ideas of (social) co-operation through the invisible price mechanism with 'record-type games' that pursue excellence or competitive advantage, while rejecting 'struggle-type games' which determine winners in zero-sum games.[6]

The ordoliberal concept of competition has two important shortcomings with respect to these different conceptions of competition. First, while Eucken explicitly mentions the idea of prevention competition, he limits the downsides of an incomplete competition to the emergence of monopolistic or oligopolistic market structures.[7] Successive authors added emphasis on the problem of rent-seeking,[8] arguing that the rules of the game of politics needed to be constrained by a constitutional order that prevented government from becoming the target of special interest groups.[9] Neither of these arguments provides, however, a rationale for *why* performance competition should be the rule rather than the exception. In fact, in the

---

[1] Werner Bonefeld, 'Freedom and the Strong State: On German Ordoliberalism', (2012) 17 *New Political Economy*, pp 633–656.

[2] Walter Eucken, *Grundsätze der Wirtschaftspolitik*, (Tübingen: J.C.B. Mohr (Paul Siebeck), 1952).

[3] Franz Böhm, *Reden und Schriften*, (Karlsruhe: C.F. Müller, 1960), p 22, cited in Vanberg, n 5 below.

[4] Walter Eucken, 'Die Wettbewerbsordnung und ihre Verwirklichung', (1949) 2 *ORDO Jahrbuch*, pp 1–99, at 25.

[5] Viktor J. Vanberg, 'The Freiburg School: Walter Eucken and Ordoliberalism', (2004), *Freiburger Diskussionspapiere zur Ordnungsökonomik* 04/11.

[6] Yuichi Shionoya, 'The Ethics of Competition', (1995) 2 *European Journal of Law and Economics*, pp 5–19.

[7] Eucken, n 4 above.

[8] Franz Böhm, *Freiheit und Ordnung in der Marktwirtschaft*, (Baden-Baden: Nomos Verlag, 1980); Manfred E. Streit, 'Economic Order, Private Law and Public Policy—The Freiburg School of Law and Economics in Perspective', (1992) 148 *Journal of Institutional and Theoretical Economics*, pp 675–704.

[9] Vanberg, n 5 above.

traditional ordoliberal view, non-peaceful competition somehow appears to be an artefact that is easily avoided by an appropriate institutional order.

Oliver Williamson, however, reminds us that opportunism and malfeasance are common phenomena among individuals, and will, therefore, affect market outcomes:[10] 'Economic man is a much more subtle and devious creature than the usual self-interest seeking assumption reveals.' To him, economic opportunism is 'self-interest seeking with guile'[11] or 'the incomplete or distorted disclosure of information, especially to calculated efforts to mislead, distort, disguise, obfuscate, or otherwise confuse'.[12] In this neo-Hobbesian setting,[13] the outcomes of a competitive market order are no longer clear-cut because opportunism creates transaction costs, which may distort market choices and social welfare maximisation may not succeed.[14]

Second, the ordoliberal concept of competition is very much in line with the traditional economic thinking about the win-win aspects of exchange and the gains from trade. These arise, however, only when competition is based upon perfectly specified and perfectly enforced property rights.[15] Accordingly, the task of the competitive order is then to establish the appropriate rules for efficient market processes; for instance, by unambiguously assigning property rights. While this appears plausible at first glance and the implementation of these rules may, indeed, be feasible, the underlying assumption that market actors can only produce and trade to make a living is far from being self-evident.

Even in standard models of imperfect economic competition with a particularly large deadweight loss or a significant waste of consumer and/or producer rents, the possibility of a trade-off between production and what may be called *conflict activities* is usually excluded. Market actors neither engage in appropriation, nor do they grab the production of others, nor do they have to defend what they themselves have produced.[16] They do not even invest in conflict technologies. This is somewhat surprising as substantial parts of the economic literature on conflict(s) relies on contest models that are also used in the rent-seeking literature.[17]

---

[10] Oliver E. Williamson, *Markets and Hierarchies: Analysis and Anti-trust Implications: A Study in the Economics of Internal Organization*, (New York: Free Press, 1975), p 47.

[11] ibid, p 255.

[12] idem, *The Economic Institutions of Capitalism*, (New York: Free Press, 1985), p 47.

[13] Samuel Bowles, 'The Production Process in a Competitive Economy: Walrasian, Neo-Hobbesian, and Marxian Models', (1985) 75 *American Economic Review*, pp 16–36.

[14] Oliver E. Williamson, 'Transaction-Cost Economics: The Governance of Contractual Relations', (1979) 22 *Journal of Law and Economics*, pp 233–261; see, critically, Geoffrey M. Hodgson, 'Opportunism is not the Only Reason Why Firms Exist: Why an Explanatory Emphasis on Opportunism may Mislead Management Strategy', (2004) *Industrial and Corporate Change*, pp 401–418.

[15] Michelle R. Garfinkel and Stergios Skaperdas, 'Economics of Conflict: An Overview', in: Todd Sandler and Keith Hartley (eds), *Handbook of Defense Economics, Volume 2: Defense in a Globalized World*, (Amsterdam: North Holland, 2007), pp 649–709.

[16] Gordon Tullock, 'Rent-seeking as a Negative-sum Game', in: James Buchanan, Robert D. Tollison and Gordon Tullock, *Toward a Theory of the Rent-seeking Society (No. 4)*, (College Station TX: Texas A & M University Press, 1980), pp 16–36; Shmuel Nitzan, 'Modelling Rent-seeking Contests', (1994) 10 *European Journal of Political Economy*, pp 41–60.

[17] Jack Hirshleifer, 'Conflict and Rent-seeking Success Functions: Ratio vs. Difference Models of Relative Success', (1989) 63 *Public Choice*, pp 101–112.

Modelling conflicts as a contest implies a game in which the participants expend resources on arming to increase their probability of winning if conflict were actually to take place.[18] This 'arming' can be understood within a larger economic context when investments are not productive but aim at improving a firm's relative bargaining power to win a conflict or contest in the next round. For instance, it requires investments either to become or to fight a 'patent troll' (ie a party that attempts to enforce a patent far beyond its actual value).[19] Neither of these investments has any productive value, since the troll, seeking to extract rents from a firm, spends money on an otherwise useless patent, while the firm does everything (for example, hiring expensive attorneys) to avoid becoming the target of the troll.

Against this background, recent advances in the economic literature on conflict are a good starting-point to extend the traditional ordoliberal perspective on competition. On markets, in which non-peaceful forms of conflict co-exist with, or even dominate, peaceful competition, the traditional outcomes of competitive processes come under scrutiny and may no longer hold. If this is the case, the policy recommendations and (normative) claims of ordoliberalism may no longer hold or be effective. In the following, we will analyse how introducing conflict activities into a competitive market changes the market equilibrium; then, we discuss the consequences for the ordoliberal model of a competitive market order.

Our argument will be based upon a very broad concept of conflict that is compatible with many real-world situations. We are less interested in the specific micro-technology of conflict (ie the weaponry) than in the more general issue that market actors may invest resources in a conflict in order to increase their chance of winning the 'market game'. Unlike in the economics-of-conflict literature, we do not emphasise physical violence as the essence of conflict. However, the obstruction, damage, expropriation or destruction of competitors may be the actual strategies chosen by some market actors, typically aiming at a non-market driven re-allocation of existing property-rights assignments. Some of these strategies may mainly be observed in illegal markets, but it would be naïve to believe that they not to occur in regular markets or that illegal activity (for example, protection rackets) would not feed back into regular markets. Often, the simple threat of potentially destructive activity suffices to make market actors comply. Again, the example of a patent troll is striking because the mere threat of suing a firm may already make the firm accept excessive demands by the troll.

This is clearly very different from market competition in the traditional sense, in which—based upon the assumption of clearly assigned property rights—scarce resources are to be allocated on consumption and production activities in the most beneficial way for society as a whole. This market competition may turn into a conflict scenario once the market actors are negatively able to affect the cost structures of their competitors, or when they use excessive resources to avoid market entry by

---

[18] Garfinkel and Skaperdas, n 15 above.
[19] Randall R. Rader, 'The State of Patent Litigation', address at the E.D. Texas Judicial Conference, 2011, available at: www.patentlyo.com/media/docs/2011/09/raderstateofpatentlit.pdf.

competitors. More generally, the distinction between conflict and competition boils down to the difference between bilateral, beneficial exchange, on the one hand, and unilaterally taking advantage of a power asymmetry in the market, where power results from threatening or actively combating a competitor, on the other. Of course, in real-world markets, the line between fierce competition and mild conflict may be blurred.

Even if one expected laws, institutions and norms to emerge in order to limit and shape the use of force by economic agents,[20] the outcomes of the competitive process will still be influenced by the always-existing possibility of increasing one's influence by additional conflict investments. In the following section, we will provide a simple model that shows that the predictions of the competitive model are no longer valid once conflict is introduced.

II. HOW TO INTRODUCE CONFLICT IN A SIMPLE MODEL OF COMPETITIVE MARKETS

One of the simplest models of allocation and (production) efficiency in competitive markets is the *Edgeworth Box*, shown in Figure 1. The model considers two firms and two factors of production (for example, capital and labour). In their attempt to fulfil consumers' demands, firms typically realise that the initial factor endowment is not sufficient to maximise their profits. For a given production technology, exchanging or trading production factors upon a voluntary basis with another owner of these factors may help to utilise them more effectively. At some point in time, trading further factors is no longer advantageous for the firms because the profit loss from giving up one unit of the first factor equals the profit gain from obtaining additional units of the other factor in exchange. Graphically, the isoquants of both firms as a representation of their production technologies become tangent and their marginal rates of technical substitution equalise. The contract curve represents the *locus* of all efficient trade outcomes and thus all possible Pareto-optimal allocations.

Under these circumstances, there is no need for government intervention because trade leads to the social welfare optimum. Starting from the initial endowment, moving into the lens spanned by the isoquants of both firms increases the profits of each of these firms. If at all, the role of government is to facilitate and maintain Pareto improvements and Pareto efficient allocations, ie processes towards and solutions on the contract curve. Hence, the government should promote voluntary and peaceful exchange and trade of goods, services and production factors by providing exchange institutions such as a market infrastructure or secure well-defined property rights, which, in turn, reduce the transaction costs of market exchanges. As shown above, ordoliberals favour, among other things, sound constitutional rules and effective anti-trust legislation to set an institutional framework within which social welfare can flourish.

---

[20] Garfinkel and Skaperdas, n 15 above.

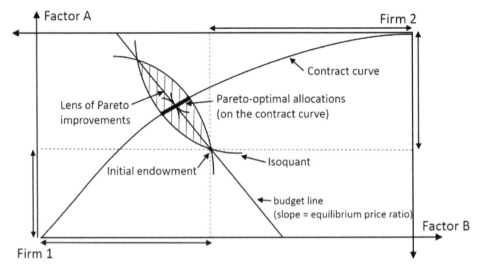

Figure 1: Edgeworth Box of Voluntary Exchange

Figure 1 represents not only a pure exchange economy, but also a competitive market once a price mechanism is introduced. For a given initial endowment, prices evaluate the amount of available and tradable resources that may be used in the production process. At the same time, they determine the budget line for each firm. Only if the exchange ratio of the production factors in terms of prices and marginal profits is equalised, do any remaining incentives to continue trading factors disappear and total profits (and thus social welfare) are maximised. The underlying reason for this outcome is that profit-oriented firms, while competing for scarce resources, are aware of the potential profit gains from trade, which they do not want to forgo.

This simple theoretical framework can be expanded by integrating conflict activities directly into the Edgeworth Box. This allows us to analyse how conflict affects the outcomes of a competitive market. The basic assumption of this approach is a *guns-versus-butter* scenario, ie producers can transform any endowment (or resources or abilities) into a conflict good or into conflict behaviour. By definition, conflict goods ('guns') are neither productive nor can they be used to fulfil consumers' demands ('butter'). Their only purpose is to secure a powerful position in a conflict or to threaten other market actors; just as the patent troll acquires a patent only in order to extract rent from another firm by threatening to sue it, but does not intend to use the patent for production purposes. Clearly, this implicitly assumes that property rights are diluted, ie they are not always fully attributable to one market actor.

Figure 2 shows different scenarios that may arise when conflict activities are included in the model. The figure makes the simplifying assumption that Firm 1 is endowed only with Factor B, while Firm 2 is endowed only with Factor A, implying that the point of initial endowments is in V.

The first scenario is shown in Panel 2a, which corresponds to Figure 1. Although conflict investments are possible, neither of the two firms actually invests. Instead, the firms take the initial factor endowment as the basis for trade (here, the isoquants

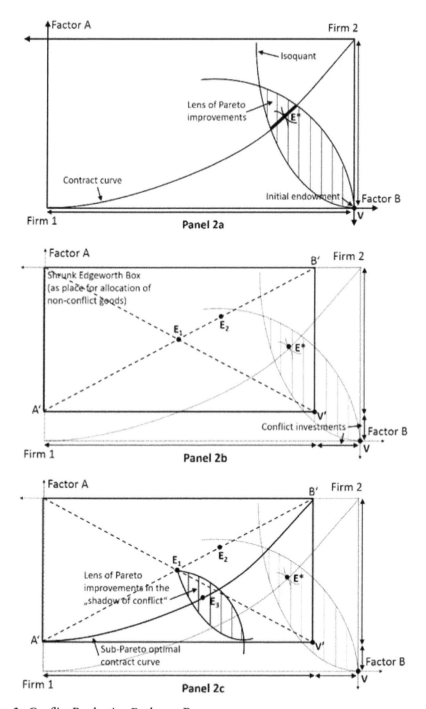

Figure 2: Conflict-Production Exchange Box

span the potential settlement region) and achieve a Pareto optimum with maximum total profits at point E*. In comparison, Panel 2b shows a case in which some of the initial factor endowment is transformed into conflict goods. The graph already presents the outcome of an arms race, ie a conflict game in which both players choose to invest in conflict activities as a dominant strategy. This interpretation results from the following logic: if Firm 1 (for example, the patent troll) gives up some units of Factor B and invests these units into conflict activities, it will win all available resources, ie it will own both the remaining units of Factor B and all units of Factor A which were previously owned by Firm 2. The reason for this outcome is the assumption that an exclusive investment in conflict activities on behalf of Firm 1 results in the overwhelming power of Firm 1 to appropriate the property rights of Firm 2 for Factor A. Losing everything is not a very attractive perspective for Firm 2, so it will also invest in conflict goods by diverting some units of its initial endowment with Factor A (for example, by hiring an attorney, instead of investing in research and development).

Investing in conflict if the other firm does the same is an optimal strategy because it helps to avoid a complete loss of resources. Investing if the other firm does not invest would even allow additional resources to be gained. Hence, investing in conflict is the dominant strategy for both firms; however, from a welfare perspective, this outcome is clearly inferior, in that it represents a classic prisoner's dilemma situation. The unproductive conflict investments let the Edgeworth Box shrink, indicating that fewer resources are available for production (and consumption) purposes.

This does not say, however, that there cannot be winners and losers in this game, although society, as a whole, will lose. The dashed lines in the shrunk Edgeworth Box in Panel 2b provide a first idea of possible allocations of consumption goods depending on the actual conflict outcomes. If conflict investments lead to power equality, ie an equal relative force of conflict players, the midpoint E_1 of the shrunk Edgeworth Box will be reached (implicitly, we assume here that both firms value factors equally strongly). Here, both firms will capture exactly the same amount of Factors A and B, respectively. If, *after* conflict investments, one firm is more powerful than the other firm, it will be able to appropriate more than half of the available resources (at point E_2, Firm 1 is more powerful than Firm 2). Most importantly, however, we observe that neither allocation E_1 nor E_2 corresponds to the optimal allocation E* that would result without any conflict investments.

Panel 2c provides yet another possible outcome of competitive markets with conflict investments. Again, both firms invest into conflict leading to a shrunk Edgeworth Box. In contrast to the previous scenario, however, they do not decide to enter into conflict, but continue trading, instead. That is, starting from a position of equal power (E_1), they trade toward E_3. This is an impure conflict outcome called 'exchange in the shadow of conflict'.[21] This outcome rests, however, on the assumption that both firms actually prefer exchange to conflict, otherwise the market outcome will be an allocation akin to E_2. An alternative interpretation of this scenario

[21] Charles H. Anderton, Roxane A. Anderton and John R. Carr, 'Economic Activity in the Shadow of Conflict', (1999) 37 *Economic Inquiry*, pp 166–179.

is a *simultaneous conflict-exchange equilibrium* in which E_1 is the allocation that occurs after a conflict of equally powerful firms. Despite the previous open conflict, the firms realise that entering into trade is beneficial to them. In fact, this situation may even occur for a post-conflict allocation such as E_2, in which Firm 1 dominated Firm 2, because trade of non-conflict goods and factors remains attractive.

One can think of several extensions of this model. According to Anderton and Anderton,[22] the conflict technology plays a role. Some firms have a comparative advantage in offensive, and others in defensive, conflict technologies (for example, the patent troll acts offensively, while the attacked firm responds defensively). Similarly, the asymmetric availability of conflict technologies may affect the outcomes. Finally, the timing of the attacks will certainly matter to the success probability of the market actors.

Regardless of the model variant under consideration, there is a basic unilateral incentive to invest in conflict goods in order to realise an allocation, which is strictly preferred to pure bilateral exchange. Even if the firms know that pure factor trade without any conflict investments (and without competition under the shadow of conflict) leads to the highest social welfare by the maximum sum of profits, each of them has the unilateral (ie non-cooperative) incentive to invest in conflict goods. Hence, in general, any trade or exchange only exists in the shadow of the conflict.

What follows from this exercise is that traditional wisdoms of welfare economics and ordoliberalism are challenged when conflict is introduced. The two welfare theorems on competitive economies, ie (i) any equilibrium in competitive markets is Pareto-optimal and (ii) any Pareto-optimal allocation can be sustained under competitive markets with an appropriate adjustment of initial resources, do no longer hold when conflict is introduced into the Edgeworth Box.[23] The Edgeworth Box is instead endogenous and depends on the intentions of the firms to enter conflict or the fear to become involved in a conflict. In fact, there is a family of Edgeworth Boxes and only one of these boxes is Pareto-optimal, namely the one with zero conflict investments. That is, in general, one observes *sub-Pareto optimal* competitive markets, which contradict the *First Welfare Theorem*.[24]

The major question for any (welfare) economist is, therefore, how to get from sub-Pareto optimality to Pareto-optimality. At first glance, it appears reasonable to let the government provide society with, for instance, a sound protection of property rights and a governmental conflict management. More generally, one might argue that the idea of a protective state should be extended to economic policy as well. It should be noted that, in neoclassical economics, it is generally assumed that the problem of the protective state is solved, but this assumption appears doubtful. If conflict is at least partly inevitable because there is no, or only an incomplete, protective state when it comes to market transactions, government has (i) to foster exchange in the shadow of the conflict, and (ii) to implement and manage institutions in a world of

---

[22] Charles H. Anderton and Roxane A. Anderton, 'The Economics of Conflict, Production, and Exchange', in: Jürgen Brauer and William G. Gissy (eds), *Economics of Conflict and Peace*, (Aldershot: Avebury, 1997).
[23] ibid.
[24] ibid.

simultaneous conflict and exchange activities. Assuming that the ordoliberal agenda shares the interest in moving from a sub-optimal to an efficient allocation, one will furthermore have to ask how (constitutional) rules which do not restrict the welfare-enhancing forces of competition, while simultaneously avoiding the negative impact of conflict on the market mechanism, need to be designed.

III. ENVY-FREE ALLOCATIONS AS A POTENTIAL CONSTITUTIONAL SOLUTION TO CONFLICT IN COMPETITIVE MARKETS

There are many reasons why conflict could occur. In psychology, conflict is assumed to follow from strong emotions, such as anger, hatred, guilt, shame, pride, regret, joy, grief, malice, indignation, jealousy, contempt, disgust, fear or love.[25] In economics, envy, as one particular emotion, has attracted quite a lot of attention, because it can be generalised as a common feeling of individuals and groups of individuals (such as employees and managers of a firm that is being attacked by a patent troll) that is closely interrelated with concepts such as inequality and relative deprivation.[26] While Hirschman assumes relative deprivation to be identical with envy, other authors acknowledge that (minor) differences may exist.[27] Whether or not the two concepts are identical or are only closely interrelated, however, does not matter for our argument. Rather, since Gurr's seminal contribution on the genesis of conflict from relative deprivation, this link is also broadly accepted in economics.[28]

Against this background, it is important to note that, while envy is considered an emotion in psychology, in economics, the concept is made free of emotion by defining it in strictly behavioural terms.[29] It is assumed that the members of group i depict a 'feeling of envy' towards the members of group j (or a single person j), if they prefer to change their position, ie their access to a specific commodity bundle, with that of group j (or individual j). If group or individual i reveals a preference for a change in position with group or individual j, i is said to envy j. Or, to put it loosely, a distribution of goods is envy-free if every group is satisfied with the commodity

---

[25] Jon Elster, 'Emotions and Economic Theory', (1998) 36 *Journal of Economic Literature*, pp 47–74.

[26] Runciman explains relative deprivation as follows: 'The magnitude of a relative deprivation is the extent of the difference between the desired situation and that of the person desiring it'; see Walter G. Runciman, *Relative Deprivation und Social Justice: A Study of Attitudes to Social Inequality in Twentieth Century England*, (London: Routledge and Kegan Paul, 1966). See, amongst others, Christian Arnsperger, 'Envy-freeness and Distributive Justice', (1994) 8 *Journal of Economic Surveys*, pp 155–186; Jack Hirshleifer, 'The Expanding Domain of Economics', (1985) 75 *American Economic Review*, pp 53–68; Georg Kirchsteiger, 'The Role of Envy in Ultimatum Games', (1994) 25 *Journal of Economic Behavior and Organization*, pp 373–389; Vai-Lam Mui, 'The Economics of Envy', (1994) 26 *Journal of Economic Behavior and Organization*, pp 311–336; Nripesh Podder, 'Relative Deprivation, Envy and Economic Inequality', (1996) 49 *Kyklos*, pp 353–376; Hal R. Varian, 'Equity, Envy, and Efficiency', (1974) 9 *Journal of Economic Theory*, pp 63–91.

[27] Albert O. Hirschman and Michael Rothschild, 'The Changing Tolerance for Income Inequality in the Course of Economic Development: With a Mathematical Appendix', (1973) 87 *Quarterly Journal of Economics*, pp 544–566; Adhip Chaudhuri, 'Some Implications of Intensity Measure of Envy', (1986) 3 *Social Choice and Welfare*, pp 255–270; Podder, n 26 above.

[28] See, eg, Ted Robert Gurr, *Why Men Rebel*, (Princeton NJ: Princeton University Press, 1970); see, eg, Tim Krieger and Daniel Meierrieks, 'Does Inequality Lead to Terrorism?', CESifo Working Paper No. 5821, available at: www.cesifo-group.de/DocDL/cesifo1_wp5821.pdf.

[29] Podder, n 26 above.

bundle allotted to them, ie no group should (strictly) prefer the commodity bundle held by any other group to its own bundle.[30] Representative of the economics literature, Hal Varian calls the absence of envy together with Pareto optimality *fairness* and, indeed, envy-freeness has become the most relevant 'distributive companion' to the aggregative requirement of Pareto efficiency in normative economics.[31] Given the relevance of envy in the economic literature and its handy interpretation, we will use envy as our example of a potential conflict-trigger in the following. Note that we subsequently assume an implicit general agreement that allocations with no envy define a fair social state from the perspective of the market participants.

The Edgeworth Box can again be used to explain this concept. As before, we will refer to firms and their isoquants, although we have to keep in mind that the actual envy is related to the group of managers and employees working in a specific firm. Graphically, we take the midpoint of the Edgeworth Box as a starting-point. By definition, the midpoint is envy-neutral because both firms have exactly identical allocations of resources. For each group, we now have to identify the envy-free region by considering 'changing-places' situations. We do so by taking any two points, ie initial endowments, left and right of (or above and below) the midpoint of the box. For each pair of these points, it must hold that they can be connected by a straight line through the midpoint and that they have exactly the same distance to the midpoint. Furthermore, they need to lie on the same isoquant, meaning that the individuals in the firms are indifferent to them. In Figure 3, G and G' fulfil these conditions. Here, G and G' lie on the same isoquant of Firm 2, which implies that the endowments G and G' are, in fact, envy-neutral. The individuals working at Firm 2 are indifferent to changing places with workers of Firm 1 from G to G', or vice versa. If the exercise of identifying analogous endowment pairs is repeated, the envy-neutral curves of both firms' workers can be determined.

It should be noted that the workers of Firm 2 would not mind any allocation southwest of their envy-neutral curve because it would result in a position on a higher isoquant with more of both goods. The same is true for the workers from Firm 1 who prefer any endowment northeast of their envy-neutral curve to the curve itself. Combining these observations helps us to identify the mutually envy-free region, which is the region between the two envy-neutral curves in the lower right corner. Moving into this region is beneficial for both firms as there is no conflict potential if envy is the single cause of deviating from peaceful exchange (which we assume throughout this section). However, as one can easily recognise from the graph, most of the mutually envy-free region is not efficient as it lies off the contract curve. As long as the initial endowment is inside the region, this is not a problem. Firms will simply start to trade until they reach the contract curve by peaceful settlement.

This has some straightforward implications. If we assume that envy-freeness is the pre-condition for peaceful exchange and if we want to move from a sub-optimal to an efficient allocation, which is also free of conflict, then the ordoliberal policymaker has to ensure that market exchange starts within the mutually envy-free region of Figure 3. In this case, the final market outcome will be efficient *and* free

---

[30] Arnsperger, n 26 above.
[31] Varian, n 26 above; Arnsperger, n 26 above.

of envy. Here, the government only has to guarantee the proper functioning of the market game; beyond this, there is no need for any kind of intervention. However, since the initial endowments do not necessarily lie within this region, a modern ordoliberal research programme that includes the possibility of conflict would imply policy instruments (labelled as the 'ordoliberal agenda' in Figure 3) in order to help us to move from outside the envy-free zone to the inside.

This is reminiscent of the *Second Theorem of Welfare Economics* which—as we have already mentioned above—states that, out of all possible Pareto optimal outcomes, one can achieve any particular one by enacting a lump-sum wealth re-distribution and then letting the market take over.[32] That is, at least in theory, the policy-maker will choose an appropriate lump-sum re-distribution at the outset to move into the envy-free zone. The difference to the classical theorem is, of course, that the goal of the policy-maker is now a different one. It is no longer the idea of achieving/attaining a desired income distribution, but rather that of ensuring peaceful exchange. It should be noted that the latter is an allocative goal here in the first place, not a distributional one.

Since the implementation of a lump-sum tax (or subsidy) is nearly impossible, however, one has to resort to distortive taxes which are second-best according to optimal-tax theory.[33] Here, the negative welfare effects of distortional taxation would be countered by positive welfare gains from the avoidance of the allocative harm from conflict.

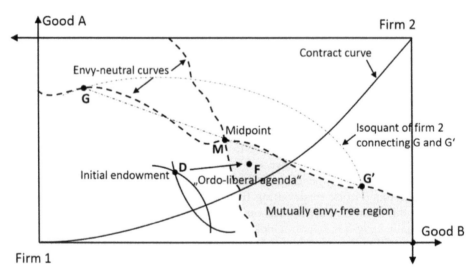

Figure 3: An Ordoliberal Agenda to enter the Mutually Envy-Free Region

---

[32] See, eg, Andreu Mas-Colell, Michael D. Whinston and Jerry R. Green, *Microeconomic Theory*, (Oxford: Oxford University Press, 1995).

[33] For attempts to derive optimal envy taxes, see, eg, Dieter Bös and Georg Tillmann, 'An Envy Tax: Theoretical Principles and Applications to the German Surcharge on the Rich', (1985) 40 *Public Finance*, pp 35–63; Yukihiro Nichimura, 'Optimal Commodity Taxation for Reduction of Envy', (2003) 21 *Social Choice and Welfare*, pp 501–527, and idem, 'Optimal Non-linear Income Taxation for Reduction of Envy', (2003) *Journal of Public Economics*, pp 363–386.

IV. THE NEW ORDOLIBERAL AGENDA: REBUILDING THE INSTITUTIONAL FOUNDATIONS FOR A PEACEFUL MARKET ECONOMY THROUGH PRE-DISTRIBUTIONAL POLICIES

Based upon the preceding considerations about envy-free allocations as a means of decreasing the conflict potential in the market, we now turn to the wider question of how to facilitate further market exchange in a world of simultaneous conflict and exchange activities. Admittedly, an economy is a complex order in which it is epistemologically impossible and practically too costly to reach a situation by means of lump-sum re-distribution in which the market participants' social preferences will be satisfied to a degree that any conflict investment becomes individually irrational. We might be successful with regard to envy in a narrowly defined market, but, of course, economic agents can hold all sorts of social preferences (for example, inequality aversion, Rawlsian fairness, and reciprocity, to name but a few) that may motivate conflict investments in complex market situations. Consequently, in a second-best world with transaction costs in which property rights are diluted, there will always be a certain minimal level of conflict activities that is acceptable from a social welfare perspective.

Having said this, there is still a more general implication of our previous discussion. Although it is true that re-distributing initial endowments in many areas of an economy would be costly, would change incentive structures and would often lack the necessary knowledge on the part of the social planner, it shifts the general logic of the market participants away from 'exchange in the shadow of conflict' to 'exchange in the shadow of pre-distribution'.[34] This line of reasoning follows Jacob Hacker and Paul Pierson in that it focuses on market reforms that encourage a more equal distribution of (economic) power before individuals freely enter into market transactions.[35] The idea goes back to the notion of a property-owning democracy developed by James Meade and philosophically extended by John Rawls.[36] Conflict-laden market segments in which players have an individual incentive to invest strategically in a 'struggle-type' competition now turn into segments in which 'record-type' competition becomes more attractive since the players anticipate the new distributional situation, which, in turn, diminishes or cancels out returns on conflict investments in the first place.

From a welfare economic perspective, one could argue that any governmental re-distribution makes individual property rights less stable or secure. Although this

---

[34] In general, the idea of 'pre-distribution' draws attention to policies and institutions that are designed to improve the resources and opportunities of economic agents before entering the market game (eg through education or workers' participation on the individual level or lowering the market entry costs on the firm level), which, in turn, reduces the need for redistributive tax-and-transfer mechanisms or antitrust measures ex post. For a recent summary article, see Gavin Kerr, "Predistribution', Property-Owning Democracy and Land Value Taxation', (2016) 15 *Politics, Philosophy and Economics*, pp 67–91.
[35] Jacob S. Hacker and Paul Pierson, *Winner-Take-All Politics; How Washington Made the Rich Richer—And Turned its Back on the Middle Class*, (New York: Simon and Schuster, 2011).
[36] James E. Meade, *Efficiency, Equality and the Ownership of Property*, (New York: Routledge, [1964] 2013); John Rawls, *A Theory of Justice*, rev'd edition, (Oxford: Oxford University Press, 1999), and idem, *Justice as Fairness: A Restatement*, (Cambridge MA: Harvard University Press, 2001).

observation has some merit in competitive markets, it neglects the dynamic inefficiencies stemming from the constant threat of conflict activities in simultaneous conflict-exchange markets. In addition, government interference ideally is a pre-distributional, one-shot interference with the aim of yielding an envy-free (or any other socially desired equivalent) market situation that strengthens, in particular, the market and/or the bargaining power of the relatively-deprived market actors at the outset.[37] Such a policy enables all market participants to focus on exchange activities in the market game since it raises their opportunity costs of conflict investments. Once the mutually envy-free allocation is reached, the government abstains from further interfering and allows the free market to define the final distributional outcome. In contrast, if we have a situation with high conflict investments by the market participants without any pre-distributional efforts, the potential window for welfare improving market exchange becomes increasingly smaller and, more importantly, the degree of property rights security deteriorates and unilateral protection measures (such as lawyers, lawsuits, or pre-emptive safety arrangements) become more costly over time.

The crucial advantage of a pre-distributional account to conflict-laden markets is that it allows for a *rule-based solution*: At a market constitutional level, one can establish mutually advantageous rules that constrain the possible transactions to the 'peaceful settlement region' (in our example: the zone of envy-freeness). Consequently, all market participants know, *ex ante*, the rules of the game (in particular, the range of property rights becomes common knowledge) and they can adjust their individual behaviour accordingly.[38] If market participants know in advance that strategic behaviour is limited to the envy-free choice set, incentives for investments in conflict efforts are significantly reduced, if not completely eliminated. This raises utility at the individual level, in that it enables economic participation and planning, and it raises potential gains from trade for firms, since market instabilities are decreased and firms abstain from entering a wasteful arms race. Resources that had previously been invested in conflict activities can now be productively funnelled into alternative value-generating uses.[39] In addition, this rule-based enhancement of 'record-type' competition can propagate peaceful market solutions (for example, industry specific codes of fair conduct that rule out harmful business models and strategies, including those chosen by patent trolls, or informal rules against deceptive advertising) which, in turn, re-inforce the stability of the constitutional framework over time.

As a matter of course, the government has to secure the 'peaceful settlement region' of the market and enforce the constitutional rules of the game through the punishment of property rights violations. However, it lies in the self-interest of the

---

[37] In their research published by the IMF, Michael Kumhof and Romain Rancière, 'Inequality, Leverage and Crises', IMF Working Papers, (2010), argue, eg that the best way of flattening pre-tax inequalities is to raise the bargaining power of wage-earners before entering the market game.

[38] James M. Buchanan, 'Generality as a Constitutional Constraint', in: idem, *The Collected Works of James M. Buchanan, Vol. 1: The Logical Foundations of Constitutional Liberty*, (Indianapolis IN: Liberty Fund, 1999), pp 419–428; and idem, 'The Constitution of Economic Policy', (1987) 77 *American Economic Review*, pp 243–250.

[39] Buchanan, 'Generality as a Constitutional Constraint', n 38 above, p 427.

market participants not only to support and finance a property rights regime by means of an effective police force (*protection of property right*) and an independent judiciary system (*management of conflict situations*), but also to address and agree on the establishment of pre-distributional policies at the constitutional level in order to secure welfare-gains from peaceful market exchanges. Therefore, the normative benchmark for pre-distributional policies should always be the criterion of (potential) mutual agreement on constitutional rules within which peaceful market transactions are allowed to emerge freely. Consequently, market participants would stick to the rules of the game, if, on balance, over the whole sequence of discrete 'plays', the pre-distributional policies serve their interests more effectively than unilateral conflict activities.[40] This shift in the political agenda from *re*-distributive corrections of extremely unjust market results to *pre*-distributional efforts to secure a fair, ie envy-free, competition, serves to facilitate agreement on the general rules of the game and may remove conflicts among individuals or firms in strategic actions in the game itself.[41] In this respect, they support the ordoliberal concept of the competitive order even in a setting with potential conflict activities.

V. CONCLUSION

Very early on in the intellectual history of ordoliberalism, Eucken argued in favour of *performance competition* and against *prevention competition* ('hand-to-hand combat'); however, the proponents of the Ordoliberal School have never fully paid attention to the implications of this important distinction. Ordoliberals have mainly focused their scholarly attention on the necessity to protect the competitive order against the emergence of monopolistic or oligopolistic market structures, and against rent-seeking activities in the political arena. In doing so, they have long neglected the possibility that a non-peaceful struggle-type competition might be the rule rather than the exception, even in competitively organised markets.

In fact, recent literature in conflict economics emphasises that competition can trigger conflict, rather than have an appeasing effect: market actors often expend resources on arming to increase their probability of sustaining market shares or simply to damage a more powerful competitor. These *conflict activities* are not productive, but resource wasting instead. On markets, in which conflicts co-exist with or even dominate peaceful competition, classic ordoliberal policy recommendations, such as antitrust laws to secure competition or property rights protection to stimulate investments, may no longer be sufficient or may lose their effectiveness; the outcome of the market will be 'in the shadow of conflict', ie it will be influenced by the ever-existing threat of the loss of market shares to a competitor in the arms race,

---

[40] idem, 'The Constitution of Economic Policy', n 38 above, p 248.

[41] Buchanan, in: 'The Constitution of Economic Policy', n 38 above, p 248, gives the following explanation: 'To the extent that the individual reckons that a constitutional rule will remain applicable over a long sequence of periods, with many in-period choices to be made, he is necessarily placed behind a partial 'veil of uncertainty' concerning the effects of any rule on his own predicted interests. Choice among rules will, therefore, tend to be based on generalizable criteria of fairness, making agreement more likely to occur than when separable interests are more easily identifiable.'

including a generally too high level of (unproductive) investments in conflict activities, which lowers overall welfare.

In order to grasp this observation theoretically, we have introduced conflict into a simple Edgeworth Box model of competitive markets in order to show how the market equilibrium changes if we allow for a struggle-type competition. In such a competition, investing in conflict is the dominant strategy for all market actors, yet, from a welfare perspective, this outcome is clearly inferior since fewer resources are available for production and consumption purposes. We then discussed envy and its link to relative deprivation as a potential conflict-trigger in markets. Based upon the Edgeworth Box model of competitive markets, we identified the envy-free market segment as a potential solution to struggle-type market situations.

Given these theoretical insights, we advocated *pre-distributional policies*, ie measures that increase the economic opportunities of actors on markets before entering into bilateral market transactions, as a way of decreasing conflict potential and enhancing peaceful market exchange. In general, the normative discussion has been rather abstract. Examples for pre-distributional policies might range from educational minimum standards at individual level to decreasing disparities in access to infrastructure or repealing market-entry barriers for firms. The crucial advantage of such measures is their *rule-based* character: one can establish mutually advantageous rules on the market-constituting stage that constrain the subsequent transactions on the market to the 'peaceful settlement region'.

Admittedly, it might be difficult to find a clear-cut distinction between peaceful and conflict-laden competition. However, acknowledging the conflict aspect of competition and the institutional challenge that comes with it could spur the research agenda of a new ordoliberal programme.

16

Ordoliberalism and the Quest for Sacrality[1]

JOSEF HIEN

ABSTRACT

Ordoliberalism has been identified as an important ideational force during the European sovereign debt crisis. A lively scholarly and public debate has erupted on how much influence the ideology had on the German position during the crisis. This chapter concentrates on an aspect that this debate has so far omitted: the cultural foundations and the ethical provisions of ordoliberalism. The chapter explores the genealogy of ordoliberal thinking and shows that it has profound roots in German Protestant social teachings. The religious connection ensured the political survival of ordoliberalism in the highly religious environment of post-WWII Germany. With the decline of organised religion form the 1960s onwards, ordoliberalism adopted the myth of the social market economy as a civil religion to ensure the ideology's survival.

I. INTRODUCTION

WHY DO WE need to know more about the religious 'connection' of ordoliberalism? Fifteen years after Philip Manow's seminal article on the Protestant *Tiefengrammatik* of ordoliberalism, the connection between Protestantism and ordoliberalism has received a new spin. A European banking-crisis, a sovereign debt crisis, and a crisis of the euro all hold the European Union in an iron grip and have brought it to the brink of collapse. Ordoliberalism might not be responsible for harsh austerity, the rules-based approach to the crisis, or the conditionality of the *Troika*, but a great deal of the verbal wars surrounding the crisis both in and outside of Germany has been informed by ordoliberal and counter-ordoliberal arguments.

[1] This paper has been written in the context of the RESCEU Project (Reconciling economic and social Europe, www.resceu.eu), funded by the European Research Council (Advanced Grant no 340534).

These ordoliberal arguments—launched primarily by Northern European governments, central banks and epistemic communities—follow a Protestant *Tiefengrammatik* which clashes with the prevailing ideas on the economy, the state and society in the Catholic and Orthodox Southern periphery of the Eurozone. These verbal wars are as important as the responses to the crisis because they alienate European citizens from one another and give rise to extremists on both sides of the political spectrum.

The following chapter categorises ordoliberalism as an ideology and explores the function that religion and Protestantism play in ordoliberal thought. The contribution argues that ordoliberalism needed Protestantism, especially in the post WWII period, to form an attractive value base and to attract large parts of population, élites and the Protestant electorate. Once the legacy of the social market economy had been constructed, ordoliberalism gradually relaxed its direct references to Protestantism in favour of a crypto-Protestantism. Ordoliberalism's new *civil religion* became the myth of the social market economy,[2] one which fulfilled the emotional and cultural appeals that ideologies need to bind their followers and legitimise their provisions once the churches and organised religions began to enter into crisis in Germany from the late 1960s onwards. This 'metamorphosis of the sacred'[3] also broadened the appeal of the ordoliberal conception of the social market economy beyond the Protestant camp in post-war Germany.

The study shows not only how important (crypto-) Protestant values still are in today's ordoliberalism, but also advances our understanding of the religious origins of seemingly secular ideologies, about which we know little.

The chapter first discusses why we should classify ordoliberalism as an ideology, and what this implies for the methodological approach of this chapter. Second, the religious connection of ordoliberalism, both at a biographical level and at a conceptual level, is introduced. Third, it shows how ordoliberalism became a civil religion by adopting the social market economy as a foundational myth. Fourth, it elaborates on how ordoliberalism and the social market economy have become a transposition machine that transports Protestant values and assumptions on individualist behaviour into the present.

---

[2] I call it a myth since the social within the *praxis* of the social market economy (the German welfare state) has nothing to do with the original ordoliberal conceptions of the social in ordoliberal thought. The German welfare state was instead re-introduced by the social Catholic wing of the Christian Democratic Party against the fierce resistance of ordoliberals such as Ludwig Erhard, who threatened to resign several times; see Philip Manow, 'Modell Deutschland as an Interdenominational Compromise, Minda De Gunzburg Center for European Studies. Harvard University'. CES Working Paper, Programme for the Study of Germany and Europe, 2001; Werner Abelshauser, 'Erhard Oder Bismarck? Die Richtungsentscheidung Der Deutschen Sozialpolitik Am Beispiel Der Reform Der Sozialversicherung in Den Fünfziger Jahren'. (1996) 22 *Geschichte und Gesellschaft*, pp 376–92; Josef Hien, 'The Ordoliberalism that never was', (2013) 12 *Contemporary Political Theory*, pp 349–58; and Frank Bösch, *Die Adenauer-CDU : Gründung, Aufstieg Und Krise Einer Erfolgspartei ; 1945–1969*, (Stuttgart-Munich: DtVerl-Anst, 2001).
[3] Emilio Gentile, 'Political Religion: A Concept and its Critics—A Critical Survey', (2005) 6 *Totalitarian Movements and Political Religions*, pp 19–32.

II. TAXONOMY AND METHOD

Ideologies 'are clusters of ideas, beliefs, opinions, values, and attitudes usually held by identifiable groups, that provide directives, even plans, of action for public policy-making, making it an endeavour to uphold, justify, change or criticise the social and political arrangements of a state or other political community'.[4] Ordoliberalism is neither complex nor coherent enough to be a philosophy, but it is more encompassing and has more real-world aspirations than economic theory. Like philosophers, ordoliberals developed positions about the good life, but their provisions do not exclusively target epistemic communities but were, instead, made to be used in politics. The involvement of ordoliberals in the economic policies of the 1950s in West Germany, the fight against economic governance in Europe in the 1960s, and the attempts to influence Euro politics during the recent European crisis are all examples of this.[5] One could say that ordoliberal's 'theoretical weakness ensures its political survival'.[6]

During the European debt crisis, ordoliberals engaged in 'de-contestation', presenting value judgements as if they were not potentially controversial but truth statements, another trademark of ideologists.[7] Ideologies are not only held together by reason, values and common assumptions about society, but they also tend to think that their assumptions and values are superior to others. This is why disputes between ideologists are so heated and seldom lead to an alteration of ideological content. Freeden reminds us that the 'language of ideologies' is 'couched in terms of truth-assertions'.[8] However, since ideologies are not philosophies, they 'do not attain truth-value status'.[9] This inherently 'justificatory' nature of ideologies poses a great challenge for analysts. Can the student of ideologies avoid falling into the trap of normative assertions? How can we study ideologies without constantly measuring and interpreting their provisions against our own ideological background(s)? Weber considered this seemingly solvable but in the end irresolvable. Gerald Gaus argues that '[t]he student of ideology and political theory is like an anthropologist confronting a native culture that she does not share, but is trying to make sense of'.[10]

---

[4] See Michael Freeden, 'Ideology, Political Theory and Political Philosophy', in: Gerald F. Gaus and Chandran Kukathas (eds), *Handbook of Political Theory*, (London: SAGE Publications, 2004), p 6.

[5] See Abelshauser, n 1 above; Brigitte Young, 'German Ordoliberalism as Agenda Setter for the Euro Crisis: Myth Trumps Reality', (2014) 22 *Journal of Contemporary European Studies*, pp 276–287; and Alexander Nützenadel, *Stunde Der Ökonomen. Wissenschaft, Expertenkultur und Politik in Der Bundesrepublik 1949–74*, (Göttingen: Vandenhoeck & Ruprecht, 2005).

[6] Christian Joerges and Florian Rödl, '"Social Market Economy" as Europe's Social Model?', EUI Working Paper Law No. 2004/8, p 14, available at: http://cadmus.eui.eu/bitstream/handle/1814/2823/?sequence=1.

[7] See Michael Freeden, 'The Morphological Analysis of Ideology', in: Michael Freeden, Lyman Tower Sargent and Marc Stears (eds), *The Oxford Handbook of Political Ideologies*, (Oxford: Oxford University Press, 2013), pp 115–37.

[8] idem, *Ideologies and Political Theory: A Conceptual Approach*, (Oxford-New York: Oxford University Press, 1998), p 98.

[9] ibid.

[10] See Gerald F. Gaus, 'Ideology, Political Philosophy, and the Interpretive Enterprise: A View from the Other Side', in: Ben Jackson and Marc Stears (eds), *Liberalism as Ideology Essays in Honour of Michael Freeden*, (Oxford: Oxford University Press, 2012), p 20.

Anthropological fieldwork fails once the anthropologist assumes the 'superiority of one's subjects' because her 'field journal will be a study in obvious errors'.[11] He proposes a benevolent interpretative stance as the way out, in allegiance to the principle of charity 'and so to help make sense of what others think, rather than to reveal their errors and follies'.[12] It is in this spirit that the following study approaches the connection between ordoliberalism and Protestantism.[13]

III. ORDOLIBERALISM AND RELIGION

Ordoliberalism had, since its very beginnings, the claim not only to be an economic theory, but also a theory of society. As a theory of society, it needed ethics. In one of the rare comments on the ethical content of ordoliberalism, Rainer Hillebrand states that:

> [e]ven the ideal principle-based economic order, however, is not the ultimate goal of economic policy. In fact, ordo liberals perceive of the market economy as a means to an end rather than an end in itself, which allows people to conduct their lives self-dependently and with dignity.[14]

Ordoliberals did not buy the idea of 'the self-regulation of society through the self-interest of the individual'.[15] The 'spiritualisation' of the invisible hand would lead to an 'atomised' society.[16] '[S]ociological liberalism' should replace 'sociologically blind' classic liberalism and help to 'embed' the market economy into a 'higher total order'.[17] Ultimately, this should lead to a 'moralisation of economic life'.[18] This is why ordoliberals paid so much attention to social cohesion, economic traditions, values, culture, nature, religion, kinship, and other social formations that they saw threatened by modernity.[19] In this sense, the first generation of ordoliberal thinkers shared with its social Catholic and Polanyian counterparts the view that

---

[11] ibid, p 27.

[12] ibid.

[13] Everyone has normative assertions and biases, only few defend them in their scientific work. A critical theory approach would make the normative leaning of the author explicit.

[14] See Rainer Hillebrand, 'Germany and its Eurozone Crisis Policy: The Impact of the Country's Ordoliberal Heritage', (2015) 33 *German Politics & Society*, pp 6–24, at 11.

[15] See Alfred Müller-Armack, 'Die Wirtschaftsordnung Sozial Gesehen', (1947) 1 *ORDO Jahrbuch*, pp 125–54.

[16] See Alexander Rüstow, *Ortsbestimmung Der Gegenwart : Eine Universalgeschichtliche Kulturkritik. 1. Ursprung Der Herrschaft*, (Erlenbach-Zürich: Rentsch, 1950), p 111.

[17] See Wilhelm Röpke, cited in: Dieter Haselbach, *Autoritärer Liberalismus und Soziale Marktwirtschaft : Gesellschaft und Politik im Ordoliberalismus*, 1. Aufl, (Baden-Baden: Nomos Verlag, 1991), p 172.

[18] Müller-Armack, n 14 above, p 147.

[19] The Protestant theologian Traugott (trust-god) Jähnichen states that we can find numerous 'normative-anthropological considerations in the early texts' of the ordoliberals with a 'high affinity to a freedom oriented and overwhelmingly Protestant Ethos', Günter Brakelmann and Traugott Jähnichen (eds), *Die protestantischen Wurzeln der Sozialen Marktwirtschaft. Ein Quellenband*, (Gütersloh: Gütersloh Verlaghaus, 1998), p 11 and 13. See Wilhelm Röpke, *Gesellschaftskrisis der Gegenwart*, (Erlenbach Zürich: Eugen-Rentsch Verlag, 1948); idem, *Civitas Humana : Grundfragen der Gesellschafts- und Wirtschaftsreform*, 3. Aufl, (Erlenbach-Zürich: Rentsch, 1949); Müller-Armack, n 14 above; idem, *Das Jahrhundert Ohne Gott : Zur Kultursoziologie Unserer Zeit*, (Münster: Regensberg, 1948); and Rüstow, n 15 above.

the capitalist economy has to be socially embedded. However, all of them had very different ideas about how this embeddedness should take place.

The early ordoliberal thinkers had strong ties to Protestantism.[20] Dieter Haselbach comments on Alfred Müller-Armack that his 'Protestant confession was not without impact on his scientific work'.[21] Wilhelm Röpke was a descendent of 'Protestant-rural notability',[22] and Alexander Rüstow had a Pietist mother and published, during his early Communist period, preferably in the *Bätter für Religiösen Sozialismus*. Writing a letter to Rüstow in 1942, Walter Eucken claimed that, 'I could neither live nor work if I did not believe that God existed'.[23] After the *Reichskristallnacht*,[24] the ordoliberals worked together with the Protestant resistance movement. Dietrich Bonhöffer, a prominent Protestant theologist later murdered in a concentration camp, asked the Freiburg circles to hammer out a plan for a post-war economic order, and the leading ordoliberals who did not go to exile worked with Protestant theologians in Freiburg on the documents. The result was the 'Freiburger Denkschrift' whose Annex IV is widely acknowledged as one of the founding documents of ordoliberalism.[25]

The biographical connection between ordoliberalism and Protestantism is well established in the literature. There is slightly more controversy about the conceptual connection between ordoliberal ideology and Protestantism.

Fifteen years ago, Philip Manow convincingly argued that ordoliberal ethics are rooted in mainline Lutheranism. Manow makes his point by linking the ordoliberal idea of the indispensability of the state for structuring the conduct of human and economic interaction, to the inherently pessimistic view of mainline Lutheranism of the individual. He neatly works out the differences with the freedom doctrine of the Anglo-American ascetic dissenting sects.

Nonetheless, if, for a second, we disregard the strong role of the state in ordoliberalism when looking from the perspective of the individual action model (ordoliberal's assumptions about individual behaviour), ordoliberalism still bears a dose of ascetic Protestant doctrine.[26] Manow argues against ascetic Protestant influences

---

[20] See Heinz Rieter and Matthias Schmolz, 'The Ideas of German Ordoliberalism 1938–45: Pointing the Way to a New Economic Order', (2010) 1 *Journal of the History of Economic Thought*, pp 87–114; Hans-Rainer Reuter, 'Vier Anmerkungen zu Philip Manow die Soziale Marktwirtschaft als Interkonfessioneller Kompromiss? Ein Re-Statement', (2010) 1 *Ethik und Gesellschaft*, pp 1–7; Philip Manow, 'Ordoliberalismus als Ökonomische Ordnungstheologie', (2001) 29 *Leviathan*, pp 179–98; and Nils Goldschmidt, 'Christlicher Glaube, Wirtschaftstheorie und Praxisbezug. Walter Eucken und die Anlage 4 der Denkschrift des Freiburger Bonhoeffer-Kreises', (1998) 5 *Historisch-Politische Mitteilungen*, pp 33–48.

[21] Haselbach, n 16 above, p 119.

[22] ibid, p 162.

[23] Walter Eucken cited in Rieter and Schmolz, n 19 above, p 105.

[24] The pogrom against Jews in Nazi Germany, 9–10 November 1938, Free City of Danzig, 12–13 November 1938.

[25] One of the authors, Constantin von Dietze later became the head of the German Protestant church (Präsens); Philip Manow, 'Die Soziale Marktwirtschaft Als Interkonfessioneller Kompromiss? Ein Re-Statement', (2010) 1 *Ethik und Gesellschaft*, pp 1–22, available at: https://open-journals.uni-tuebingen.de/ojs/index.php/eug/article/view/1-2010-art-1; and Jähnichen, n 18 above.

[26] Ordoliberals did not share the same affinity to all churches. In his book *Civitas Humana*, William Röpke discusses the pros and cons of different branches of Christianity with a preference for ascetic Protestantism; (see Röpke, *Civitas Humana*, n 18 above, p 210).

since reformed Protestants are disciplined by religion alone. Hence, they do not need state institutions to do the disciplining. He has a point, as Calvinists often radically rallied against the state or against state-driven social security solutions.[27]

However, this misses out on some disciplinary aspects of reformed Protestantism. The strong individualism of ascetic Protestantism was countered by rigid morals and social disciplining mechanisms by early ascetic Protestant leaders. These disciplining techniques were not only individual and inward looking, but were also applied to the congregation as a whole. Calvin ordered that each congregation should have a consistory, or council, to supervise 'the morals of the congregation',[28] and to do so the consistory 'interviewed individual church members several times a year in order to ascertain whether they were fit to receive communion. Errant members—for example, drunkards, adulterers, wife beaters, and tax cheats—were excluded from communion'.[29] Disciplining was not solely left to the consistory but 'each individual was not only made responsible for his or her own conduct but was charged to keep a watchful eye over other members of the congregation and to remonstrate with those who strayed from the path of righteousness'. However, this was not enough for Calvin. He also wanted to transmit discipline beyond the congregation. If the ungodly could not be saved, he reasoned, then they could at least be compelled to obey God's laws. Together, church and magistrate were to work towards the establishment of a 'Christian polity' (*res publica christiana*) to affect a thoroughgoing Christianisation of social life.[30] In the seventeenth century, some Protestant state leaders imported reformed Protestant bureaucrats which made their state bureaucracies highly efficient. The 'disciplinary revolutions'[31] that the reformed Protestants unleashed in Lutheran Prussia and in the Netherlands were so successful that other Lutheran states (and even some Catholic ones) tried to emulate these reforms.

Ordoliberalism might bear the imprint of both mainline Lutheranism and ascetic Protestantism. The source could be the blend of Lutheran and reformed Protestantism typical to German Pietism. This would explain the schizophrenia of ordoliberalism when considering the strong institutions that they advocate to correct for moral hazard and the enduring calls for a moral-ethic (*sittliche*) grounding of society and economy. If you had a morally grounded economy in the *Sittlichkeit* of the people, then strong institutions to 'discipline the peccator'[32] would be obsolete. Moreover, the theology of Bonhöffer, the Protestant host of the ordoliberal circles during the last years of WWII in Freiburg, was not mainline Lutheran, and his arguments for a lay church were not very well perceived by large parts of the German Protestant church.

---

[27] Often because their state tended to persecute them.
[28] Philip Gorski, *The Disciplinary Revolution: Calvinism and the Rise of the State in Early Modern Europe*, (Chicago IL: University of Chicago Press, 2003), p 21.
[29] ibid.
[30] ibid.
[31] idem, 'The Protestant Ethic Revisited: Disciplinary Revolution and State Formation in Holland and Prussia', (1993) 99 *American Journal of Sociology*, pp 265–316.
[32] See Bernhard Emunds, 'Ungewollte Vaterschaft. Katholische Soziallehre und Soziale Marktwirtschaft', (2010) 1 *Ethik Und Gesellschaft*, pp 1–26.

The ascetic Protestant elements (next to the mainline Lutheran elements) in ordo-liberal thought become more tangible if we look at what the early ordoliberals had to say about the welfare state. Ordoliberals argue that traditional social policy creates moral hazard, by setting wrong incentives which undermine personal responsibility, the 'mainspring' of society.[33] Social insurance and the welfare state would ultimately lead to the 'total catastrophe of state and society'[34] and degrade citizens to 'slaves of the state'.[35] Instead, the state should limit itself to establishing a framework that creates 'equality of opportunity' and fosters help to self-help.[36] These positions not only echo Luther's '[n]o one should live idle on the work of others',[37] but also the more individualistic lay responsibility principles of reformed Protestantism in which 'God helps he who helps himself'.[38] As Sigrun Kahl analysed:

> [t]he Calvinist creation of the Protestant work ethos and the strict systematic requirements about what constitutes a life that increases the glory of God (e.g., personal responsibility, individualism, discipline, and asceticism) made poverty appear to be the punishment for laziness and sinful behavior.

Therefore,

> [b]oth predestination and its marks—the ethics of worldly life—have in common the fact that the poor are sinners and the rich are not. Predestination implied that the community has no positive responsibility for the poor. Calvinist moralism even implicated that the poor needed to be punished and corrected.[39] Beggars were to be whipped and forced to work.[40]

For the original ordoliberals with their Protestant connection, personal responsibility is the 'mainspring' of society. Help can only be granted if it induces self-help. The same goes for contemporary ordoliberalism. Alms giving and transfers from one social group to another is detrimental because it induces moral hazard. When Jens Weidmann, head of the *Bundesbank*, was awarded the Wolfram-Engels prize, by the ordoliberal *Kronenberger Kreis* in 2014, he insisted that 'personal responsibility' should be the 'second fundamental principle of the currency union'.[41] In a recent speech, Weidmann said that he admired Prussia for its early reforms of the state

---

[33] Röpke, *Gesellschaftskrisis der Gegenwart*, n 18 above, p 364.

[34] Röpke, *Civitas Humana*, n 18 above, p 258.

[35] ibid, p 257.

[36] idem, *Gesellschaftskrisis der Gegenwart*, n 18 above, p 264.

[37] See Sigrun Kahl, 'The Religious Roots of Modern Poverty Policy: Catholic, Lutheran, and Reformed Protestant Traditions Compared', (2005) 46 *Archives Européennes de Sociologie*, pp 91–126, at 111.

[38] See Max Weber, *Gesammelte Aufsätze Zur Religionssoziologie I, Photomechanischer Nachdruck Der Erstauflage von 1920*, (Tübingen: Mohr Siebeck UTB, 1988).

[39] What matches with this is Erhard's public radio speech from 1962: 'Während diese (andere Länder) sich kraftvoll anschicken, durch zuchtvolle Ordnung über die Sünden ihrer Vergangenheit hinwegzu-finden, wissen wir nichts Besseres, als in der so oft angesprochenen Maßlosigkeit unseres nationalen Charakters das selbstverdiente Glück wieder zu zerstören.'

[40] Kahl, n 36 above, p 107.

[41] Jens Weidmann, 'Deutsche Bundesbank—Reden—Marktwirtschaftliche Prinzipien in Der Währungsunion, Presentation during the Award Ceremony for the Wolfram-Engels-Preis at the Stiftung Marktwirtschaft', Kronberg, 28 March 2014, available at: www.bundesbank.de/Redaktion/DE/Reden/2014/2014_03_28_weidmann.html.

because those started with an amnesty for prisoners, but this amnesty excluded 'blasphemers, murderers, persons guilt of high treason and—debtors'.[42]

Philip Manow roots the normative opposition of ordoliberalism to the welfare state to the hijacking of the Bismarckian welfare state institutions through Social Catholicism and Social Democracy during the Weimar Republic. This alienated the Protestant camp from the Welfare state which it had supported in Bismarckian times, and this is the basis of the anti-welfarism of ordoliberalism. It is a convincing argument, however, Manow might be overstating the purity of the Protestant camp's support for the Bismarckian welfare state. So argued the Protestant and influential bureaucrat Theodor Lohmann against the Bismarckian welfare ideas in a way that anticipated ordoliberal arguments against the welfare state already in the 1880s. Moreover, the Protestant camp might already have been alienated even before the Weimar Republic from the welfare legislation of the 1880s since Catholics were able to water down and transform so many parts of the initial proposals.[43] Bismarck himself called parts of the welfare legislation a 'child foisted on him' and did not mention his great project with a single word in his memoires.

IV. SOCIAL MARKET ECONOMY AS CIVIL RELIGION

The strong anchoring in the *Sittlichkeit* and the Protestant religion that the ordoliberals point at begs the question of why they searched for such a profound value anchorage? Were they not liberals? Why this quest for sacrality? I argue that the answer lies, in part, in the ordoliberals' project to build an ideology that could be successfully received in the post-WWII religious climate in Germany.

Given the highly religious climate of the post-WWII period, the ordoliberals searched for an ethical embedding of their new economic concepts in Christianity. Many Germans were convinced that Weimar had failed because of the secularising tendencies that had prevailed during the Weimar Republic.[44] The Holocaust, the Second World War and the Nazi dictatorship all triggered a strong thirst for traditional concepts of morality. Regular church attendance climbed to 60% for Catholics.[45] The Berlin Programme, one of the first party manifestos of the CDU, was of the view that:

> From the chaos of guilt and disgrace, in which the deification of a criminal adventure has thrown us, an order with freedom can only evolve if we remember the cultural, ethical and moral force of Christianity.[46]

[42] idem, 'Deutsche Bundesbank—Reden—Stabiles Geld Für Europa', Bremen, 14 February 2014, available at: www.bundesbank.de/Redaktion/DE/Reden/2014/2014_02_14_weidmann.html.
[43] See Josef Hien, 'Competing Ideas: The Religious Foundations of the German and Italian Welfare States', thesis, available at: http://cadmus.eui.eu/handle/1814/24614.
[44] See F. Bösch, *Macht und Machtverlust : Die Geschichte der CDU*, (Stuttgart-Munich: DtVerl-Anst, 2002).
[45] See Florian Tennstedt and Günther Schulz, *Geschichte Der Sozialpolitik in Deutschland Seit 1945, Band 3: Bundesrepublik Deutschland 1949–1957. Bewältigung Der Kriegsfolgen, Rückkehr Zur Sozialpolitischen Normalität*, (Baden-Baden: Nomos Verlag, 2007).
[46] CDU (1945) Gründungsaufruf der CDU Berlin 26. Juni 1945. available at: www.kas.de/upload/ACDP/CDU/Programme_Beschluesse/1945_Gruendungsaufruf-Berlin.pdf, p 1.

Hence, the post war economic order had to start with a 're-rooting in faith',[47] and Walter Eucken identified the churches as one of the 'three regulating powers' of the new economic order.[48]

These calls resemble the attempts of many liberals in Southern Europe in the eighteenth century that tried to reconcile liberalism with religiosity. They were shocked by how the Catholic church's resistance had undermined the Napoleonic occupation regime in Southern Italy. Despite being liberal and anti-clerical, they were convinced that, without an alliance with the Vatican, they would not succeed in nation- and state-building.[49] Thus, they searched for ways to accommodate religion into their liberal ideas. The results were various forms of enlightened Catholicism and crypto Protestantism.[50] Only later in the nineteenth century could they break with the church, when they had developed a set of national foundational myths that became 'a civil religion'.[51]

In addition, the ordoliberal use of Protestant concepts and imaginary can be understood as an attempt to form a *civil religion*. A civil religion is the adaptation of 'religious habits to secular ends'.[52] Michael Freeden reminds us that 'ideologies have to deliver conceptual social maps and political decisions, and they have to do so in a language accessible to masses as well as intellectuals, to amateur as well as professional thinkers',[53] and Gerald Gaus adds that this is why 'they freely mix appeals to reason and emotions'.[54] Since ordoliberal bibles such as Walter Eucken's *Grundsätze der Wirtschaftspolitik* did much to lay the ground for the academic and élite appeal of ordoliberal ideology, these books certainly did not provide emotional appeal for the masses. On the contrary, it was the foundational myth of Germany's Post-WWII social market economy which provided the emotional appeal that the ordoliberals needed in order to pursue their political project.

In the rather a-religious climate of the Weimar Republic of the 1930s, ordoliberals still looked towards various deisms to find a fertile ground for their values and theory of society. Eucken was also the chairman of the *Euckenbund*, a club based upon 'fragments from Luther, Kant, Hegel, Fichte and Goethe'.[55] Wolfgang Streeck remarks that the concept of the ordoliberal state 'represents how deist theology, in its Leibnitzian version, imagined God, as an all-powerful clockmaker limiting himself

---

[47] See Alfred Müller-Armack, *Diagnose Unserer Gegenwart: Zur Bestimmung Unseres Geistesgeschichtlichen Standorts*, 2., erw Aufl, (Bern: Haupt, 1981), p 171.

[48] Eucken, cited in Rieter and Schmolz, n 19 above, p 105.

[49] See Roberto Romani, 'Liberal Theocracy in the Italian Risorgimento', (2014) 44 *European History Quarterly*, pp 620–50; and Maurizio Isabella, 'Review Article Rethinking Italy's Nation-Building 150 Years Afterwards: The New Risorgimento Historiography', (2012) 217 *Past & Present*, pp 247–68.

[50] See Maurizio Isabella, 'Citizens or Faithful? Religion and the Liberal Revolutions of the 1820s in Southern Europe', (2015) 12 *Modern Intellectual History*, pp 555–78.

[51] Gentile, n 2 above.

[52] ibid, p 19.

[53] Freeden, n 6 above, p 30.

[54] Gerald F. Gaus, *Political Concepts and Political Theories*, (Boulder CO: Westview Press, 2000), p 35.

[55] See, Uwe Dathe, 'Walter Euckens Weg Zum Liberalismus (1918–1934)', (2009) 60 *ORDO Jahrbuch*, pp 53–86, at 9.

to watching the operation of the perfect clock he has made, without intervening in it', because '[a]fter all, if he had to intervene, the clock would not be perfect'.[56] In the religiously-loaded climate of Post-WWII and against the backdrop of the Holocaust and the horrors of both WWII and totalitarianism, ordoliberals themselves made a religious turn which was later supplemented by adopting, fostering and nurturing the myth of the social market economy, and the emotional attraction of this civil religion went beyond the Protestant camp and even beyond Germany.[57]

V. CONCLUSION

The chapter has highlighted the religious connection of ordoliberalism. The rooting in Protestantism explains why the Southern Catholic and Orthodox countries react so alien to it. The religious *tiefengrammatik* might explain the 'heat' in the debate about the alleged influence of ordoliberalism in Europe and why it comes with a high dose of nationalism in a way not witnessed since WWII. The chapter conceptualised ordoliberalism as an ideology in the political theory understanding of ideology and argued that it not only transports Lutheran values, but also ascetic Protestant values. It then proposes that the popularity of ordoliberalism and the sacralisation of writers such as Eucken was less a function of their writings but more due to the connection of the key figures of ordoliberalism with the civil religion of the social market economy. The adoption of the social market economy as civil religion by ordoliberals has replaced direct religious references in ordoliberal writings in the secular period in Germany after the late 1960s.

The ordoliberal conception of the social market economy can, therefore, be understood as what I would like to call here a transposition-machine, a vehicle that transforms religious values into crypto-religious content and transports this content to the present where it can flourish also in a largely secularised or at least de-confessionalised environment. The transposition of such values makes ordoliberalism not only appeal to the élites, but also to a wider public audience. What role the recently emerging myths of the Hartz IV reforms ('*Hausaufgabenmachen*') entail for this still remains to be seen, whether this marks a further neo-protestantisation of the German economy will have to be discussed.

---

[56] See Wolfgang Streeck, 'Heller, Schmitt and the Euro', (2015) 21 *European Law Journal*, pp 361–70, at 362.

[57] See Manow's discussion of the craziness of a social market economy as the fundament of the European Union, discussed by the German Christian Democrats, n 24 above, p 15.

Section V

Government without Law

17

Ordoliberalism and Political Theology: On the Government of Stateless Money*

WERNER BONEFELD

ABSTRACT

The euro is a stateless currency. In the context of European Union, the ordoliberal argument that economic liberty amounts to a political practice and that the state is the predominant power in the relationship to free economy appears dated. This is however not the case at all. The Euro rests on the capacity of the federated Member States to operate in concert as executive states of Monetary Union. The notion of an executive state belongs to Carl Schmitt's political theology. It also characterises the ordoliberal idea of freedom as a practice of government. European Union incorporates the role of the state in sustaining supranational relations of law, market and money.

I. INTRODUCTION

THE FOUNDING ORDOLIBERAL thinkers inherited from Carl Schmitt a keen understanding of the crucial role of the state as the concentrated power of a free labour economy.[1] For them, the market economy is not independent from state authority. On the contrary, it amounts to a practice of government,

---

* I completed the paper with the support of a Leverhulme Research Fellowship. I am grateful to the Leverhulme Trust for its award. The final version owes a great debt to Chris Engert's most careful editing. I am most grateful to him.

[1] Walter Eucken, 'Staatliche Strukturwandlungen und die Krise des Kapitalismus', ((1932) 36 *Weltwirtschaftliches Archiv*, pp 297–321, at 307) refers to Carl Schmitt's *The Guardian of the Constitution (Der Hüter der Verfassung*, (Berlin: Duncker & Humblot, 1931)) as the authoritative source behind his thinking. Friedrich von Hayek, *The Constitution of Liberty*, (London: Routledge, 1960), p 485), considers Schmitt's *Guardian of the Constitution* as the most learned and perspective account of the ills of Weimar democracy. Alexander Rüstow's notion of the liberal state as 'market police' (Alexander Rüstow, 'General Social Laws of the Economic Disintegration and Possibilities of Reconstruction', Afterword, in: Wilhelm Röpke, *International Economic Disintegration*, (London: W. Hodge, 1942), pp 267–283) bears the stamp of Schmitt's 'strong state' as the concentrated force of 'sound economy', (Carl Schmitt, 'Sound Economy—Strong State', Appendix to Renato Cristi, *Carl Schmitt and Authoritarian Liberalism*, (Cardiff: University of Wales Press, 1998).

that is, a politics of order, an *Ordnungspolitik*, and the regulation of this order by market-facilitating liberal interventionism. Franz Böhm thus likens the free economy to a political event (*Veranstaltung*).[2] Leonard Miksch is most explicit on this point.[3] He asserts that economic freedom does not manifest some natural propensity, as in classical liberalism. Rather, it is a 'political event'.

In the founding ordoliberal argument, the emergence of mass democracy is a fundamental threat to free economy. Weimar mass democracy weakened the liberal character of the state by transforming it into a legislative state of mass demands. In Schmittean phraseology, the legislative state of mass democracy supplanted the executive state of a sound economy. The repercussions of this change are fundamental. Mass democracy inserted the claim for general social equality and welfare into the machinery of the state, transforming it into an 'economic state'.[4] The taming of mass democracy, its transformation into liberal-democracy, was therefore considered essential to the restoration and maintenance of economic liberty.

In the context of the European Monetary Union (EMU), the ordoliberal argument that economic freedom is a practice of government appears not to hold. Just as the euro is a stateless currency, European law is stateless law. There is neither a European government nor a European state. The European Central Bank (ECB) is not a political institution. It is a technocratic institution that conducts policy according to set objectives and requirements, which are rule-based and law-governed. It does not recognise what Wilhelm Röpke called the 'enemies'.[5] It makes monetary policy upon the basis of expert judgement and economic insight. The absence of central political power does not, however, entail that the euro is non-political currency. On the contrary, its establishment amounted to a political decision and its maintenance amounts to a practice of government. A functioning monetary order requires political authority to sustain it. Monetary union depends on the capacity of its Member States to implement the demands of supranational money internally, securing balanced budgets and achieving competitive levels of labour productivity. This effort at implementation is a matter of continued and sustained solidarity between the Eurozone Member States. Monetary Union thus depends on their capacity to act in concert as a form of 'market police'.[6] I argue that monetary union strengthens the liberal character of the democratically constituted Member States. It absorbs the traditional forms of mass democracy into a European '*Ordnungspolitik*', emasculating them.

This chapter examines the political character of the European '*Ordnungspolitik*' in three steps. The next section presents Carl Schmitt's political theology, focusing on his critique of mass democracy and the characterisation of the strong state.

---

[2] Franz Böhm, *Ordnung und Wirtschaft*, (Berlin: Kohlhammer, 1937), p 34.
[3] Leonhard Miksch, *Wettbewerb als Aufgabe. Grundsätze einer Wettbewerbsordnung*, (Bad Godesberg: H. Küpper, 1947), p 9.
[4] Eucken, n 1 above, p 301.
[5] Wilhelm Röpke, *A Humane Economy: The Social Framework of the Free Market*, (Wilmington DE: ISI Books, 1998), p 66.
[6] Rüstow, n 1 above.

The following section introduces the ordoliberal notion of free economy as a moral order that is created and sustained by *'political decision'*.[7] The final section is the conclusion. It discusses the political character of monetary union, arguing that it amounts to a federated political system in which each Member State operates as an 'executive state' of supranational rules and requirements.[8]

II. AUTHORITARIAN LIBERALISM AND POLITICAL THEOLOGY

Carl Schmitt's political theology does not address pastoral questions. It identifies modernity as a desacralised and graceless manifestation of rationalism, egalitarianism, legal positivism, and mass democratic usurpation of legitimate Rights (*Rechte*). Political theology entails a political metaphysics; it has to do with authority, transcendence, and freedom, too, that is in the sense of freedom under God. His political theology holds that 'the central concepts of modern state theory are all secularised theological concepts'.[9] In line with the conservative critics of the Enlightenment, from Juan Donoso Cortes and Joseph de Maistre to Benjamin Constant, he asserts that, with the French Revolution, political concepts started to lose their metaphysical quality. The old concept of legitimacy, which had to do with divine Rights of social distinction based upon property ownership and social propriety, had given way to rational-legal forms of legitimation that supplanted loyalty to King and country with principles of equal rights. Nothing sacred remained. Legitimate Rights succumbed to mass demands for employment contracts and material satisfaction. In modernity, politics has become mass politics. The sacred was replaced by the profane. In mass democracy, the rule of law has no definite values to instil and regulate. It can be the rule of socialist law or liberal law. Legal formalism replaced a constitutional order founded on Right. In mass democracy, the legitimacy of law is a matter of rightful procedure, not of Right.[10] By reducing the legitimacy of law to process-law, law becomes arbitrary and profane. Instead of stating what is right and proper, law collapses into mere formalism. Political power thus ceases to be understood on, and accepted as, the model of God's creation. Thus, in mass democracy, the 'theistic and

[7] Franz Böhm, 'Die Kampfansage an Ordnungstheorie und Ordnungspolitik. Zu einem Aufstaz im Kyklos', (1973) 24 *ORDO Jahrbuch*, pp 11–48, at 39.

[8] Schmitt, *The Guardian of the Constitution*, n 1 above.

[9] idem, *Political Theology. Four Chapters on the Concept of Sovereignty*, (Chicago IL: University of Chicago Press, 1985), p 36.

[10] Schmitt argued his case against especially Kelsen, who was the outstanding advocate of democratic law making and of procedural-democracy (on this, see Ingeborg Maus, *Bürgerliche Rechtstheorie und Faschismus. Zur sozialen Funktion und aktuellen Wirkung der Theorie Carl Schmitts*, (Munich: Wihlhelm Fink Verlag, 1976). Franz Neumann and Otto Kirchheimer agreed with aspects of Schmitt's analysis of the crisis of Weimar and differed entirely in the prescription of how to resolve the crisis, calling for further democratisation, legal protection of workers' rights, etc (See Keith Tribe, *Strategies of Economic Order: German Economic Discourse, 1750–1950*, (Cambridge: Cambridge University Press, 1995); William E. Scheuerman, *The Rule of Law Under Siege*, (Berkeley CA: University of California Press, 1996). See Ernst-Joachim Mestmäcker, *A Legal Theory without Law*, (Tübingen: Mohr Siebeck, 2007) for an ordoliberal defence of these Schmittean conceptions in ordoliberal legal thought.

the deistic idea of God is unintelligible'.[11] In Schmitt's argument, the liberal state of Right had become the prey of an irrational mass society that identifies the state as the means by which everybody tries to enrich himself.[12]

Schmitt's political theology does not intend to restore to modern mass democracy a theological dimension. Rather, the point of Schmitt's political theology is to recover the elements of metaphysics in opposition to a mass democratic age. He argues that unlimited mass democracy abolishes the distinction between state and society, leading to the 'socialisation' of the state and therewith the disappearance of the political as a sacred sphere of sovereign authority, power and Right.[13] The 'de-theologised' world is a 'de-politicised' world,[14] a world without divine authority, certainty of moral values, ready acceptance of social position, etc. Whereas Man used to accept his 'responsibility to the state', now 'the state is responsible to man', as Herbert Marcuse put it in his account of Schmitt's authoritarian liberalism.[15] In the modern world, existential problems appear as 'organisational-technical and economic-sociological ones'.[16] Right is reduced to egalitarian notions of distributive justice and material security. In the words of Schmitt,

> [t]he state as an outgrowth of society, and thus no longer objectively distinguishable from society, occupies everything societal, that is, anything that concerns the collective existence of human beings. There is no longer any sphere of society in relation to which the state must observe the principle of absolute neutrality in the sense of non-intervention.[17]

In mass democracy, the state is at the mercy of the social forces. It is a total state of pure quantity.[18]

Schmitt's call for the recovery of the elements of metaphysics in the government of mass society argues for a total state of pure quality. Its establishment pre-supposes the separation of society and state as separate institutions. As Marcuse recognised, its accomplishment pre-supposes the 'existentialisation and totalisation of the political sphere', politicising the state as the independent and indisputable power of socio-economic de-politicisation.[19] The politicised state reacts to the 'threatened freedom and security of private property' and acts with unbound authority.[20]

---

[11] Carl Schmitt, quoted in Cristi, n 1 above, p 112.

[12] This part paraphrases Röpke's dictum that the state is '"the great fiction by which everybody wants to enrich themselves at the expense of everybody else"'; see Röpke, *The Social Crisis of our Time*, (New Brunswick NJ: Transaction Publishers, 2009), p 164). Röpke is quoting Bastiat, a French political economist of liberal persuasion.

[13] See, also, Carl Schmitt, *Hugo Preuss: Sein Staatsbegegriff und seine Stellung in der deutschen Staatslehre*, (Tübingen: Mohr, 1930), pp 19–21.

[14] idem, Political Theology II: The Myth of the Closure of any Political Theology, (Cambridge: Polity Press, 2008), p 128.

[15] This designation is Heller's; see Hermann Heller, 'Authoritarian Liberalism', (2005) 21 *European Law Journal*, pp 295–301. See Strauss for a conservative critique of Schmitt as an authoritarian liberal thinker; Leo Strauss, 'Notes on Carl Schmitt', in: Carl Schmitt, *The Concept of the Political*, (Chicago IL: University of Chicago Press, 1996), pp 97–121. Herbert Marcuse, 'The Struggle against Liberalism in the Totalitarian View of the State', in: idem, *Negations: Essays in Critical Theory*, (London: Free Association Books, 1988), pp 3–42, at 36.

[16] Schmitt, n 9 above, p 65.

[17] Schmitt, *The Guardian of the Constitution*, n 1 above, p 79.

[18] Schmitt, 'Sound Economy', n 1 above.

[19] Marcuse, n 15 above.

[20] ibid.

The decision to act reveals the political sovereign. For Schmitt, the sovereign is the one who declares the state of exception, a commissarial dictator, whose decision to govern by unbound authority sets aside the formalism of law in order to establish law as an expression of Right (*Recht*). The purpose of dictatorship is thus to 'pro-duce law' as a manifestation of Right (*Recht zu schaffen*). For Right to prevail, the creation of a rightful social order *beyond* mass democracy is of the essence. Law does not make order. It expresses and regulates a social order. It does not apply to disorder. Order is a political category of disorder in the mode of being denied. Schmitt thus insists 'all law is situational',[21] and, at unpredictable times 'the power of real life breaks through the crust of a mechanism that has become torpid by repetition'.[22] The state of exception recognises the unpredictable power of real life in the reality of the political situation. It spills blood for a return of order, peace and tranquillity. Above all, it asserts unbound political authority for Right over the legal formalism of a mass democratic age. It thus opposes the 'democratically equal popu-lace' with the 'myth of a hierarchically ordered and unified people, which the excep-tional act of the sovereign would instantiate', as Tracy Strong put in his account of Schmitt's political theology.[23] In a state of exception, the sovereign bestows the so-called eternal values of the nation with a will and a consciousness. It thus asserts the autonomy of the nation as a community of transcendent interests over the mass democratic quarrels, class struggles, and in-fighting between socio-economic pres-sure groups. As such, the politicised state of authoritarian direction represents the veritable democracy of a national people in being and becoming, restoring not only tranquillity, order, and stability, but also certainty of values, respect for private prop-erty, and acceptance of social hierarchy and distinction.[24]

In distinction to the social democratic demand for economic justice and social equality in the here and now, the politicised state of divine Right demands ser-vice, loyalty and unquestioned commitment to the destiny of the nation. Any doubt in the veracity of the action is eliminated by pursuit of the doubter. As Ernst Forsthoff put it, 'attempts to dispute the state's newly gained effective right signify sabotage ... Relentlessly to exterminate this sort of thought is the noblest duty of the state today'.[25] Political theology, which had become unthinkable in a democratic con-text, re-asserts itself in the forceful restoration of the politicised state and de-politicised social relations, in which people know their place and comply willingly with the demands and values of the system of private property. The point of political theology in mass democracy is to draw a distinction between the 'friends' of private prop-erty and its 'enemies', and govern accordingly. Under conditions that are deemed to

---

[21] Schmitt, n 9 above, p 13.

[22] ibid, p 15.

[23] Tracy B. Strong, 'Foreword', in: Carl Schmitt, *Political Theology*, n 9 above, p xxvii.

[24] On the idea that democracy is synonymous with the autonomy of the state as the embodiment of the national interest beyond pluralist mass democracy, see, also, Röpke, n 12 above, p 101.

[25] Ernst Forsthoff, *Der totale Staat*, (Hamburg: Hanseatische Verlags-Anstalt, 1933), p 29. Forsthoff was a student of Schmitt's. He held various professorship during Nazism and was dismissed from his teaching post by order of the American military government. He resumed teaching at Heidelberg University in 1952. Forsthoff was the leading author of the Constitution of Cyprus and was President of the Supreme Constitutional Court of Cyprus from 1960 to 1963.

threaten social anarchy and turmoil, the sovereign governs for the restoration of Right under the rule of law, but is *itself* not constrained by law.[26]

In the *Guardian of the Constitution*, Schmitt argues that the old liberal state possessed elements of an 'executive state' (*Regierungsstaat*) that was 'strong enough to stand above and beyond all social forces'.[27] In Schmitt's argument, the liberal state of old comprised a dual structure that embodied two different forms of state: a parliamentary 'legislative state' (*Gesetzgebungstaat*), which was the representative body of the propertied classes and the educated classes (*Besitz und Bildung*), and an 'executive state' (*Regierungsstaat*), which expressed monarchical interests and was administered by aristocratic office-holders. The dualist structure comprised thus a democracy of liberal friends and government by the *ancien régime*. Schmitt acknowledges that this structure was contradictory and tension-ridden with traditional economic and political élites battling a liberal *bourgeoisie* demanding reforms in support of their own economic interests. Nevertheless, this conflict was between different property owners. It excluded the property-less. Schmitt argues that the dual structure of the liberal state fell apart with the German democratic revolution of 1918. He thus argues that, with the assertion of mass democracy, the legislative state supplanted the executive state, making government dependent on the governed. With mass democratisation, the capacity to sustain substantive liberal values was lost. Politics became mass politics. Following William Scheuerman, 'the democratisation of parliament in conjunction with the simultaneous parliamentarization of the state means that no element of the state now "stands above and beyond the social forces"'.[28] For Schmitt, society had taken possession of the state with profound socio-economic consequence: 'if society organises itself into the state, if state and society are to be basically identical, then all social and economic problems become immediate objects of the state.'[29] Paraphrasing Schmitt, the stranger, this figure of 'the enemy within', enters the liberal state and asserts his interests as an equal, that is, in mass democracy, control is exercised by those who need to be controlled. With mass society asserting itself within the state, the state loses its quality as a liberal state. It is no longer able to distinguish between the friends of private property and their enemies, legitimate Rights and process-law, sacred values and coarse demands for material security.

[26] Schmitt, n 9 above.

[27] Schmitt, *The Guardian of the Constitution*, n 1 above, p 73. On the Schmitt's notion of the *Regierungsstaat*, see, also, his *Legality and Legitimacy*, (*Legalität und Legitimität*), (Berlin: Duncker & Humblot, 1932).

[28] See William E. Scheuerman, *Carl Schmitt: The End of Law*, (Boulder CO: Rowman & Littlefield, 1999), p 89, citing Schmitt.

[29] Schmitt, *The Guardian of the Constitution*, n 1 above, pp 78–9. The executive state of liberty transforms into a democratic welfare state, that is, an 'economic state' with total responsibility for social well-being, from the cradle to the grave. The term 'economic state' is Eucken's. He describes it with reference to Schmitt as quantitatively total state (compare Eucken, n 1 above, p 301, n 78 with Schmitt, 'Sound Economy', n 1 above). The economic state is a state of 'lamentable weakness'; it is 'pulled apart by greedy self-seekers. Each of them takes out a piece of the state's power for himself and exploits it for its own purposes'. (Alexander Rüstow, 'Die staatspolitischen Voraussetzungen des wirtschaftspolitischen Liberalismus', in: idem, *Rede und Antwort*, (Ludwigsburg: Hoch, 1963), pp 249–258, at 255.

In the Schmittean argument, majoritarian democratic law making de-theologises the rule of law as the law of divine Right. In its stead, it manifests law as process-law, reducing the rule of law to a procedural formalism. Legality is the principle of mass democracy law-making, which attributes legitimacy to legal-rational processes and procedures. It is, says Schmitt,[30] 'nothing more than mob rule'. Schmitt recognises the time of egalitarian mass democracy as mob rule and identifies it as a time of exception. The identification of a state of exception is a matter of sovereign judgment. The judgement is true because the decision to suspend the rule of law and govern unbound by law has to eliminate any doubt in its veracity, at least this is its sovereign requirement. Decisionism, in which an unregulated act of power is taken, suspends the 'legislative state' of mass democracy and casts aside the formalism of law as the basis of government. Restoring order, peace and tranquillity, 'whatever it takes', is a matter of political judgement and decision. It is not a matter of law. The (unbound) executive state governs with 'authority and leadership'[31] on behalf of his 'following'.[32]

Decisionism has reached its limits once the decision has been taken. Decisionism is not an alternative to the suspended system of majoritarian parliamentary democracy. Decisionism is bound to the identified exception to order and tranquillity. Once the Nazi dictatorship was established, its time had passed. Now, the focus shifts to the establishment of a concrete order as a robust 'alternative' to the mass democratic de-thronement of Right by legal formalism.[33] As Georg Schwab explains, concrete order thinking focuses on 'devising a constitutional order that would once and for all drain society of political forces that could challenge the state's monopoly on politics'.[34] Schmitt's concrete order is hierarchically structured, based upon the leadership principle. It stands for entirely de-politicised socio-economic relations, from which 'all orderlessness' has been eradicated.[35] That is, the 'segregation of the state from non-state spheres ... is ... a political procedure', and the 'disengagement from politics is a specifically political act'.[36] The organisation of a de-politicised societal order was, for Schmitt, an outcome of politics in the specific use of state authority. It includes the establishment of de-politicised social organisations and political institutions, such as professional bodies, including labour unions, occupational interest groups and holiday camps. These establishments are part

---

[30] Schmitt, n 14 above, p 119.

[31] Alexander Rüstow, 'Diktatur innerhalb der Grenzen der Demokratie', (1959) 7 *Vierteljahreshefte für Zeitgeschichte*, pp 87–111, at 100.

[32] This part draws on Marcuse, n 15 above, p 37. The designated enemy defines the political friend. That is, the friends have to be followers so that they may not be designated as enemies, too. In dictatorship, 'reality is not admit of knowledge, only of acknowledgment' (Ernst Forsthoff, *Das Ende der humanistischen Illusion*, (Berlin: Furche-Verlag, 1933), p 25). Friedrich von Hayek argues that Schmitt's conception of sovereignty is a plausible one; see Friedrich von Hayek, *The Political Order of a Free People*, (Chicago IL: University of Chicago Press, 1979), p 125.

[33] Cristi, n 1 above.

[34] See George Schwab, 'Introduction', in: Schmitt, *Political Theology*, n 14 above, pp xxxvii–li, at l–li.

[35] This formulation derives form Böhm, n 2 above, p 150. Depoliticisation of socio-economic relations is an eminently political practice of social fabrication.

[36] Schmitt, 'Sound Economy', n 1 above, p 221.

of the state-organised societal order, and operate according to a centrally devised set of purposes. The notion of a concrete order does not recognise extra-political forms of interaction.[37] Rather, extra-political forms of social interaction are political constructions. Concrete order thinking is about the establishment of institutional complexes that discharge specific functions of social organisation and oversee the conduct of its members according to regulative principles that derive their authority and legitimacy from a legally unregulated sovereign, the leader. This figure of will and charisma commands not through the rationality of law, but, rather, through the illusion of omnipotence.[38]

The state of concrete order governs through the institutionalisation of diverse social practices, which manifest federated socio-economic forms of a political order. Since anybody could be designated the role of enemy, doubt in the veracity of the national friend evaporated for reasons of personal security. In this manner, the concrete order holds together because it succeeds in creating the people's adherence to the way things are. The concrete order is more than just a structure of government. It reaches into the inner recesses of the governed. It instils a certain type of relationship to a certain type of authority. The social fabrication of the individual as a disciple projects the eternal riches of life in the 'heroism' of poverty and 'service', of sacrifice and discipline. In this manner, the vigilant state of constant surveillance is internalised and governs the mentality of the governed. Schmitt's concrete order appeared thus as a 'concrete mode of existence', that is, as the 'unified and closed system of supreme and ultimate norms'.[39] In Schmitt's concrete order, the political state is the 'concrete order of orders, the institution of institutions'.[40] His leadership principle, therefore, is the secularised substitute for the monarchical principle. It unseats the democratic legal state and establishes a metaphysical executive state. The federated system of concrete institutions does not, therefore, fragment the unity of the state. Rather, it establishes channels for the decisions of sovereign power.[41]

III. POLITICAL AUTHORITY, MORALITY AND FREEDOM

In the ordoliberal view, the free economy is a 'universal form of life'.[42] That is, 'man exchanges because he is the only living being that is capable of this form of transaction without being in any way aware of the ingenious character of his behaviour'.[43] Ordoliberalism does not, therefore, conceive of the free economy in

---

[37] Alfred Müller Armack, argues along these Schmittean lines; see Alfred Müller Armack, *Staatsidee und Wirtschaftsordnung im neuen Reich*, (Berlin: Junker & Dünnhaupt, 1933), pp 20–21 and 31.
[38] Following Scheuerman's account Schmitt endorsed 'the Nazi labor reforms of 1934' enthusiastically as 'the clearest expression of concrete order thinking'. The reforms stripped workers of 'basic workplace protection, reclassified them as 'disciples' (*Gefolgsschaft*) and introduced 'Leader (*Führer*) as the concept of the legally unregulated leader'; Scheuerman, n 28 above, p 123.
[39] See Carl Schmitt, *Über die drei Arten des rechtswissenschaftlichen Denkens*, (Hamburg: Hanseatische Verlagsanstalt, 1934), p 4 and 7.
[40] ibid, p 47.
[41] The final part draws on Cristi, n 1 above, pp 162–65.
[42] Walter Eucken, *Grundsätze der Wirtschaftspolitik*, (Tübingen: Mohr Siebert, 2004), p 321.
[43] Böhm, cited in Eucken, n 42 above, p 321.

narrow economic terms. Rather, it conceives of it as a definite moral order. Without the freedom to compete, 'man [is] not a "human being"'.[44] In this claim, there is a deeper meaning. If competition defines what it is to be a human being, then those who set out to diminish it diminish humanity. It is dangerous to speak in the name of universal forms of humanity since all those who oppose must perforce appear as speaking against humanity. As an outlaw of humanity, this figure of 'the other' is not an adversary, opponent or competitor. Rather, this *other* manifests as the enemy—the disturber and disrupter of order, peace, tranquillity and Right.

The 'friend and enemy' constellation is central to ordoliberal concrete-order thinking,[45] from the more 'economic leaning' idea of an *Ordnungspolitik* (ORDO), that is, about the constitutionalisation of the free economy and the achievement of complete competition as a legal obligation, via the ideological formation of self-responsible entrepreneurship as a character trait, and the fabrication of society as an enterprise society, to the creation of de-politicised institutions that, removed from democratic influence and accountability, regulate and enforce the conduct of the liberal economy upon a rule-based and law-governed basis.[46] ORDO is a meta-physical concept, an *ordo mundi*. Although it is founded on some assumed eternal human condition of a freedom to exchange and compete, its conduct has to be 'firmly contained within an all-embracing order of society', encompassing 'ethics, the natural conditions of life and happiness, the state, politics and power'.[47] The pur-pose of *Ordungspolitik* is to 'subordinate' society to the 'ethical' effects of the free economy.[48] For the ordoliberals, 'civil society is the society of liberty'. It 'is reigned by sovereign consumers', and 'the proper task of government is to provide the insti-tutions necessary for a "society of private law", namely, private law and [competi-tion] law'.[49] ORDO combines nature with power, order with happiness, freedom with politics. ORDO also combines the freedom to compete with surveillance, osten-sibly to prevent misconduct.

In the free economy, the struggle for protection from competitive pressures and for material security is constant. If allowed to fester, it tends to politicise the social relations, which leads to powerful demands for employment protection and welfare security, including 'false incomes and labour market policy' by the manipulation of currency exchange rates.[50] In this argument, the politicisation of social relations

---

[44] Walter Eucken, 'What kind of Economic and Social System?', in: Alan Peacock and Hans Willgerodt (eds), *Germany's Social Market Economy: Origins and Evolution*, (London: Palgrave, 1989), pp 27–45, at 34.

[45] Müller-Armack, n 37 above, p 31; Röpke, n 5 above, p 66; Eucken, n 42 above, p 185.

[46] For detailed account, see Werner Bonefeld, 'Authoritarian Liberalism: From Schmitt via Ordolib-eralism to the Euro', (2016) *Critical Sociology*, Online First, DOI 10.1177/0896920516662695. The German original of complete competition is *vollständige Konkurrenz*. On the meaning of '*vollständig*', see David Gerber's useful account: 'Constitutionalizing the Economy: German Neo-Liberalism, Competition Law and the 'New' Europe', (1994) 42 *American Journal of Comparative Law*, pp 25–83.

[47] Röpke, n 5 above, p 91.

[48] Alfred Müller-Armack *Diagnose unserer Gegenwart*, (Stuttgart: Paul Haupt, 1981), p 124.

[49] Christoph Engel, 'Imposed Liberty and its Limits—The EC Treaty as an Economic Constitution for the Member States', in: Talia Einhorn (ed.), *Spontaneous Order, Organization and the Law: Roads to a European Civil Society: Liber Amicorum Ernst-Joachim Mestmäcker*, (The Hague: Asser Press, 2003), pp 429–437, at 430.

[50] See Lars P. Feld, 'Europa in der Welt von heute: Wilhelm Röpke und die Zukunft der Europäischen Währungsunion', (2012) 63 *ORDO Jahrbuch*, pp 403–428, at, 412.

'reinforces the general tendency towards state slavery (*Staatsklaverei*)'.[51] The worst outcome of this struggle for material security is, however, the 'decomposition of the human substance' (ibid, citing Köstler).[52] Indeed, the free economy, as Alfred Müller-Armack states, does not create social value orientations in support of its further progress.[53] Instead, the free economy destroys those same values, habits, loyalties and belief systems upon which its market-liberal conduct depends in its entirety. The free economy is the dynamic behind the transformation of society into a graceless, disenchanted world of 'greedy self-seekers'[54] and proletarianised workers.[55] It encourages the pursuit of only 'earthly objectives' that tend to replace competition by protectionism and the heroism of poverty by demands for welfare support.[56] There is thus the danger that, instead of social enterprise, 'the increasing exploitation of the government for the satisfaction of the desires of parties or groups' increases, 'which in the end leads to the management of the whole nation by these organised and powerful groups'.[57] The resulting 'pathological and degenerate form' of a capitalism in which the freedom to compete has been supplanted by a democratic welfare state is a consequence of this struggle for social equality and material security.[58] 'Constant surveillance of the total economic process'[59] is thus needed to sustain the system of complete competition against what Viktor Vanberg calls 'special interest rent-seeking'.[60]

In the ordoliberals' conception, the capitalist economy is a moral economy because 'man is free if he needs to obey no person but solely the law' (Kant). However, they recognise that its freedom expresses a definite social order. For freedom to prevail, it has to express this order in its practice. Man is thus free if he complies with the order of freedom. The ordoliberals endorsement of Kant's dictum entails a critique of unlimited mass democracy.

> [E]ven if individuals are only obliged to follow the law, their freedom is always threatened if these laws can be changed arbitrarily by … duly elected parliamentary majorities (that is, minorities) [that] are allowed to introduce new laws or change old ones relating to any sphere of human existence.[61]

The danger, then, of mass democracy is that law (*Gesetz*) and legitimacy (*Recht*) collapse into a purely formal rule of law. Alexander Rüstow's rejection of *laissez-faire* liberalism makes clear the danger that mass democracy holds for the liberal

---

[51] Eucken, n 42 above, p 193.

[52] ibid, citing Köstler: no details available.

[53] Alfred Müller-Armack, *Wirtschaftsordnung und Wirtschaftspolitik*, (Stuttgart: Paul Haupt, 1976), p 299.

[54] Rüstow, n 29 above, p 255.

[55] Röpke, n 1 above.

[56] Alfred Müller Armack, *Religion und Marktwirtschaft*, (Stuttgart: Paul Haupt 1981), p 556.

[57] Wilhelm Röpke, *The Moral Foundation of Civil Society*, (New Brunswick NJ: Transaction Publishers, 2002), p 92.

[58] Alexander Rüstow, *Freiheit und Herrschaft*, (Münster: LIT, 2005, p 364; see, also, Eucken, n 1 above.

[59] Müller-Armack, n 48 above, p 124.

[60] Viktor Vanberg, 'Ordnungspolitik. The Freiburg School and the Reason of Rules', Diskussionspapiere zur Ordnungsökonomie, 2014, no 1, p 7.

[61] Peter Bernholz, 'The Slow and Hidden Road to Serfdom', *Frankfurter Allgemeine Zeitung*, 2013, available at: http://blogs.faz.net/fazit/2013/06/20/the-slow-and-hidden-road-to-serfdom-1933.

rule of law.[62] He charges *laissez-faire* liberalism with suffering from the delusion of freedom, according to which private vices transform, as if by magic, into public virtues. In his view, the belief that the invisible hand creates social order is illusory. The invisible hand pre-supposes a definite social order and expresses this order in the regulation of individual preference by competitive price movements. Freedom is an expression of order. Order is a political category. It amounts to a political practice of *Ordnungspolitik*. Concerning the idea of unrestrained democratic freedom, '[t]he enemies profit by it, too, and are in the name of freedom given every conceivable opportunity to put an end to liberal democracy'.[63] Röpke argues his case along Schmittean lines, that is, the mass democratic demand for 'equality' transformed the liberal executive state into a legislative state (*Gesetztgebungsstaat*) of mass opinion and mass demands. Mass democracy is based upon the 'principle of sovereignty of the people, ascertained by majority decision and intended to realise the identity of people and government'. *Laissez-faire* liberalism 'gives a free hand to all trouble makers and agitators, therefore condemning itself to death with open eyes ... this absolute tolerance even towards intolerance, this intransigent dogmatism of the liberals ... must ultimately reduce "pure democracy" to the defenceless victim of anti-liberalism'.[64] In particular, monetary policy and credit policy should not 'be operated like a switchboard by a government directly dependent upon a parliamentary majority or, worse still, upon some non-parliamentary group posing as the representative of public opinion'.[65] Tyranny belongs to democracy; authority to liberalism (von Hayek). Like Schmitt, Röpke posits that democracy works best as a democracy of friends. To govern for the freedom of competition means to govern with a clear conception of 'the enemies' of that freedom.[66]

In the ordoliberal argument, the (liberal) state is the independent power of the free economy. It 'creates the living space for individual life'.[67] Freedom amounts thus to an eminently political practice.[68] It includes the embedding of competitiveness into the mentality of the governed.[69] The liberal state 'knows exactly where to draw the line'.[70] It decides. That is, the freedom to compete and the willing adjustment of individual forms of behaviour to the signals coming from the free price mechanism involve the state as the political power of that freedom. Eucken offers a succinct account of the political character of economic freedom.[71] He identifies the freedom to compete as an intrinsic human property and argues that 'nobody is authorized to abandon his or her moral autonomy' and thereby become a mere

---

[62] Rüstow, n 58 above.
[63] Röpke, n 12 above, p 50, and idem, n 5 above, p 66.
[64] idem, n 12 above, p 50.
[65] Röpke, n 5 above, p 223.
[66] ibid, p 66.
[67] Müller-Armack, n 37 above, p 22.
[68] Böhm, n 7 above.
[69] Alfred Müller-Armack, 'The Social Market Economy as an Economic and Social Order', (1978) 36 *Review of Social Economy*, pp 325–331.
[70] Röpke, n 12 above, p 85.
[71] Eucken, n 42 above, p 178 and 179.

tool for somebody else. 'But no one must also force the others to waive his or her moral autonomy'. Freedom is an (authorised) moral obligation. It 'serves' (*dient*) man as a 'self-responsible' being.[72] Self-responsible freedom is a function of order. 'Freedom and order are not opposites. They depend upon one another. *Ordering means the ordering of freedom*'.[73] For the sake of the order of freedom, therefore, 'Man has to behave in a disciplined manner',[74] and such behaviour is possible only under conditions in which 'the necessity of a willed order is affirmed in the mentality of a properly understood freedom'. Only upon this basis can 'the coordination of the economic participants be achieved, which is the essence of a competitive order'.[75] Eucken thus argues that the freedom to compete is a function of order. Freedom therefore has 'its limits, namely, there where the order is threatened by it'.[76] Whether freedom persists as an expression of order is a matter of sovereign decision.[77] If, therefore, a decision needs to be made between freedom and order, freedom has to give way for the benefit of order.[78] Eucken grants that the pursuit of liberty might establish 'new forms of order. These are justified for as long as they are in conformity with the order of competition'.[79] Here, too, a decision needs to be made as to whether socio-economic developments are in accordance with the principles of the economic constitution. *Ordungspolitik* amounts thus to a sustained political decision about the character of the economy and the conduct of the market participants. Government constitutes the competitive order, governs for the completeness of competition, secures the self-responsible conduct of the individuals in support of this order, curtails the excess of freedom, and, if required, re-asserts the order of freedom by limiting its scale, re-ordering freedom. Government is thus a constant presence. It keeps the market participants under surveillance and facilitates their freedom to compete, steadily monitoring them as self-responsible entrepreneurs of a free labour economy, which the ordoliberals moralise as a 'human economy'.[80]

During the 1930s, the ordoliberal denunciation of Weimar democracy as an 'economic state' and their call for a strong state to 'recover' the free economy, changed into what Schmitt (1934) called 'concrete order thinking'.[81] As Müller-Armack had already put it in 1932,[82] we need to 'invent (*erfinden*) an objective order constellation (*Ordnungsgefüge*)' to institutionalise free economy. The Freiburg School

---

[72] ibid, p 178.

[73] ibid, p 179, (my emphasis).

[74] ibid, citing Miksch, p 197.

[75] ibid.

[76] ibid.

[77] Eucken, n 1 above.

[78] 'In a conflict between freedom and order, order is the unconditional priority', Böhm, n 2 above, p 101.

[79] Eucken, n 42 above, p 197.

[80] Röpke, n 5 above.

[81] On this call for the strong state, see, eg, Eucken, n 1, p 318, Rüstow, n 31 above, p 100 ff., and Röpke, n 1 above, pp 246–47. For an assessment, see Werner Bonefeld, 'Freedom and the Strong State', (2012) 17 *New Political Economy*, pp 633–656.

[82] Alfred Müller-Armack, *Entwicklungsgesetze des Kapitalismus*, (Berlin: Junker & Dünnhaupt, 1932), p 42.

Ordnungspolitik and the sociological liberalism associated with Rüstow, Röpke, and Müller-Armack developed different aspects of concrete order thinking from the mid-1930s onward. These efforts included arguments for an *Ordnungspolitik* based upon an economic constitution of complete competition, de-politicised forms of market supervision and enforcement, such as, the later West-German monopoly commission, and de-politicised forms of policy-making, such as, the conduct of monetary policy by an independent central bank with statutory obligation for sound money, akin to the later West-German *Bundesbank*, and restriction of majoritarian parliamentary law-making through an extra-parliamentary legal framework of constitutional norms and values that are enforceable by a de-politicised and extra-democratic institution in the form of an independent Constitutional Court. It further included commitments for a market facilitating conduct of social policy and ideological cohesion of the social relations upon the basis of Christian values, and the establishment of a liberal-democratic state that does not tolerate the enemies of its basic constitutional value commitments—to wit, a 'militant democracy'.[83] That is to say, 'trust in freedom must be accompanied by a distrust of forces that abolish freedom or interfere with it'.[84] Surveillance is the condition of trust.

IV. ON THE *ORDNUNGSGEFÜGE* OF THE EUROPEAN UNION

Ernst Mestmäcker conceives of European Economic Community in terms of a comprehensive decision (*Gesamtentscheidung*) about the economic constitution of Europe.[85] Its principle elements are the free movement of goods, capital, services, and labour, and competition law. Competition between territorialised labour markets also includes the institutional systems, from taxation to social protection.[86] The regulative institutions of EU are law, money, and market. They are developed, administered, and enforced by European organisations that operate removed from the traditional democratic principles of parliamentary law-making, oversight and accountability. Within the 'concrete order' (*Ordungsgefüge*) of Europe, only the European Parliament is directly elected.[87] It is a forum for public discussion, argument, and self-important deliberation. It represents the spectre of democratic pluralism at its most harmless. It has no executive to control, lacks the right of legislative initiative, cannot change the constitution of Europe because none exists, a least not in a traditional form. European integration is based upon international treaties

---

[83] See Johannes Agnoli, *Die Transformation der Demokratie*, (Freiburg: Ca Ira), 1990; Jan-Werner Müller, 'Militant Democracy', in: Michel Rosenfeld and András Sajó (eds), *Oxford Handbook of Comparative Constitutional Law*, (Oxford: Oxford University Press, 2012), pp 1253–69.

[84] Hans Otto Lenel, 'Evolution of the Social Market Economy', in: Alan Peacock and Hans Willgerodt (eds), *German Neo-liberals and the Social Research Market Economy*, (London: Palgrave, 1989), pp 16–39, at 21.

[85] Ernst Mestmäcker, *Wirtschaft und Verfassung in der Europäischen Union: Beiträge zur Rechtstheorie und Politik der Europäischen Integration*, (Baden-Baden: Nomos Verlag, 2003).

[86] See Pierre Dardot and Christian Laval, *The New Way of the World: On Neoliberal Society*, (London: Verso Books, 2013), pp 208–212.

[87] The part draws on Streeck's insightful account; see Wolfgang Streeck, 'Heller, Schmitt and the Euro', (2015) 21 *European Law Journal*, pp 361–370.

between sovereign states. In the European Parliament, the democratic groupings do not comprise governing majorities and opposition parties since there is no European government in the traditional sense. As a mass democratic body, it is without bite or consequence, and ordoliberal mantra about the dangers of 'mass democratic inter-ference' with the free economy is pointless. In Schmitt's terms, it is not the institution of a European legislative state (*Gesetzstaat*). It is, I argue, a deliberative institution of a union of executive states (*Regierungsstaaten*).

In this system, the European Commission, too, is a most curious institution. The Commission has 27 commissioners that are proposed by national governments, one for each state. It operates akin to a technocratic cabinet government. It is the execu-tive body of the EU and the sole institution that has legislative initiative in the EU. It is responsible for proposing legislation, implementing decisions, upholding the EU Treaties and managing the day-to-day business of the EU. It holds collective responsibility for the EU. The European Court of Justice, now the Court of Jus-tice of the European Union, emerged from being the authoritative interpreter of European competition law of the kind developed by German ordoliberalism to be the legal guardian of the European market society.[88] The European Central Bank is the sovereign institution of European money. It is the most independent and de-politicised Central Bank. It is a stateless central bank and not answerable to any government nor to any other European institutions. It regulates a stateless currency which, according to its founding treaties, is 'Austrian, ordo-liberal and neoliberal money'.[89] The characterisation of the ECB as the sovereign institution of European money has to do also with its decision-making during the Euro-crisis, which violated a number of legal obligations, ostensibly to preserve them in the long run. In the context of the Greek crisis, its decision in the summer of 2015 to terminate financial life-lines to the Greek banking system, leading to its enforced closure, was instru-mental in compelling the Greek government to submit to punishing conditions of (temporary) debt relief.

The political institution of the EU is the European Council, which comprises the Heads of the Member State governments. It is supported by various ministerial Coun-cils. The Council is the membership organisation of national executives. It is the de facto European legislator and policy-maker. National parliaments may oppose the ratification of binding policy-decisions made by European Councils, but their pow-ers remain purely negative. Member State parliaments do not make European policy or law. The Council operates akin to a medieval conclave of sovereign kings and queens who are united in their efforts to find resolutions to conflicts that, in the past, pitted them against each other. Their efforts are supported by a number of legal and technocratic organisations that act upon the basis of the agreements that they have reached. The troublesome populace is kept out of the bargain.

The concrete order of the EU—its *Ordnungsgefüge*—forecloses, as Michael Wilkinson has argued, the 'route of parliamentary, political contestation that might

---

[88] Gerber, n 46 above.
[89] Streeck, n 87 above, p 369.

have democratically legitimised redistribution from the bottom-up'.[90] In its stead, it establishes a top-down framework for market liberalisation, individual economic rights and processes of competitive adjustments, '[imposing] liberty' on territorial-ised labour markets.[91] Within this framework, the national Member States act as the executive states (*Regierungsstaaten*) of a European regime of liberty, and they do so akin to the ordoliberals characterisation of the liberal state as the concentrated power of 'liberal interventionism',[92] as a 'planner for competition'.[93]

In 1933, Hermann Heller had argued that the authoritarian liberal scheme could not be maintained in democratic form.[94] A state 'that is determined to secure "the free labour power of those people active in the economy" will ... have to act in an authoritarian way'.[95] The concrete order of the EU suggests that it is, however, pos-sible to achieve the freedom of labour within a democratic form. Its *Ordnungsgefüge* respects in its entirety the traditional forms of parliamentary democracy in Member States. Indeed, it makes the establishment of parliamentary democracy a condition of membership. Nevertheless, it places economic governance into a supranational structure and retains parliamentary sovereignty in the Member States that in effect operate as federated executives of Union rules.[96] As argued by Friedrich von Hayek, a federated system of containing mass democracy does not in any way curtail the state as the independent power of society.[97] Rather, it provides the means for its independence from society. In the EU, the Member States govern through European structures of money, law, and market forces.

The Euro crisis revealed that, contrary to appearances, the Euro is a politically constituted currency. It is not at all helpful to conceive of it as a technical institution that functions according to some presumed systemic automaticity. It amounts, rather, to a practice of governments to sustain and maintain the euro, especially in a context of debt and contestation. The creation of the euro as a stateless currency amounts to an eminently political decision. The statutory rules of the euro are not just technical and economic. They, too, are the outcome of political decisions, and, as the (Greek) crisis has shown, they remain politically founded and sustained rules. During the Euro-zone crisis, the European Council asserted itself as Europe's sovereign political

---

[90] Michael A. Wilkinson, 'Authoritarian Liberalism in the European Constitutional Imagination', (2015) 21 *European Law Journal*, pp 313–339, at 323.

[91] For a systematic argument setting this out, see Friedrich von Hayek, 'The Economic Conditions of Interstate Federalism', in: idem, *Individualism and Economic Order*, (London: Routledge, 1939), pp 255–73.

[92] Rüstow, n 28 above, p 252 ff.

[93] Friedrich von Hayek, *The Road to Serfdom*, (London: Routledge, 1944), p 31.

[94] Heller, n 15 above.

[95] idem, p 301, citing Schmitt, 'Sound Economy', n 1 above.

[96] As Streeck put it, '[w]here there are still democratic institutions in Europe, there is no economic governance any more, lest the management of the economy is invaded by market-correcting non-capitalist interests. And where there *is* economic governance, democracy is elsewhere'; Streeck, n 87 above, p 366. See, also, Werner Bonefeld, 'European Economic Constitution and the Transformation of Democracy', (2015) 21 *European Journal of International Relations*, pp 867–86.

[97] F. von Hajek, n 91 above.

power. In cohorts with the ECB in that it acted freely to do 'whatever it takes' to preserve monetary union.[98]

I have argued that the institutional structure of the EU has given national executives independence from majoritarian parliamentary law-making. Union law overrides national law. It is made by national executives as members of a supranational Council. The heterogeneous parliaments of the Member States have been transformed—to a considerable degree—from majoritarian law-makers into debating chambers. In contrast to the heterogeneous character of national parliaments, the Council assumes the role of an assembly of friends—each committed to the bargain in—at times heated—debate on how best to sustain the European idea. With the Greek case in 2015, however, the fundamental homogeneity of Council interests was broken. Instead of containing the mutinous character of the Greek opposition to austerity through the institutional *Ordnungsgefüge*, it gained entry not only into the Greek parliament, but also gained the seat of government in Greece and thus became a member of the Council, shattering its homogeneity of interests. Concerted action between the ECB and Council majority forced the Greek government to heel.[99] Indeed, by accepting the conditionality of the bail-out agreements, the Greek state has, to all intents and purposes, become an executive state of the European Council.

For its stability and future prospects, the federated order of Europe requires unbending solidarity between its Member States—'whatever it costs'. For as long as the populist backlash on the left and on the right is contained in national parliaments, the basic structure of the European order will not be threatened, unless Council solidary weakens in the face of national populist backlash. The question of who is the European sovereign will then be asked again. Only the state has the power to stop people running through the door. What is the name of the state that has the courage and the power of authoritative enforcement of the rules agreed upon? Clearly, this state is not the UK. It had never fully committed itself, and, lacking courage, it caved in at the first sign of serious trouble, first to populist flagbearers and then to the populist backlash, both rejecting the free movement of labour, and projecting its buccaneering spirit of old. Hans Tietmeyer's warning that 'sustaining monetary union might need perhaps more solidarity than beginning it' says more than it seemed at first.[100]

---

[98] 'Whatever it takes' is a now famous phrase used by Mario Draghi, who, in his role as President of the ECB, offered this Schmittean phrase in answer to the question of what the ECB would do to sustain the Euro. See www.ecb.Europa.eu/press/date/2012/html.sp120726.en.html.

[99] On Eurozone crisis resolution, see Kaarlo Tuori and Klaus Tuori, *The Eurozone Crisis: A Constitutional Analysis*, (Cambridge: Cambridge University Press, 2014).

[100] Cited in Walter Eltis, 'British EMU Membership would Create Instability and Destroy Employment', in: M. Baimbridge, Brian Burkitt and Philip Whyman (eds), *The Impact of the Euro: Debating Britain's Future*, (London: Palgrave, 2000), pp 139–159, at 146.

18

Policy Between Rules and Discretion

JONATHAN WHITE

ABSTRACT

The chapter examines how efforts to design a policy regime governed by rules may lead on the contrary to recurrent and far-reaching political discretion. Where re-orientations of policy are formally excluded, as in the ordoliberal perspective, unforeseen situations will typically provoke last-minute unconventional actions, whether in the form of temporary exceptions to the existing framework or moves to constitute a new one. In order to preserve the ideal of a rule-governed order, such actions must be cast as extraordinary measures for exceptional times—as the politics of emergency, that is. Whereas modern political thought of various stripes tends to defend constitutional rules as the condition of policy discretion, here one sees the converse scenario of constitutional discretion pursued in the name of policy rules. These themes are elaborated in connection with the ongoing crisis of the European Union.

I. INTRODUCTION

THE POLITICS OF the Euro crisis, and Germany's role within it, are commonly described in two diverging ways: on the one hand, as displaying new heights of executive discretion, on the other, as exhibiting an extreme attachment to the imposition of constraining rules.[1] How are we to account for these apparently contrasting depictions?

Currently, the most popular interpretation seems to be this: that the prominence of rules both in discourse and practice derives from the influence of ordoliberal thought, while the prominence of discretion results from the incomplete application

---

[1] See, on the one hand, Fritz Scharpf, 'Political Legitimacy in a Non-optimal Currency Area', in: Sara Hobolt and Olaf Cramme (eds), *Democratic Politics in a European Union under Stress*, (Oxford: Oxford University Press, 2014), and, on the other, Kalypso Nicolaïdis and Max Watson, 'Sharing the Eurocrats' Dream: A Demoicratic Approach to EMU Governance in the Post-crisis Era', in: Damian Chalmers, Markus Jachtenfuchs and Christian Joerges (eds), *The End of the Eurocrats' Dream: Adjusting to European Diversity* (Cambridge: Cambridge University Press, 2016), pp 50–77, especially p 52: 'rules now reign supreme'.

of these ideas.[2] Ordoliberalism is the structuring ideal, but remains only partially realised. There is at least one further possibility, of course, which is that the combination of discretion and rules is itself characteristic of ordoliberalism. On this reading, both rules and extraordinary measures have their place in the ordoliberal outlook, and the presence of both in the contemporary EU is consistent with the structuring influence of ordoliberalism. This is the possibility that I would like to explore here.

II. THE IDEA OF AN ECONOMIC CONSTITUTION

If there is a core idea in the ordoliberal tradition, present in one form or another throughout its various incarnations, it is the commitment to a stable system of rules for socio-economic activity. *Ordnungspolitik* evokes an ideal of political order in which agents of the state design an enduring framework to underpin the functioning of market society.[3] As is well known, ordoliberals have typically referred to this framework as an 'economic constitution' (*Wirtschaftsverfassung*), drawing on ideas already in circulation by the early 1900s and fashioning them into the cornerstone of their construction.[4]

Adjacent to this concept in the ordoliberal tradition are a range of more abstract ideas informing it, as well as a set of more specific prescriptions. Amongst the former is the assumption that the economy forms an integrated system, that the market and the state can exist in a complementary relation,[5] and various underlying ethical ideas including the view that fairness requires the alignment of risk and responsibility, an emphasis on individual freedom, and a corresponding current of scepticism towards democracy. Amongst the more concrete prescriptions are a range of policy commitments, such as the endorsement of private ownership, opposition to monopoly power, and the central importance ascribed to price stability, as well as evolving views on the monetary policies that can foster this and the institutions conducive to upholding them in a given time and place.[6] The idea of *Ordnung* expressed in

---

[2] See, eg, Lars P. Feld, Ekkehard A. Köhler and Daniel Nientiedt, 'Ordoliberalism, Pragmatism and the Eurozone Crisis: How the German Tradition Shaped Economic Policy in Europe', CESIFO WORKING PAPER NO. 5368, 2015.

[3] For historical and analytical overviews, see David J. Gerber, 'Constitutionalizing the Economy: German Neo-liberalism, Competition Law and the 'New' Europe', (1994) 42 *The American Journal of Comparative Law*, pp 25–84; Viktor J. Vanberg, 'The Freiburg School: Walter Eucken and Ordoliberalism', Paper 04/11, 2004 (Freiburg: Walter Eucken Institut); Werner Bonefeld, 'Freedom and the Strong State: On German Ordoliberalism', (2012) 17 *New Political Economy*, pp 633–56; Thomas Biebricher, 'Europe and the Political Philosophy of Neoliberalism', (2013) 12 *Contemporary Political Theory*, pp 338–75.

[4] On the history of the concept before its adoption by Franz Böhm, see Knut Wolfgang Nörr, '"Economic Constitution": On the Roots of a Legal Concept', (1994) 11 *Journal of Law and Religion*, pp 343–54.

[5] That the market-economic and the constitutional are, as one might say, 'co-original'; let us set aside the question of whether this interdependence is conceptual or empirical.

[6] See, eg, on competition law, Gerber, n 3 above, pp 52–3.

an economic constitution mediates all these features of ordoliberal thought: it is a central concept in the tradition, notwithstanding the tradition's evolution.[7]

This commitment is commonly understood to express deep opposition to executive discretion, as ordoliberal thinkers themselves have emphasised. Franz Böhm wrote warmly of an 'automatically functioning coordination system' that would 'restrict [the state] to the task of defining the structural framework' and 'severely limit political discretion'.[8] Walter Eucken, in a discussion of monetary policy, evoked the ideal of 'rational automatism'.[9] Political agents were to operate within sharply demarcated parameters. Partly as a function of a technocratic concern for the coherence of economic policy,[10] partly the consequence of fears of state capture by private interests, for ordoliberals the point has always been to constrain political action with rules. Following a foundational moment of adoption—the point at which a market economy, by 'an explicit and uncompromising decision',[11] was embraced by the community and thereby put beyond further contestation—things were to unfold in a closely-constrained fashion.

To be sure, this was never a model of social order without the state. There is a class of initiatives that political agents *were* expected to engage in—those 'formal' actions which serve to maintain, to perfect and to update the economic constitution. These were to be formal in the sense that they did not serve particular economic ends, but established the conditions under which such ends could be pursued. They would shape the 'framework' of economic activity, but not entail efforts to 'control the

---

[7] See Vanberg, n 3 above, p 6.

[8] As Böhm writes: 'the individual plans of members of society would be controlled with the help of an automatically functioning coordination system. This would relieve the state of the task of central economic control and would restrict it to the task of defining the structural framework which would preserve and enforce observance of the control laws. Moreover, the role of the state in the overall enforcement of this system would be so constituted that it would severely limit political discretion. If a political decision was taken to adopt such a system, then the rules would be laid down as to: (i) the task of the legislator, (ii) the role and duties of the government and (iii) the principles by which the courts would interpret the law. This system is based upon an instrumental and procedural "score" of a predominantly standard character which has been worked out to the last detail. The margin of discretion given to the autonomous members of society is limited by the peculiarity of their coordinated actions and by the consequent special feature of objective mutual interdependence. The margin of discretion given to persons with political authority is limited by the compulsion to submit to the mechanism of control which is laid down as in a musical score, as a modest-I should like to say both socially and politically harmless-minimum. This minimum, though it leaves many options open to the creative imagination which conforms to the system, nevertheless severely restricts the possibilities of ignoring the score and acting in a manner which does not conform to the system by setting the furies of economic and political disaster on the heels of the sinners.' (See Franz Böhm, 'Rule of Law in a Market Economy', in: Alan T. Peacock and Hans Willgerodt (eds), *Germany's Social Market Economy: Origins and Evolution*, (London: Palgrave Macmillan, 1989), pp 62–3 (a translation of Böhm, 'Privatrechtsgesellschaft und Marktwirtschaft', (1966) 17 *ORDO Jahrbuch*, pp 75–152.)

[9] Walter Eucken, *Grundsätze der Wirtschaftspolitik*, (Reinbek: Rowohlt, 1965), p 263.

[10] See Walter Eucken in: Peacock and Willgerodt, n 8 above, p 32. Note also the religious inspiration behind Ordoliberalism which further promotes the holistic outlook: see Philip Manow, 'Ordoliberalismus als ökonomische Ordnungstheologie', (2001) 29 *Leviathan*, pp 179–98.

[11] Wilhelm Röpke, 'Is the German Economic Policy the Right One?', in: Horst Frierich Wünsch (ed), *Standard Texts on the Social Market Economy—Two Centuries of Discussion*, (Stuttgart-New York: Gustav Fischer, [1950] 1982), p 39.

productive process itself'.[12] They were to be indifferent to the substantive outcomes to which they led, and were certainly not to be responsive to public opinion.[13] Thus, there was a category under which significant state action could be envisaged—but always on behalf of *constraining* discretion in conformity with the principles of the economic constitution.[14]

The reluctance with which political agents should consider breaking with the principles of their economic system—though also the suggestion that sometimes they may have to—was well expressed by Wilhelm Röpke:

> Any emphatic call for a homogeneous national economic policy implies that the various segments of this policy (prices, marketing, foreign trade, agriculture, money and banking, the capital market, etc) must correlate with each other so as to present a uniform whole rather than various parts reciprocally cancelling each other out. [...] It seems a cheap argument to designate this demand and its concomitant policy "doctrinaire". Naturally, economic policy ought to remain flexible in regard to its details and guard against the danger of tarring everything with the same brush. A systematic consistent policy such as that recommended here does not signify that no exceptions should or could be made. Nevertheless, it must at the same time always be dominated by the fear that concessions on the crucial points or even a series of concessions will militate against the overall system which will disrupt it and finally generate further concessions in the direction of government controls.[15]

The approach chimes well with a conception of the market economy as something that, if sufficiently well-ordered, achieves a measure of equilibrium. If one can assume that such an economy does not feature endogenous tendencies towards periods of extreme upheaval and unacceptable social costs, it may be tenable to conceive good policy as purely 'formal' in the sense described.[16] What, though, if there are destructive forces in the economy that threaten moments of great instability and distress? The work of Keynes and others has long emphasised the volatile aspects of the market economy—the centrality of 'confidence', the problem of 'speculation',

---

[12] Eucken 1986/1948, p 275.

[13] Franz Böhm, Walter Eucken and Hans Großmann-Dörth, 'The Ordo Manifesto of 1936', in: Peacock and Willgerodt, n 8 above, p 23; see, also, Röpke, n 11 above, on the difference between 'market-conforming' and 'non-conforming' measures. See, also, Michel Foucault, *The Birth of Biopolitics: Lectures at the Collège de France*, 1978–9, (Basingstoke: Palgrave Macmillan, 2008), p 171.

[14] It is noticeable that in some of the earliest formulations of these ideas, the scope for legitimate state intervention was drawn quite inclusively. In the proto-Ordoliberal thought of Alexander Rüstow, the state is bound in its actions simply by the 'laws of the market': 'I think there exists a third type of attitude, which would be the correct and modern mode of production. If we were agreed that every new condition of equilibrium which arose in the normal way was the most appropriate solution even though many frictional losses and disagreeable phases had to be overcome en route, it would seem highly advisable to try to achieve this condition without delay and to reduce to zero the interim period which would otherwise slowly pass until a new and durable set of circumstances could be established—an interim period marked by hopeless struggle, by decline and by distress. That would be interference in precisely the opposite direction to that in which we have hitherto proceeded, ie not contrary to the laws of the market but in conformity with them: not to maintain the old situation but to bring about a new one, not to delay the natural course of events but to accelerate it. With this in mind, our recommendation is for a form of liberal interventionism under the motto 'fata volentemducunt, nolentemtrahunt' [*the fates lead the willing and drag the unwilling*].' Alexander Rüstow, 'Liberal Intervention', in: Wünsch, n 11 above, pp 184–5.

[15] Röpke, n 11 above, p 38.

[16] Leaving aside for now the question of democracy.

and so on.[17] An economic model committed to *constraining* the sphere of state action may clearly face a distinctive set of challenges should it ever have to confront these more volatile tendencies in the market economy—features all the more visible in more recent forms of financial capitalism, where contagion has become a thematic problem.

Moreover, the ordoliberal policy regime is only ever likely to be applied in a world that is not wholly ordoliberal—where other countries pursue different models, that is, or imperfectly execute the same. The context of ordoliberalism's enactment is likely to be one that, if not outright hostile, is at least liable to present frictions. Where rival powers pursue policies that deviate from ordoliberal precepts, an important source of uncertainty is introduced into the economic system. How then does the ordoliberal declared aversion to political discretion fare in the context of the pathologies and distortions of a market economy, and what options does it leave available in the face of an economic shock?[18]

The question carries added relevance given the prospect that the ordoliberal emphasis on stable rules of policy itself contains the seeds of instability, at least when applied in certain settings.[19] An accent on strictly 'formal' interventions alone arguably entails a degree of blindness to contextual variations in economic conditions. This may be true cross-spatially, as numerous critics of 'one-size-fits-all' policy-making in the EU have observed.[20] Rules intended to be neutral in their treatment of actors always carry the risk of treating unequals equally, with difficult implications, both economically and politically. The point holds also cross-temporally: an emphasis on a stable policy regime inevitably faces the problem of how to adapt to changing conditions. It has long been argued that the proliferation of policy rules leads to rigidity, and where periodic major shifts in policy are excluded, unforeseen situations will typically provoke last-minute unconventional actions. Even if the idea of an economic constitution admits the possibility of periodically introducing new rules, it may suggest a reluctance to expunge old ones, with similar challenging implications. I do not wish to suggest that ordoliberals are without resources to

---

[17] See John Maynard Keynes, *The General Theory of Employment, Interest and Money*, (London: MacMillan, 1936), especially Ch 12. The emphasis is on tendencies that depart from what might be viewed objectively rational—how, for instance, assessments of value involve predictions of how others will assess the same, introducing a degree of uncertainty that detaches behaviour from the economic fundamentals and creates the potential for great fluctuations (see pp 100 et seq.).

[18] This is often said to be a weak point of ordoliberalism: see Mathias Siems and Gerhard Schnyder, 'Ordoliberal Lessons for Economic Stability: Different Kinds of Regulation, Not More Regulation', (2014) 27 *Governance: An International Journal of Policy, Administration, and Institutions*, pp 377–396, at 386 and 389, on 'doubts about whether a rigid Ordoliberalism can help to address severe financial crises'. See, also, the sympathetic analysis in Feld et al, n 2 above, p 14, where contagion—undiscussed in the founding texts of ordoliberalism—is noted to be at the heart of the mismatch between responsibility and liability that ordoliberals abhor.

[19] Given that ideas are never perfectly instituted in practice, this idea is more an intuition than a testable hypothesis.

[20] Christian Joerges, 'What is Left of the European Economic Constitution II? From Pyrrhic Victory to Cannae Defeat', in: Poul F. Kjaer and Niklas Olsen (eds), *Critical Theories of Crisis in Europe: From Weimar to the Euro*, (Lanham MD: Rowman & Littlefield, 2016), pp 143–60; Wolfgang Streeck, *Gekaufte Zeit. Die vertagte Krise des demokratischen Kapitalismus*, (Berlin: Suhrkamp Verlag, 2013).

address these questions, but it remains the case that the prospect of disequilibrium must be reckoned with for reasons *internal* as well as external to the core commitments of ordoliberalism.

III. THE PLACE OF THE EXTRAORDINARY IN THE ORDOLIBERAL TRADITION

For the committed Ordoliberal, clearly one response to difficult times is to stand by the existing rules framework. The advice to political agents will be to restrict themselves to actions regarded as merely formal, preserving thereby an order in which discretion is highly constrained.[21] This may be rationalised with the idea that more harm than good is done by putting the integrity of the framework in question, combined with efforts to downplay the negative outcomes arising.

There are a number of reasons why this response may be unsatisfactory, even from within the ordoliberal outlook. Not only may it involve ignoring high socio-economic costs, but it may sit badly with other ordoliberal commitments, including the ethical principle that actors be held responsible for their actions (the *Haftung-sprinzip*). Upholding this principle may require interventions hard to conceive as merely 'formal': indeed, it may require reconfiguring economic relations precisely so as to influence substantive outcomes. When mechanisms such as contagion are in play—or simply when they cannot be excluded—interventions may need to be targeted at particular actors if these wider principles are to be maintained. Clearly, the point is only further underlined if one accepts that an ordoliberal preference for stable rules may itself be a contributing factor to economic instability.

Is there scope then for more radical actions? One possibility is to declare an exception to the rules framework, thereby seeking both to uphold the framework and to stave off the effects of its dogmatic application.[22] This is the kind of response implied by Röpke in the passage cited above, and is mirrored in other more recent ordoliberal writings.[23] Importantly, such a move is likely to depend on casting the situation as a wholly exceptional one in which the usual constraints on political discretion do not apply.[24] The ordoliberal presumption that the state's relations with the market can be founded on stable rules requires that difficult times be framed as moments of emergency. Precisely because the model is so wary of permitting exceptions, the situations in which discretionary initiatives are pursued must be cast as

---

[21] Such a position may in practice look rather similar then to Austrian neoliberalism and its avowed wariness of all kinds of political intervention in the market.

[22] See David M. Woodruff, 'Governing by Panic: The Politics of the Eurozone Crisis', (2016) 44 *Politics & Society*, p 97, on exceptionalism as the implication of ordoliberal rule consequentialism.

[23] See, eg, Viktor J. Vanberg, 'Ordnungspolitik, The Freiburg School and the Reason of Rules', (2014) 14 *Freiburger Diskussionspapiere zur Ordnungsökonomik*, p 15: 'prudence does indeed require us to acknowledge that there may be emergency situations in which we need to temporarily disband rules that in ordinary times we consider binding.'

[24] For a closer discussion of ideas of exceptionalism and emergency powers in Röpke's thought, see Werner Bonefeld, 'Authoritarian Liberalism: From Schmitt via Ordoliberalism to the Euro', (2016) *Critical Sociology*, online early.

exceptional—situations in which actions are grounded in necessity. In this way, the ordoliberal emphasis on a constitutional framework of policy-making would seem to invite the escalation of political rhetoric—a politics of emergency—when interventions hard to subsume under the heading of 'formal' are pursued.

A second coherent response from within the ordoliberal viewpoint is to deny that a genuine rules framework is in existence, previous impressions notwithstanding, and to assert that it now needs to be *established*. The present generation may be repositioned, in other words, not as the inheritor of an economic constitution but as being back at the founding moment when a decision for the (ordoliberal) model is to be taken. As we have noted, ordoliberal thought has tended to cast this moment as one of legitimate political discretion—the moment of discretion to end discretion.[25] Also a form of 'extraordinary' politics,[26] it is not quite the same as exceptionalism: the rules to which it is oriented are those-to-come rather than those already in force. But like the exceptionalist response, it invites the framing of the situation as one of urgent necessity. To commit decisively to a new framework of rules generally requires viewing the status quo as wholly unsustainable, as a state of disorder to be contrasted with the order-to-come.

It is in the nature of arguments from *exception* and *foundation* that they are difficult to ward off. Deciding whether a situation warrants extraordinary action is clearly a matter of judgement—nothing in the objective nature of the circumstances themselves or in the political apparatus that confronts them can settle this. A departure from the rules framework is therefore a *persistent* possibility, not one restricted to a particular context. Moreover, as those with a privileged vantage-point on political developments, and typically with claims to expertise in the socio-economic issues at stake, decision-makers are well placed to make this judgement in a way that others may struggle to refute.

It is worth emphasising in this context that both scenarios of extraordinary politics are well in keeping with the technocratic tendency in ordoliberalism. Already in its early formulation by the Freiburg thinkers, the approach was consciously conceived as a project to be advanced by the 'men of science' of law and political economy as those able to stand back from private interests and take an objective view of the economic system in all its complexity.[27] The very idea of an economic constitution, as a project of finding the technical means to institutionalise principles taken as agreed and settled, reflects this general inspiration. If the ordoliberal aspiration in times of uncertainty is to stick with the existing rules framework, this demands that initiatives be cast as simply technical adjustments to existing constitutional commitments (as 'formal' in the sense described). Standards of democratic political justification, involving comparison of competing options and the acknowledgement of competing

---

[25] This is how the West German currency reform of 20 June 1948 tends to be portrayed in the ordoliberal tradition: see, notably, Ludwig Erhard, 'The New Facts', in: Wünsch, n 11, especially p 35.

[26] Kalyvas 2008.

[27] See the Ordoliberal Manifesto of 1936, with its explicit aim to combat fatalism and relativism and to renew confidence in what science could achieve (in Peacock and Willgerodt, n 8 above, p 16 and 21). The position of the Austrian neoliberals was, of course, quite different, with von Hayek tending to denounce such aspirations as 'scientism'.

values, are likely to be deliberately eschewed. To the extent, on the other hand, that adhering to the rules framework is deemed unfeasible, and the ordoliberal encounter with crisis leads to exceptionalism and/or re-constitution, the technocratic tendency is again undergirded. Suspending rules, as well as adopting new ones as an indivisible package, typically relies on a claim to special insight—not just the knowledge of how rules are to be followed, but an understanding of the ideas that inform them (the 'spirit' of the rules) so that the decision to waive them can be presented as authoritative. It is exactly in such moves that the claim to expertise is performed.

I have suggested that the ordoliberal tradition invites economic situations to be approached in a dichotomous fashion: either as part of the 'normal' conditions which can be handled by the merely formal state interventions associated with the economic constitution; or—should such efforts prove unworkable—as exceptional situations warranting an extraordinary response of some sort. Being strongly committed to a certain understanding of order encourages any challenge not easily absorbed within that framework to be cast as the threat of far-reaching disorder, to be staved off by radical means. The attempt sharply to constrain political discretion paradoxically makes thinkable the possibility of far-reaching discretion unconstrained by the usual norms of politics and political justification. Missing, we might say, is the third position, in which it is recognised that even the best policy regimes will always be challenged by difficult situations necessitating discretion (not to mention the democratic rationale for change), and that the question is therefore how to ensure such situations are *not* cast as wholly exceptional but rather are handled in accordance with political norms.

The ordoliberal emphasis is, one may note, on an *economic* constitution rather than a political constitution structuring the procedures of the polity more generally.[28] It primarily seeks to constrain the *kinds* of economic policy that political agents can pursue rather than the ways in which they may initiate and enforce policy. This is an important distinction, since there is nothing in the idea of fidelity to a certain set of economic principles that implies constraints on political discretion more generally. Indeed, it may be that a strong commitment to upholding rules of policy may invite great latitude in the procedures by which this is achieved. The early phases of ordoliberal thought famously emphasised the importance of a strong state that was, as it were, (legally) unencumbered to do what (economically) it must—hence the familiar depiction of it as tending towards authoritarian liberalism.[29] Even if we acknowledge that later iterations of the tradition were more interested in questions of an overarching rule of law,[30] it remains true that these larger aspects of constitutionalism have been relatively neglected in ordoliberal thought.

---

[28] Although the notion of an 'economic constitution' looks something like a bid to draw on the prestige of constitutional terminology to describe what is ultimately a policy regime, the distinction is additionally blurred in English by the use of the same word to translate *(Wirtschafts)verfassung* and *Grundgesetz*.

[29] Classically, see Hermann Heller, 'Autoritärer Liberalismus', (1933) 44 *Die Neue Rundschau*, pp 289–298; see, also, Dieter Haselbach, *Autoritärer Liberalismus und Soziale Marktwirtschaft: Gesellschaft und Politik im Ordoliberalismus*, (Baden-Baden: Nomos Verlag, 1991). See, also, Bonefeld, n 24 above.

[30] See, also, Volker Berghahn and Brigitte Young, 'Reflections on Werner Bonefeld's "Freedom and the Strong State: One German Ordoliberalism"', (2013) 18 *New Political Economy*, pp 768–78, (*contra* Werner Bonefeld, n 3 above).

IV. DISCUSSION: RULES AND DISCRETION IN THE EURO CRISIS

Has the handling of the Euro crisis been consistent with the picture described? Certainly we have seen major departures from existing policy regimes pushed through by executive discretion. Some have been defended as temporary measures intended to restore short-term stability, such as the European Financial Stability Facility. Such instances are consistent with the logic of *exception*: understood as responses to exceptional circumstances, they are treated as restorative moves, intended merely to reset the existing rules framework. Often their proponents have gone to great lengths to avoid actions that might resemble a decisive break with the pre-crisis order—the reluctance to approve debt write-offs, or even bail-outs, being a well-known example.

Other measures on the other hand—the later ones especially—instead look rather more like efforts to initiate a substantially *new* rules-based regime. Prominent amongst these are the Fiscal Compact, the Six-Pack and the Two-Pack. These moves have typically been coupled with the portrayal of the pre-crisis regime as essentially dysfunctional, as rules-based only in name. Emblematic in this respect was the blueprint for the future of the Eurozone released by the head of the European Council in 2012, entitled 'Towards a Genuine Economic and Monetary Union'.[31] Exactly by suggesting that the existing rules-order was bogus, its authors invoked the licence needed to wield far-reaching discretion in the service of establishing a new one. The creative re-deployment of EU institutional powers (notably of the Commission), the circumvention or compression of national-parliamentary debate, as well as the use of extra-EU mechanisms to marginalise the European Parliament, are just some of the actions taken to this effect.

By framing the economic situation as one of emergency, unconventional moves at odds both with a commitment to stable rules of policy and with basic constitutional norms have been adopted as last-minute responses to urgent problems.[32] To the extent that these problems are indeed pressing, arguably they arise in significant part from a reluctance to confront the pathologies of financial capitalism, with structural problems of state capture, speculation and contagion overlooked in favour of the localisation of blame and an insistence on the avoidance of moral hazard.[33] The new policy regimes arising are intended to bind decision-makers more tightly to 'responsible' economics by giving it the status of a constitutional commitment.[34]

In short, using the only justifications that ordoliberals could accept, interventions anathema to their instincts have been employed, to handle challenges that their own

---

[31] 'Towards a Genuine Economic and Monetary Union', Report by President of the European Council Herman Van Rompuy, 5 December 2012, available at: www.consilium.europa.eu/uedocs/cms_Data/docs/pressdata/en/ec/134069.pdf.

[32] Jonathan White, 'Authority after Emergency Rule', (2015) 78 *Modern Law Review*, pp 585–610, idem, 'Emergency Europe', (2015) 63 *Political Studies*, pp 300–18, and idem, 'Politicizing Europe: The Challenge of Executive Discretion', in: Sara Hobolt and Olaf Cramme (eds), *Democratic Politics in a European Union under Stress*, n 1 above, pp x.

[33] See, for example, Matthias Matthijs, 'Powerful Rules Governing the Euro: The Perverse Logic of German Ideas', (2016) 23 *Journal of European Public Policy*, pp 375–91.

[34] On the relevant aspects of the Fiscal Compact, see White, 'Authority after Emergency Rule', n 32 above.

ideas allowed to develop, with the aim of re-constituting the economic system to be immune to such threats in future.

One line of argument treats the actions of the German government in the context of the Euro crisis as directly inspired by ordoliberal thinking. As one author puts it, 'The crisis initially got worse as a result of too close an adherence to ordoliberalism, and it only started to go away as those same ideas were partially deserted'.[35] Compelling as this thesis may be, the risk is that it overstates the influence of one agent—the German government—in a situation characterised by the interplay of multiple agents not always with converging agendas.[36] Also, it understates the influence of other brands of liberal-economic thought, particularly the Chicago-School neoliberalism that has been a major influence on the ECB and branches of the Commission in recent decades. If anything, these ideas are *more* conducive to the politics of emergency, since they foresee large scope for executive discretion in the service of an agenda of 'competitiveness'.[37] There is a problem of over-determination, in other words, that should make us cautious in linking the EU's crisis management too closely to one body of thought alone.[38]

But one does not need to evoke unity of programme in this way, and attribute to it causal status, in order to concede the relevance of ordoliberalism to recent EU decisions.[39] The significance of this set of ideas, it can be said, lies rather in encouraging the avoidance or postponement of certain lines of action, in suggesting certain kinds of justification for actions once undertaken, and in prompting limited resistance to such manoeuvres from others (be they parliamentary figures in the political mainstream or opinion leaders in the media). Ordoliberalism establishes a sensibility, possibly largely tacit, for certain kinds of response. If the EU's politics of emergency in this period has sources well beyond the influence of one ideological tradition, it remains possible that, at least in this sense, ordoliberalism was an enabling factor.

Importantly, and as I have tried to argue, it is *not* plausible to discount the influence of ordoliberalism simply by observing that the Euro crisis has been as much about acts of executive discretion as about the constraining force of binding rules. Certainly, the emphasis in the ordoliberal tradition has always been on this latter aspect—on a system sufficiently structured by rules that it becomes 'automatically

---

[35] See Matthijs, n 35 above, p 380. See, also, David Schäfer, 'A Banking Union of Ideas? The Impact of Ordoliberalism and the Vicious Circle on the EU Banking Union', (2016) 54 *Journal of Common Market Studies*, pp 961–80, and supporting quotations therein concerning Schäuble's own ordoliberal convictions; see, also, Peter Nedergaard and Holly Snaith, '"As I Drifted on a River I could not Control": The Unintended Ordoliberal Consequences of the Eurozone Crisis', (2015) 53 *Journal of Common Market Studies*, pp 1094–1109; for critical discussion, see Feld et al, n 2 above.

[36] See the IMF and ECB as two agents whose actions are hard to subsume under the ordoliberal label.

[37] See, eg, William Davies, *The Limits of Neoliberalism: Authority, Sovereignty and the Logic of Competition*, (London: Sage Publications, 2014).

[38] Though, on this, see Biebricher, 'Europe and the Political Philosophy of Neoliberalism', n 3 above, and, idem, 'The Return of Ordoliberalism in Europe—Notes on a Research Agenda', (2014) 9 *I-lex*, pp 1–24.

[39] I take some inspiration here from Quentin Skinner, 'Moral Principles and Social Change', in: idem, *Visions of Politics Vol I: Regarding Method*, (Cambridge: Cambridge University Press, 2002).

functioning'—and the recurrent calls to strengthen the rules of the Eurozone are the features of the crisis period most in tune with the ordoliberal outlook.[40] The fact that the exercise of discretion has in no sense been banished from the emerging Eurozone regime[41] is testament certainly to its imperfections from an ordoliberal perspective. But the larger observation, I suggest, is that the very commitment to the idea of a stable and binding economic constitution has always implied the prospect of challenging situations being handled in far more discretionary fashion (in the service, of course, of strict rules), coupled with their framing as matters of high emergency. It is exactly the dialectical *combination* of rules and extraordinary discretion which is arguably characteristic of ordoliberalism in its 'actually existing' form.

The distinctiveness of the EU setting, as a post-sovereign order, is that it makes this entwinement more pronounced and visible. Although at one level there would seem to be a special affinity between the ordoliberal tradition and the transnational context—the voluntarily-embraced rules of an 'economic constitution' promise to substitute for the absence of political hierarchy, and to establish order without popular interference—at the same time this context raises peculiar challenges for it. The disparity of economic conditions across the Eurozone makes the principle of limiting intervention to merely formal, rule-based approaches more difficult than ever to sustain. The insistence for political reasons on territorialising ordoliberal ideas of responsibility and liability, so that states become their carriers,[42] creates pressure for conditionality requirements and national vetoes that have more to do with discretion than rules.[43] The problem of contagion is more pronounced given the interdependence of Eurozone economies. The weakness of the EU as a constitutional order in the conventional sense means there are fewer legal constraints on what agents can do in the service of an 'economic constitution'. The lack of a dominant political agent able to exercise uncontested authority, in the manner of the government of a nation-state, means that the exercise of political discretion can be especially chaotic, involving as it must the collaboration of multiple agents, and the appeal to the politics of emergency especially tempting as a means to galvanise action. All these are ways in which the combination of rules and extraordinary discretion becomes especially clear in the EU context; the combination itself though seems a characteristic implication of the ordoliberal standpoint.

The discretionary handling of legal and political norms—of sovereignty, democracy and others—in the name of strict policy rules: if this is what one witnesses today, then arguably it is the inverse of how many would want things to be. Instead of constitutional discretion to entrench a certain set of policies, a strong constitutional

---

[40] See Feld et al, n 2 above, p 10.
[41] See Scharpf, n 1 above.
[42] See Schäfer, n 35 above.
[43] On the asymmetric bargaining and threat of force involved, see Scharpf, n 1 above; Damian Chalmers, 'Crisis Reconfiguration of the European Constitutional State', in: Damian Chalmers, Markus Jachtenfuchs and Christian Joerges (eds), *The End of the Eurocrats' Dream: Adjusting to European Diversity*, (Cambridge: Cambridge University Press, 2016); Magnus Ryner, 'Europe's Ordoliberal Iron Cage: Critical Political Economy, the Euro Area Crisis and its Management', (2015) 22 *Journal of European Public Policy*, pp 275–94; and Woodruff, n 22 above.

order that enables the orderly *contestation* of policies is arguably a preferable arrangement, certainly more in keeping with ideals of collective self-determination. Rather than aiming to reduce political discretion to the bare minimum, with all the potential for extraordinary action that this entails, there would seem to be no substitute for establishing the institutional structures that enable it to take legitimate form, as the considered interventions of agents responsive to contending opinion rather than as the last-minute improvisations of technocratic élites.

19

How Monetary Rules *and Wage* Discretion *get into Conflict* in the Eurozone (And What—If Anything—Ordoliberalism has to do with it)*

PHILIP MANOW

ABSTRACT

Post-war Germany's political economy was never ordoliberal, and this remains to be true for its role in the Eurozone. Much of the functioning of the German political economy depends on an encompassing welfare state, vehemently opposed by ordoliberals in the 1950s and 1960s and ever since. The German 'social market economy' therefore always represented a compromise between a non-interventionist economic policy and a substantially redistributive social policy, and their interaction produced something not at all resembling a (ordo-)liberal outcome. The position of the German government in the Eurocrisis reflected core ingredients of this Modell Deutschland, namely the importance of a non-accommodating monetary policy and fiscal restraint to secure wage moderation (essential for Germany's export-led growth model). It was thus rational interest in the protection of a successful economic model, not ordoliberal ideology or irrational German inflation angst, which explained the German position during the crisis.

I. INTRODUCTION

WHAT CAUSED THE Euro-crisis? One might think that most, if not everything, has already been said on this topic. Six years after the onset of the Euro-crisis (and eight years after the onset of the Great Recession),

* Paper presented at the workshop 'Der Ordoliberalismus: Chance oder Gefahr für Europa?', 14 September 2016, University of Freiburg, and at the conference 'Ordoliberalism—An Irritating German Idea', 13–14 May 2016, Hertie School of Governance, Berlin. I thank all the participants for the helpful discussion. Furthermore, I would like to thank Martin Höpner, Susanne Schmidt, Stephan Siepe, Fritz W. Scharpf, Tim Krieger and Josef Hien for helpful comments.

something like a 'consensus view' seems to have emerged among economists.[1] It differs from an understanding that is still prevalent in the public—and particularly so in the German public—namely, that the Euro-crisis was, and continues to be, essentially a sovereign debt crisis caused by a continuous violation of the Maastricht criteria, if not by flagrant fiscal forging over many, many years, as in the case of Greece. Instead, the consensus view among economists stresses the increasing divergence among the euro Member State's current accounts, with increasing deficits in the periphery and increasing surpluses in the Eurozone centre, which were exposed and then triggered a 'sudden stop' of capital flows from the centre to the periphery in the wake of the Lehman Brothers bankruptcy. Baldwin and Giavazzi summarise the key insight of this emerging consensus:

> debt levels were not the determinant issue when it came to which nations got in trouble. The nations with the highest debt ratios were not the ones hit; current account deficits were what mattered.[2]

Yet, this account also raises a couple of subsequent questions, in particular with respect to the 'causes of causes'. If the increasing current account imbalances between Eurozone members caused the crisis, what caused these imbalances?

I would like to stress an explanation that points to the importance of wage bargaining—an argument that has, over the last years, been developed in the Comparative Political Economy literature.[3] In brief, the argument runs as follows. The Member States of the Eurozone have institutionally different wage-bargaining regimes,[4] *systematically* different regimes. On a very general level, one could distinguish co-ordinated and uncoordinated regimes. Both differ in their capacity to deliver wage restraint. Yet, different growth rates in wages (growth of [nominal] unit labour costs) translate into different growth rates in prices. These diverging inflation

---

[1] Richard Baldwin and Francesco Giavazzi (eds), *The Eurozone Crisis: A Consensus View of the Causes and a Few Possible Solutions*, (London: CEPR Press, 2015).

[2] ibid, p 40.

[3] See Bob Hancké and Andrea Monika Herrmann, 'Wage Bargaining and Comparative Advantage in EMU', in: Bob Hancké, Martin Rhodes and Mark Thatcher, *Beyond Varieties of Capitalism: Conflict, Contradictions, and Complementarities in the European Economy*, (Oxford: Oxford University Press, 2007), pp 122–144; Fritz W. Scharpf, 'Monetary Union, Fiscal Crisis, and the Preemption of Democracy', MPIfG Discussion Paper 2011/11, Max Planck Institute for the Studies of Societies, Cologne; Wendy Carlin, 'Real Exchange Rate Adjustment, Wage-setting Institutions, and Fiscal Stabilization Policy: Lessons of the Eurozone's First Decade', (2013) 59 *CESifo Economic Studies*, pp 489–519; Bob Hancké, *Unions, Central Banks, and EMU: Labour Market Institutions and Monetary Integration in Europe*, (Oxford: Oxford University Press, 2013); Martin Höpner and Mark Lutter, 'One Currency and Many Modes of Wage Formation. Why the Eurozone is too Heterogeneous for the Euro', MPIfG Discussion Paper 2014/14; Alison Johnston, Bob Hancké and Suman Pant, 'Comparative Institutional Advantage in the European Sovereign Debt Crisis', (2014) 47 *Comparative Political Studies*, pp 1771–1800; Torben Iversen, David Soskice and David Hope, 'The Eurozone and Political Economic Institutions', (2016) 19 *Annual Review of Political Science*, pp 163–185; and Torben Iversen and David Soskice, 'A Structural-institutional Explanation of the Eurozone Crisis', in: Philip Manow, Bruno Palier and Hanna Schwander (eds), *Worlds of Welfare Capitalism and Electoral Politics*, (Oxford: Oxford University Press, 2017 forthcoming).

[4] Jelle Visser, 'Data Base on Institutional Characteristics of Trade Unions, Wage Setting, State Intervention and Social Pacts, 1960–2014 (ICTWSS)', (2015) University of Amsterdam, Amsterdam Institute for Advanced Labour Studies.

rates within a common currency area with a uniform monetary policy have a couple of important consequences, the most important being a divergence in the 'real exchange rate', and that means in competitiveness, and thus in the trade balance (and subsequently in the current account). Another important consequence of inflation differentials within a common currency area are differences in the real interest rate (see the famous Walters critique of monetary union).[5] Countries (regions) with higher inflation enjoy lower real interest rates, given uniform nominal interest rates within the currency area. Lower real interest rates, in turn, lead to higher investment, to higher growth, to more employment, to higher wages, and in this way again to higher inflation and thus to lower competitiveness (and further declining real interest rates) and so on. So, here, inflationary wage settlements trigger a self-enforcing feedback-loop.

Note, however, the specific consequences in the wage-moderation scenario: moderate wage settlements lead to low inflation, low inflation to a low 'real exchange rate', increased competitiveness, more exports, and subsequently a current account surplus. This, in the medium-term, would translate into (export-led) growth. But, interestingly, in the short-term, the 'real interest rate'-feedback loop has a counter-vailing effect. Low inflation in a uniform nominal interest rate environment means higher real interests, which dampens investment, and thus dampens growth and employment, and wages in their turn.[6] If this stylised account captures what happened in the low and high wage-inflation countries after the introduction of the common currency, we should be able to observe an immediate boom period in countries with above average inflation combined with a steady erosion of their cost competitiveness, whereas we would expect to observe a steady improvement in the current account of countries with below average inflation, combined with an initial period of sluggish growth.[7]

Somehow tragically, the increasing gap between the current accounts of the centre and the periphery in the Eurozone was sustained because the surpluses in the centre financed the deficits in the periphery. Massive capital flows from north to south fed the increasing trade imbalances, until the breakdown of Lehman Brothers first caused a sudden stop to these capital flows and then, even worse, a massive repatriation of capital, first, across the Transatlantic, and then within Europe from south to north. Within the Eurozone, this sudden reversal of capital flows was facilitated as capital flows remained unaffected by exchange rates. Selling an Italian state bond and buying in its stead a German one affected no exchange rate and therefore involved no exchange rate risk.[8] The sudden stop of capital flows quickly

---

[5] Alan Walters, 'Walters Critique', in: John Eatwell and Murray Milgate and Peter Newman (eds), *The New Palgrave Dictionary of Money and Finance*, (Basingstoke: Palgrave Macmillan, 1992), pp 781–783.

[6] See, Walters, n 5 above, Scharpf, n 3 above, and Carlin, n 3 above.

[7] We may also note that, in the long-run, the low-inflation and the high-inflation trajectories result in different growth models—export led *vs* domestic demand—and correspondingly, different sizes of exposed *versus* sheltered sectors of the economy; see Barry Eichengreen, 'Institutions and Economic Growth: Europe after World War II', in: Nicholas Crafts and Gianni Toniolo (eds), *Economic Growth in Europe since 1945*, (Cambridge: Cambridge University Press, 1996).

[8] See Paul De Grauwe, *Economics of Monetary Union*, (Oxford: Oxford University Press, 2104).

translated into a sudden and dramatic decline of economic activity in the periphery. This process was partially attenuated by Europe's TARGET2-payment system, which secured the continuation of capital inflows. Keynesian crisis management, rescue programmes for the collapsing banking systems and the automatic increase in welfare spending and the decrease in tax revenue in a recession then led to the dramatic increase in public debt, and *now*, and *only now*, did the crisis transform itself into a sovereign debt crisis—which then took on a particular intensity due to the fact that the Eurozone Member States were indebted in a currency over which they had lost national control. But in this account the sovereign debt crisis is not a *cause*, but a—albeit particularly dramatic—*consequence* of the crisis (again, with the exception of Greece, where the crisis had been a sovereign debt crisis right from the start—but this is a different story).

This account is relatively well supported empirically.[9] It is also in basic agreement with Mundell/Flemming's theory of optimal currency areas (OCA),[10] as the Eurozone violates one of the central OCA assumptions, namely, labour mobility and/or wage flexibility. Moreover, the account does not contradict the emerging consensus view on the causes of the Eurocrisis;[11] rather, it would claim to complement it with a 'cause of the cause': wage inflation as a cause of the current account imbalances, which, in turn, made the deficit-countries so vulnerable to a withdrawal of capital. This, then, is a structural explanation of the Eurocrisis,[12] with a particular emphasis on the importance of the differences in wage-bargaining systems within the common currency area.

However, a couple of questions lead on from this, which I will try to address in this chapter. First, as an empirical question: Do we observe, for the pre-crisis period, the expected development of wages and prices and current accounts? Can they be explained with differences in the institutional set-up of national wage-bargaining regimes? If the answer is yes, what reason can be given for their systematic variation between the centre and the periphery? Moreover, and here we enter the (empirically) still rather uncharted terrain: What happened *after* the onset of the crisis? How did wages and prices develop after 2009–2010? We should expect that wages in the periphery have grown at lower rates than in the Eurozone-centre, but to what extent can we observe these processes of real de- and re-valuation? Were they sufficient to recalibrate the current accounts or did the various wage-setting regimes continue to make a difference—as we would expect—so that wage growth was still too low in the centre and too high in the periphery? This is important if we are to distinguish the institutional effects—the impact of the wage-bargaining

[9] See Hancké and Herrmann, n 3 above; Scharpf, n 3 above; Carlin n 3 above; Hancké, n 3 above; Höpner and Lutter, n 3 above; Johnston, Hancké and Pant, n 3 above; Iversen, Soskice and Hope, n 3 above; and Iversen and Soskice, n 3 above.
[10] See Paul De Grouwe, 'The Political Economy of the Euro', (2013) 16 *Annual Review of Political Science*, pp 153–170; and idem, n 8 above.
[11] Baldwin and Giavazzi, n 1 above.
[12] Iversen and Soskice, n 3 above.

regimes—from pure business-cycle effects, namely, inflationary tendencies during boom periods and deflationary tendencies during recessions.

Assuming the wage-bargaining explanation that I propose here holds true, one would also ask whether this was, at any moment, an issue 'on the road to Maastricht'?[13] Were the decision-makers aware of the systematic variation in wage-setting regimes and its potentially destructive consequences? Anything else would be somewhat surprising, given that the OCA theory emphasises the importance of labour mobility and wage flexibility. And, in this context, ordoliberalism finally enters. Since I claim that the decision-making élites were aware of the problem of different wage growth within the Eurozone (see below), there is also ample evidence that the euro was meant as a means to overcome these differences. As I will argue below, the common currency had indeed been conceived as a credible self-commitment device, especially by those who had heretofore lacked the possibility of credibly committing themselves to a low-inflation equilibrium (ie Italy and France, in particular). But this would offer a very ironic conclusion. Our focus on the fiscal consequences of EMU leads us to forget how much the independence of monetary policy had been directed as a signal towards market actors, rather than governments, namely, at those setting wages: monetary rules directed at wage discretion. Yet, the obsession of the Eurocrisis debate with the *fiscal* rules of *allegedly* ordoliberal origin that are said to have prevented an appropriate response to the crisis[14] tends to obfuscate the main motivation behind the French or Italian push for a common currency, namely that European monetary rules should effectively discipline domestic wage discretion. Fiscal discipline, by the way, has to complement a non-accommodating monetary policy for this to work.[15] Hence, it was not the austerity-obsessed German ordoliberals, but French and Italian political élites, besides the Commission of course, that had pinned all their hopes on *rules*.[16] For Germans, the *fiscal* rules (as well as the 'no bail-out' provision) served only as an assurance against the danger of being made liable for other nations' debt(s)—an understandable position, I think (even one with substantial normative democratic value), and one which has nothing to do with ordoliberalism in particular.

This chapter is organised as follows. In a first descriptive part, I start by giving an overview based upon selected indicators for the development of nominal labour unit costs, prices, current accounts, between 1999 and (including) 2008, and then since 2009. I also address the question of whether differences in wage-bargaining regimes can explain the differences in wages and prices. This will then be answered with the help of a multi-variate analysis. It will also address the question how much

[13] See Kenneth Dyson and Kevin Featherstone, *The Road to Maastricht: Negotiating Economic and Monetary Union*, (Oxford: Oxford University Press, 1999).
[14] See Mark Blyth, *Austerity: The History of a Dangerous Idea*, (Oxford: Oxford University Press, 2015).
[15] See Philip Manow, *Social Protection, Capitalist Production: The Bismarckian Welfare State in the German Political Economy, 1880–2010*, (Berlin-Bremen-Cologne: Bookmanuscript, forthcoming).
[16] See Fritz W. Scharpf, *Forced Structural Convergence in the Eurozone—Or a Differentiated European Monetary Community*. MPIfG Discussion Paper (forthcoming).

pre- and post-crisis times differ with a view to wage inflation and deflation in both the periphery and the centre of the Eurozone. I then turn to a brief discussion of what motivated decision-makers to bind two rather different political economies with two rather different wage-setting logics together under a single currency. A short summary of the argument concludes.

II. WAGES, PRICES, INTEREST RATES, AND CURRENT ACCOUNTS IN THE EUROZONE: THE INCREASING DIVERGENCE BETWEEN CENTRE AND PERIPHERY

If we compare the development of nominal unit labour costs between Germany and the crisis-countries of Ireland, Greece, Spain, France, Italy and Portugal (Figure 1), or between two variants of political economies, namely, continental-coordinated and southern-uncoordinated ones (Figure 2), we can see the hypothesis of a systematically higher development of unit labour costs before 2008 confirmed. In particular, if we look at how different wage growth rates accumulated over time, we can see how the south was confronted with an increasing cost competitiveness problem. As Martin Wolf had pointedly put it:

> it really did *not* make sense for countries whose industries were competing with those of China to allow their labour costs to rise faster than in countries, like Germany, whose industries were complementary to those of China.[17] [emphasis in the original]

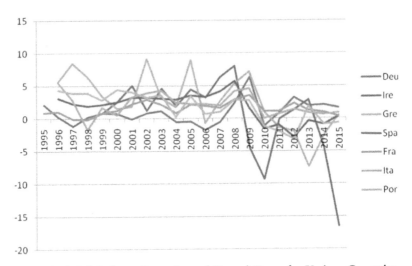

Figure 1: Nominal Unit Labour Costs, Annual Growth Rates for Various Countries
Source: Eurostat.

---

[17] See Martin Wolf, *The Shifts and the Shocks: What we've learned—and have still to learn—from the Financial Crisis*, (New York: Penguin Books, 2014), pp 293–294; see, also, 63–64.

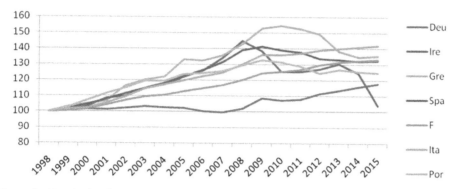

Figure 2: **Nominal Labour Unit Costs, Annual Growth Index (1998 = 100)**
Source: Eurostat.

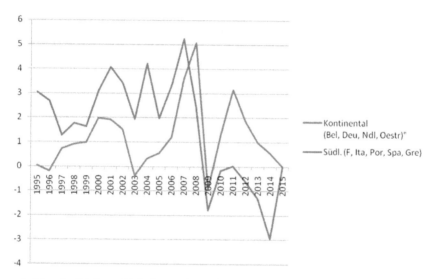

Figure 3: **Nominal Labour Unit Costs, Annual Growth in Continental and Southern Member States of the Eurozone**
Source: Eurostat.

Standard assumptions in economics would lead us to expect that different growth rates in wages translate into different growth rates in prices, ie inflation. This, then, is re-inforced by the interest rate effect of higher inflation under uniform nominal interest rates. Higher prices in a uniform 'nominal interest rate' environment mean lower real interest rates. These fuel investment, growth and employment, and, in turn, put pressure on wages and, in so doing, put pressure again on prices. It therefore comes as no surprise that we find higher consumer price inflation in the Eurozone periphery—at least in a first simple 'eye-balling' approach (compare Figures 4 and 5; for the multi-variate analysis, see below). As an initial and intended effect of the euro, we first observe the convergence of different inflation rates at a low level. Yet, over time, small, but persistent and therefore cumulative differences in inflation can be observed between the co-ordinated and the un-coordinated political economies of the Eurozone's centre and periphery, respectively. These accumulated differences, in the medium term, then lead to differences in competitiveness and, subsequently, to current accounts deficit and surpluses, respectively. Everything else then follows.

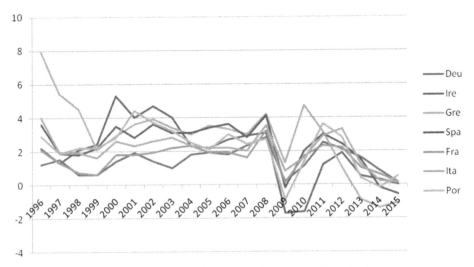

Figure 4: Inflation, Various Countries (Harmonised Consumer Price Index)
Source: Eurostat; annual growth rates in %.

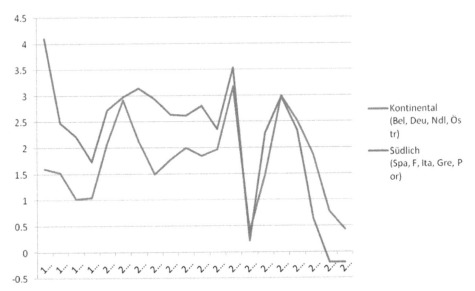

Figure 5: Inflation, Centre and Periphery (Harmonised Consumer Price Index)
Source: Eurostat; annual growth rates in %.

This becomes quite clear if we now turn to trade balances (see Figures 6 and 7). Instead of the general economic convergence that had been predicted, amongst others, by the European Commission in their 'One Market, One Money' study of 1990,[18] we see, quite to the contrary, divergence, partly dramatic divergence.[19] For instance, the German surplus doubled between 1999 and 2015 from 4 to more than 9% of GDP today. That is dramatic.

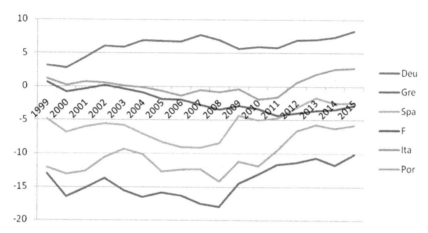

Figure 6: Trade Balance in Percentage of GDP, Various Countries
Source: Eurostat.

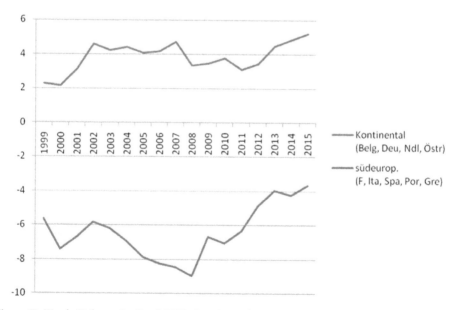

Figure 7: Trade Balance in % of GDP, Continental *Versus* Southern Euro-Member States
Source: Eurostat.

[18] The European Commission (1990), 'One Market, One Money. An Evaluation of the Potential Benefits and Costs of Forming an Economic and Monetary Union', (Brussels, EU Commission, 1990).

[19] Interestingly, the authors of this study list among the preconditions that they deem necessary for convergence to happen: 'the costs of absorbing country-specific economic shocks will be minimized if labour costs adjust relatively flexibly' (Commission note 18 above, p 13). This—as we know by now—they do not.

310   *Philip Manow*

Figures 6 and 7 also show reduced trade deficits in the periphery after 2009, but this will, in all likeliness, be an 'automatic' recessionary effect (a shrinking GDP leading to a reduction of imports). In any case, the surpluses of the continental countries continued to increase at the same time, so that convergence is still far from happening.

So, let us now turn towards an explanation and see whether the argument that is proposed here survives a more rigorous testing.

III. ADJUSTMENT PROCESSES OF TWO DIFFERENT POLITICAL ECONOMIES: THE CENTRE AND THE PERIPHERY OF THE EUROZONE

Much of what has been said above is hardly new.[20] Less well-known, however, are the institutional configurations concerning wage bargaining and the labour market, which underlie the different economic trends that were sketched above. Let me provide some indicators and rough measures that highlight the systematic differences between the Eurozone Member States in this respect. I basically refer to variables which capture the way in which wages are set and co-ordinated between capital and labour and—sometimes—government, and across industries and sectors. The variables are taken from the ICTWSS-*Data Base (Data Base on Institutional Characteristics of Trade Unions, Wage Setting, State Intervention and Social Pacts, 1960–2014)* in its most recent version.[21] I distinguish between a period before 2010 and a period after the onset of the crisis. I start by reporting some summary indicators. Subsequently, I ask whether a panel regression can confirm a systematic institutional effect of wage-bargaining systems on wage growth.

Table 1 again supports an argument that puts the different wage-bargaining regimes at its centre. Up until the crisis, annual wage growth was higher in the southern countries of Greece, Italy, Spain, Portugal and France—on average almost three-times as high as in the continental countries of Germany, Belgium, Netherlands and Austria. As a consequence, inflation rates differed as well. In the south, they had been on average 0.8 above the ECB's 2% inflation target in each year. Not surprisingly, this went hand in hand with higher growth rates in the periphery up until the crisis—whereas Germany went through a recession after the year 2000, due, amongst others, to the higher real interest rate that came with the common currency.[22] Higher growth in the south—however—came with higher deficits, but this was mainly due to the outlier Greece.

With respect to the—rather sticky—institutional variables, I report summary statistics for the entire period, from 1999 to 2014. The institutional variables show, with respect to the Industrial Relation (IR) systems, systematic differences with respect to centralisation, union density and union fragmentation, as well as ideological

[20] For a concise summary of the general argument, see Carlin, n 3 above.
[21] Compare with Visser, n 4 above.
[22] Scharpf, n 3 above.

Table 1: Some Indicators of Economic Performance and Some Measures for Institutional Characteristics of Wage-Setting Regimes in Continental and Southern Europe annual averages 1999–2009 and 2010–2014 (for the institutional variables. 1999–2014)

Indicators of economic performance	continental		southern	
	−2009	2009–	−2009	2009–
Wage growth (annual)	1.04	1.72	2.87	0.17
Inflation	1.9	1.5	2.78	1.15
Trade balance	3.7	4.03	−7.2	−5.26
GDP growth (annual)	2.28	0.17	2.57	−1.86
Budget deficit	−1.96	−2.82	−3.84	−6.79
Wage-setting institutions				
Coordination	4.18		2.76	
Type	3.5		2.94	
Union Density	30.47		20.78	
Eff. N. of Trade Unions	10.51		31.22	
Coverage private	77.14		57.59	
Coverage public	99.0		99.9	
Deme (ideological division among unions)	1.37		1.72	
Centralisation	0.598		0.322	

Sources: Eurostat and (Visser 2015, note 4 above).

fracture that point to the varying degree to which these systems are capable of delivering wage restraint. Wage co-ordination is less prominent in the Eurozone periphery, union density lower, union fragmentation (effective number of unions) is, at the same time, higher, and all this obviously makes wage co-ordination more difficult; in the south, the relative weights between public and private sector unions tilt stronger towards the public sector, and, again, this makes wage moderation less likely because of the higher job protection standards in the public sector and because the often close partisan-political, partly clientelistic links between public unions and socialist (and Communist) parties. Moreover, if public sector unions do not engage in wage moderation, private sector unions have less of an incentive to do so, too.[23]

---

[23] The Employment Protection Index displays for the Southern-European countries particularly high values (see Gayle Allard, 'Measuring Job Security over Time: In Search for a Historical Indicator of EPL (Employment Protection Legislation)', IE Working Paper WP05-17, 2005). See, also, the OECD indictors of employment protection, available at: www.oecd.org/els/emp/oecdindicatorsofemploymentprotection.htm.

Last, but not least, the ideological polarisation between unions is particularly strong in Southern Europe.[24] This reflects the division between radical, Communist, partly anarcho-syndicalist unions, on the one hand, and reform-oriented social-democratic unions, on the other. This all sums up to a centralisation-variable that is almost twice as high in the Eurozone's centre as in the southern periphery.

If we ask for the reasons for these substantial differences, the division on the left between a reform-oriented and a radical wing, which can be found in both the party systems and in the industrial relation systems of these countries,[25] explains their much lower degree of corporatist co-ordination, and their much higher degree of political polarisation. Historically, this division, in turn, refers back to the particular polarisation of the fundamental political conflict between an anti-clerical republican left and a pro-clerical anti-republican right, a conflict that in all countries—Greece, Italy, Spain, Portugal and also France—turned violent in the first half of the twentieth century. In this polarised constellation, and in the early twentieth century, in a period in which the agricultural sector still accounted for a huge share of employment, or, to put it differently, in which no political majority could be formed against the pious peasants under the close tutelage of the Catholic (or Orthodox) church, a substantial part of the left lost confidence in a legal-parliamentary reform-agenda and chose the radical option. This, then, translated into a post-WWII constellation with strong Communist unions and parties, if these countries turned democratic at all after 1945 (as Spain and Portugal only did in the mid-1970s, and as Greece did earlier, but only partly, after a violent, ferocious civil war, and then with an intermittent totalitarian episode later on).

We can now turn to the question of whether the causal chain that was depicted above will also show up in a multi-variate analysis. Of particular interest is whether the two different political economies distinguished here continue to leave their imprint on the adjustment to the crisis. This is important in order to distinguish pure business-cycle effects from structural ones. So, did the wages in the centre (periphery) increase (decrease) too little after the crisis set in, mirroring that wages had increased too much (too little) in the periphery (in the centre) in their respective boom and slump periods before, ie before 2009?

So, let's turn now towards the panel-regression (compare Tables 2 and 3). In Tables 2 and 3, I report the results of a random effects, time-series, cross-section analysis. The specification controls for the standard economic factors: lagged growth, lagged inflation and the level of unemployment, and then either includes a dummy variable for the northern or southern Eurozone Member States (Table 2)

---

[24] Compare the DEME-variable of the ICTWSS dataset: 'External demarcations between union confederations 2 = sharp (political, ideological, organisational) cleavages associated with conflict and competition 1.5 = moderate (occupational, regional, linguistic, religious) cleavages, limited competition.'
[25] See Jonathan Hopkin, 'Hard Choices, Mixed Incentives: Globalization, Structural Reform, and the Double Dilemma of European Socialist Parties', Manuscript, on file with the author. See, also, Philip Manow, 'Workers, Farmers, and Catholicism: A History of Political Class Coalitions and the South-European Welfare State Regime', (2015) 25 *Journal of European Social Policy*, pp 32–49.

or includes an index for the centralisation of wage bargaining (Table 3). I report clustered standard errors. Table 3 also includes a time variable, which accounts for the trend in the data (via a variable that measures years since introduction of the common currency).

Table 2: TSCS-Regression, the Determinants of Nominal Unit Labour Costs, 1995–2015, a Comparison Between the Eurozone's Periphery and Centre, 1995–2015

Nominal Labour Unit Costs	Model 4 <2009, South	Model 5 <2009, Centre	Model 6 >=2009, South	Model 7 >=2009 Centre
Lag.GDPGrowth	0.390	0.357	0.295	0.285
	(7.68)***	(6.87)***	(3.95)***	(3.80)***
Unemployment Rate	−0.260	−0.281	−0.292	−0.272
	(5.61)***	(5.69)***	(4.59)***	(3.87)***
Lag.Inflation	0.579	0.531	0.169	0.102
	(6.72)***	(6.12)***	(1.33)	(0.81)
Southern Europe	1.158		1.527	
	(2.29)**		(2.05)**	
Continental Europe		−1.250		−0.647
		(2.15)**		(0.72)
constant	1.852	2.888	3.200	3.715
	(3.29)***	(4.27)***	(4.36)***	(3.74)***
N	289	289	119	119

* $p < 0.1$; ** $p < 0.05$; *** $p < 0.01$.

Both specifications are in line with the proposed argument, and both report an even stronger effect of wage-bargaining institutions—either comparing north and south or by looking at the effect of wage centralisation—for the period *after* the onset of the crisis, ie after 2009. The standard economic factors show the expected signs and are significant throughout: labour unit costs rise with growth (in the previous period) and prices (in the previous period) and fall in unemployment.[26] In both specifications, we can observe additional institutional effects beyond business-cycle effects. And these provide little hope for the economic convergence that had originally been envisioned in the 'One Market, One Money' scenario of EMU.

---

[26] Results remain robust under various specifications, eg with a smaller country sample (only the Euro-12), and restricting the observations from 1999 to 2015.

Table 3: TSCS-Regression, the Determinants of Nominal Unit Labour Costs, the Effects of Wage-Bargaining Centralisation, 1995–2015

Nominal Labour Unit Costs	Model 1 1995–2015	Model 2 1995–2008	Model 3 2009–2015
Lag.GDPGrowth	0.487	0.443	0.439
	(2.88)***	(2.49)**	(3.55)***
Unemployment Rate	−0.242	−0.264	−0.334
	(4.40)***	(2.85)***	(4.60)***
Lag.Inflation	0.594	1.011	−0.044
	(5.25)***	(4.82)***	(0.13)
Centralisation	−3.027	−2.037	−4.155
	(2.93)***	(1.00)	(2.15)**
T (index for time)	0.173	0.261	−0.150
	(2.34)**	(2.27)**	(0.46)
Constant	−344.821	−521.453	307.836
	(2.32)**	(2.26)**	(0.47)
N	230	168	62

* $p < 0.1$; ** $p < 0.05$; *** $p < 0.01$.

IV. DISCUSSION AND OUTLOOK

I would like to summarise the argument and to provide a brief outlook. The discussion about the Eurocrisis has, in my view, a fiscal bias. In this context, the German insistence on fiscal rules appears as stubborn, rule-obsessed, based upon irrational inflation-angst, and contrary to the most basic of all textbook-wisdom of macroeconomics, namely, that you cannot save yourself out of a recession. The literature seems to be only in disagreement as to whether one should interpret this as outright stupidity or as part of a bigger German plot for economic domination. A common culprit in this interpretation is ordoliberalism, an odd German economic doctrine, whose intellectual roots reach back to the 1920s and 1930s, which is poorly understood, often mystified, but clearly identified as the doctrine that can be held accountable for all that is going wrong in Europe.[27]

The debate's fiscal bias, so it seems, mirrors the preoccupation with questions of public finance in the Maastricht negotiations themselves—in which everything focused on intergovernmental moral hazard problems and in which decision-makers thought that the 'no bail-out'-provisions of the EMU Treaty would provide

---

[27] Blyth, n 14 above. For a more nuanced statement, see Markus Brunnermeier and Harold James, *The Euro and the Battle of Ideas*, (Princeton NJ: Princeton University Press, 2016).

protection against fiscal free-riding among Member States. Dyson and Featherstone in their authoritative account of these negotiations depict them as a 'Core Executive Activity'.[28] Since negotiations were about monetary policy, political élites assumed that governments had an exclusive responsibility in these matters. One consequence was that sectoral interests were 'very much excluded from the EMU negotiations. Employer organizations, trade unions, and industrial and banking associations were not incorporated in the process, either at national or EC levels'.[29] That these actors remained outside was—according to Dyson and Featherstone—not only due to the fact that monetary policy was perceived as 'high politics', but also because organised labour and capital and other sectoral interests had difficulties in assessing the consequences which a common currency would have for 'exchange rates and interest rates'.[30] This last point, however, seems highly implausible.

The consequences of price stability, which the euro was going to bring to all Member States, should have been fully obvious to anyone. If national central banks lose their say over monetary policy, they could no longer accommodate inflationary wage settlements. The common currency was the maximally credible self-commitment vis-à-vis capital and labour. It was directed against the inflationary spiral comprising wage increases, subsequent increases in the supply of money, the depreciation of the currency (because of lower interest rates), imported inflation, and then again high wage settlements in order to recoup the real-wage loss due to (imported) inflation. It was exactly those inflationary spirals that had haunted countries such as Italy and France in the 1970s and 1980s. The euro was meant to put an end to this.[31] The German *Bundesbank* had shown how to break the inflationary cycle in the early 1970s after the breakdown of Bretton Woods,[32] and this had made the *Deutschmark* the anchor currency in the emerging European Monetary System. Now, this trick was supposed to be emulated at European level, since neither the Italian nor the French central banks had proven capable of achieving this on their own:

> in the eyes of French technocrats, the EC could serve as an external discipline forcing overdue domestic policy reforms on France. This theme of vincolo esterno was even more clear in the Italian case, where the ERM and EMU could be seen as instruments of economic and political modernization.[33]

---

[28] Dyson and Featherstone, n 13 above. This is also why an interest-group based explanation of EMU is not particularly persuasive. See Jeffrey A. Frieden, *Currency Politics. The Political Economy of Exchange Rate Policy*, (Princeton NJ: Princeton University Press, 2015, Ch 4).

[29] ibid, p 14.

[30] ibid.

[31] De Grauwe, n 8 above.

[32] See Fritz W. Scharpf, *Sozialdemokratische Krisenpolitik in Europa*, (Frankfurt aM: Campus Verlag, 1987).

[33] Dyson and Featherstone, n 13 above, p 22. *cf*, 'The customs union, the single market, the ERM, and, then, EMU were means of breaking domestic political, economic, and industrial deadlock by relying on external discipline' (Dyson and Featherstone, n 13 above, p 73).

One could name numerous other comments with the same general thrust, for instance, those by Daniel Gros and Niels Thygesen in their 'classical' 1998 textbook on EMU:

> In sum, labour market flexibility is always useful and if EMU forces labour market reforms that are needed anyway, the economy of EU can only gain.[34]

In a different context, Niels Thygesen, a member of the Delors Committee, stated that monetary union would be 'a way of 'reducing the scope for the kind of lax and divergent monetary policies' that characterized Europe in the 1970s'.[35] In other words, the consequences which a common currency would have, in particular for organised capital and labour, were fully obvious.

However, what is perhaps less known is that fiscal restraint is usually part of an institutional structure in which unions are 'price takers', because (a) an independent central bank would also have an interest in sanctioning the inflationary dangers inherent in fiscal profligacy with interest-rate hikes (as the German *Bundesbank* did in the post-unification boom in 1992), and (b) because unions in exposed sectors have an interest that their wage moderation is not undermined by aggressive wage demands by public unions (per definition in the sheltered sector).[36] To this extent, fiscal discipline, as enshrined in the Treaty of Maastricht, did not only reflect worries about intergovernmental moral hazard, but was part of the package that was supposed to bring low-inflation to all of Euroland. The tragedy, if one wants, was that the constraints of the euro on domestic wage-bargaining in the periphery became only binding after a prolonged period of high inflation and high growth, which made the adjustment then necessary so extreme and politically unbearable. But it then appears that it had been foremost French and Italian decision-makers, not crazy German ordoliberals, who had pinned all their hopes on monetary rules against fiscal discretion.

In this context, then, the current polemic against ordoliberalism,[37] an economic doctrine which had nothing to do with the emergence of wage co-ordination in the 1950s and 1960s,[38] nor with the new equilibrium that established itself after the breakdown of Bretton Woods in the early 1970s, nor with the 'rescue policy' during the Euro-crisis itself,[39] seems to be mostly a placeholder for something else.

---

[34] Daniel Gros and Niels Thygesen, *European Monetary Integration: From the European Monetary System to Economic and Monetary Union*, (London, Prentice Hall, 1998), p 288.

[35] Quoted from Harold James, *Making the European Monetary Union*, (Cambridge MA: Belknap Press, 2012), p 7.

[36] Wendy Carlin and David Soskice, 'German Economic Performance: Disentangling the Role of Supply-side Reforms, Macroeconomic Policy and Coordinated Economy Institutions', (2009) 7 *Socio-Economic Review*, pp 67–99; Carlin, n 3 above.

[37] Blyth, n 14 above.

[38] Manow, n 15 above.

[39] Lars P Feld, Ekkehard A. Köhler and Daniel Nientiedt, 'Ordoliberalism, Pragmatism and the Eurozone Crisis: How the German Tradition Shaped Economic Policy in Europe', (2015) 2 *European Review of International Studies*, pp 48–61.

Index